CATASTROPHIC GRIEF, TRAUMA, AND RESILIENCE IN CHILD CONCENTRATION CAMP SURVIVORS

A Retrospective View of Their Holocaust Experiences

"This book captures the voices of some of the last living survivors of the Holocaust. These in-depth interviews provide valuable testimony to how the catastrophic losses and trauma suffered by children and youth in the context of a genocide shaped their life trajectories, and how these early experiences impact their engagement with the final developmental challenges of the late years in life. Farber's gentle and compassionate relationships with the survivors are an inspiration to all who know or work with trauma survivors."

— Irit Felsen, PhD, Clinical Psychologist,
Co-Chair of the Trauma Working Group at the NGO
on Mental Health in Consultative Relationship
to the United Nations

"A must-read for those interested in a rich combination of unique perspectives on theories of childhood development and trauma, including the impact on aging for those who were children during the Holocaust. The Survivor narratives are gripping and haunting, and command the reader to pause in honor of their testimonies. Be prepared to be inspired by their resilience. This book contributes to a deeper understanding of the experiences of grief and hope among those who survived the atrocities of the Holocaust as children."

— Jenni Frumer, Ph.D.,
LCSW, MSEd; Director,
NOW for Holocaust Survivors Initiative/
MorseLife Health System USA

CATASTROPHIC GRIEF, TRAUMA, AND RESILIENCE IN CHILD CONCENTRATION CAMP SURVIVORS

A Retrospective View of Their Holocaust Experiences

Tracey Farber, PhD,
Gillian Eagle, PhD,
and Cora Smith, PhD

BOSTON
2023

Library of Congress Cataloging-in-Publication Data

Names: Farber, Tracey Rori, 1966- editor. | Eagle, Gillian, editor. |
  Smith, Cora (Adjunct Professor of Psychiatry), editor.
Title: Catastrophic grief, trauma, and resilience in child concentration
  camp survivors : a retrospective view of their Holocaust experiences /
  edited by Tracey Rori Farber, Gillian Eagle, and Cora Smith.
Description: Boston : Academic Studies Press, 2023. | Includes
  bibliographical references.
Identifiers: LCCN 2023009301 (print) | LCCN 2023009302 (ebook) | ISBN
  9781644696347 (hardback) | ISBN 9781644696354 (adobe pdf) | ISBN
  9781644696361 (epub)
Subjects: LCSH: Holocaust survivors--Psychology. | Holocaust
  survivors--Mental health. | Holocaust survivors--Interviews. | Jewish
  children in the Holocaust--Interviews. | Holocaust, Jewish
  (1939-1945)--Psychological aspects. | Psychic trauma.
Classification: LCC RC451.4.H62 C38 2023 (print) | LCC RC451.4.H62
  (ebook) | DDC 940.53/18019--dc23/eng/20230414
LC record available at https://lccn.loc.gov/2023009301
LC ebook record available at https://lccn.loc.gov/2023009302

ISBN 9781644698761 (paperback)
ISBN 9781644696354 (adobe pdf)
ISBN 9781644696361 (epub)

Book design by Lapiz Digital Services
Cover design by Ivan Grave

Published by Academic Studies Press
Academic Studies Press
1577 Beacon Street
Brookline, MA 02446, USA
press@academicstudiespress.com
www.academicstudiespress.com

In memoriam of my family who were killed during the Holocaust with the six million:

> my great-grandmother Meryl Farber and my great-uncle Yehuda Farber, who were shot and killed in mass graves in a forest near Janova, Lithuania;

> my great-grandfather Shimon "Yuri" Diner and my great-grandmother Channa Diner, who were killed in the Dvinsk Ghetto in Latvia.

I honor the memory of my beloved grandfathers Dave Farber and Max Diner, who suffered these tragic losses.

I was their firstborn grandchild and I carry their stories told and untold.

My younger brothers were their pride and joy, a reminder of their younger masculine selves who survived pogroms and antisemitism.

They are remembered with love, and their legacy lives on in their grandchildren and great-grandchildren.

—Tracey Farber, first author

To say that survivors were fortunate would not be fair. In not perishing with their family members, friends, and fellow Jews, these survivors were destined for what can, at the very least, be described as an uncertain future. More accurately, they were to live a life sometimes filled with boundless happiness, bottomless sadness, torturous guilt, an urge to die, and an urge to strive; destined to live with only death marking the end of their suffering.

Tracey's work opens our eyes to the suffering of so many, ensures that their suffering was not in vain, and documents the importance of the resilience that enables people to transcend incredible trauma. In recent years, I have seen how much energy Tracey has expended on seeing that good comes from evil, and that her years of pain gathering up stories of suffering contribute to a pool of knowledge that can help others overcome emotional challenges and live more functional lives. Just as Tracey's work has given me the opportunity to understand the processes that so many endured, I hope that this book will do the same for others.

Our Jewish history is littered with an endless stream of perpetrators of antisemitism who inflicted tremendous suffering on victims. Amongst these victims were my grandparents Jack and Rose Shankman and Shmuel and Sora Musikanth, who arrived in South Africa in the 1930s having preemptively escaped the Lithuanian pogroms that predated the arrival of the Einsatzgruppen. While my recollections of my grandparents are in some ways limited, they are always of happy times. In hindsight, my grandparents likely masked the terrible suffering of living with memories of childhoods destroyed by the sudden disappearance of parents. Only recently have I come to understand the incredible mental sacrifices they made to give me a stable foundation—as well as the bravery and strength they drew upon to protect me from their traumas.

They arrived in South Africa defeated, desolate, and for all purposes orphaned. Against all odds, and without the benefit of psychologists, social workers, or therapists, they made new lives for themselves and, one has to imagine, buried the past beneath their new lives. While I was fortunate to unearth remnants of their memories of Lithuania, the culture and traditions of their early years, although recreated to an extent in South Africa, was seldom mentioned. While

I regret having been spared the details of their loss, Tracey's work has shown me the value of their suffering and the extent of their bravery and strength in charting new lives.

Against incredible odds, my grandparents made lives worth living, as did millions of others. In building families on solid foundations, they made certain that their experience meant something. We, and generations to come, sit in their dust. May we forever remember their courage—and the anguish they must have felt—in allowing us our opportunities and freedom. May the memories of my grandparents, and all those who made similar journeys, be forever blessed.

—Jeff Shankman, community leader, Johannesburg

Figure 1. Rose and Jack Shankman.

Figure 2. Shmuel and Sora Musikanth.

This book is based on a thesis submitted to the Faculty of Humanities, in fulfillment of the requirements for the degree of doctor of philosophy in clinical psychology, University of Witwatersrand, Johannesburg.

A qualitative study was conducted into the long-term impact of the Holocaust on nine child survivors who were interviewed in their old age with a focus on how their life trajectory had shaped their engagement with the life tasks associated with "integrity versus despair." The survivors comprised a community rather than a clinical sample of individuals and consisted of those who volunteered to take part in the study on the basis of an invitation from a Jewish community leader. All of the participants had been interned in concentration camps for periods during their childhood or adolescent years and all were resident in South Africa at the time that they were interviewed. A case study method was employed to examine the experiences of aging survivors and extended, in-depth, semi-structured interviews were used to generate data on the following features: pre-Holocaust life and family of origin; Holocaust and concentration camp trauma exposure, impact, and coping; life post-liberation; and experiences of aging. Thematic analysis, informed broadly by psychodynamic theory, was used to extrapolate themes relating to trauma and resilience, and to understand how participants appeared to be navigating old age specifically in relation to Erikson's (1965) formulation of the life stage of "ego integrity versus despair."

Aspects of each participant's developmental trajectory were explored in order to better understand the impact of Holocaust trauma as experienced during the life stages of childhood or adolescence. Both within-case and across-case features were identified. Findings demonstrated that survivors who had stable attachments in early life seemed to be more resilient in their coping after liberation. Participants varied in their capacity to function adaptively for a range of reasons, but significantly many of those who had led apparently productive lives had employed repression, suppression, or compartmentalization to keep Holocaust-related recollections at bay. Responses to negotiating ego integration and despair fell on a continuum, with some participants evidencing the capacity to view their lives with a sense of acceptance and retrospective appreciation, and others experiencing extreme despair.

All survivors reported some symptoms consistent with complex traumatic stress. It was significant that all the participants have suffered with significant post-traumatic symptoms, such as depression and continuous PTSD, over their lifetimes. These symptoms were visceral and deeply haunting. A ubiquitous finding was that all survivors expressed catastrophic grief for the loss of their parents and siblings enduring into the present, many decades after the Holocaust. This catastrophic grief had consequences for the structure of the self, for the quality of their interpersonal relationships, and for their spiritual relationship with religion and God. This impacted aging child survivors' experience of despair in old age in a profound way—the continuous unresolved grief led to a sense of existential loneliness. The findings of this study indicated that the burden of catastrophic grief was a defining theme in the life trajectories of child survivors and the present research identified a "trauma trilogy" that linked catastrophic grief to anger and survivor guilt contributing to their sense of despair in old age. Finally, the study examined the process of reflexivity, as this proved very significant in conducting the research, and also recommended potential interventions to better support aging child Holocaust survivors.

Contents

Acknowledgments

Our deep gratitude goes to the research participants—child Holocaust survivors—who opened their hearts and shared their stories with such generosity.

We also would like to thank the following people. Don Krausz, chairman of the Johannesburg Holocaust Survivors Association, who helped to develop and refine the questionnaire used in this study. His insight and collaboration added depth to this research and his input is deeply appreciated. Jeff Shankman for funding the social services for Holocaust survivors based on the findings of this research and for his support in funding the publication of this book. The Christa Maria Trust for funding and in particular for supporting the launch of this book, and the public lectures that ensure the ongoing value of Holocaust education that this book provides. The management and social workers at the Chev, Jewish Welfare services, Johannesburg for establishing a service for Holocaust survivors as a recommendation of this research. Tali Nates, director of the Holocaust and Genocide Museum, for assisting in the selection of research participants and her help in advising how testimony should fully capture and reflect the full extent of Holocaust trauma. The volunteers from the Holocaust and Genocide Museum for the work they do in reaching out to help Holocaust survivors during the COVID-19 pandemic. Dr Jenni Frumer, director of Holocaust Survivors Now, United States, for her specialized knowledge about services available to survivors in the United States. Professor Irit Felsen for her valued input and contribution. Evelyn Pieprz for encouraging us to tell Shlomo Pieprz's story and for giving us access to his pictures and signed permission to tell his story. We thank orthodox Chabad Rabbi Ari Keivman for his advice on how to respectfully write about sensitive spiritual aspects of this research. Professor Diana Shmukler for her encouragement regarding the publishing of this research, and the understanding and acknowledgement of the difficulty of the work.

Finally, we thank our beloved families and friends for their support during the writing of this book.

Foreword

This book finds itself placed within the ever-increasing data collected on various aspects of the Holocaust, its impact on survivors, perpetrators, and witnesses, both immediate and long-term, conveyed in numerous accounts, documentaries, film footages, movies, photographs, memoirs, biographies, and various forms of fiction. The Holocaust remains a significant and relevant topic with aspects still not fully recorded and/or the implications and impacts yet to be described. At this time, almost eighty years since the end of World War II, the generation of survivors, even those who were very young, are now dying out, adding to the poignancy and urgency of still collecting their stories and eyewitness experiences. Needless to say, engagement in this material remains extremely difficult by the nature of the horrors that were perpetrated. This is more particularly so in the light of the fact that this is not a product of imagination or fiction but reflective of true accounts of events that continue to amaze and shock generations who came afterwards, generations who were often fortunate not only to have escaped, but to be far from the survivors in time and space. It is nearly eighty years since the full horror of the mass extermination of six million European Jews became widely known. This crime, planned and executed largely during World War II by Hitler and his allies, has come to be known as the "Holocaust." There are and have been other mass murders of ethnic and religious populations but there are a number of reasons why this atrocity still burns and lives on in the minds and memories of so many survivors and their children, across now at least four generations, as well as holding emblematic status in modern history. One of the horrors is not only the number and the scale of death, but the systematic, cold-blooded, planned, and ruthless nature of execution using modern methods on an industrial scale. Following on from this fact is that the survivors, near survivors, and the generations that came after them are spread throughout the Western World. These groups, of mainly European Jewish extraction, are largely articulate, sophisticated populations, who are psychologically aware, well-educated, and recognize the impact and long-term effects directly and indirectly in themselves and those who are near to them, as well as in those who more widely identify with the victims of the Holocaust.

The particular value of the work elaborated in this book is that it can be seen from both a research and a clinical lens, producing findings by way of eyewitness testimony and reports of profound personal experience. The accounts of child survivors find resonance with theories of lifespan development and the long-term effects of early trauma and the nature of resilience, and in addition, the findings of this research have produced relevant clinical and practical outcomes for survivors and their families. The book is written and produced by three talented, well-informed psychologists, all recognized for their clinical acumen and experience. Going deeper than the immediate brief of describing the nature of this particular horror of child Holocaust survivors, they provide valuable guidance and support for ongoing professional intervention with those who experience early and massive trauma by demonstrating the lifelong effects of this kind of traumatization. The individual case histories make moving and poignant stories. Herein lies the importance of, and difficulty with, the material. The strength and courage of the authors in exposing themselves to a number of years of immersion in these accounts and in engaging with the participants' current lives and their aging situation, with its own sets of emotional impact, is to be highly commended. Also, to be commended are the research assistants, who undoubtedly must have been deeply impacted in helping process the material. In reading these cases it is clear that the authors were sensitive to the individuals and able to hold them and their emotional reactions as they reexperienced, remembered, and described some of their ongoing nightmares, guilt, and terrible sadness at the loss of close family and communities, and in many cases of belief and hope in human nature and trust in the world. The writing shows that the interviews proved to be largely beneficial, or even therapeutic for the participants through the processing and containment of the material often previously never spoken of or told to others, even if therapy as such was not the aim of the project.

Once a clear picture has been drawn showing how the experiences of the children and adolescents would fit into current understandings of trauma, including the symptoms of trauma known as PTSD and those associated with complex and ongoing trauma (CPTSD), the authors further consider the lifelong consequences within an Eriksonian framework. Erik Erikson's theory of child and adult development, although developed and described shortly after World War II, remains one of the best-established theories of lifespan psychology. Using Erikson's theory as a base provides a well-established foundation from which to describe the participants' life courses, both clinically and in comparison, with normal expectable life trajectories in the context of the developmental crises individuals are usually required to navigate. One is thus able to compare how these participants were affected and irrevocably changed by their traumatic early life experiences.

A further strength of the research elaborated in the book is that it explores the Holocaust-related experiences and life trajectories of a group of nine participants, who met broad criteria in the sense that they were all exposed to similar Holocaust-related trauma, encompassing, massive, widespread, and most severe degrees of loss and horror. Within this collective group of nine child survivors, both individual differences and similarities can be shown. This highlights the understanding and provides confirmation that, although there are things in common across the group, each participant is also an individual. Their unique history, circumstances, and particular episodes of luck, as well as of misfortune, can be shown to play a part in their subsequent lives and how they were able to process their situations and attempted to make sense of what had happened to them. Furthermore, there are other findings of interest, which corroborate well-reported clinical facts. As an example, very few of the survivors sought professional psychological help after the war. It has been previously reported that often, rather than the direct survivors, it is the second or even the third generation of survivors who seek psychotherapy as they still find themselves plagued by parents' and grandparents' histories. This fact powerfully supports the clinical and theoretical understanding of the transgenerational transmission of trauma.

Publishing the body of a doctoral thesis in the form of a book makes the material available to a wide audience. As indicated, the text also includes some practical outcomes that may inform clinical practice, further research, and comprehension of the impact of other genocides. The book may assist in the training of clinical psychologists and mental health workers to work in more depth, with greater empathy, and hopefully with more containment, guided by the theory and backup provided from this work.

It is a privilege to write this foreword to an important contribution to the ever-accumulating worldwide literature on Holocaust and genocide impact and for a book that helps us to move forward in the recognition of past and prevention of future tragedies.

—Professor Diana Shmukler, PhD, associate
professor (Wits.) and visiting professor
of psychotherapy (UK), senior clinical
psychologist, supervisor, and trainer
(SA Medical and Dental Council), UKHPC
(Health Professions Council, UK)

Preface

Tracey Farber

This book is based on PhD research that explored the experiences of aging Holocaust survivors who were children or adolescents during the Holocaust and who had been interned in concentration camps at least for some period. Since the study was retrospective in nature, aging survivors were interviewed about their pre-Holocaust life as young children and special focus was given to the loss and trauma that they endured during the Holocaust. Their adjustment post-liberation was of interest, most specifically the way in which the Holocaust appeared to have impacted them in the final developmental phase of "integrity versus despair," as described by Erikson (1982). "Integrity versus despair" is the developmental stage whereby aging people look back at their lives and seek to integrate their experiences and make meaning. This retrospective view leads to a sense of wisdom and acceptance, or a sense of despair. At the time of the research interviews all of the child survivors interviewed for the purposes of the study were in this eighth stage of "integrity versus despair," and the impact of Holocaust trauma was understood within this context.

I completed the doctorate on which the book is based in Johannesburg in 2019. I worked full time as a psychologist in private practice while completing this research. Working as a clinical psychologist in Johannesburg, I had specialized in practicing as a psychodynamically oriented individual psychotherapist and also in the treatment of trauma. This included seeing victims of car hijacks, house invasion, rapes, and robberies. I also worked on a long-term basis with victims of child abuse and second-generation Holocaust survivors. My choice to embark on Holocaust research was influenced by being Jewish and of Ashkenazi lineage. I grew up in Johannesburg with two traumatized grandfathers who had left Eastern Europe before the Holocaust; I was interested in the Holocaust on a personal and professional level.

The seeds of this book were sown many decades ago in Johannesburg. As a young child I watched my two grandfathers playing cards at the dining room table and I heard them speaking Yiddish, as they sipped on black tea with strawberry jam. I watched them speaking in an animated way, in a language that had a beautiful sound but I didn't understand a word. They both called me "Trace-kela," a Yiddish diminutive of my name that no one has called me before or since. I knew I belonged—they had put their stamp and the sounds of their Eastern European accents—on my English name. I felt connected to them and to their culture, and this sense of identification made me want to know about their families. My journey to understand my lost great-grandparents who had been killed in the Holocaust led me to this research. In an effort to prepare for this research I met survivors in Johannesburg, Cape Town, Tel Aviv, and Buenos Aires. In addition, I went to visit Warsaw, and Auschwitz and Majdanek concentration camps in Poland.

After completing my PhD research on child concentration camp survivors, I felt compelled to write a book so that their stories could be widely read. It was a privilege to meet with nine elderly child survivors who had endured the horrors of the concentration camps in their childhood/adolescence. They shared their stories with me with such honesty, intensity, and generosity. I collected seventy-four hours of taped testimony and was deeply disturbed by the horror and loss that they had endured. However, I was also greatly inspired by the stories of love and connection that they shared about their families who had been killed by the Nazis. Many also shared the compassionate humanity of the righteous gentiles who saved them. I found myself to be a witness to their trauma and loss and their stories will forever be etched on my soul. At the same time, I was also a witness to their capacity to adapt and survive and rebuild their lives after the Holocaust. It was a testament to their resilience and fortitude; their stories were deeply moving and I was absorbed in understanding their resilience. As aging people looking back at their lives, I was able to hear both the wisdom that they had gleaned and the sense of meaning they had salvaged as well as their despair about their losses, particularly of family members, whom they continued to mourn for several decades after the Holocaust. I felt I wanted to share the wealth of knowledge and wisdom as well as the stories so that this knowledge could be witnessed by the readers of this book. This is a book about horrific trauma, deep despair, and the triumph of love and hope.

I had the privilege of having my PhD supervised by two senior professors who have joined me in writing this book. Prof. Gillian Eagle is a professor of psychology in the Faculty of Human and Community Development at the University of the Witwatersrand. She is also a clinical psychologist who specializes in trauma and she has published widely on this subject. She joins me in describing the psychological defenses that were used by survivors, and in addition she has written about the contribution of this research in understanding complex traumatic stress (CPTSD). Prof. Cora Smith is a joint professor of psychiatry in the Faculty of Health Sciences at the University of the Witwatersrand and chief clinical psychologist at Charlotte Maxeke Johannesburg Academic Hospital. She has been my clinical supervisor for over two decades, and in the present research she was faced with the difficult task of having to debrief me. She also had to deal with the nearly impossible task of pushing me to finish the research. Prof. Smith has written a chapter about the contribution of the research to appreciating retrospective construction of trauma across the lifetime developmental trajectory. Both supervisors came from a different religious background than mine and they have invested so much of their energy and time in this research, for which I am forever grateful.

The narrative of this book includes me writing about my interactions with the Holocaust survivors—when I do this, I refer to myself as "I." This book is an adaption of my PhD research, and when I refer to "we," I mean Gillian Eagle, Cora Smith, and myself.

This book introduces the theory and research around developmental trauma, child Holocaust survivors, and aging in an initial section and describes the qualitative research methodology that was used to generate the case material presented in the book. It then moves on to discuss the findings generated. First, a description of each participant's case history is provided, after which there is a discussion of some of the common themes found in the narratives of these child Holocaust survivors. The rich case histories tell the stories of the nine survivors and include observations of my clinical impressions of being with them over several hours in each case. Each story is different and forms a unique picture of trauma, grief, and resilience. However, common themes have emerged that have warranted discussion such as evidence of a "trauma trilogy" of catastrophic grief, anger, and survival guilt and how existential questions were engaged in this late stage of their lives. I wrote a chapter about my own reflexivity countertransference experiences and a chapter on the clinical interventions that were implemented as a result of this research. Both Gillian Eagle and

Cora Smith as senior academics have written their own chapters to interpret the research and extrapolate the understandings from their own experience. In writing their chapters I feel that they have elevated the level of my research and given it new meaning, for which I am deeply grateful. Finally, we have written a joint chapter presenting the summary, conclusions, and the recommendations stemming from this research. We collaborated on this book after I had left to live in Israel—working over Zoom and email—and I am so grateful for their years of investment in my research and now finally this book, which they have co-authored.

Firstly, I want to thank the Creator for giving me the opportunity to do this meaningful work. One of the survivors sang "Ani ma'amin" (I believe) during his testimony and I echo this prayer with hope. My grandmother Dolly Farber was a beacon of light during the difficult years of completing the interviews of this research and her love and devotion built my resilience and made it possible for me to finish. My loving father Mervyn believed in my abilities and constantly encouraged me. They are both sorely missed and their memory is a source of comfort and inspiration for me. Hessie Gordon was my mentor and she is remembered with gratitude for teaching me about the importance of dignity for Holocaust survivors who have suffered extreme dehumanization. In addition, my thanks go to my beloved family—my mother Sandra and my brothers Ashley, Gordon and Rowan. My nieces, cousins—and friends for their support and encouragement, in particular my aunt Hilary Kahn and my friend Jane Newcombe who spent many hours proofreading the research. Finally I would like to thank my friends, colleagues and the director at Tel Aviv University, Psychological Services for their encouragement of my work during the writing of this book.

We as authors hope that students of mental health will benefit from knowledge generated in a study that has sought to understand the long-term impact of trauma across the life cycle. This book is written from a psychodynamic perspective, and the nine case histories and the cross-case analysis can be used as valuable course content in subjects such as psychology, psychoanalysis, and social work. This book will also be of interest to students of the Holocaust. It offers unique testimony from child survivors about concentration camp life and brings the history of the Holocaust alive.

The research participants were promised anonymity and confidentiality in the write-up of the material unless otherwise requested. One of the participants requested that his real name be used and his story told—Shlomo Pieprz appears with authentic pictures.

In addition, the participants had personal wisdom to offer after a lifetime of struggle. For example, Dave, who was liberated at fourteen and had been interned in three concentration camps, where he was responsible for collecting dead bodies, spoke of his experience of human nature: "We all have an angel and a devil inside us. I know that because I saw it in others and in myself. I saw that I was capable of rescuing my friend and sharing my food and I was also capable of beating the gypsy and the young Jewish boy who betrayed us." Dave had never read Melanie Klein or Freud, yet he was aware of the human capacity for good and evil. The wisdom in survivors' retrospective reflections will hopefully be conveyed through their stories, which are at the core of this book.

In this book nine case histories tell the stories of trauma, grief, survival, and resilience. Each story is different and they are rich with nuanced paradox. In the stories there are examples of cruelty and dehumanization by Nazis, and yet many of the child survivors were rescued by Germans and righteous gentiles who risked their lives to save them. These saviors were "islands of hope" in a world that had lost empathy and compassion. All the participants continued to grieve for the parents that they lost when they were children. This is their story . . .

Introduction

Tracey Farber, Gillian Eagle, Cora Smith

Understanding the long-term effect of trauma on child survivors is important for both clinicians and researchers and in the case of Holocaust survivors has become urgent as this population has reached old age and end of life stage (Barak 2013). The trauma of the Holocaust was extensive and there cannot be hope of complete healing or cure, however, we need to understand as much as possible about the Holocaust to try to alleviate some of the ongoing suffering (Tauber 1996).

The word Holocaust is derived from the Greek composite word *holoskaustos*, from roots meaning "whole" and "burnt." It refers to a burnt offering. In Hebrew, the Holocaust is referred to as *ha-Shoah*, which translates to "the catastrophe" (Kellermann 2009). The Holocaust is the commonly used term to describe the destruction of European Jewry during the World War II. Six million Jews were systematically persecuted and exterminated, including one and a half million children (Barel, Van Ijzendoorn, Sagi-Schwartz, and Bakermans-Kranenburg 2010; Gutterman and Shalev 2008). Jews were tormented, maltreated, and murdered solely based on their identity as Jewish people. The genocide was perpetrated primarily by forces operating under, or in conjunction with, Adolph Hitler's Nazi Germany army during World War II lasting from 1939 to 1945. From 1941 to 1945 Jews were systematically murdered, as were Romani, homosexual, and mentally and physically disabled populations (Gutterman and

Shalev 2008). "That attempt at the systematic destruction of an entire people falls like a shadow on the history of Europe and the entire world; it is a crime which will forever darken the history of humanity" (Pope John Paul II, in Kellermann 2009, 1).

The Holocaust was a tragic, humanmade catastrophe, where human beings were exposed to destruction on a vast scale (Gutterman and Shalev 2008). The Nazis perpetrated atrocities against Jews and other minority groups who were forcibly rounded up and transported in cattle cars to concentration camps. Here, those who managed to survive witnessed the murders of their families and friends, suffered humiliations, and endured dehumanizing living conditions, including starvation, cold, and disease. Others lived in hiding or fought as partisans (Barel et al. 2010; Gutterman and Shalev 2008). Research concerning Holocaust survivors provides a framework for understanding the long-term consequences of massive trauma for aging genocide survivors (Carmil and Breznitz 1991). Insights from this understanding may be applied to helping victims of more recent genocides (Barel et al. 2010). Brice (2005) argues that the Holocaust was different from other genocides and processes of ethnic cleansing, as the primary aim of the Holocaust was the physical extermination of the Jewish people. He explains that killing in war ends with surrender, however, in the Holocaust, killing was aimed at the most defenseless and there was no mercy. As such, the extermination of Jews justifies the name "Holocaust" (Brice 2005).

Nobel Prize winner Eli Wiesel wrote about his experiences as a fifteen-year-old boy during the Holocaust in his book *Night* (1960). He was in the same age group as some of the participants who took part in this study. Here is how he describes the trauma he endured when he was interned in Auschwitz and Buchenwald:

> Never shall I forget that night, the first night in the camp, which has turned my life into one long night, seven times cursed and seven times sealed. Never shall I forget that smoke. Never shall I forget the little faces of the children, whose bodies I saw turned into wreaths of smoke beneath a silent blue sky. Never shall I forget those flames, which consumed my faith forever. Never shall I forget that nocturnal silence which deprived me, for all eternity, of the desire to live. Never shall I forget those moments, which murdered my God and my soul and turned my dreams to dust. Never shall I forget these things, even if I am condemned to live as long as God Himself. Never. (Wiesel 1960, 43)

Wiesel (1960) conveys very evocatively how as a fifteen-year-old boy he experienced the devastation of the Holocaust and the impact it had on the rest of his life. He describes how he has been forever scarred by what he witnessed and how the trauma impacted his worldview and his spiritual relationship with God. Based on his experience he maintains that "time does *not* heal all wounds; there are those that remain painfully open" (Wiesel 1978, 222). Kellermann (2009) states that no mental health professional can capture the human predicament of the Holocaust with the level of intensity conveyed by authors like Eli Wiesel and Primo Levi. As such, their words are used in this thesis to highlight experiential aspects of living through the Holocaust and their reflections upon this as now elderly child survivors (although both authors are now deceased).

Since time immemorial humankind has endured trauma and tragedy as expressed in art and literature (Van der Kolk and McFarlane 2007). In accordance with Laub (2002): "The massive psychic trauma of genocide produces excessive fragmentation in its survivors—fragmentation of perception, fragmentation of a sense of coherence in their life histories, fragmentation of their relationships to their families, and to the wider human community" (p. 1). Such observations suggest that significant life trauma continues to be a legitimate area of study for psychologists and other social scientists.

In her book *Trauma and Recovery*, Herman (1992) pointed out that: "Atrocities refuse to be buried. They keep penetrating the conscious and unconscious minds of survivors and their offspring until they are properly remembered, mourned and worked through within a safe, healing relationship" (1). Kellermann (2001) says that the long-term effects of Holocaust traumatization have been evident several decades after the war in both survivors and their children and even grandchildren, as explored from a range of psychological perspectives. This perspective was substantiated by Klein[1] (2012) and Wardi (1992), who also wrote about Holocaust survivors and second- and third-generation effects. Van der Kolk and McFarlane (2007) state that traumatic experiences alter individuals' physiological equilibrium and observe that traumatic memories affect the appreciation of present positive experiences. All of these authors have highlighted that the trauma of the Holocaust had significant impact on the lives of Holocaust survivors. The trauma of the Holocaust caused a shattering of the psyche that did not necessarily heal with time and impacted later generations (Wardi 1992).

---

1 In this text "Klein" will refer to Hillel Klein. When referring to Melanie Klein, her first name will be specified.

Herman (1992) argues that the study of trauma represents a cycle of episodes over historical time in that knowledge about traumatic stress is periodically forgotten and then reclaimed. She explains that trauma evokes intense controversy, involves the unthinkable, and raises basic questions of belief. The study of trauma exposes human vulnerability and humankind's capacity for evil. Herman (1992) suggests that a predictable pattern emerges after an atrocity. The victim is blamed and there is a collective denial surrounding the trauma. In addition, victims feel alienated and isolated and this exacerbates their suffering (Herman 1992). Such conditions were true of gender-based violence, for example, until feminist activism brought such trauma into prominence. The Holocaust is a mass trauma that also produced considerable denial. For example, within the broader Jewish community it was not widely discussed until the 1980s with the establishment of the Spielberg foundation that requested that survivors give testimony to memorialize their Holocaust experiences. Danieli (1984) argues that even mental health professionals contributed to the "conspiracy of silence" by not acknowledging the trauma of the Holocaust. At its most extreme there has been a denial that the events of the Holocaust took place at all.

While aspects of Holocaust impact have been quite widely researched, there is limited research on the long-term impact on child survivors. The study of the long-term effects of the Holocaust facilitates the understanding of how trauma impacts the life cycle, starting with young children and ending in the phase of old age (Fridman, Bakermans-Kranenburg, Sagi-Schwartz, and Van Ijzendoorn 2010).

During the Holocaust, children were segregated with their parents in ghettos and were subjected to starvation, overcrowding, cold, lice, poor hygiene, shootings, and humiliations. Some went into hiding and survived, whist others were captured. Some were gathered with their parents and put in cattle trucks to be sent to concentration or extermination camps (Valent 1998). Within the camps individuals were subjected to horror and death (Gutterman and Shalev 2008; Valent 1998; Wiesel 1978). Children were treated with cruelty and brutality. For instance, in the Lodz Ghetto children were thrown out of hospital windows and used for target practice (Chalmers 2015). Of those interned in Auschwitz concentration camp many were subjected to medical experimentation (Gutterman and Shalev 2008).

One and a half million children were killed during the Holocaust (Gutterman and Shalev 2008; Valent 1998). Those that survived were generally separated from their parents and many children were orphaned (Valent 1998). Children lost extended family and were uprooted from their homes. The loss experienced was enormous, and, in addition, school and play were disrupted. This massive trauma halted the normal developmental process (Valent 1998). Wardi (1992) explains that survival was the ultimate goal of individuals in the ghettos, forced labor camps, and concentration camps. Those imprisoned used all their physical and psychological resources to survive. This survival focus was sustained for months and years, involving terrible physical suffering, including coping with illness, cold, ravenous hunger, and exhaustion. The psychological warfare of the Nazis involved individual dehumanization and "the destruction of the identity and personality of each individual as a person and as a Jew" (Wardi 1992, 8). Wardi (1992) details the way in which Holocaust survivors were repeatedly traumatized. The traumatization began with the transportation to the camps and extended into the selection upon arrival at the camps where family members were separated. Life in the camps involved ongoing traumatization, which was intended not only to physically eliminate the prisoners but also to obliterate the inner reality of the survivors. In addition, life in the camps annihilated all representations of an external, familiar world (Klein 2012). Auerhahn and Laub (1998) state that "failed empathy" (p. 1) was a central theme in the Holocaust survivor's experience. The empathic response was absent from the Nazis and society at large, including in many instances from the Allies. The victims felt there was "no longer anyone to count on" (Wiesel 1970, 229). The Nazi ideology defined Jews as subhuman and in this respect the Holocaust represented a socially sanctioned sadistic racism that had pervasive effects (Auerhahn and Laub 1984).

Hillel Klein (2012), a psychiatrist and psychoanalyst born in Krakow, Poland, was sixteen years old when the Holocaust began. He survived internment in the Krakow ghetto. After joining the resistance, he was captured by the Germans and interned at Plaszow concentration camp, where he experienced many horrors (Klein 2012). After he was taken on a "death march," he spent time in Theresienstadt concentration camp, where he was later liberated by the Soviet Army. He was twenty-two years old when the war ended, his health was poor, and he was the only survivor of his large family. After studying medicine, psychiatry, and psychoanalysis in Israel, his professional interest was drawn to Holocaust survivors. Klein's writing has considerable relevance for this study as he endured the Holocaust in his late teenage years. Klein's strength was that he resisted generalizations and avoided discussing Holocaust survivors as a group. Rather, he viewed survivors as individuals within a group, each survivor having a different personal history and consequently, a unique psychological reaction to his or her Holocaust experience (Klein 2012). Klein wrote about survivors from a psychodynamic point of view and reported that the psychotic nature of the concentration camps produced a trauma of catastrophic proportion. Both Hillel Klein and Eli Wiesel wrote prolifically about their experiences as adolescent survivors during the Holocaust from their different perspectives, Klein as a psychiatrist and psychoanalyst and Wiesel as a writer and Nobel Prize laureate. Their testimony and insight have special relevance for this research project as this was a retrospective study where aging survivors described their experiences as children and adolescents in the concentration camps and their impressions of how this experience had impacted their life trajectories.

Chalmers (2015) writes about massive trauma during the Holocaust. She quotes Desbois, a Catholic priest who has researched the deaths of Jews in the Ukraine and Belarus during the Holocaust:

> I am convinced that there is only one race: a human race that shoots two-year-old children. For better or for worse I belong to that human race and this allows me to acknowledge that an ideology can deceive minds to the point of annihilating all ethical reflexes and all recognition of the human in the other. (Desbois in Chalmers 2015, 256)

It would seem that humankind is unable to learn from experience. While technology has advanced, humanity is still unable to protect children from genocides. Chalmers (2015) states that ideological fanaticism is evident worldwide and continues to be a destructive force for humankind, including for young people growing up in such contexts.

As authors we aimed to explore the psychological effects of the Holocaust experience on child survivors who were now in late life stages of development in terms of the following features:

1. developmental life cycle processes including early childhood experiences prior to the Holocaust;

2. subjective accounts of exposure to traumatic events during the Holocaust;

3. mental health impacts including post-traumatic stress symptoms and related conditions;

4. patterns of affective experiences, with particular reference to loss and mourning and exposure to further traumatic stimuli;

5. the development of (adaptive) coping mechanisms;

6. the negotiation of "integrity versus despair" and existential beliefs.

The testimony in this book challenges the false assumption that child Holocaust survivors were "too young to remember" (Felsen 2017). On the contrary many of them described their visceral memories with clarity and their emotional experiences of loss and trauma remained palpable for many decades.

This book is being published at a point in history where the United Nations general assembly has adopted an Israeli resolution to combat Holocaust denial (*Times of Israel*, January 2022). The testimony in this book vividly describes the tragedy of the Holocaust told through the eyes of children and adolescents and serves to memorialize their stories.

1

Literature Review

Tracey Farber

Introduction

This initial theoretical discussion will present theories concerning trauma exposure and its impact largely as understood from a psychodynamic perspective, as well as covering some diagnostic aspects of post-traumatic stress and complex traumatic stress. Thereafter, a focus will be drawn to the existing research into the trauma of Holocaust survivors specifically. Because this study views trauma through a developmental lens, aspects of Erikson's psychosocial theory of human development will be outlined with attention to previous research that describes the impact of massive trauma on the developmental process. Child Holocaust survivors' experiences will be discussed with a particular focus on the themes of trauma and loss and resilience. Themes related to trauma and affective impact will be presented. In addition, coping strategies such as defense mechanisms will be explored together with debates concerning resilience in child survivors. Since the focus of the book is on aging survivors, special emphasis will be given to the developmental stage of aging and end of life, that is, the stage of "integrity versus despair" (Erikson 1965).

The inclusion of psychologists, psychiatrists, and psychoanalysts who were also Holocaust survivors or child survivors is particularly meaningful as the writers who survived the Holocaust were able to use their experiences of loss and trauma to make a contribution to the body of literature. Their wisdom is highlighted and acknowledged in the literature review, as they open an important lens to help us to gain some deeper insight into the world of child survivors (Cyrulnik 2009; Dasberg 1992/2001; Durst 1995; Frankl 1962; Klein 2012; Krell 2013; Laub 1992/2002; Valent 2014) For example, Viktor Frankl (1962) who was an adult survivor developed his existential theory based on his experiences. These authors had a lived experience regarding their subject matter and their contribution to the understanding of child Holocaust survivors is underscored in this book.

Traumatic Stress

Introduction to Traumatic Stress

Owing to the constant challenges that mental health professionals face to meet the needs of survivors of ongoing trauma, the field of traumatic stress is an area that continues to grow in research, theory, and practice. Ongoing wars, terrorist attacks, and genocides ensure that this field is called on to address human suffering in its most extreme form. Eagle (2000) states: "It is evident that the experience of post-traumatic stress impacts at multiple levels from neurological and biological to the social and spiritual" (9).

Herman (1992) argues that traumatized victims are overwhelmed with helplessness and traumatic events disrupt the individual's sense of control, connection to others, and sense of meaning. Two central aspects of traumatization have been described as helplessness and terror. Herman (1992) continues to explain that traumatized people feel and behave as if their nervous systems have been "disconnected from the present" (35). She explains that the symptoms of trauma, such as hyperarousal, intrusive thoughts, and emotional constriction, are connected to the nervous system. Hyperarousal represents the continuous expectation of danger; intrusive thoughts reflect the enduring imprint of the traumatic experience; and emotional constriction represents the numbing response of helplessness or surrender. These effects are often enduring and extensive, demonstrating that perhaps trauma seems to alter the human nervous and psychic systems, in some instances more severely than others depending on the extent of the trauma exposure and the developmental capacities of the individual concerned.

The following discussion will offer a primarily psychodynamic view of trauma in keeping with the overarching theoretical frame of the study.

The Psychodynamic Approach to Traumatic Stress

Proponents of the psychodynamic approach include classical theorists such as Sigmund Freud, as well as object-relations theorists such as Melanie Klein, Wilfred Bion, and Donald Winnicott. The psychodynamic school of thought emphasizes unconscious conflict, memories, and feelings. Psychic determinism is a basic tenet that underscores the view that to a large extent we are characters, living out a script written by our early experiences and informed by our unconscious. Early infancy and childhood are considered to be defining influences in the development of an adult personality. Defense mechanisms are understood to be a core function of the psyche and play a role in reducing anxiety in relation to threatening experiences. Eagle (2013) singles out three theoretical bodies within the psychodynamic tradition that have contributed to our understanding of how trauma impacts the psyche: classical psychoanalytic, ego-psychological, and object-relations perspectives. Each of these perspectives will be elaborated in the discussion that follows.

Psychoanalytic Contributions to Trauma

Freud (1920) developed his psychoanalytic theory regarding trauma as a result of working with "shell-shocked" combat veterans after World War I. As his theory of trauma influenced many later theorists, it is important to outline his conceptualization. Freud (1920) described the conflict between the life instinct and the death instinct, Eros and Thanatos. In his opinion, the goal of the psyche is to optimize pleasure and minimize pain. To maintain balance and lessen anxiety, the ego attempts to mediate and moderate the individual's experience of the external world, guarding the person from becoming overwhelmed by anxiety. The impact of traumatic stress is sudden and overwhelming for the ego, and its function in the containment of anxiety becomes compromised (Eagle 1998).

Freud (1920) described the protective shield of the ego as a "stimulus barrier." When trauma impacts the individual, the stimulus barrier is overwhelmed, which ruptures the protective interface between the self and the external world. Freud described trauma as a consequence of a breach in the "protective shield" against overwhelming stimuli. This conceptualization of trauma emphasizes the core issues of disruption and the breaks in continuity of experience (Benyakar, Kutz, Dasberg, and Stern 1989) as well as the manner in which it compromises overall functioning. Once the rupture has happened, the ego is weakened and its ability to mediate inner and outer reality is compromised.

Thus, in the immediate aftermath of trauma the ego is unable to contain anxiety and becomes overwhelmed. The individual's reality contact is impaired (Eagle 1998). Primitive regressed forms of thinking may be dominant, as more id-driven primary process thinking and impulsivity are apparent. Freud (1920/1948) made an important contribution to our present understanding of traumatic stress in explaining that catastrophic trauma causes regression, leading to cognitive deficits and primitive defenses, which lean toward dissociation.

Freud (1920) coined the term "repetition compulsion" to describe the way in which memories about the trauma continued in the form of intrusive thoughts and nightmares, usually evoking high anxiety levels. Freud speculated that the function of repetitive memory was "to work over in the mind some overpowering experience so as to make oneself master it" (Freud in Gay 1995, 600). Later, his formulation included the way in which trauma survivors reenact their trauma as an attempt to gain mastery over it. Van der Kolk (2007) explains that Freud thought that the aim of repetition compulsion was to achieve mastery, but clinical experience demonstrates that the opposite happens: the repetition tends to cause more suffering for the victims and those around them.

Herman (1992) states that survivors do not consciously seek to relive the trauma to gain mastery; in fact, they fear and dread it. Whether the traumatic experience is relived in the form of images, dreams, or actions, it involves reexperiencing the accompanying emotional intensity of the traumatic event. The survivors are overwhelmed with feelings such as terror and rage, to the extent that they may become unable to process or tolerate the emotion involved. Because the experience of reliving the trauma is so distressing, survivors go to great lengths to avoid these kinds of emotional experiences. In the attempt to avoid the trauma, further symptoms of post-traumatic stress are caused, such as depersonalization, avoidance, and dissociation. This leads to a withdrawal from relationships and an "impoverished life" (Herman 1992, 42).

Ego Psychology Writers

As indicated by Eagle (1998), Horowitz (1992) extended aspects of Freud's thinking on trauma impact as he clarified the way in which trauma overwhelms an individual, specifically, the individual's ability to process information, and to connect adaptively to the external world. Horowitz (1992) contributed to our understanding of both intrusion and avoidance symptoms of post-traumatic stress. As far as traumatic stress symptoms are concerned, he demonstrated that an individual can have a mixed experience of both avoidance or suppression and intrusive thoughts and emotions. Horowitz argues that in order to "live with" the impact of traumatic experiences the psyche is compelled to integrate (assimilate and accommodate) the disturbing information into long-term memory. The process of integration requires finding a balance between engaging with traumatic material and becoming overwhelmed by anxiety and moving away from this kind of information. The attempt to absorb the traumatic material is often reflected in cycles of intrusion and avoidance. Horowitz argues that both the intrusion- and avoidance-related symptoms of trauma disrupt meaning systems, interfere with memory, and challenge the capacity to integrate experience. His theory set the foundation for a theoretical model of understanding that included intrusion-related, avoidance, and numbing symptoms as part of the diagnostic picture of post-traumatic stress (American Psychiatric Association 2000).

Lifton (1979), after World War II, described the reaction to death anxiety after catastrophic trauma. His experience was in working with survivors of Hiroshima and Nazi doctors. He described trauma with reference to the "death imprint." Lifton argues that a traumatic experience can damage the capacity for libidinal investment in the world and the capacity for thinking. Dissociation occurs as a result of severe death anxiety in reaction to overwhelming trauma and comprehension of mortality and leads to a deadening of the mind. Dissociation becomes an intrapsychic phenomenon when affect is severed from knowledge or awareness of reality. Parts of the self is severed from the individual's personal history. In addition, the self is detached from compassion for others, community involvement, and other important values (Lifton in Wilson and Raphael 2013).

For both Lifton (1979) and Horowitz (1992), severe trauma affects the individual's worldview, relationships with others, and sense of self. For both authors, exposure to traumatic life events creates a preoccupation with mortality and the purpose of life or lack of it. In addition, interpersonal relationships become the focus of concerns surrounding harm and protection, isolation and solidarity, as well as issues of dependence and trust. Thus, there appears to be consensus regarding a fundamental questioning of issues pertaining to human existence, the self, and others (Eagle 1998). Eagle (1998) describes that Freud, Horowitz, and Lifton explain that trauma is an attack on biological and psychic survival, particularly the personality organization of the individual. In addition, the capacity for symbolization, the capacity to think in metaphors, and basic thought is compromised. This is reflected to some extent in a propensity to favor dissociation.

Object-Relations Understanding of Trauma

In accordance with Garland (1998), a combination of Freudian and Kleinian thinking offers a useful theoretical framework to understand trauma. A deep understanding of the impact of traumatic events upon the human psyche can be derived from a knowledge of what the particular meaning was for the individual of their traumatic experience. From this perspective, detailed attention is given to childhood memory and developmental history, as they are understood to form the foundation of the psychic structure and internal world. This psychic structure will receive the wounding from the external world in an idiosyncratic way, which will have a bearing on how the trauma is understood and interpreted. Central to this view is the understanding that an external trauma will trigger unresolved emotional pain and conflicts from infancy and childhood.

In Garland's (1998) view trauma disrupts the core of the survivor's identity and compromises the individual's capacity to filter reality and process anxiety. There is a breakdown of a sense of a predictable external world where the established defensive system is overwhelmed and shattered. "Thus, a trauma is an event which does precisely this: overwhelms existing defences against anxiety in a form which also provides confirmation of those deepest universal anxieties ... and has long term consequences for the entire personality" (Garland 1998, 11). A further aspect of such experiences is that trust in the protective role of the internal and external "good object" is shattered. This will lead to an escalation of fears about the cruelty and power of "bad objects." In this way, trauma resonates with all past injuries in object relations (Garland 1998).

The object-relations perspective understands trauma through the lens of early developmental experiences and difficulties, such as difficulty in the mother-infant relationship. From the perspective of a Kleinian lens, trauma leads to splitting and a regression to the paranoid-schizoid position. Eagle (2013) explains that the object-relations view of trauma will emphasize a way in which trauma echoes difficulties in relation to early developmental parental introjects or objects within the theater of the psyche. For example: "the trauma can be experienced as an absence of or abandonment of the 'good object' introject" (Eagle 2013, 124) Eagle (2013) says: "The fact that one has been allowed to suffer so terribly suggests the failure and/or impotence of good objects to protect one and this may lead to the sense that such objects have been destroyed or cannot be trusted" (124). Laub and Auerhahn (1993), who worked with Holocaust survivors, offer observations that resonate with this formulation:

> Trauma disrupts the link between the self and empathic other, a link first established by the expectation of mutual responsiveness in the mother-child bond and "objectified" in the mother child introject. Indeed we ... proposed that the essential experience of trauma was the unravelling of the relationship between the self

and nurturing other, the very fabric of psychic life. (Laub and
Auerhahn 1993, 287)

A major contributor to the object-relations school was Donald Winnicott
(1960), who spoke about the infant's experience of a "good enough mother."
The internalization of this experience leads to the establishment of the first
structure of the ego. In addition, Winnicott (1971) emphasized the importance
of the maternal attunement to the infant's needs. Winnicott also spoke about
the establishment of hope in a predictable environment where the child's needs
are met. Hillel Klein (2012) believed that all traumatic events hold a personal
meaning for survivors, based on their background and personal history. This
perspective clearly resonates with Garland and other object-relations theorists.
Auerhahn and Laub (1993) and Eagle (2013) each explain how trauma
damages the relationship to the good internalized introject (providing one has
had "good enough" early developmental experiences), shattering subsequent
trust in others for the trauma survivors.

Garland (1998) draws on Bion's formulation of the centrality of the containing
function of the maternal object. Garland (1998) explains that when trauma
occurs the external and internal containers are shattered—the world becomes
experienced as dangerous and persecutory. The dangers are overwhelming
and good internal objects are powerless to protect and prevent a calamity
from occurring. The capacity to symbolize is shattered, rendering the internal
container powerless to function in the realm of thinking and understanding.
Trauma thus shatters the internal container and in addition compromises the
trust in external containment.

Garland (1998) makes an important contribution to the object-relations view
of traumatic loss. She explains that from a psychoanalytic view all relationships
reflect both loving and hostile feelings, which are conscious or unconscious.
Garland notes that survivors of traumatic events have often lost family or loved
ones. These survivors are faced with the traumatic event as well as the traumatic
loss. Mourning, in this context, is difficult. The individuals are unable to mourn
as they may be in a fight for their own survival and their coping resources are
stretched. "Some of this mourning, as has often been pointed out, must be for
himself—for his own lost world, his own pre-trauma life and identity" (Garland
1998, 17).

Garland (1998) indicates that some survivors are overwhelmed by survivor
guilt and rage about being abandoned by their lost loved ones. In addition,
survivor guilt is intensified if prior relationships were problematic or deeply
ambivalent. The task of mourning for both their loved objects and the loss of

their pre-trauma self may be overwhelming for survivors. Consequently, they may well develop a pathological form of mourning—melancholia. In the case of chronic melancholia, as Freud wrote in *Mourning and Melancholia* (1917), a survivor may overidentify with the dead love object and carry unconscious guilt about survival that precludes the ability to mourn appropriately. Garland (1998) states that chronic post-traumatic stress, or complex traumatic stress and its symptoms of numbing and dissociation, are reminiscent of Freud's (1917) concept of melancholia. Temple (1998) adds that melancholia resembles the modern-day picture of clinical depression. As described by Pines (1986), many survivors of severe trauma use regression and splitting. They have an impaired ability to symbolize in fantasy and "return to a state of psychic death to avoid overwhelming and unbearably painful feelings" (304). Melanie Klein (1935/1952) described how the inability to mourn losses and retain a relationship with the internalized good object may lead to a paranoid-schizoid mode of functioning. This results in a strong "splitting" into "good object" and "bad object" representations both internally and interpersonally (Klein 1935).

Gerson (2009) describes the experience of a massive trauma in the case of genocide in the following terms: "When the container cracks" there is no continuity (1343). The experience of a genocide shatters the survivor's ability to regain faith and has an extensive impact on the sense of human relatedness. Andre Green's (1986) concept of the "dead mother" is used by Gerson, both literally and figuratively, to describe the impact of such mass individual and social trauma. Green's (1986) metaphor was used to describe a mother who was so preoccupied with her own traumatic loss that she was experienced by the infant as "blank and dead . . . a distant figure, toneless and practically inanimate . . . a mother who remains alive but who is psychically dead so to speak in the eyes of the young child in her care" (170). Gerson (2009) explains that the "dead mother" can symbolize the traumatic loss of a nurturing object. This could be a parent, a significant other, a doctor, or even a community at large. The loss of this nurturing leaves the survivor with fundamental anxiety that their needs will not be met. Thus, Gerson's work elaborates the theorization on the damage done to "good object" introjects by trauma and also resonates with Melanie Klein's formulation that the world is experienced as pervasively persecutory and threatening, as in the paranoid schizoid position.

Both Laub (2005) and Gerson (2009) use the metaphor of the "dead mother" to describe the psychodynamics of infantile maternal loss and the traumatic loss of the internal good object at any age in the life cycle. Laub and Auerhahn (1989) and Gerson (2009) each use the term "dead mother" to describe an aspect of the experience of survivors of genocide, who see the world as unconcerned in relation to their fate and unconcerned about their suffering. Survivors of genocide experience humankind as the universal "dead mother," as humankind in general remains silent and unresponsive to the pain of the victim.

For Laub and Auerhahn (1993), trauma ruptures basic trust and creates barriers in intimacy. Gerson (2009) describes a state of catastrophic loss, where "the absence of an involved and caring other leaves only a dense and collapsed heap of destroyed internal and external objects for whom no one mourns" (1349). He uses this metaphor to describe the internal world of the genocide survivor, as well as the infant born to the survivor. He describes the way in which dissociation is experienced by Holocaust survivors in relation to their unprocessed loss and describes how this state is transmitted to the second generation. Gerson's (2009) central point is that survivors of genocide live with a sense of "unfinished business" and a sense of permanent "damage done to the experience of goodness" (1350).

As discussed just previously, from the psychoanalytic perspective, the unresolved traumatic grief associated with significant trauma can be understood to take the form of melancholia; as described by Freud (1917): "the shadow of the object fell upon the ego" (Freud in Gerson 2009, 1351). Gerson (2009) explains that the unfinished business of melancholia "leaves life devoid of meaning through an unconscious and tragic embrace of deadliness" (Gerson 2009, 1351). From this perspective survivors of genocide are unable to "work through" the loss, as it is too traumatic and overwhelming for the psyche to encompass. They struggle with the ongoing challenge of bearing or living with the enormity of the losses and violations they have endured and witnessed.

Herman's Contribution to Theorization of Trauma and its Impact

Herman (1992) describes the importance of understanding the effects of captivity on the traumatized survivor:

> Traumatized people suffer damage to the basic structures of the self. They lose their trust in themselves, in other people, and in God. Their self-esteem is assaulted by experiences of humiliation, guilt and helplessness. Their capacity for intimacy is severely compromised by intense and contradictory feelings of need and fear. (56)

Herman (1992) explains that traumatic events impact the psychological structures of the self, as well as on attachments and meaning systems that connect the individual to the community. In addition, victims of chronic trauma may feel that their sense of self has been entirely violated. They have repeated experiences of trauma and suffer from intense hyperarousal symptoms, feeling constantly anxious and agitated. The intrusive symptoms of post-traumatic stress may continue for many years after liberation from an ongoing traumatic experience. Goldstein, Van Kammen, Shelly, Miller, and Van Kammen (1986) found that soldiers who were taken prisoner in World War II and the Korean War were suffering from nightmares, flashbacks, and extreme reactions to memory triggers thirty-five to forty years after their release from captivity. Their symptoms were more severe than those of soldiers of the same era who had not been imprisoned (Sutker, Winstead, Galina, and Allain 1991).

Herman (1992) states that the diagnosis of PTSD fails to capture the ongoing intense symptoms of prolonged and repeated trauma and the psychological damage on the personality of the victim in captivity. One population that Herman understood to have suffered prolonged and chronic trauma exposure was that of Holocaust victims. She cites the observations of psychiatrist Emmanuel Tanay: "The psychopathology may be hidden in characterological changes that are manifest only in disturbed object relationships and attitudes towards work, the world, man and God" (in Herman 1992, 120). Herman (1992) proposed and elaborated the syndrome of what she terms complex traumatic stress disorder or CPTSD. She describes seven features that characterize this syndrome (Herman 1992, 121):

1. a history of subjugation to totalitarian control over a prolonged period—months or years (examples include: hostages, prisoners of war, concentration camp survivors, and survivors of religious cults, as well as those subjected to totalitarian systems in sexual and domestic life, including survivors of domestic battering, childhood physical or sexual abuse, and organized sexual exploitation);

2. alterations in affect regulation, including persistent dysphoria, chronic suicidal preoccupation, self-injury, exploitative or extremely inhibited anger (may alternate), and compulsive or extremely inhibited sexuality (may alternate);

3. alterations in consciousness, including amnesia or hyperamnesia of traumatic events, transient dissociative episodes, depersonalization/ derealization, and for reliving events, either in the form of intrusive post-traumatic stress disorder symptoms or in the form of ruminative preoccupation;

4. alterations in self-perception, including sense of helplessness or paralysis of initiative, feelings of shame, guilt, and self-blame, a sense of
defilement or stigma, and a sense of complete difference from others
(which may include a sense of specialness, utter aloneness, a belief that
no other person can understand, or non-human identity);

5. alterations in perception of perpetrator, including preoccupation with
the relationship with the perpetrator (includes preoccupation with revenge), unrealistic attribution of total power to the perpetrator (cau-
tion: victim's assessment of power realities may be more realistic than
clinician's), idealization or paradoxical gratitude, a sense of special or
supernatural relationship, and acceptance of belief system or rational-
izations of perpetrators;

6. alterations in relations with others in general, including isolation or
withdrawal, disruption in intimate relationships, repeated search for a
rescuer (may alternate with isolation and withdrawal), persistent distrust, and repeated failures of self-protection;

7. lastly, alterations in systems of meaning, including a loss of sustaining
faith and a sense of hopelessness and despair.

As will be evident, the impact of prolonged subjugation and exposure to
traumatic stimuli can have a profound, far reaching, and enduring symptomatic
and psychological effects.

Herman's (1992) understanding of complex traumatic stress is important
in explaining how ongoing trauma impacts the personality over time and
is particularly relevant in understanding child Holocaust survivors, as
Kellermann (2009) states explicitly. Child Holocaust survivors were interned in
concentration camps and became victims and witnesses of immense cruelty. The
specific relevance for Kellermann (2009) was that Herman (1992) emphasized
the impact of ongoing traumas over an extended period of time leading to the
fragmentation of the self and "the loss of a sense of safety, trust and self-worth"
(Kellermann 2009, 60).

Summary of Psychodynamic Theorization of Trauma Impact

In summary, it is apparent that many psychodynamic writers use metaphors
and symbols associated with shattering and destruction to describe the way
in which trauma damages the psyche, most especially in the case of severe

trauma exposure, as was the case for most of those who were victimized during the Holocaust. Freud (1920) described the shattering of a protective shield, Melanie Klein (1935/1952) described splitting as part of movement into the paranoid-schizoid position, and Bion (1985) described the destruction of the internalized container. Garland (1998), Benyakar et al. (1989), and Herman (1992) explain the way in which trauma disrupts the core identity of survivors. Benyakar et al. (1989) also subscribe to the notion of trauma as a psychological wound that shatters the self-structure. This structure includes the capacity to operate autonomously, the sense of a coherent identity, and the capacity to self-regulate affective states. Trauma leads to a sense of helplessness and disrupts internal continuity. Trauma shatters the individual's sense of self, and in addition can destroy their sense of meaning (Frankl 1962) and their core assumptions about the world (Janoff-Bulman 1985). Trauma carries different levels of injury associated with loss, rupture, and unpredictability. Traumatized individuals not only sustain losses in the external world but also in many instances lose their sense of dignity or humanity and their sense of a self with a continuous personal history and future. The sense of unpredictability that arises with exposure to traumatic events disrupts the capacity to self-regulate. "When events lose their lawfulness, faith in one's self-regulating capacity is diminished or lost completely, hopelessness and helplessness prevail, and one resigns, not only to the events but also to the loss of one's former capacity and identity" (Benyakar et al. 1989, 439).

In a related but somewhat different vein, Garland (1998) emphasizes the shattering of internalized good objects because violation to the self has occurred and there has been an absence of protection against this. She also emphasizes that current trauma is mapped onto and processed through early relational templates. Laub and Auerhahn (1993) describe the way in which trauma disrupts attachment; and in keeping with others, Eagle (2013) also elaborates how the trauma survivor feels abandoned by the good object. Such formulations are amplified by Gerson (2009) who applies the concept of the "dead mother" to describe the trauma survivor's feeling of desolation in relation to having to live in a world that has abandoned them without empathy, recognition, or care.

It is evident that many object relations authors describe the loss of trust (Erikson 1965; Herman 1992) in the good object and in the world at large (Gerson 2009; Herman 1992) as being a fundamental aspect of traumatization. Psychodynamic writers agree that trauma ruptures the self and the attachment to the outside world, leading to a sense of mistrust and vulnerability to feelings of abandonment and loss (Benyakar et al. 1989; Eagle 1998; Erikson 1950; Garland 1998; Herman 1992; Laub and Auerhahn 1993). All of these observations about the impact of severe and mass traumatization are important to acknowledge with regards to the present study. One begins to understand that when a Holocaust survivor is struggling to symbolize, for example, because of trauma-related dissociation, they may consequently struggle with ego integration in Erikson's (1950) stage of "ego integrity versus despair" (Dasberg 2001). It is likely that exposure to severe and prolonged trauma in early life may have lifetime effects, including influencing negotiation of end-of-life psychological tasks.

Having discussed the work of several key psychodynamic writers and their understanding of trauma, the discussion turns to formulations of traumatic stress associated with more psychiatric or clinically focused diagnostic models, with a particular emphasis on post-traumatic stress disorder (PTSD).

Diagnostic Formulations of Traumatic Stress Conditions

Given that the primary lens through which the interview material was interpreted was psychoanalytic, the discussion of diagnostic formulations of traumatic stress-related conditions is rather brief. However, since the research addresses aspects of the mental health impact of childhood internment, it is considered important to address some more psychiatrically focused understandings of trauma impact.

Van der Kolk and McFarlane (2007) explain that the diagnosis of post-traumatic stress aims to establish a commonly accepted formulation or structure that is understood to describe the impact of trauma on an individual's personality features, biological functions, and understanding of the world. The central issue in the diagnosis of traumatic stress conditions is the recognition of the reality of exposure to an extraordinarily stressful event. Although the reality of the traumatic event is central to diagnosing traumatic stress, for psychologists the subjective aspect, meaning that the survivor attaches to the event, is as important as the nature of the trauma itself. In addition, it has also been recognized that the individual's interpretation of the trauma is ongoing and continues after the initial processing, and that traumatization can occur sometime after the event, and in some instances even years later. This retraumatization is often triggered by a new event in the present that resonates in some way with the prior trauma. Van der Kolk and McFarlane (2007) state that the post-traumatic stress syndrome represents "the failure of time to heal all wounds" (7).

Regarding psychiatric diagnosis, post-traumatic stress disorder, or PTSD, as it is commonly referred to, requires that a specific symptom set is present in order for diagnosis to take place. While traumatic stress-related responses to traumatic events are common and perhaps almost inevitable, the translation of such responses into full-blown PTSD, with its associated compromising of everyday functioning, is less frequent. While individual vulnerability plays a part, it is also recognized that severity of exposure is predictive of the likelihood of development of PTSD and the events characteristic of the Holocaust would certainly be of the kind of severity that would produce PTSD in most people exposed to such stimuli. However, as has been discussed previously with reference to Herman's work, it appears that the prolonged nature of captivity and multiple forms of traumatization suffered by camp survivors may more likely have produced complex forms of trauma syndromes, such as CPTSD, a condition recognized by clinicians even if not formally included in the diagnostic manual of the American Psychiatric Association. In addition, it is also important to note that PTSD has high comorbidity with mood, dissociative, and anxiety disorders, as well as with substance abuse and personality disorders (Davidson, Hughes, Blazer, and George 1991; Green, Lindy, Grace, and Leonard 1992; Kulka et al. 1990).

Since the participants in this study were interviewed while the Diagnostics and Statistical Manual, fourth edition revised (DSMIV-R) (American Psychiatric Association 2000) was in use, in the writing of this book the DSM-5 (American Psychiatric Association 2013) was utilized to understand the PTSD for each participant. Interesting to note is that DSM-5 places greater weight on negative beliefs arising as a consequence of trauma (American Psychiatric Association 2013). Since most readers familiar with the traumatic stress field will be cognizant of the diagnostic features of the condition, these are not detailed in the text.

Depression as an Associated Feature of PTSD in Child Survivors

In a large North American-based National Comorbidity Survey, it was evident that most subjects who met the criteria for PTSD also met the diagnostic criteria for clinical depression (Kessler, Sonnega, Bromet, Hughes, and Nelson 1995). Kellermann (2009) states that the most appropriate diagnostic category for Holocaust survivors who form part of a clinical population is "chronic post-traumatic stress disorder" (Kellermann 2009, 35) with depression as a commonly associated feature (Conn, Clarke, and Van Reekum 2000; Yehuda, Kahana, Southwick, and Giller 1994). Yehuda et al. (1994) found that Holocaust survivors with PTSD had a greater number of depressive symptoms. In addition, a high proportion of Holocaust survivors experienced major depression and most of the remainder were found to have experienced symptoms of subclinical depression (Trappler, Cohen, and Tulloo 2007).

Research has demonstrated that aging survivors are more prone to depression as they age (Barel et al. 2010; Joffe et al. 2003; Trappler, Cohen, and Tulloo 2007). Aging child Holocaust survivors were found to have higher levels of depression when compared to older adults in general in Israel and Canada. Significantly, the experience of early life trauma increased depressive affect and the absence of wellbeing in Holocaust survivors (O'Rourke, Carmel, and Bachner 2018). In addition, an increased risk of suicide was found among aging survivors with depression (Barak et al. 2005). It's important to note that not all child survivors suffer from depression, however, those who were depressed also suffered from significantly worse psychosocial functioning than non-depressed survivors (Trappler, Cohen, and Tulloo 2007).

Erikson's Psycho-Social Theory of the Life Cycle

Introduction to Erikson's Theory

Erikson was a student of Anna Freud. His contribution to ego psychology emphasizes the adaptive function of the ego (Erikson 1959). Erikson focuses on the normal developmental crises that an individual faces at each of the lifespan developmental stages that he identifies as significant. Mastery of the challenge posed by the crisis leads to the acquisition of psycho-social skills, whereas failure leads to fixation in relation to the issues associated with this life phase. Erikson argues that successful resolution of lifespan stages from birth to death leads to a sense of identity that constitutes a core sense of self (Goldstein 1995). Erikson emphasizes the role of the social context in the individual's lifespan development (Smith and Osborne 2008).

Erikson (1965) postulated eight significant consecutive developmental stages from infancy to late adulthood. Erikson's (1950/1965) first stage begins in infancy and prioritizes trust versus mistrust, and the final stage ends in old age with integrity versus despair. Negotiation of the final stage is dependent upon the cumulative outcomes of the previous seven stages. From this perspective, Erikson (1950) proposed his theory of epigenesis, arguing that personality development unfolds, in part as a consequence of environmental influences, with each developmental stage impacting on the next and so forth. "Integrity versus despair" is based on the form of resolution of the previous stages and the capacity to find meaning and glean a sense of wisdom based on previous life experience (Cheng 2009). Since many readers are likely to be familiar with Erikson's developmental theory, a fairly brief exposition of the life stages is offered here, with some emphasis on issues that may have relevance for this particular book.

Stage One: Hope, Basic Trust versus Mistrust

In accordance with Erikson (1965), this stage occurs in the first year of life. The foundation of personality development is established where the infant develops a sense of trust in having his or her needs met in a predictable manner (or not). Intrinsic to this stage is developing a sense of hope that the maternal figure will respond to primary needs. Erikson (1964) said: "Hope is both the earliest and the most indispensable virtue inherent in the state of being alive. If life is to be sustained hope must remain, even where confidence is wounded, trust impaired" (115). Thus, for Erikson, this is a time when, in addition to having physical needs met, the baby is hopefully soothed and the mother regulates the infant's sense of safety in the world (Erikson 1977).

Erikson (1982) goes on to describe the early origins of projection and introjection: "In introjection we feel and act as if outer goodness had become our inner certainty. In projection, we experience an inner harm as an outer one; we endow significant people with the evil that is in us" (223). He emphasizes the importance of the facilitative maternal relationship in infant development of a sense of trust and states that this sense of trust will form the core of the individual's identity. Erikson (1982) also identifies basic trust as lying at the core of religious faith. For Erikson, the opposite of trust is a sense of mistrust. For him, this state characterizes an individual who withdraws from relationships and is uncomfortable with themselves and others (Goldstein 1995). The child who has a sense of mistrust is fearful, empty, depressed, and has an inner sense of badness (Erikson 1977). Erikson (1982) explains that hope emerges when the conflict of "trust versus mistrust" is successfully negotiated.

Stage Two: Will, Autonomy versus Shame and Doubt

Although the child strives to be autonomous, they have dependency needs, which mobilize them to turn to parental figures for protection and nurturing. This coincides with Freud's (1920) "anal stage" of development: at this stage, the child is exposed to the imperative to conform to societal rules and regulations. As such, the child's will and the parent's control may come into opposition. Erikson (1982) describes the sensitive dynamic of control that enters the parent-child relationship during the process of toilet training. A child's rudimentary sense of will begins at this stage and children come to establish a sense of faith in self, as they practice autonomous self-control. Erikson (1977) explains that young toddlers are very sensitive to shame about both their lack of control and their smallness in relation to adults. If children are excessively shamed within the family, lack of confidence and/or defiance may ensue.

Stage Three: Purpose, Initiative versus Guilt

This stage describes the developmental process of a four- or five-year-old child and tallies with what Freud (1920) described as the "phallic/oedipal stage." At this stage, the child is concerned with taking the initiative and conquests. Children's identity begins to strengthen and they embrace fantasies about the future. Conquest, competition, and behavior is driven by a sense of purpose. Gender role modelling also becomes important and sexual curiosity intensifies (Goldstein 1995). The core of a superego is formed at this stage, and the ego defense of repression is used to cope with excessive guilt.

Stage Four: Competence, Industry versus Inferiority

This stage coincides with Freud's "latency stage." Erikson (1965) views this as an active stage where the child engages socially and intellectually at school. The child strives to develop a sense of competence, particularly intellectual competence (Erikson 1982). The child learns perseverance in relation to the completion of tasks. This is essential to the attainment of ego mastery. The opposite of the mastery of industry is inferiority. Erikson (1982) explains that when a child has a sense of inferiority, he/she loses hope in his or her ability and begins to view the future negatively.

Stage Five: Fidelity, Identity versus Role Confusion

Erikson (1982) describes how the ego starts to integrate at the stage of adolescence when there is sufficient stability and continuity in the social environment.

Identity forms around self-confidence, sexual identity, commitment to social values, and the anticipation of a career. When there is acceptance within the social group, the individual can separate from the family to some extent and take their place in the world apart from family of origin. In addition, the individual tends to move towards a chosen ideology to fortify a personal sense of identity. Role confusion occurs when the environment is not able to offer opportunities for the individual to adaptively form this identity. As such, low self-esteem may be reinforced. Role confusion may lead to antisocial behavior in some young people who fail to resolve this life stage (Goldstein 1995).

Stage Six: Love, Intimacy versus Isolation

The consolidation of an ego identity enables the individual to engage in an intimate relationship without losing a sense of self (Goldstein 1995). In Erikson's (1982) view, a rewarding relationship should enable a couple to include sex in a trusting relationship, where work, procreation, and recreation are regulated and mutually satisfying. This stage also entails the ability to be intimate and is, to a considerable extent, predicated on the early negotiation of "trust versus mistrust."

Stage Seven: Care, Generativity versus Stagnation

For Erikson (1982), the establishment of a sense of guiding the next generation is central to this stage. In specific terms, in its early phase generativity is often associated with child-bearing and -rearing. However, generativity can also take other forms such as engaging in mentoring or formal or informal teaching. Productivity, creativity, and caring are the core developmental tasks of this stage. After experiencing old age, Erikson revised his theory and realized that generativity deserved more emphasis than he had originally thought. Erikson said, "Much of older people's despair is, in fact, a continuing sense of stagnation" (1982, 63). Recent research has suggested that attaining generativity may be the most important factor in establishing and attaining ego integrity (James and Zarrett 2006). Lenna, Domino, Figueredo, and Hendrickson (1996) studied predictors of ego integrity in a large sample of men and women aged fifty-five to eighty-four years. Results showed that ego integrity was preceded by generativity, intimacy, identity, autonomy, and trust. However, generativity alone accounted for seventy-eight percent of the variance in ego integrity

Stage Eight: Wisdom, Integrity versus Despair

Ego integrity is understood by Erikson to be associated with a sense of wisdom that is gleaned from a retrospective view of one's life. This involves a sense of acceptance of what "was"; in the face of accepting physical changes related to aging, and the final stage of death. Erikson (1982) points out that in infancy a sense of trust engenders hope; and in old age a mature hope and faith is included in a sense of integrity and wisdom. Erikson states that the opposite of wisdom is a sense of despair and hopelessness. "In this case the old person mourns for autonomy weakened, initiative lost, intimacy missed, generativity neglected . . . an all too limiting identity lived" (Erikson 1982, 63). For individuals to integrate their experiences of the previous stages they look back on their lives and hopefully find a sense of meaning, despite the physical and psychological deterioration associated with old age.

Integrity represents the ego's need to establish a sense of order and meaning. "It is the acceptance of one's one and only life cycle as something that had to be and that, by necessity, permitted no substitutions" (Erikson 1977, 241). Despair is described as the acknowledgement that one faces death, without the time to "attempt to start another life and try out alternate roads to integrity "thus there is a hopelessness about the future (Erikson 1977, 242). Despair is often expressed in the individual's expression of disdain or even disgust on multiple levels.

Erikson's theory has been criticized for cultural biased and the description of lifespan development in the United States as if it were universal. However, a questionnaire study in South Africa, that included both Black and White men and women, established that Erikson's stages could be universally applied (Ochse and Plug 1986). In addition, many criticize his theory for being unclear. For example, there is overlap between autonomy and initiative. Nevertheless, the continuing widespread employment of his life stage theory in both scholarly and applied settings suggests that despite its flaws, his life stage formulation has considerable merit.

A more specific critique of Erikson's (1982) theory of the life stage of "integrity versus despair" is offered by Loevinger (1987), who observed that few aging people reach full integrity. Fillit and Butler (2009) criticize the idea that identity is established and remains consistent throughout the lifespan. They argue that an identity can be transformed as a result of significant life events, such as the lived frailty of old age. The increasing occurrence of illness and loss of energy that is associated with old age challenges the individual's identity, invoking perceptions of frailty and the need to come to terms with a new identity as an "old person" (Fillit and Butler 2009, 349). Fillit and Butler (2009) make a valuable criticism in arguing that the physical vulnerability associated with aging may deeply influence the individual's experience of aging and may block the capacity for acceptance and making meaning—the hallmark of integration. Loevinger (1987), who develops her theory of ego and moral development based on Erikson's psychosocial model, calls the final stage of aging the "integrated stage," where the ego has a capacity to demonstrate wisdom and empathy towards the self and others. She offers a somewhat more positive perspective than that of Fillit and Butler. However, in keeping with others Loevinger cautions that full resolution of this stage is rarely attained as it involves the capacity to tolerate inner conflict and ambiguity and an acceptance of destiny.

It would seem that Erikson (1982) was more optimistic in his belief that aging people could reach a stage of ego integration than many subsequent theorists. His critics are more pessimistic in their view that aging individuals can attain full resolution leaning towards a sense of wisdom and ego integration. In spite of these cautions there would be few who would argue against the fact that this end-of-life stage tends to involve a degree of stock-taking and a retrospective reconciliation with personal history. The present study tends to view the developmental theory of Erikson's (1982) stage of "integrity versus despair" on a continuum rather than as a fixed stage.

The discussion now moves to look at previous research conducted into child Holocaust survivors.

Child and Adolescent Holocaust Survivors

Introduction

Of the six million Jews who died in the Holocaust, an estimated one million were below the age of fourteen. Child survivors were rare, as only eleven percent of Jewish children survived in Nazi-occupied Europe (Dwork 1991).

Despite developmental differences, such as different family histories and different actual experiences in the Holocaust, when children were faced with the reality of their own and other's deaths psychological regression was universal. Van der Kolk (2007) asserts that the experience of trauma during childhood can disrupt normal developmental processes. Children have unique patterns of reaction to trauma because of their dependence on caregivers for survival, as well as their biological and psychological vulnerability (Van der Kolk 2007). Van der Kolk (2007) describes the child as developing a sense of "self" in the process of interacting with his or her caregivers. Therefore, trauma during childhood may interrupt the development of a self and a coherent ego identity and thwart the capacity to develop trusting relationships. Trauma also interferes with the child's ability to self-regulate emotional arousal levels (Herman 1992).

McFarlane and Van der Kolk (2007) observe that "Emotional attachment is probably the primary protection against feelings of helplessness and meaninglessness" (24). Such attachment is critical for the biological survival of children and vital for the attainment of existential meaning in adulthood. Early secure attachment can operate as a defense against trauma and aids in buffering and protecting the individual, assisting in building psychological resources to face further distressing situations. Secure attachments enable children to self-soothe and self-regulate their emotions (Van der Kolk 2007). McFarlane (1988) states that the quality of the parental bond is the most important predictor of long-term damage in children, who have been traumatized. The secure parent-child bond serves as a foundation for teaching the child a host of skills, including emotional regulation, and extends to facilitate the capacity to derive comfort from social support. Coping with trauma necessitates a group of skills such as self-care and accessing social support. Research states that traumatized adults with a history of childhood neglect had a poor long-term prognosis in terms of mental health when compared with traumatized adults who had a history of secure attachments in their childhoods (Van der Kolk, Hostetler, Herron, and Fisler 1994).

Klein (2012) describes how child survivors of the Holocaust, in many, if not most instances, faced the destruction and loss of their entire families, including the loss of parents, siblings, grandparents, and extended family. The loss experienced was not only of loved ones, but of familiar social structures like school and friends. They were often physically uprooted from their country of origin and could not speak the language of countries in which they relocated after the Holocaust, contributing to a diminished verbal capacity for the expression of feelings in general, including grief. They emerged from the camps starved, exhausted, and sick, with a reduced cognitive ability to process what was happening in their world. Many remember their inability to cry and a sensation of living in a dazed state. In some cases, growth had been stunted owing to malnutrition, and many children and adolescents had a damaged body image. Those survivors who returned to their homelands confronted the death of their families and the eradication of their communities, which resulted in feelings of rage and helplessness, without an opportunity for retribution or justice. For many decades, child survivors struggled to accept the death of their parents. Mourning was avoided because of the overwhelming pain it engendered (Klein 2012).

Owing to their young age at the time of persecution, there was an assumption among some theorists and clinicians that child survivors did not have clear memories of their experiences and therefore that their trauma was not as great as that of older survivors (Durst 2003). This meant that despite the fact that many children did have vivid memories of what had occurred their experiences were minimized. Further complications involved the German reparation system that failed to consider child survivors' legal claims as they were less easily able to present specific factual memories or validated evidence of persecution (Shklarov 2013) and to represent their experience to others in these settings. This outward lack of validation of experience only served to exacerbate the ongoing traumatic experience child survivors faced after the Holocaust ended.

Traumatic Stress and Developmental Disruption

Pynoos, Steinberg, and Goenjian (2007) emphasize that it is important to understand the impact of trauma on child and adolescent development. Trauma exposure can disrupt the child's sense of safety in the world and has potential to cause long-term psychiatric difficulties. Pynoos et al. (2007) state that research into PTSD in children has found evidence to suggest that children experience a full clinical spectrum of post-traumatic stress symptoms. The intensity of the trauma is strongly linked to the severity and duration of the post-traumatic stress reactions. Bereavement, PTSD, depressive mood, and separation anxiety are related but independent of each other and may all occur in children faced with loss and damage.

It is important to understand the context of the developmental issues at the onset of the trauma and to see the psychodynamic symbolism of the threats, along with the possible cognitive implications, fantasy, emotional, and physiological reactions. For example, when there is a threat of injury children may become preoccupied with issues about the injury and the need to rescue and make reparation. In violent situations, children may be forced to repress wishes to retaliate out of the fear of provoking more violence. Adolescents are particularly at risk in terms of threats to nascent ideological belief formation and need to be understood in terms of how the trauma may impact their identity development and consolidation (Erikson 1968). Pynoos et al. (2007) emphasize the "existential dilemma" of the adolescent regarding, for example, the conflict between rescuing others or prioritization of self-protection. Durst (1995) argues that the fact that pre-adolescents and adolescents endured the Holocaust during the phase of identity formation was critical in their later developmental trajectory. "These children experienced personal suffering, starvation, dehumanization and daily confrontations with death" (Durst 1995, 296). The experience of loss and danger forced them to become adults prematurely and they lost their faith in humanity.

Van der Kolk (2007) states that childhood trauma plays a major causative role in the development of adult psychiatric difficulties. Klein (2012) observes that all young children, age two to eight, who survived the Holocaust, were injured in areas of psychosocial development, being unable to negotiate the fundamental tasks of development, from the establishment of basic trust to the negotiation of an identity. In all cases there was an element of developmental regression. Hillel Klein (2012) explains that universally, there was regression in children who survived the Holocaust: "Normal childhood sadomasochistic fantasies paled in comparison to the nightmares of the Holocaust" (56). There was unlimited horror and cruelty and basic trust at an existential level was destroyed. For Klein (2012), the child's capacity for fantasy became a hallmark of ego functioning and those who had lost the capacity for fantasy were dehumanized. They were unable to hold onto a sense of self (Klein 2012) and to use fantasy or the sense of an internal world to ward off some of the external pressures.

Both Herman (1992) and Erikson (1977) emphasize the establishment of trust in the earliest developmental phase of infancy. Herman (1992) explains that trust is developed in relation to the caretaker and sustains an individual in all the developmental phases of the life cycle. It is the foundation of all interpersonal relationships, as well as the cornerstone of faith in a God.

Caretaking in infancy allows the individual to trust in a world in which they belong and a world that embraces and sustains human life. "Basic trust is the foundation of life, the order of nature and the transcendent order of the divine" (Herman 1992, 52). Herman (1992) explains how the experience of trauma breaks basic trust in that it produces a primitive loss of comfort and protection. When traumatized people are desperate, they call out for their mothers or for God. When their cry remains unanswered, their sense of basic trust is shattered. Traumatized people feel abandoned by both humankind and God and feel cast out. As a result, a sense of alienation and disconnection becomes pervasive in all close relationships across the spectrum, extending to a sense of alienation regarding community and religious links (Herman 1992).

In addition to compromises to the negotiation of trust, trauma also affects the negotiation of other developmental tasks. Herman (1992) explains that in child development, competence, mastery and the ability to take initiative builds self-esteem. Guilt and inferiority result when there is unsatisfactory resolution of these motivations. A traumatic experience blocks initiative and thwarts the individual's competence. The individual is aware that, no matter how brave or competent their actions were, they were unable to prevent disaster. Herman (1992) explains that it is universal for trauma victims to critically assess their conduct at the time of the trauma, thus being vulnerable to guilt and inferiority. Lifton (1980) finds "survivor guilt" to be common in survivors of war, natural disaster, or nuclear holocaust. Feelings of guilt are severe when the survivor has been a witness to the suffering of others or in a situation in which it was equally likely that one may have been injured or died oneself. Survivors struggle with mental images of those who they could not save. In addition, they feel guilty for not risking their lives in order to rescue others or for surviving at all, even if by chance or fate.

Durst (1995) described the way in which child survivors' developmental processes were disrupted during the Holocaust. There was almost no continuity or predictability. Children learned that the future was unknown and that they could not expect anyone to comfort them in moments of terror, and they were frequently overwhelmed by loss. They used defense mechanisms such as dissociation to "forget" their losses. The children who survived with parents were forced to witness the humiliation and degradation of their parents who could not save themselves or their children from immense suffering. The frequent reversal of child and parent roles, or taking on of premature responsibility by young children, often evoked anger and guilt, even when child survivors appreciated that such behaviors were necessary under the circumstances. Hass (1995) adds that unconsciously in many instances child survivors felt anger towards their parents for not protecting them from harm.

After liberation, child survivors were often not allowed to discuss their experiences, nor were they provided the opportunity to mourn and grieve within a supportive environment (Durst 1995; Felsen and Brom 2019). This void made it difficult for child survivors to integrate their past and their present experiences. Their environments encouraged them to construct new lives, and they coped by using denial and suppression of their trauma and grief. The loss of family and lack of "space" gave child survivors a sense that "a part of them is dead and empty" (Durst 1995, 300). Thus, there was a numbing of feelings in response to ongoing inhibited mourning.

Dasberg (2001) describes the three severe types of "traumatic impact" on child survivors. First, he indicates that childhood deprivation as the result of no home and exposure to dirt, lice, and inadequate hygiene was significant. In addition, enduring hunger, cold, and exposure to dangerous infectious diseases was traumatic in terms of physiological survival. Secondly, Dasberg (2001) argues that the experience of traumatic stress, as a result of exposure to death and horror, caused the child to feel terrified, unprotected, and helpless. Thirdly, children suffered massive loss on many levels, including the loss of parents and family. The extensive loss resulted in lifelong, unresolvable mourning. The grief was generally repressed or experienced in unanticipated bouts (Dasberg 2001). In addition, child survivors experienced a sense of loneliness and anhedonia. The trauma was experienced at physiological, psychological, and existential levels and required engagement not only with threats to the self, but also with threats to and loss of significant others.

Dasberg (2001) argues that in adapting to new environments and suppressing traumatic memories the child survivor developed a split self. On the outside, they appeared to be adapting however, inside they had an inner sense of loneliness, low self-esteem, anxiety, and insecurity. They were under pressure to learn a new language and adapt to a new environment. Many were deprived of the opportunity of finishing school and were vocationally disadvantaged. Dasberg (2001) coined the term "child survivor complex" (5) to describe both the trauma and deprivation children experienced and their impact on the developmental process. Deprivation was understood to occur in relation to the lack of functioning parents, who were initially anxious and traumatized themselves by the threats within their environments, and then later unable to protect their children. Either the parent died or was unable to carry out their parental functions when reunited with the child, being themselves deeply affected by massive traumatization. Child survivors felt an enormous pressure to please their caretakers and to be accepted in their communities based on their need to belong and succeed. The suppression of their mourning and traumatization, as well as the pressure to adapt, left them feeling an inner sense of loneliness and estrangement, contributing to identity problems (Dasberg 2001).

Dasberg's (2001) reference to "splitting" as a form of coping mechanism differs from Melanie Klein's understanding of "splitting" that may be familiar to many clinical theorists. Dasberg (2001) states that child survivors used splitting to enable them to cope, and as such, splitting became the characteristic feature of child survivors: "This split is a feature of incomplete and postponed mourning, and also between a traumatized inner core and outward adaptation" (Dasberg 2001, 6). There is a split between outward apparent psychosocial adaption and an inner self that has unmet dependency needs and remains highly traumatized. Survivors hid their vulnerabilities in an attempt to adapt to their new environments as refugees. This left them at risk for bouts of depression and symptoms of post-traumatic stress, and for experiencing emotional outbursts that alternated with emotional detachment. In addition, survivors experienced anhedonia, guilt, and amnesia regarding periods of their childhood. According to Dasberg (2001), child survivors struggled to regulate aggression and experienced conflict with authority figures, as well as experiencing frequent marital conflicts. Thus, when child survivors presented clinically, they were often given diagnoses such as those of chronic depression, anxiety disorders, personality disorders, PTSD, and in rare cases, psychotic disorders. In accordance with Brom (2001, 1), Dasberg's (2001) concept of the Child Survivor Syndrome is helpful as it encapsulates the full picture of "the psychosocial consequences of the Holocaust in those who grew up under Nazi occupation."

A Psychodynamic Perspective on Child Holocaust Survivors

Although psychodynamic perspectives on traumatization and on Holocaust trauma have been discussed to a considerable extent previously, it is useful to elaborate more specifically on psychodynamic research findings related to child Holocaust survivors in particular. It was Winnicott (1960) who coined the term "protective shield" to describe the way in which parents protect their children against psychological harm. Based on this, Hillel Klein (2012) stated that during the Holocaust parents were not able to function as "protective shields" for their children, nor as strong caretaking models for identification. Children witnessed their parents being ridiculed and shamed in their role as adults. In addition, children witnessed mass extermination. "The child was forced to be a witness of the massive destruction of his family and community and first became aware of himself as a 'victim' when he perceived his parents' intensified anxiety and intense preoccupation with survival" (Klein 2012, 54). Thus, not only were parents unable to provide barriers to traumatic experiences for their children, they were also directly traumatized in front of their children, contributing to a profound sense of loss of functioning "good objects" who could provide a source of containment and optimism.

Klein argues that dealing with survival issues of life and death led to a lessening of more conventional intrapsychic conflicts. Thus, tensions relating to intrapsychic aggression and to conflicts within the family were directed outward towards the oppressor or "outside group" (Klein 2012). While this may have been helpful to a degree, it also precluded the likelihood of integrating conflicting feelings towards the same person or working through aggression. The latency-age child was often burdened with responsibilities of finding food for their families or making decisions in dangerous situations. This led to an intensified fidelity to their family, or gang, and a lack of feeling towards those outside their family circle, contributing to potential forms of isolationism and out-group prejudice. Children's fantasies were concerned not so much with pleasure as with safety. The Holocaust comprised a series of many traumas that overwhelmed the child's ability to cope in multiple respects (Klein 2012).

Klein (2012) contends that psychoanalytic insights may deepen the understanding of the specific conflicts and psychological defenses utilized, as well as the meaning of life during and after the Holocaust for child survivors. It is essential to take account of pre-internment family structure and experience and the vicissitudes of life in the pre-Holocaust period, as well as the personality attributes and stage of development of the individual when the traumatization occurred. Dasberg (1987), Kestenberg and Brenner (1986), and Valent (1998) all align themselves with Klein's (2012) psychodynamic formulation of child survivors, agreeing that child survivors were uniquely influenced by their family histories as well as the developmental disruption caused by the Holocaust trauma. From this perspective, early history and quality of attachments are crucial in understanding the long-term impact of the Holocaust. In addition, risk and ameliorating factors need to be considered when assessing post-liberation adjustment of child survivors. For example, when evaluating the survivor's experience, one needed to pay particular attention to the time between persecution and the time that followed liberation, as the psychosocial environment could either be rejecting or supportive and might worsen or ameliorate the impact of Holocaust experiences (Klein 2012; Felsen and Brom 2019).

Expanding on the importance of developmental life stages for appreciation of Holocaust impact, Kellermann (2001) divides child survivors into three groups: infants and children who were younger than six; child survivors who were between six and twelve; and adolescents who were between twelve and eighteen at the end of the Holocaust. The age at which trauma was experienced is important to take cognizance of as it draws attention to the child's cognitive ability to understand as well as other capacities. "Apparently the younger the survivor, the more traumatic the circumstance, and the more damaging the war experience" (Kellermann 2001, 8). From Kellermann's (2001) understanding, the lack of safety and trust instilled from experiences in the camps left the child feeling powerless and this affected their sense of autonomy and subsequent development. Older children were better able to comprehend their circumstances and as a consequence their sense of a just world in which there is a balance of good and evil was severely compromised, contributing to a kind of existential alienation. This also had enduring effects.

Dasberg (1987) explains that child survivors may be well adjusted in their current daily, lives however, they are a group that is vulnerable regarding emotional distress and instability. They differ with regard to relating to their past. For example, some are obsessively preoccupied with traumatic memories, while others are avoidant in this regard. When confronted with current stress, memories of loss and separation may be retriggered and they may suffer from increased anxiety and depression. As reported by Kellermann (2001), the clinical depiction of child survivors has features similar to that of complex post-traumatic stress.

Empirical Research on Child Survivors of the Holocaust

Keilson (1979), a Dutch researcher, did a follow-up study on child survivors twenty-five years after liberation. He randomly selected a non-clinical group of 204 child survivors who had become orphaned during the war. Some were in hiding, while others were in concentration camps during the Holocaust. His findings showed that children aged eleven to fourteen at the time of liberation suffered from anxiety, while those who were over fourteen tended to suffer from reactive depression. He found that, generally, the younger the child was at the time of the Holocaust, the more harmful the effects on their later personality development. This finding is in keeping with the premises advanced by Kellermann (2001).

Keilson (1979) described three phases or "traumatic sequences" that could be observed in the accounts of the children he researched. The first phase of distress or traumatization in the group's accounts related to the disruptive and anxious atmosphere before the outbreak of World War II. This included suffering from discrimination or antisemitism, including ghettoization. At this stage, parents were overwhelmed, anxious, and worried about being able to protect their children. Older children and adolescents felt the threat of danger and death, resulting in their frequently taking over adult responsibilities. The second sequence began after children were separated from their parents, uprooted from their schools and communities, moved into concentration camps, or had to go into hiding. In this second phase, children were exposed to terror and persecution (Dasberg 2001; Keilson 1979). The third sequence began at liberation and reentry into the post-war world, involving adaption and adjustment to new environments as refugees. Dasberg (2001) emphasized that at this third stage childhood deprivation was experienced because of the impact of massive loss, chaotic post-war conditions, and the difficulty of confronting the world with a refugee status. Keilson (1979) found that a positive and supportive post-war environment was a mitigating factor and children who found themselves in a favorable environment coped well, even if their trauma during the Holocaust had been great (Durst 1995; Felsen and Brom 2019). Both Durst (1995) and Dasberg (2001) mention the importance of Keilson's (1979) contribution in the understanding of child survivors. Traumatic experiences can cause developmental regressions or catapult the child or adolescent into developmental processes that are inappropriate. In addition, post-traumatic symptoms may disturb the development of peer relationships, leading to social isolation. Furthermore, when a child survived the Holocaust with a parent, they suffered their own loss and trauma as a survivor in addition to absorbing the stress and trauma of their surviving parent (Sossin 2007). However, despite these vulnerabilities Keilson's work was also able to demonstrate that access to a supportive environment post-trauma had substantial benefits in ameliorating trauma scars. While Keilson's research involved investigation of a similar population to that on which we focused in the present study, his research took place some forty years ago when survivors were much younger than those interviewed for the current research project and it was thus not possible to establish implications for longer-term life trajectories.

Moskowitz (1983) did a follow-up study of young children who spent the war in concentration camps, as well as in hiding, and who were placed in an orphanage after liberation. Twenty-four subjects were interviewed thirty-five years after liberation. Some had successful careers and many were married with families. Moskowitz (1983) stated that, as a group, his participants were resilient and had adapted well to their new environments, however, they continued to suffer from the loss of their parents, as well as a loss of faith. They felt that nobody could adequately grasp the extent of their trauma. Although they had high levels of anxiety and family problems, none had sought psychiatric or psychological help.

Hemmendinger and Krell (2002) took care of a group of male child concentration camp survivors (from the Buchenwald children's camp) at an orphanage in Paris. Initially the boys who were orphaned seemed chaotic due to extreme neglect. They interviewed fourteen child survivors thirty years later: most were married and had never received psychiatric help, although they reportedly suffered from depressed moods, anxiety, and nightmares. This indicates that, although child survivors seemed well adjusted, in many instances they suffered ongoing PTSD and related symptoms in keeping with Klein's description of internal-external splits. There was some evidence of a kind of dual existence of adaptive functioning alongside periodic symptomatic expressions of distress related to past trauma exposure and bereavement.

Mazor, Gampel, Enright, and Ornstein (1990) also researched child survivors, thirteen of whom had been in concentration camps and two in hiding during the Holocaust. Many experienced late grief and some experienced anger and depression, reporting strong feelings of early abandonment and loss.

Valent (2002) interviewed ten child survivors. The survivors described how their childhood experiences during the Holocaust had shattered their lives. In addition, they described how being surrounded by death and torture became a normalized experience in the psychotic world of the Holocaust. Tauber (1996) described the compound personality of child survivors, suggesting they in some respects remained fixated at the developmental stage of the trauma while continuing to function reasonably effectively in their adult worlds.

From 1967 to 1969 Klein (2012) conducted a three-year study on Polish Holocaust survivors and their families who were living in *kibbutzim* in Israel. All the participants had been adolescents at the time of the Holocaust. He observed that adolescents during the Holocaust did not have a moratorium on responsibility and did not have the opportunity to experiment with different roles in their peer group. In addition, they were not able to express sexual curiosity because of the abnormal circumstances. In these respects, aspects of their development had been foreshortened.

What appears evident from the several previous empirical and generally interview-based studies into the experiences of child Holocaust survivors is that the nature of the damage they suffered and how this manifested was complex, with many appearing more functional in subsequent life than may have been anticipated. However, it was evident that there was simultaneously fairly extensive evidence of vulnerability to mental health difficulties and the possibility of triggering of traumatic memories and significant losses by stimuli in the present.

Loss and Grief Experiences of Child Survivors

The intrapsychic, psychodynamic view is that a loss of a parent figure and adversity in childhood necessarily has serious pathological consequences (Bowlby 1973; Nelson et al. 2007). However, Pynoos et al. (2007) have indicated that it is important to differentiate between post-traumatic stress symptoms and the reaction to loss and related grief that may be observed in child trauma survivors. The research of Pynoos (1992) and Goenjian et al. (1995) established that children can experience both complicated grief and bereavement-related depression, such as that found in adults (Prigerson et al. 1995). In addition, they observed the way in which PTSD complicated grief by distracting from the experience of loss and drawing psychological resources to focus on processing the trauma (Pynoos 1992).

Child Holocaust survivors lost their families and their communities. For many, there was, and still is, a lack of closure, complicated, for instance, by the fact that there are no gravesites to visit, nor family pictures to retain. This lack of closure complicates the process of grieving (Sicher 1998/2000). Kellermann (2001) states that child survivors suffered multiple losses, which subsequently loomed over them for the rest of their lives. Children were torn away from their parents and siblings in tragic and brutal ways. Separation was often sudden, with little preparation and ongoing threats to self, which made it difficult for mourning to take place. In this interruption to grief many child survivors used defense mechanisms to block feelings of overwhelming loss, contributing in some instances to shallowness or distancing in subsequent interpersonal relationships (Kellermann 2001/2009).

Wardi (1992) explains that after liberation survivors of concentration camps began moving around Europe. Some went to their hometowns searching for family, but most landed up in displaced persons' camps that had been set up in different parts of Europe. Many hoped to find lost family members but, in many cases, found that their families had perished during the Holocaust. They suffered unbearable loneliness and isolation, as they had lost their immediate and extended family connections, their communities, their friends, and their homeland. Wardi (1992) explains that the survivors needed to continue the process of splitting that started in the camps, as their psyches could not cope with the extent of loss. According to Davidson (1987), the experience of profound loss left a sense of emptiness that engulfed and overwhelmed them. Wardi (1992) explains that the capacity to dissociate enabled the survivors to cope with this overwhelming loss: "All those who were unable to dissociate themselves from their memories—all those whose hearts did not turn to stone—did not survive" (23). In keeping with both Wardi and Kellermann, Lifton (1980) explains that in the process of dissociation the survivor's capacity for trust and dependence became limited. To form loving attachments again was not only a betrayal of the dead, but also represented the threat of being overwhelmed by emotions in intimate situations and the possibility of having to bear future loss.

Wardi (1992) describes the trauma of separation from family as the deepest wound a person can suffer and the most difficult to treat. The experience of separation from families caused survivors to feel "pain, anger, guilt feelings, and feelings of loss and emptiness. It remained a wound in their souls, which may seem to have been covered by a scab, but still gives them no rest" (9). He observed the intensity with which Holocaust survivors held on to the memories of their final moments with their loved ones who were later killed. Owing to the overwhelming nature of these traumatic situations, survivors experienced intrusive nightmares and psychosomatic and related symptoms linked to family separation and loss (Durst 2003). Mazor et al. (1990) also reported that the process of remembering intensified post-traumatic stress symptoms, such as nightmares, flashbacks, sadness, and crying. In a long-term follow-up study with child survivors Krell (1985) found that the loss of parents was a central issue, leaving what he termed "a gap" in the core of the survivor's identity (Krell 1985). However, remembering the Holocaust experience may create a narrative cohesion in the personal histories of survivors, which some people may find beneficial. Lifton suggests that, despite being painful and perhaps triggering intrusive recollections, experiencing distress and anger in remembering may be representative of the fact that a necessary mourning process, which these adults did not experience as children, is taking place (Lifton 1967).

Witztum and Malkinson (2009) challenge the psychoanalytic assumption that Holocaust survivors were unable to mourn their losses. They present research to demonstrate that an inner relationship is maintained with the deceased person throughout life (Klass, Silverman, and Nickman 1996). In contrast, Klein (2012) spoke from his clinical experience of working as a therapist and psychoanalyst with Holocaust survivors observing that many survivors were not able to face the grief related to the loss of their parents as the mourning was too painful.

Survivors of traumatic loss need to mourn as failure to grieve perpetuates the traumatic symptoms (Herman 1992). In normal bereavement there are rituals and social support for the mourners. By contrast, there is often no common ritual for mourners after a traumatic experience such as the Holocaust. Herman (1992) explains that when there is a bereavement with no social support, the potential of developing pathological grief and severe depression is extremely likely. As discussed earlier, the deliberate rupture of familial and community structures entailed in the Holocaust precluded externally containing rituals from being performed and compounded difficulties in grieving in a population that was enjoined to move on and put their camp experiences behind them.

Loss and traumatic bereavement nevertheless remain core themes in relation to Holocaust survivors (Witztum and Malkinson 2009). Recent research suggests that trauma and bereavement very often coexist, particularly when loss is under traumatic circumstances such as that exemplified in 9/11 (Cohen and Mannarino 2004), terror attacks in Israel (Karniel-Lauer 2003), and the Holocaust. Research on Cambodian survivors also indicated that prolonged grief was linked to ongoing PTSD in genocide survivors (Stammel 2013). Based on their clinical findings, Witztum and Malkinson (2009) indicate that Holocaust survivors experience "continuous bereavement." Malkinson and Bar-Tur (2005) observed that elderly Holocaust survivors continued to express their loss and grief. Witztum and Malkinson (2009) propose that Holocaust survivors be understood through a lens of "traumatic bereavement" that allows for acknowledgement of both experiences of catastrophic trauma and of devastating loss.

Having looked at theory and findings related primarily to bereavement and loss this discussion moves on to focus more carefully on traumatic stress-related aspects of child survivors' experiences.

Difficulties in Engaging with Lack of Agency in Victimization and Perpetration

A particular area of risk for some trauma survivors, and Holocaust survivors in particular, is when they have been compelled to become involved in their own or others' suffering in some way. Herman (1992) points out that the final point of psychological control is when individuals are forced to violate their moral principles and betray their basic human attachments. When a victim is forced to participate in sacrificing others, they develop self-loathing and become psychologically devastated and "broken." Herman (1992) quotes Eli Wiesel (1960), who writes about his experiences at Auschwitz-Birkenau with his father. Wiesel reports that he and his father supported each other through terrible experiences yet he is tormented by memories where he feels that he let his father down, and when he felt angry with his father for being unable to protect himself from the violence of the camp guards. Herman (1992) points out that Wiesel was humiliated by his own helplessness. In this instance the betrayal was of a more cognitive kind, taking the form of critical judgement of his father, but in other instances betrayal took more concrete material forms. Victims in captivity report that in the process of being "broken" they relinquish autonomy, their principles, or their connection to others, in order to survive (Herman 1992). As will become apparent in subsequent discussion, there were groups of prisoners and individuals who either cooperated with the Nazis in some way in order to survive or who felt that they compromised their own principles in competing with other inmates for survival or in failing to intervene on their behalf.

Krystal (1978), who worked with Holocaust survivors, described the emotional shutdown of many of those interned as "robotization." As described by the Holocaust survivor Primo Levi (1959), the final stage of being "broken" is losing the will to live. Survivors of Nazi concentration camps describe this fatal condition as evident in what were termed *Muselmanner*: "Prisoners who had reached this point of degradation no longer attempted to find food or warm themselves, and they made no effort to avoid being beaten. They were regarded as the living dead" (Levi 1959, 85). Klein (2012) writes that survivors who witnessed exterminations "spoke about hell, literally not metaphorically" (51) and carried an enduring sense of helplessness at their failure to intervene. A state of impotence to protect or intercede on behalf of those one is attached to produces a kind of psychotic state or negated self.

Chalmers (2015) argues that the severe living conditions, including starvation, fear, danger and humiliation, often led to "understandably inhumane behaviour among some prisoners" (203) towards each other. She attributed the "untoward behaviour" among some Jews to the camp or ghetto conditions created by the perpetrators, where Jews were forced to fight for their own survival. Levi (1989) has indicated that it is unfair and inappropriate to judge the behavior of Jews in concentration camps where the impact of the perverted world of the Nazi doctrine and related practices is difficult to comprehend. This is a controversial topic as some of the Jewish *Kapos* (prisoners who were given authority by the Germans to police the inmates in the camps) were reportedly self-serving, or worse, collaborated with the Nazis.

Gideon Greif, a historian from Yad Vashem, and the author of *We Wept without Tears* (2005), interviewed survivor inmates who were part of the Jewish *Sonderkommando* in Auschwitz. The *Sonderkommando* consisted of mainly Jewish prisoners who were forced by the Germans to facilitate mass exterminations and to work with dead bodies after killings in gas chambers. They described ongoing complex traumatic stress as a result of their experiences. In addition, they faced moral and human challenges while being involved with this appalling work. Greif (2005) interviewed eight survivors of the *Sonderkommando* regarding their experiences. Although his perspective was historical, the testimonies revealed that the survivors were suffering from severe post-traumatic stress decades after their experiences. "You cannot dwell on it too long . . . if it would help to cry then I would cry, but it doesn't help" (quoted in Greif 2005, 8). Leon Cohen was one of those interviewed by Greif (2005). He said that, some sixty years after the Holocaust ended, he was still troubled by intrusive memories and post-traumatic stress.

Herman (1992) indicates that, when an individual is forced to violate another human being, the risk of PTSD is very high. This is because the survivor has not only witnessed but is also an active participant in the violent murder or atrocity. In addition to risk of PTSD there is the risk of becoming almost permanently dissociated or alienated from the self.

Greif (2005) explains that *Sonderkommando* members felt forced to adapt to their "occupation" and settled into a daily routine. They came to accept their situation with "total indifference." Greif quotes a survivor of the *Sonderkommando* who described the experience of numbing in the following way:

> We were human beings devoid of human emotion. We were really animals, not people. It's frightening, but that's how it was—a tragedy. None of us went insane in Auschwitz since we had stopped being human. We'd become robots. (305)

It is evident that the range of damage to survivors of the camps varied fairly extensively but that those who might have been viewed as complicit in some ways were very vulnerable to later PTSD or CPTSD.

Guilt and Survivor Guilt in Child Survivors

Primo Levi (as cited in Hass 1995) described the emotional torment of survivor guilt in the following way:

> Are you ashamed because you live in the place of another? It is more than a supposition, indeed the shadow of a suspicion: that each man is his brother's Cain, that each of us has usurped his neighbour's place and lived in his stead. It is a supposition, but it gnaws at us; it has nested deeply like a woodworm; although unseen from the outside, it gnaws and rasps. (Primo Levi in Hass 1995, 17)

The term "survivor guilt" was first coined by Niederland (1964). It was used to describe the moral dilemmas faced by Holocaust survivors, who may have made choices for the sake of self-preservation that they felt to be personally compromising (Ayalon et al. 2007).

As indicated by Hass (1995), "survivor guilt" captures the cognitive and emotional experience of those who are fortunate enough to emerge from a catastrophe that mortally strikes down others. Researchers have different views about the pervasiveness of this phenomenon. Harel, Kahana, and Kahana (1993) wrote extensively about its prevalence among Holocaust survivors, while Hass (1995) claimed that it was not prevalent among the survivors with whom he worked. Hass suggests that the prevalence of survivor guilt was strong after the war, but faded as the survivors moved on to building post-war lives.

Klein (2012) offers a unique contribution to an understanding of how one views guilt in Holocaust survivors. For him, guilt was a sign of "recovery" as it signaled the survivor's engagement with the mourning process. "I believe that guilt for surviving is the only possibility to start the process of mourning and to promote a process of individuation" (Klein 2012, 13).

It is evident that while survivor guilt may have indicated that some form of mourning was taking place, physical survival in the face of the annihilation of others was often felt to be at the expense of psychological integrity.

This discussion will now move on to exploring anger and rage in child survivors, as these affects were identified as significant in addition to the pain and anxiety already mentioned.

Anger and Rage in Child Survivors

For the past two decades anger has been emphasized as an important feature of PTSD. For example, arousal symptoms of PTSD, which may include anger, have been earmarked as a predominant predictor of severity in PTSD (Schell, Marshall, and Jaycox 2004). Some other studies have specifically named anger as a predictor of severe PTSD intensity (Andrews, Brewin, Rose, and Kirk 2000; Orth and Maercker 2009). Various phenomena have been highlighted regarding anger and PTSD such as its enduring nature and both personality and pre-trauma-related variables (McHugh, Forbes, Bates, Hopwood, and Creamer 2012).

Herman (1992) explained that because of the difficulty in regulating intense anger, survivors of significant trauma move between expressions of uncontrolled rage and intolerance of aggression. This split seems to be indicative of the struggle of the trauma survivor who identifies with both the victim and the aggressor.

Lifton (1967) and Auerhorn and Laub (1984) state that anger and rage have a role in the integrative "working-through" process and in reaching mastery. However, if these feelings become fixed and repetitive, an embittered worldview develops. Auerhorn and Laub (1984) suggest that anger may represent a reaction to abandonment and unresolved mourning for the loss experienced.

Survivors had to suppress their anger and rage towards their Nazi persecutors, which had a destructive impact on self-esteem (Klein 2012). This was particularly true for adolescent males who were struggling to create a masculine identity. As stated by Herman (1992), the prisoner in captivity cannot afford to express humiliated rage at the perpetrator as this will threaten his or her survival, however, this does not mean that the feelings are not present. Their identity becomes contaminated with shame, self-hatred, loathing, and a sense of embodying a failure. Former prisoners internalize the hatred expressed by their captors and sometimes continue being self-destructive. In addition, the prisoner may also carry unexpressed rage at bystanders. The survivor may withdraw in an effort to control rage, deepening social isolation. Survivors may also direct rage against themselves, leading to depression and suicidal feelings. It is evident that many Holocaust survivors carried feelings of rage during their internment but were unable to express or act on these feelings for fear of retaliation and annihilation. Thus, they became vulnerable to a range of the kinds of outcomes described here—including self-hatred and a propensity to perhaps displace aggression onto others in the present.

Helplessness, Humiliation, and Shame in Child Survivors

There is ample evidence that powerlessness is a central theme for people who are traumatized (Eagle 1998). Krystal (1978) described the infantile helplessness of people who had experienced catastrophic events, such as the Holocaust. The loss of power, especially over an extended period and of an extreme kind, such as that evident in the camps, may result in a general attitude of submissiveness, which may manifest in symptoms similar to clinical depression. The impact of helplessness may depend on pre-existing personality factors as well as the recovery environment (Eagle 1998). Herman (1992) defined and explained ongoing trauma in the context of captivity: "A single traumatic event can occur anywhere. Prolonged, repeated trauma, by contrast, occurs only in circumstances of captivity. Such conditions obviously exist in prisons, concentration camps and slave labour camps" (74). Captivity sets the stage for repeated trauma and coercive control of the victim by the perpetrator. The victim is enslaved while the perpetrator exerts total control over every aspect of the victim's life. Psychological domination is inflicted through repetitive psychological trauma.

As previously mentioned, Benyakar et al. (1989) argue that the loss of autonomy is a central theme in the experience of trauma. Its impact causes a shattering of personal identity, continuity, and self-regulation. Herman (1992) links the idea of humiliation to the experience of helplessness. Herman indicates that in states of captivity fear is induced by episodes of unpredictable violence and the enforcement of meaningless rules. The perpetrator becomes so omnipotent that the victim realizes that resistance is futile. The perpetrator instils in the victim a fear of death. Moreover, the perpetrator controls the victim's bodily functions and destroys the victim's sense of autonomy. The perpetrator is in control of what the victim eats, wears, and when he or she goes to the toilet.

Van der Kolk and McFarlane (2007, 15) argue that trauma generally engenders feelings of shame and humiliation; "Shame is the emotion related to having let oneself down." The emotional intensity of shame is so unbearable that it often leads to dissociation. Hass (1995) also notes that feelings of powerlessness, humiliation, and being at the mercy of another person cause some survivors to carry an enduring sense of inadequacy. Herman (1992), too, emphasizes the sense of shame and helplessness that arises from ongoing dehumanization in captivity. Chalmers (2015) conducted an extensive study of women in the Holocaust and based her research on diaries, archives, and testimony of concentration camp survivors. A central theme in the testimony involves the experience of dehumanization, entailing emotional and physical humiliation. Chalmers includes "excremental attack" as part of the abuse and dehumanization. The excremental attack involved dirty public toilets and restricted toilet use times. If concentration camp inmates lost bladder or sphincter control, this would lead to further beating and humiliation. She quotes the testimony of Holocaust survivor Des Pres, who said that the excremental attacks caused disgust and self-loathing in the inmates and were a major weapon of psychological dehumanization (Chalmers 2015).

The humiliation of existence in the camps included the shaving of body hair, body searches, and nakedness. Forced nudity was particularly humiliating for female concentration camp inmates who were forced to strip and parade naked in front of soldiers in order to be "disinfected," and were often subjected to taunting, searches, and inappropriate touching. In addition, the inmates were poorly clothed, starving, and cold. They were not given an opportunity to bath and were lice-infested. Chalmers (2015) states that it is overwhelming to conceive of the physical suffering, in addition to the psychological humiliation, that was inflicted on concentration camp inmates. As just discussed, Herman (1992) explains that, when the persecutor targets the bodily functions of the victim, this type of attack contributes to dependence and regression that may instill further shame.

Having discussed the main affective impacts of Holocaust-related trauma as identified in the literature it is important to look at the function of coping defenses in the face of trauma.

Coping and Defenses against Trauma Impact

Laub and Auerhahn (1993) explains that trauma shatters the functional barrier created by the ego and leads to a fragmentation of the self. Constructing defenses against knowing is often an initial response to a trauma. From a psychodynamic perspective repression and suppression are understood to be psychological defenses that remove uncomfortable thoughts or feelings from awareness (Boag 2010). Repression is understood to be largely unconscious, whereas suppression is considered to be more conscious, although Boag (2010) suggests that the differences may be unclear. Erdelyi (2006) suggested an "unconscious-conscious continuum" to clarify this definition (169). Laub and Auerhahn (1993) explained that in the case of massive trauma, primitive defense mechanisms such as denial, amnesia, splitting, depersonalization and derealization are used by the survivor to block out the reality of the event(s). For Laub and Auerhahn (1993) also refer to a continuum in relation to the manner in which the memory of atrocity is preserved, reflecting the degree to which the observing ego is involved in "knowing and not knowing, massive psychic trauma" (1). Thus, some survivors may recall a traumatic event in great detail whereas others may be amnesic regarding the entire event. They suggest that the more severe the trauma the stronger the pull towards "not knowing."

Herman (1992) states that victims in captivity develop altered states of consciousness to cope with their unbearable reality. They use coping defenses such as dissociation, denial, thought suppression, and minimization. These coping defenses are used to withstand cold, hunger, cruelty, and pain. They narrow the individual's focus of attention to limited goals. A concentration camp inmate's range of initiative narrowed to plans to get a pair of shoes, a spoon, or a blanket. Thinking about the future brought up yearning and hope that prisoners found unbearable, as it made them feel vulnerable to disappointment and desperation (Herman 1992). Herman describes the psyche of the survivor in captivity in the following way: "The past, like the future, becomes too painful to bear, for memory, like hope, brings back the yearning for all that has been lost" (Herman 1992, 89). Thus, Herman suggests that in such contexts it may be functional to restrict one's consciousness and to live in a psychologically constricted world that matches the external environment. Herman explains that these alterations in consciousness are central to constriction or numbing, symptoms associated with PTSD. "Sometimes situations of inescapable danger may evoke not only terror and rage but also, paradoxically, a state of detached calm, in which terror, rage and pain dissolve" (Herman 1992, 42). Although the trauma victim is aware and conscious of events that occur, these events are detached from emotional experience and personal meaning. Perceptions may be numbed and sense of time may be experienced in slow motion. The survivor may feel as though the event is not happening to him or her, as though he or she is observing it from outside their body. While this kind of psychological way of being would normally be considered dysfunctional, it may be helpful in inescapable situations of ongoing traumatization. Numbing and hypnotic dissociation was described in Holocaust literature as pertaining to the way of being of *Muselmanner* as previously described, thought to characterize a necessary way of being for those who had no sense of agency and were likened to walking dead.

Klein (2012) explains that in an attempt not to draw attention to themselves within the concentration camps victims compromised their self-esteem, judgement, and desire for self-expression. Thus, a cultivated invisibility was understood to be adaptive in this context. Victims disconnected emotionally to cope with the overwhelming loss and terror in the camps. Klein says that most Holocaust survivors had continuous experiences of derealization and depersonalization as a result of being confronted with a reality that exceeded their most awful nightmares and, in many senses, felt surreal. In addition, as reported by Wardi (1992), the concentration camp inmate constructed a kind of psychological armor around him/herself as a protection from feelings of pain. Thus, the inmate became rigid and emotionally shut down. Wardi (1992) explains that the camp inmates suffered physically and lived in constant fear, compromising their capacity for empathy and attachment. The ability to mourn friends or family was lost, and primary process or primitive thinking dominated the inmates' internal world. In accordance with Wardi (1992), "Denial, repression and emotional isolation . . . became appropriate and vital mechanisms for psychological survival" (19).

Herman (1992) explains that after liberation there was a rupture in continuity between past and present, and observes that many prisoners remained psychologically imprisoned. The sense of the power of the perpetrator continued to exist in the victim's inner life long after liberation. The victim struggled to integrate their experience in captivity into their present lives and used powers of thought control to avoid thinking about it. These observations are similar to those of Laub and Auerhahn concerning the capacity to engage or "know" one's experience. Krystal (1984) found that concentration camp survivors were generally unwilling to talk about their past, confirming that the integration of the material was perhaps felt to be beyond the capacity to process or comprehend.

In relation to child survivors, Kellermann (2001), in particular, suggests that as a consequence of overwhelming emotional trauma, powerlessness, and isolation, they employed defense mechanisms to help them disconnect on an emotional level, in part because they observed that "children, who cried, died." Thus, similar to adults, children were aware that emotional constriction and invisibility were functional within the context. When they were overwhelmed with "speechless terror," the emotional experience was dissociated. In adulthood, this sometimes manifested as emotional numbing and a need to fit in and not be "seen." The cultivation of this way of being at an early age may have made it more difficult to generate a more flexible way of being in later life. It may have also produced a constricted emotional range of expression.

Isserman, Hollander-Goldfein, and Horwitz (2013) comment on the defense mechanisms used by the ninety-five Holocaust survivors interviewed in their qualitative research. It is clear from the interviews that, amidst the terrible circumstances of the Holocaust, defense mechanisms could be an effective way of dealing with difficult and life-threatening situations. Numbing, compartmentalization, and dissociation were important strategies in protecting the survivors from the horrors they experienced during the war. Defense mechanisms continued to play a role in coping in later years too. Isserman et al. (2013) are one of the first sets of authors to mention compartmentalization as a specific defense.

The above discussion indicates that different writers agree that Holocaust survivors used profoundly impactful defense mechanisms to cope with their unbearable pain, many of which would be viewed as dysfunctional in non-perverse contexts but which proved necessary for survival (both physical and psychological) within the camps. While Klein (2012), Herman (1992), Wardi (1992), Kellermann (2001), and Isserman et al. (2013) describe derealization and dissociation as significant in coping, alongside affective constriction, Dasberg (2001) additionally describes internal splitting, particularly in the aftermath of the Holocaust, as useful to survivors. These writers are all in agreement that Holocaust survivors disconnected their emotional worlds from their thoughts in order to cope. However, the costs of this form of coping can be extremely high. They may include the development of CPTSD and the kinds of existential alienation that may be part and parcel of survivors' lives. Laub (1992, 82) explains the toll on the development of the self: "The loss of the capacity to be a witness to oneself and thus to witness from the inside is perhaps the true meaning of annihilation, for when one's history is abolished, one's identity ceases to exist as well."

Having examined modes of coping that involved particular kinds of defensive styles and mechanisms, the discussion will now move to exploring and describing resilience in child survivors, as this introduces a somewhat different set of considerations.

Resilience in Child Survivors

The American Psychological Association (2014) describes resilience as "The process of adapting well in the face of adversity, trauma, tragedy, threats or even significant sources of stress (para. 4 in Southwick et al. 2014, 2) Resilience includes a healthy, adaptive, or integrated positive functioning over the passage of time in the aftermath of adversity" (Southwick et al. 2014, 1). Resilience refers to a process that includes positive adaptation in the context of adversity" (Luthar, Cicchetti, and Becker 2000). "Determinants of resilience include a host of biological. psychological, social, and cultural factors that interact to determine how one responds to stressful experiences" (Southwick et al. 2014, 2). This also includes genetic, epigenetic, developmental, demographic and economic determinants (ibid.). Cultural resilience is described as the capacity of families to hold onto hope and "make meaning" of suffering (Panter-Brick and Eggerman 2012).

From these definitions it is apparent that resilience involves two important conditions: severe threat or adversity, and positive adaptation despite major disruption of the developmental process or current functioning (Luthar and Zigler 1991; Masten, Best, and Garmezy 1990; Rutter 1999; Werner and Smith 1982/1992).

Resilience has a multidimensional nature, and children may demonstrate resilience in one area while experiencing vulnerability in another facet of their lives. Researchers are cautioned to be specific about an area of resilience that is manifested, rather than making general statements regarding resilience (Luthar et al. 2000). In addition, it is important to understand nodal points of resilience across the life cycle. Research has tended to focus on resilience in children, however, resilience can be attained at any stage in the developmental life cycle (Cicchetti and Tucker 1994; Luthar 1999). Within the developmental process, areas of competency may change when new challenges are faced.

The following factors are recognized to be linked to resilience in children and adolescents: positive attachments to competent and supportive adults; the development of cognitive abilities; the capacity to self-regulate and self-soothe; positive self-esteem; capacity for behavioral control; and the ability to act effectively. In addition, the following further factors have been associated with resilience: flexible disposition; positive temperament; social cohesiveness; an internal locus of control; external attribution for blame; good coping strategies and problem-solving; degree of mastery and autonomy; special talents; spirituality and creativity (Werner and Smith 1992). Thus, as with the prior discussion of post-Holocaust adjustment, it is evident that temperamental and personality features, developmental stage, severity of adversity, and environmental features may all play a role in resilience.

McFarlane and Van der Kolk (2007) state that secure emotional attachment in childhood serves as a building block in the establishment of resilience as well as serving to provide protection against existential meaninglessness in adulthood. For young children, family attachments are a mitigating factor against traumatization, and children are often resilient as long as they have a caregiver who is available on an emotional and physical level. Cook et al. (2005) reiterate that caregiver support is a protective factor in nurturing resilience and provides a buffer against the development of PTSD (Cook et al. 2017).

In keeping with earlier descriptions, psychosocial resilience, as defined by Valent (1998), implies "springing back after having been subjected to severe stresses" (30). Valent's (1998) work on resilience is based on his personal treatment of Australian Holocaust survivors. In addition, he himself is a child survivor. He indicates that his clinical and personal experiences resonate with the literature, which reports that being appealing, having good attachments, good social supports, competent interactional skills, and raised self-esteem mitigates the long-term effects of traumatic situations. Valent suggests that child survivors of the Holocaust were by definition resilient, as an estimated ninety percent of 1.5 million children were killed. Many child survivors cited an inner search, or compulsion to live, and a will to survive as the most important factors in their survival.

During the Holocaust, children experienced dread, desolation, panic, grief, despair, anger, and guilt akin to that experienced by adults (Kestenberg and Brenner 1986). Like adults, they could also freeze and/or numb their emotions. Children over the age of four years were able to make use of splitting defenses and to live in two parallel worlds (Kestenberg and Kerstenberg 1988). They lived in the current reality while keeping alive an internal world where they fantasized about a reunion with their good parents in a good world. Gampel (1988) sees the inner urge to survive, the ability not to feel, and the ability to keep mental contact with a good object as the primary means of psychological survival.

Klein (2012) explains that fantasy formation created a defense against the massive traumatization of child Holocaust survivors. By using fantasy, children were able to distance themselves from the horror and hopelessness in their external world. This is an interesting notion given Klein's (2012) earlier observation that one of the capacities that became compromised for children in the camps was the ability to develop a fantasy life. Thus, it seems that for those who were able to retain this capacity there was a better likelihood of resilience. In trauma-free periods, hope was an essential resource in helping victims to tolerate and survive painful experiences. Klein (2012) explains that hope was based on a positive self-evaluation and memories of people who were loved and represented the safe world of past experience. Experiences of nurturing in the past helped to sustain the child, and ego strength based on earlier developmental inputs facilitated survival. It is apparent that children within the camps needed to develop introspective capacities at a stage at which this would not necessarily have been normative and that many of them had to become psychologically precocious in order to survive.

Wherever possible, children were creative. They played and did drawings in ghettos and concentration camps. The innocence and hopes expressed in children's games were precious to adults who dared not hope so openly. Valent (1998) suggests that child survivors of the Holocaust commemorated the importance of secure attachment, the appeal of spontaneity, and the ability to continue to interact with the environment despite deprivation. In addition, they symbolized the capacity to maintain hope through intense desires to reunite in the future with past attachment figures, kept alive through dearly held memories.

As discussed previously, in the post-war period most survivors' parents did not return, or, when they did, they were different to the ones remembered (Durst 2003). Many children returned to hostile antisemitic environments. For those who emigrated, adoptive countrymen were indifferent to the past sufferings and encouraged them to forget. Normal grieving processes were inhibited or curtailed. Child survivors in this phase seemed to cope by focusing on the future, repressing memories and feelings, and by restricting their thinking. Many suspended any self-reflection for the next three to four decades.

Early professional studies of child survivors tended to be pessimistic. For instance, approximately half of psychiatrically hospitalized child survivors were found to be psychotic, and overall a greater proportion of psychoses was found in younger survivors (Krell 1985). However, most child survivors belonged to a non-clinical population. Such child survivors worked hard to establish security, and most became financially successful, married, and were devoted parents. Many belonged to helping professions and were altruistic members of society (Kestenberg and Kestenberg 1988). Nevertheless, most had silently carried a variety of post-traumatic stress responses such as nightmares, physical symptoms, anxieties, and other distressing emotional states, including having disturbing disjointed memories. Valent (1998) also observed that, although survivors were able to transcend early sufferings and build productive lives, symptoms of despair existed below the surface. Most continued silently to desire to belong, to have fuller loving relationships and to enjoy the world with greater humor and optimism (Gampel 1988).

Despite their suffering, most child survivors were able to function competently later in the adult world. They were successful in work and often achieved beyond the average. Their passion for bringing up children in normal and loving circumstances and their compassion and community awareness was surprising to an extent, given what they had experienced. Valent (1998) states that each facet of resilience has a corresponding wound. He notes that the discrepancy between survivors' inner pain and outer high-functioning capability points to ambiguity in understanding and dealing with trauma impact. It also brings into question some of the prior assumptions in the trauma literature concerning the incompatibility of these two types of response. In a similar vein, Shklarov (2013) points to the paradoxical existence of good life adjustment and painful emotional memories.

Suppressing memories continued to be the key means of coping with the pain of trauma in post-Holocaust life. Suppression was aided by psychological defenses such as negation, denial and repression (Mazor et al. 1990). "Half-knowing" was achieved as a result of the isolation of affect, and depriving events of meaning, significance, and full knowledge (Kestenberg 1987). This kind of resilience, or defensive style, was shared with siblings, fellow child survivors, and parents. The silence between the generations has been referred to as the "conspiracy of silence" (Danieli 1985) and was also the term Danieli employs to describe the way in which mental health professionals who worked with survivors failed to acknowledge their suffering and colluded with the societal denial of the Holocaust in many instances.

In discussing resilience, it is important to remember what Chalmers (2015) describes as the inappropriateness of attempting to "sweeten the Holocaust" (254). She points out that the testimonies we have about life transcendence after the Holocaust are from survivors, and that emphasizing the overcoming of hardship may occlude full awareness of the tragedy represented in the millions who died. The need to deny trauma and view genocides in a more palatable way is part of the human desire to minimize this form of trauma, as it is intolerable (Chalmers 2015; Herman 1994). Research needs to honestly reflect the devastation of the Holocaust, including the cruelty of a genocide that ended in millions of deaths.

The recognition of both vulnerabilities and resilience in child survivors is important. Child survivors of the Holocaust have shown that both the will to survive and psychological adjustments were important. Psychological adjustment included the mental attachment to good objects and the hope of retrieving these objects, as well as the blunting of emotions and meanings inconsistent with survival. However, for later integrity, these mental processes had to be revisited and assimilated, and past and current responses had to be reconciled.

The fact of child survivors also highlighted higher mental and spiritual levels of resilience, illustrating the capacity to develop a unique sense of identity, existential meaning, and purpose, despite having suffered extreme degradation, cruelty, and loss in earlier life. The child survivors demonstrate how creativity can emerge from resourcefulness developed in traumatic situations and how life urge can be transformed into investment in the next generation. Klein (2012) suggests that, while the psychological effects of traumatization have been well described in the literature, patterns of resistance and recovery have been less well articulated. After the Holocaust, survivors were able to invest in building families and taking responsibility for other's welfare in the world. Klein sees this as an important step in revival and renewal after the Holocaust.

Yehuda (in Southwick et al. 2014) explains resilience as the capacity to "fight back against adversity" (Southwick et al. 2014, 5). This idea is reflected in the work of Boris Cyrulnik, French psychiatrist and psychoanalyst, who was himself a child Holocaust survivor. Cyrulnik (2009) states that resilience is also representative of an individual's ability to adapt to different environments and overcome problems, suggesting the presence of a healthily functioning ego. He further explains that suffering can evoke defiance. He says that the young child experiences trauma, and the internal narrative is "I'll get over this one day—I will get my own back one day—I will show them" (Cyrulnik 2009, 65). Cyrulnik states that trauma survivors are not doomed to an unhappy destiny and they are able to muster inner resources to transform themselves. He understands resilience as a capacity to triumph over tragedy. However, he warns that "the triumph of the wounded never exonerates the aggressors" (Cyrulnik 2009, 321), meaning that the gravity of the human tragedy should never be undermined, and the aggressors forgiven, because the trauma survivor is "coping."

Mediators of Traumatic Stress: Protective and Risk Factors

Herman (1992) argues that a supportive response from the people in the survivor's world may mitigate the impact of the traumatic event, and conversely, a negative response may exacerbate the traumatic syndrome. "Having once experienced the sense of total isolation, the survivor is intensely aware of the fragility of all human connections in the face of danger, and fears further abandonment" (Herman 1992, 62). Rutter (1985) proposes that the family could be a protective factor or a risk factor in relation to childhood adversity.

Felsen (2017) indicates that psychosocial support has been found to be crucial in the recovery of trauma survivors. Research has demonstrated that the distress of relocation and acculturation to a new environment significantly contributed to experiences of distress, but that this distress could be ameliorated significantly by access to social support (Bolton 2015; Turner 2004). Meta-analyses of research on populations exposed to mass trauma conclude that social support is the most important factor in determining adjustment and the amelioration of distress (Norris and Wind 2009). Last and Klein (1980) note that within the camps many survivors coped by forming dyads or small groups where they shared food and provided protection for one another. Chalmers (2015) suggests that women and men also formed dyads and this helped them to survive life in the camps. Klein (2012) wrote extensively about the protective factor of forming bonds with other inmates. Common activities such as praying, singing, and offering love and hope were important in representing a "new family" that supported the individual. This was an antidote to the general dehumanization.

Keilson (1979) speaks of the importance of the post-Holocaust environment in the recovery from trauma. Durst (2002) notes that the survivors had a need to speak about their traumatic experiences in order to regain a sense of relief and faith in a meaningful world. However, for many years, survivors were met with silence from their new communities and the mental health specialists who did not want to hear their experiences (Durst 2002). The silent response that survivors encountered reinforced their sense of shame, and they felt rejected by their fellow Jews and other citizens in their new environments: "For a survivor to speak about his experiences in the 1950's and 1960's invited humiliation, ridicule, and disbelief" (Durst 2002, 8). For many, the opportunity for others to bear witness to their trauma was denied and the lack of engagement with their history left them feeling isolated and disillusioned. This is in part why subsequent projects to document Holocaust experiences have been viewed as important. Bialystok (2000) describes how the Canadian Jewish community did not want to hear about the survivors' experiences, and this is echoed by Danieli (1984), who describes how the mental health professionals both in Israel and the United States at the time did not acknowledge the trauma that the survivors had endured.

Felsen and Brom (2019) interviewed fifteen child or adolescent Holocaust survivors regarding their post-war adjustment. They described the silence that followed in the post-war adjustment where the participants did not discuss their experiences during the Holocaust—not even with their own parents. This qualitative research described their adaption and resilience as well as the importance of social support in post-war adjustment.

The discussion will now move on to explore aging amongst child survivors.

Aging Survivors

Introduction to Aging Survivors

As outlined previously, there are tasks in old age that hold promise for both growth and challenges (Aarts and Op den Velde 2007). Aarts and Op den Velde (2007) have indicated that memory plays a central role in reflection and reminiscing. Memory gives a sense of continuity across developmental stages and is central in the process of reaching ego integrity. In addition, memory facilitates the process of giving meaning to past life experiences. Reminiscence is important in the aging process and may carry both positive and negative weight, but recollection is also inherent in post-traumatic symptoms.

Dasberg (1987) explains that it takes the time span of at least one generation to stimulate the willingness and motivation to return to massive collective trauma of the form that the Holocaust took. Renewed interest in the Holocaust is a worldwide phenomenon. In the later phases of the adult human life cycle reintegration and reinterpretation of the past and reminiscence comes to the fore. Although denial was adaptive for many years after the Holocaust, survivors may now want to speak out or to attempt to engage with this highly significant period of their lives. Old trauma may resurface, and unfinished emotional business requires resolution. Hassan (2013) argues that Holocaust survivors have a complex relationship with aging. With more available time on their hands, dormant memories emerge—in keeping with Van der Kolk's (2007) observations.

Engaging with the process of aging was complicated by the fact that most Holocaust survivors had no close role model of aging as their parents and older relatives had been killed in the camps. In working with elderly Holocaust survivors in England, Hassan (2013) noted that despair and hopelessness came into focus as elderly survivors faced old age and their defenses weakened. In addition, the added stresses of old age required new efforts to cope not only with past events but also with everyday demands with depleted reserves. Van der Kolk (2007) has reported that trauma has a long-term impact over time and it may become the focus of attention in the elderly as their bodies decline and their participation in the external world diminishes.

Symptoms of PTSD may worsen as traumatic memory dominates in old age. Joffe et al. (2003) did a systematic study looking at the early impact of trauma on aging in Australian Holocaust survivors and looked at the presence of PTSD. They showed that survivors suffered from depression, anxiety, intrusive thoughts, insomnia, nightmares, headaches, exhaustion, and dizziness, and that they were taking more hypnotics and anxiolytics than the general population. It appeared that symptoms did not improve with time, and psychological intervention was needed fifty years later, as symptoms appeared to worsen with age. These lessons should be applied to current survivors of other atrocities (Joffe et al. 2003).

In addition to the work of Joffe et al. (2003) and Hassan (2013) there is a considerable body of research indicating that aging Holocaust survivors are vulnerable to psychological distress. Lomranz, Shmotkin, Zechovoy, and Rosenberg (1985) compared forty-four non-clinical survivors to thirty-three controls. Findings showed that survivors had a past-orientated and more pessimistic attitude to life some forty years after the Holocaust. Levan and Abramson (1984) researched a random sample of 300 concentration camp survivors and compared them with European-born members of the same community, thirty-five years after the Holocaust. Camp survivors displayed more emotional distress and medical symptoms. They also found that women were more affected than men. Carmil and Carel (1986) found that forty years after the Holocaust the 150 survivors they had researched suffered more emotional distress and had less satisfaction in life than their matched controls.

Cohen, Brom, and Dasberg (2001) compared a non-clinical group of fifty aging child Holocaust survivors with a group of controls. The child survivor group was found to have a high level of post-traumatic stress symptoms, enough to warrant the diagnosis of PTSD in fifty percent of participants in the group. However, they coped well and did not show significant psychosocial stress when compared to controls. They did not ask for help despite the severity of their symptoms, and they continued to function well despite their suffering. Brom (2001) points out that this study showed that although the Holocaust survivor group did not show high levels of psychosocial stress, they were deeply preoccupied with their Holocaust memories, as evidenced by their high score for post-traumatic stress symptoms. Many of the survivors who appeared to be functioning well would "fulfil the Re-experiencing, Avoidance and Hyperarousal criteria for Post-Traumatic Stress Disorder" (Brom 2001, 1).

Barak (2013) elaborates on what he considers to be a central feature of post-trauma adjustment in survivors that influences aging in a fundamental way. He explains that, because survivors have strong dissociative tendencies that they have relied on over extended periods, this may well lead to a failure in integrating memories and emotional experiences. As such, dissociation may complicate the aging process and compromise the survivor's ability to integrate their Holocaust experiences fully, interfering with their capacity to successfully negotiate Erikson's (1965) stage of ego integration (Barak 2013). Barak (2013) observes that the Holocaust deprived child survivors not only of a normal childhood but also of a peaceful legacy in old age.

Research on child survivors of the Holocaust confirmed these individuals to be the most vulnerable group to lifelong personality disturbances (Dasberg 1987), suggesting that those who have now entered their seventies and eighties may well be at risk for end-of-life difficulties. Rees (2002) found that a disproportionate number of Holocaust survivors reside in Israel's mental hospitals, where they have been neglected for decades. There has been a campaign to have survivors treated for Holocaust trauma instead of being diagnosed with psychotic conditions that have been treatment-resistant, as currently tends to be the case. Recently, Israeli psychiatrists (Barak, Aizenberg, Szor, Maor, and Knobler 2005) campaigned to treat survivors as victims of trauma rather than as treatment-resistant. For example, the introduction of "testimony therapy" has helped relieve distress and alleviate depressive symptoms, as doctors listened for the first time to the inmates recounting their Holocaust internment experiences in detail. Psychiatrists (Barak et al. 2005) have had to challenge more than just a misdiagnosis made decades ago. They were also perceived to be challenging a Zionist ideology that saw Holocaust victims as "weaklings" who had gone "like sheep to the slaughter," unlike the strong "new Jews" that Israel's founders helped to create (Barak et al. 2005).

It is evident that there is a range of longer-term effects that aging survivors may present with in treatment, be this in psychiatric or less formal settings. According to Kellermann (2001/2009), the following are characteristics found in older Holocaust survivors who come for treatment: massive repression of traumatic experiences and affect; amnesia; alexithymia; intrusive memories; Holocaust-related traumatic associations; depression; suicidal ideation; a chronic state of mourning; survivor guilt; sleep disturbances and nightmares; problems with self-regulation regarding anger and difficulties in dealing with interpersonal conflicts; excessive anxieties and catastrophic fear of renewed persecution; paranoia, suspiciousness, and lack of trust; loneliness and isolation from the community; and a low threshold for coping with stressful situations. In addition, Kellermann observes the somewhat rigid deployment of defense mechanisms and survival strategies that were utilized during the Holocaust. Based on their research with aging Australian Holocaust survivors, Paratz and Katz (2011) also observe that they have a higher risk of dementia as they age. This suggests an added complication to which survivors may be particularly vulnerable.

Researchers conclude that present diagnostic systems do not adequately capture the complicated picture of the late consequences of the psychic trauma of the Holocaust for those who were children and adolescents in the camps (Cohen et al. 2001; Kellermann 2001/2009). It may be that, having functioned apparently well in respect of earlier life tasks such as establishing careers and life partnerships, the carrying of the burden of their trauma returns to haunt them in a significant way during end-of-life stages and the coloring of their internal worlds by their Holocaust experiences becomes more evident or visible.

Recent research (Forstmeier et al. 2020) has investigated the effectiveness of life review therapy in elderly child Holocaust survivors living in Israel. Participants were randomly assigned to a treatment group or a social support group or social club. The participants in the treatment group received between twenty and thirty therapy sessions and measurements were taken before and after treatment as well as at a six-month follow-up. Holocaust survivors with PTSD symptoms or a full PTSD diagnosis were included as well as participants suffering from depression and prolonged grief. Results at follow-up indicated that the treatment group had less PTSD symptoms and some improvement in depressive symptoms, which demonstrated that life review therapy was effective in treating survivors with PTSD in their aging years.

Loss and Depression in Aging Holocaust Survivors

As suggested by Krystal (1981), as Holocaust survivors look back and review their lives, repressed memories emerge, and the survivors experience emotional pain. In order for survivors to achieve "integrity in aging," they need to "work through their losses and problems of guilt and shame" (p. 7). Valent (2014) has argued that memory plays a central role in the experience of being traumatized. To demonstrate his point, he quotes Wiesel, who says: "Survivors' memories are a psychological and moral vice. To remember smashes the mind; to forget betrays the dead" (p. 3). Valent (2014) observes that survivors are caught in a double bind as they need to remember in order to make meaning of their trauma, however, part of survival involves forgetting. To draw meaning, they need to feel the weight of their tragedy, fear, despair, shame, and guilt and this increases their unwillingness to remember. However, in the final developmental stage of aging remembering becomes essential to the retrospective integration of their lives.

David (2011) suggests that Holocaust survivors move through the adjustments of aging, including illness, relocation, retirement, loss of a spouse, and loss of family and friends, as do others but that these alterations in life are complicated by prior related experiences, for example, of separation from loved ones or adjustment to new living circumstances. Like others, David (1988) also highlights the significance of engagement with earlier losses. Witztum and Malkinson (2009), as previously mentioned, conclude that, in the case of Holocaust survivors, trauma and grief exist together, creating the experience of continuous traumatic grief. In some cases, "it would seem that trauma has engulfed the mourning and terror has silenced the sorrow" (138).

Laub (1992) has suggested that when Holocaust survivors experience tragedy in their lives, they experience it as a "second Holocaust, the ultimate victory of their cruel fate, which they have failed to turn around, and the final corroboration of the defeat of their powers to survive and rebuild" (Laub 1992, 650). It is evident that later life losses of peers and difficulties with health and cognition associated with aging might represent this kind of "tragedy." There is also awareness of finite time to effect any repair to past difficulties.

After reviewing the research on aging child survivors, Dasberg (2001) observes that coping was the focus after liberation and "the denials, repressions and forgotten injuries as well as the grief for our lost ones remained hidden beneath the surface for many years" (Dasberg 1991, 32). Dasberg points to the fact that, because of resonances with earlier experiences of deprivation, loss, and isolation from supports, aging survivors were at a critical point as they reached Erikson's stage of "integration versus despair." This stage signaled renewed awareness towards their unfinished business from their past, and for these reasons survivors often needed geriatric psychiatric evaluation and potentially psychological help for their PTSD. Dasberg suggests that mental health workers need to be alert to such likely difficulties and to be willing to offer psychotherapeutic opportunities to survivors (Dasberg 2001).

In summary, it is evident that there is some disagreement in the literature about Holocaust survivors' ability to reach ego integrity in old age, given the rupture in the self and difficulties in earlier developmental task negotiation as a result of the Holocaust trauma. Trauma disrupts the capacity to symbolize, which may lead to difficulty in reaching ego integration in old age. Based on his observations, Dasberg (2001) takes a somewhat pessimistic view, as he believes that aging Holocaust survivors struggle to integrate their traumatic experiences due to entrenched defenses, such as splitting, which they used during the Holocaust in order to cope with their massive trauma. Laub and Auerhahn (1993) describe the impact of the massive trauma on the disruption of the self. In keeping with Dasberg they explain how the trauma survivor employs defense mechanisms to allow them to forget their psychic pain. However, this rupture of memory impairs the survivor's identity. On the other hand, survivors such as Frankl (1962) and Klein (2012) were more optimistic in their view of survivors' resilience and ability to preserve a sense of self in order to hold onto hope and find meaning. Although these writers were not referring to reaching ego integrity in old age, they did believe that survivors were able to make meaning despite enduring catastrophic trauma. Valent (1998/2014), also a child survivor who writes about resilience, shares the more optimistic view.

Research on Aging Survivors: Resilience versus Vulnerability

More than six decades after the Holocaust researchers continue to argue regarding the long-term effect of Holocaust-related experiences on survivors

(Barel et al. 2010). The questions that are called into consideration include the following. Do survivors suffer from long-term chronic anxiety and depression (Niederland 1964) and personality difficulties (Kellermann 2001) in general, or are the chronic psychiatric difficulties observed in some studies restricted to a small group who are not representative of survivors at large? Do most survivors have functional and successful lives despite the genocide and suffering they endured (Leon, Butcher, Kleinman, Goldberg, and Almagor 1981)? Research in the past two decades has tended to produce more optimistic findings, focusing on survivor resilience (Valent 1998/2014). The shift in research has entailed focusing on the coping of survivors as they move into old age. Robinson et al. (1990) finds that aging survivors have been successful in their work and family life, despite their mental suffering. In addition, survivors often expressed an immunity to stress, saying that their hardiness was driven by their Holocaust experiences (Robinson et al. 1994).

The theory of post-traumatic growth (Calhoun and Tedeschi 1999) provides an explanation for resilience in the aftermath of significantly traumatic experiences, capturing the idea that trauma may not only be psychologically damaging but may also serve as a positive catalyst for personal transformation. As indicated by Calhoun and Tedeschi (1999), "post traumatic growth is the tendency on the part of some individuals to report changes in perception of self, philosophy of life, and relationship with others in the aftermath of events that are considered traumatic in the extreme" (Tedeschi 1999, 321). Tedeschi and Calhoun (1999) suggest that developing a sense of meaning and understanding is part of positive adaptation. In the case of Holocaust survivors, an attempt to make meaning of their survival could contribute to successful adaptation, and from some of the research previously cited it is evident that some survivors were able to achieve this.

Isserman, Hollander-Goldfein, and Horwitz (2017) explore the coping styles of ninety-five Holocaust survivors and their families to examine how they coped, adapted, and rebuilt their lives under the auspices of the Transcending Trauma Project (TTP), conducted in Philadelphia. Findings indicated that adaptive coping mechanisms utilized by survivors during the war continued to be evident as they aged. The TTP identified that the quality of early family relationships was one of the key elements that underpinned resilience. Isserman et al. (2017) demonstrate that positive family of origin attachments helped to create adults who held positive beliefs about themselves. Attachment theorists have noted that, in a supportive family of origin, caregivers create secure children who develop stable adult personalities (Ricks 1985). These early attachments appear to continue to shape wellbeing and resilience even for older adults

(Hollander-Goldfein et al. 2012). Paris (2000) presented a biopsychological stress-diathesis model of post-traumatic stress to explain resilience in aging survivors, also suggesting that, when survivors had a pre-war positive experience with their family, this served as a protective factor against the development of PTSD. "In other words, survivors may have established secure relationships with their attachment figures, which in turn may have served as a buffer against the atrocities they have endured, enabling their proper functioning after the Holocaust" (Barel et al. 2010, 679).

Although leaning towards a pessimistic view as discussed earlier, Dasberg's (1987) review of the literature suggests a mixed picture of post-war adjustment. He describes the more resilient survivors as "hardening," with the connotation that adjustment was at the expense of a full emotional life. Dasberg (1987) maintains that survivors were emotionally constricted to avert dealing fully with trauma and mourning. An intrapsychic understanding suggests that under severe circumstances the employment of core defense mechanisms, specifically repression of negative childhood experiences, may facilitate long-term adaption (Sigal and Weinfeld 2001). As previously mentioned, Dasberg (1987/2001) suggests that survivors who coped well used splitting as a defense to deal with their inner turmoil and adapt in the outside world. In alternative language, what Dasberg (2001) refers to as "splitting" may be more clearly understood as repression, suppression, or compartmentalization.

Although Joffe et al. (2003) found positive adjustment in areas of life for the survivors they assessed, other studies do not support their findings. Amir and Lev-Wiesel (2003) compared a group of forty-three aging child survivors with forty-four non-survivors living in Israel. PTSD symptoms were measured, as well as subjective quality of life and psychological stress. Results demonstrated that child survivors had higher PTSD scores, higher anxiety, depression, anger, somatization, and lower social, psychological, and physical wellbeing scores when compared to the control group. The results suggested that the psychological damage of the Holocaust is enduring (Amir and Lev-Wiesel 2003). Thus, in this instance mental health difficulties went along with other forms of problematic life adjustment. It is probable that the two sets of difficulties were interrelated as longer-term consequences of Holocaust trauma exposure.

Barel et al. (2010) conducted a meta-analytic study looking at the long-term physical, psychiatric, and psychosocial consequences of their experiences in the camps for Holocaust survivors. In seventy-one samples from worldwide research on Holocaust survivors, 12,746 participants were compared with non-Holocaust survivors in terms of psychological wellbeing, post-traumatic stress symptoms, cognitive functioning, and physical health. The Holocaust survivors showed more post-traumatic stress symptoms and were generally less well-adjusted when compared to controls. However, the Holocaust survivors showed remarkable resilience in their general functioning, such as in enjoying good health, and in the ability to manage general stress and in their cognitive functioning. "The coexistence of stress related symptoms and good adaptation in some areas of functioning may be explained by the unique characteristics of the symptoms of Holocaust survivors who combine resilience with good defence mechanisms" (Barel et al. 2010, 677). This seems an important overview of the research findings to date, and the conclusions appear to lean towards the recognition that defense mechanisms that might be understood as maladaptive in more "normal" contexts proved to be adaptive to Holocaust survivors in their post-war adjustment.

Barel et al. (2010) go on to elaborate that their findings reflect the dynamic employment of defense mechanisms that Holocaust survivors used during and after the war. The successful use of defense mechanisms, such as denial and suppression, may have enabled survivors to successfully repress their traumatic experiences in uncontaining conditions (Shanan and Shachar 1983). Mazor et al. (1990) propose that the employment of these kinds of defense mechanisms facilitated a process whereby Holocaust survivors were able to focus on good adaptation when rebuilding their lives. Barel et al. (2010) suggest that in the process of building families and achieving in their lives, child survivors further reinforced their protective mechanisms. Rutter (2012) suggests that self-esteem and competency are constructed in childhood and adolescence. However, they are open to being reconstructed during adulthood through supportive interpersonal relationships and productivity. Barel et al. (2010) suggest that, by building their lives in a positive manner, survivors developed their "acquired self-protective mechanisms" (692), which served to protect them against "dysfunction in several domains" (ibid.).

Certain specific personality characteristics may be associated with resilience in Holocaust survivors (Ayalon 2005; Barel et al. 2010). Helmreich (1992) found ten qualities in Holocaust survivors that may have enabled them to function in an adaptive manner, despite the trauma experienced. The qualities included optimism, tenacity, flexibility, intelligence, assertiveness, distancing ability, group consciousness, integration of the knowledge that they survived, courage, and finding meaning. It is evident that these kinds of qualities would also contribute positively to the building of a sense of integrity in later life. Helmreich's (1992) analysis indicated that survivors who led successful lives demonstrated more of these qualities, although not all qualities were found in every survivor.

The discussion above illustrates that it has been unequivocally demonstrated that survivors suffer from symptoms of post-traumatic stress decades after the Holocaust (Barel et al. 2010; Cohen et al. 2001). However, the findings regarding apparently good adaptation and resilient functioning are understood differently by different theorists and groups of researchers. While some theorists affirm the resilience of survivors and explain their resilience to be a capacity that developed from early good enough attachment (Klein 2012; Valent 1998) and particular kinds of personality features and aptitudes, other writers explain survivors' adaptation and life success as a result of employment of strong defenses such as splitting (Dasberg 2001), depersonalization, and dissociation (Herman 1992; Laub and Auerhahn 1993; Wardi 1992). These defenses, which may broadly be understood as entailing a form of compartmentalization, enabled coping both within the camps and war-torn environments as well as in subsequent environments where there was some understanding that trauma associations could not be entertained either because of limited personal capacities or the absence of external supports.

The debate in the literature regarding aging survivors as resilient versus vulnerable continues. Kellermann (2009) offers a way of reconciling this debate by presenting the concept of "paradoxical integration" (34) to describe the way in which survivors as a group are both vulnerable and resilient. This concept includes the aspects of both victimhood and survival, both severe traumatization and post-traumatic growth. In Kellermann's (2009) terms, paradoxical integration includes both the legacy of courage and the trauma of victimization.

The discussion will now look at the aging survivors' capacity to make meaning in Erikson's (1965) stage of "integrity versus despair."

The Critical Issue of Ego Integrity and Meaning

In accordance with Erikson (1965), acceptance of one's life story, with all its positive and negative experiences, facilitates the process of ego integration. With the acceptance of one's life story, the individual is able to look back retrospectively and find a sense of satisfaction in the final stage (Aarts and Op den Velde 2007; Erikson 1965).

For McFarlane and Van der Kolk (2007), attachment in childhood is understood to offer a basis for protection against existential meaninglessness in adulthood. As reported by Klein (2012), a strong ideological or religious identification is helpful in coping and providing survivors with meaning, purpose, and hope for the future. McFarlane and Van der Kolk (2007) agree that religion universalizes suffering and offers a larger context for this suffering, enabling traumatized individuals to connect more with their experience of victimization. McFarlane and Van der Kolk (2007) noted that victims may emerge from a trauma feeling that the suffering they endured was meaningless: "Usually suffering does not bring an increased sense of love and meaning: rather it results in loneliness and the disintegration of belief" (26).

Many Holocaust trauma survivors felt psychologically unsupported by their families and communities after the trauma had happened. In addition, they felt blamed for their own suffering in some respects and reported that this left deeper scars than aspects of the traumatic event (Danieli 1986; Durst 2003; Lifton 1979). They carried a sense of shame and disgust about not being able to protect themselves against the perpetrators, despite their survival. As such, the experience of shame and feeling unsupported by their communities became part of the traumatic experience (Durst 2002).

Hass (1995) has indicated that many survivors who lived successfully did not forget the Holocaust. Rather, they found a sense of meaning in living to tell the story of what they endured and witnessed. Des Pres (1976, 671) suggests that motivation to survive was to speak out and "to let the world know." Laub (1992) quotes a Holocaust survivor who said: "We wanted to survive so as to live one day after Hitler, in order to be able to tell our story" (78). Hass (1995) makes the following comment about resilient survivors: "There are those among them who have much to teach us about survival and successful coping under unbelievable circumstances" (73).

Klein (2012) explains that, after the confrontation with death, the search for meaning was a defense against the threat of robotization and fragmentation as a result of Holocaust trauma. Victor Frankl, a young doctor from Austria at the time of the Holocaust, wrote about his experiences in Auschwitz in his famous book *Man's Search for Meaning* (1962). He draws attention to the importance of finding meaning as an avenue of survival. He describes his experiences on a death march and writes of how he clung to his wife's image and the hope of finding her after the Holocaust. Frankl (1962) says that in the contemplation of his beloved wife he was able to endure suffering. "The truth—that love is the ultimate and the highest goal to which man must aspire. The salvation of man is through love and in love" (Frankl 1962, 56–57). Frankl argues that, even in the desperate place of the Holocaust, humankind is able to find meaning in suffering, by choosing to engage in certain behavior even in dire circumstances.

Although Klein (2012) and Frankl (1962) write from different psychological perspectives, both give credence to attachment as a core foundation that helped survivors cope and survive terrible ordeals. Frankl (1962) names the longing for an attachment figure as a driving force behind the will to survive and understands loving attachments as imbuing life with meaning. Klein (2012), coming from a Winnicottian perspective, emphasizes the core expression of hope as a guiding factor in survival and revival after the Holocaust. While Frankl (1962) does not offer a developmental theory, Klein (2012) proposes that early, pre-Holocaust positive attachments enabled survivors to have some sense of ego mastery. This enabled them to hold onto a sense of self that was not entirely lost during the Holocaust and to hold onto a sense of hope in the rebuilding of their lives. In part this meaning was derived from creating new attachments such as to partners or offspring.

For aging survivors who had become parents the eventual separation from children who appropriately separate and leave home is colored by their tainted past of being deserted and forcefully separated from their own parents. The emptiness that emerges may become filled with the threat of abandonment and an experience of "no object." The departure of children from the home or even the country may mean that there is no longer a distraction from their own trauma. Some may feel that they are losing their families for the second time. In the South African context where rather high proportions of adult children emigrate, as is the case in a number of Jewish families over the last three decades, the survivor's feelings of loss may be reactivated. Nevertheless, on balance it seems that having children brought increased life meaning for survivors even if this left them vulnerable to the pain associated with inevitable separations.

Ultimately, it seems that attempting to engage as ethically as possible with what life brought both within the camps and thereafter was important to many survivors in the establishment of meaning. "Paradoxically, the experience of the Holocaust offers a glimpse of hope for the triumph of life over death and destruction" (Klein 2012, 31).

Hope and Creativity

Nedelmann (as cited in Klein 2012) suggests that Holocaust survivors should be approached with a perspective of "meaningful life experiences rather than psychic damage" (13). In keeping with some of the earlier discussion, Klein (2012) comments that the literature was saturated with works on the psychopathology of survivors. He told his German colleagues that hope was hardly mentioned as an analytic theme and maintained that it was critical that therapists found hope in themselves and in their patients. As Klein states, hope is an important part of ego organization in coping with active hopeless feelings in painful states. Hope is regarded as the condensation of the total reservoir of internal good objects and fantasies projected onto the future, using relevant experiences from the past and actual fragments of external information, in the service of psychic survival (Klein 1974, 300). Erikson (1965) also emphasizes the importance of hope in the life cycle, beginning as part of the establishment of trust in infancy; and hope is critical in the process of developing wisdom and ego integration in old age.

The formation of new "family networks" to provide both physical and psychological succor in the camps has been mentioned already. Common experiences such as praying, singing, and conveying universal and personal strivings for hope and love were important group activities, antidoting dehumanization and supporting the self, and the ego ideal, in attaining mastery over trauma (Klein 1983). Klein (2012) explains that, universally, Holocaust survivors identified with the idea of *kiddush ha-Shem* (sanctification of God's name), as it gave meaning to their Holocaust experience and also instilled hope for the passing of torment and the possibility of something better.

In the tradition of his Winnicottian influence, Klein (2012) says: "Creativity was a form of dealing with human losses, the loss of love, the anticipation of one's own death, and most important a way of preserving an image of God in one's self" (25). Witztum and Malkinson (2009) suggest that creative process can become a means through which meaning is constructed in the face of loss. The creative process can be used as a medium through which to express emptiness and grief and yet to generate something new out of them. Pollock (1978/1982) studies the life and work of many gifted artists and finds that creativity may be an attempt to cope with grief through reparation.

According to Giberovitch (as cited in Hassan 2013), aging Holocaust survivors are able to find a sense of meaning when they share their experiences in a public forum, educating others about the Holocaust and in this sense becoming "creative" in their narration and depiction of material for the absorption by others. Positive psychologists, as well as gerontologists, are interested in how creativity and artistic expression may contribute towards resilience in aging survivors more generally (Corley 2010).

Aarts and Op den Velde (2007) suggest that there is a parallel trajectory in the developmental task of aging and recovering from trauma. Both processes involve finding meaning in loss. Aging involves an acceptance of one's life experiences, while recovery from trauma requires a level of acceptance that events took place as they did. Both the aging process and recovering from trauma require reestablishing self-coherence and self-continuity, leading to a better sense of ego integration.

As explored to some extent previously, trauma theorists, including Krystal (1968) and Herman (1992), consider the shattering of the self to be the most damaging phenomenon in trauma survivors. Ulman and Brothers (1988), influenced by Kohution and object-relations theories, postulate that trauma causes a shattering of the self, leading to a split in "good" and "bad" self-representations. The focus of recovery is the integration of the self and the reestablishment of coherent self-other representations in trauma survivors (Krystal 1988; Ulman and Brothers 1988). Laufer (1988), who studied Vietnam veterans, argues that the splitting of the self is a result of the rupture between a pre-traumatic, traumatic, and post-traumatic self. He says that the rupture in the self is caused by the wish to deny the trauma. An attempt is made to fuse the pre-traumatic and the post-traumatic self by bypassing rather than integrating the traumatized self, and this leaves the self damaged and struggling to function optimally. Recovery can be achieved when traumatic affects and memories are acknowledged, and the loss and mourning of the pre-traumatic self can be experienced (Aarts and Op den Velde 2007; Herman 2004; Laufer 1988). Krystal (1981) says that aging Holocaust survivors need to process repressed memories as part of their life review, which involves working through the pain of loss, guilt, and shame in order to reach "integrity in aging" (187).

For Eagle (2013), the attainment of a sense of meaning is possible after a trauma when there is a capacity to assimilate both good and bad aspects of objects:

> It has been suggested that it is only in the transcending of damage and loss that human beings can develop a true sense of resilience and hope. This way of thinking resonates with some notion of what is achieved in the resolution of the depressive position as understood by Melanie Klein (1935). Coming to terms with the trauma may indeed offer an archetypal opportunity to recognize the inter-relationship between the good and bad objects and the necessity for repair and restoration in response to psychic damage. (Eagle 2013, 135)

Holocaust Survivors' Engagement with God and Religion

Much of what is written about the impact of the Holocaust on the spiritual lives of survivors is based on survivors who were religious. Little has been written on Holocaust survivors who were atheists at the outset. Nevertheless, survivors who were not religious prior to the Holocaust still experienced a change in their worldview and meaning-making beliefs, having lost trust in a benign world. Most of the research on Holocaust survivors describes the loss of trust in a benign God. Eli Wiesel (1974) describes his experience as a fifteen-year-old boy in Auschwitz:

> Some talked of God, of his mysterious ways, of sins of the Jewish people, and of their future deliverance. But I had ceased to pray. How I sympathized with Job! I did not deny God's existence, but I doubted His absolute justice. (53)

The victim of severe trauma loses trust in humankind and ultimately questions their sense of faith or systems of meaning. As reported by Janoff-Bulman (1985), the experience of trauma destroys the survivors' assumptions of safety in the world and challenges a sense of justice and faith in a benevolent creator, leaving many survivors feeling bitter and abandoned by whatever God they previously believed in. Wiesel (1974) describes attending a New Year (Rosh ha-Shanah) service in Auschwitz where he felt angry and alienated:

> My eyes were open and I was terribly alone—terribly alone in a world without God and without man. Without love or mercy . . . I stood amid that praying congregation, observing it like a stranger. (74–75)

Klein (2012) notes that Holocaust survivors came to have an ambivalent relationship to God. He quotes a survivor to demonstrate his point: "I either hate God or deny His existence because He let me go through such horrifying experiences or I trust in Him because he performed a miracle in allowing me to survive" (157–158). Klein himself describes his ambivalence towards God when he describes survivors in the following way: "They are monuments to man's destructive power untamed by centuries of European civilisation. But they are, as well, symbols of rebirth and of man's efforts to preserve within himself an image of God" (Klein 2012, 31). Greif (2005) describes the loss of faith in one of the *Sonderkommando* survivors he interviewed, Ya'akov Silberberg. This participant said he was a devout Jew before the Holocaust but had lost his faith in God as a result of his work in the *Sonderkommando*. He said, "If all the trees in the world became pens and all the oceans turned into rivers of ink, one could not write down and fully document what happened in the Holocaust" (311). He continued:

> If this German could take a baby from its mother, grab it by the leg and smash its head against the wall—then faith has lost its value. Seeing something like that, the sight of the baby with its head smashed in, broke me up and destroyed the faith I had. (Greif 2005, 330)

In these kinds of quotations, it is evident how intensely camp inmates had to grapple with issues of faith and meaning as a consequence of the extreme cruelty and depravity they witnessed. Lassley (2015) quoted a phrase that was found, carved into the wall of a prison cell at Mauthausen concentration camp, in Austria: *Wenn es einen Gott gibt muß er mich um Verzeihung bitten* ("If there is a God, He will have to beg my forgiveness")—author unknown (1). For Lassley, this quote serves as a metaphor for the way in which religious Jewish Holocaust survivors were confronted by an extreme test in their faith. As indicated by Lassley, the central tenet of Judaism is that God is omnipotent and omnibenevolent. In his view, many survivors felt that "[i]f He were omnipotent, He would have been able to stop the atrocities. And if He were omnibenevolent how could he have stood by while these atrocities occurred" (1). Lassley says that every survivor emerged from the Holocaust with a different spiritual perspective. Some found a renewed faith and others abandoned their faith in God. However, many became atheist Jews: they renounced their faith but remained culturally identified.

Juni (2015) describes the way in which Holocaust survivors view God as a father figure who let them down. He believes that it is helpful for trauma victims to face their pain on this level. He describes the dynamics and interprets the defense mechanisms related to the sense of abandonment by potent figures evidenced by survivors in the following ways: "I was punished for my sins and misdeeds. God is righteous and I deserved what I received" (Juni 2015, 158). Juni understands this position as justifying God's actions and accepting culpability. In this way, the survivor identifies with the aggressor: "The Holocaust was a punishment for the sins of the Jewish nation" (ibid.). Juni (2015) interprets this as a rationalization whereby the survivor accepts the punishment as part of a group, rather than feeling personally attacked: "God does not micromanage world events. People have free will to harm others" (Juni 2015, 158). Juni explains that this contradicts the Jewish view of God being omnipotent and is an example of splitting: "A mortal cannot judge and evaluate God's ways. Our intellect and knowledge are minimal compared to his infinite attributes." Juni maintains that the way in which God's wisdom is defended to circumvent personal reactions to adversity is a manifestation of intellectualization: "Rather than focus on the hardships and pain I suffered, I choose to focus on God's beneficence, grace, and kindness in saving me." In Juni's view, this manner of thinking blocks negative feelings while focusing on positive feelings and is an example of reaction formation (ibid.). From Juni's various formulations it is evident that there were different ways of attempting to reconcile what was witnessed during the Holocaust with the idea of a God who existed and was present and that people might vacillate in adopting different positions.

Juni (2015) makes the point that defense mechanisms are not curative, they allow disturbing experiences to recede from consciousness to facilitate effective functioning. However, the underlying dynamics remain and will influence personality, relationships, and self-concept on a covert level. From his clinical knowledge from working with Holocaust survivors and their children, Juni argues that object relations can be extended from a human dimension to include the relationship one has with God: "We have found consistently that the subjective phenomenological relationship one has with God parallels, and is an extension of, the relationship one has with significant others—particularly parents" (170). For example, in his experience with religious patients, Freud's (1910) observation that "belief in an omnipotent and caring God is a developmental continuation of the all-superhuman archetype of the father in the child's psyche" (Juni 2015, 170) was reinforced. Juni says that the growing children transfer the notion of an infallible parent onto an omnipotent and omnibenevolent God figure, who later also seems to betray them. Their feeling of anger and disappointment can be likened to that of children who feel anger at a parent who they feel has betrayed their trust by failing to protect them from the viciousness of others (Juni 2015).

Holocaust survivors were "left with a disturbed sense of theistic object relations. God was no longer trustworthy to interact with them predictably" (Juni 2015, 171) since, without warning, trauma could strike, and God be absent, relegated to *hester panim* (hiding His face) (Besdin 1993). Just as one cannot trust a parent who has betrayed this trust, "trust of God as the kind father thus becomes precarious, at best" (Juni 2015, 171). Juni (2015) suggests that there are religious Holocaust survivors who feel a sense of "betrayal by the very God whom one has relied upon for sustenance and protection" since early childhood (171). Juni (2015) states that this psychodynamic applies for both adults and children where "feelings of neglect and abuse" prevail (172), but that the damage is more serious in the case of children, as they are at a vulnerable developmental stage in which internal object-relational dynamics become disrupted by the failure of protective objects.

As mentioned previously, Laub and Auerhahn (1989) say that "failed empathy" (1) is the central experience of Holocaust survivors. They refer to the rupture between the self and the "other." However, the above writers have explained how this rupture may extend to the survivor's spiritual relationship with God. From this perspective, the destruction and rupture of the trauma begins with the self and extends to interpersonal and spiritual relationships (Herman 1992).

As child survivors reach old age, they have a final opportunity to review their life process and attain a sense of meaning regarding their trauma. However, the process of meaning-making is particularly complex for this population who are forced to integrate the reality of having lived through one of the greatest tragedies of humankind, of human origin, inflicted upon them because of a particular cultural identity. Their grappling with existential issues is thus very profound and their previous defensive strategies may become inappropriate, inadequate, or even compromise their capacity to engage with the task of "ego integrity versus despair."

2

Research Approach

_____

Tracey Farber, Gillian Eagle, Cora Smith

We decided that, given the small number of living child/adolescent Holocaust survivors in South Africa and the interest in subjective recollections and aspects of experience, a qualitative, case-study based research design should be employed. The cases presented in subsequent chapters represent a cohort of nine South African Holocaust survivors. "The survivors comprised a non-clinical sample of individuals and consisted of those who volunteered to take part in the study on the basis of an invitation from a Jewish community leader" (Farber et al. 2018, 60). It was my (Tracey Farber's) privilege to meet Don Krausz, who is a Holocaust survivor and the community leader of the Holocaust survivors in Johannesburg. Don introduced me to potential participants who fitted the criteria for participation in the research study. In addition, after we had constructed the initial draft questionnaire, Don sat with me and checked all the questions to see that they were appropriate and easy to understand. I told Don that I felt anxious about interviewing survivors, fearing that the questions would open up areas of pain and cause distress. He responded to the effect of: "Tracey, these survivors have been through concentration camps—they are not going to get upset by a young girl like you! Don't worry!" Don was a constant source of encouragement, and his involvement in recruiting the survivors and approving the questionnaire was much appreciated. Tali Nates, the director of the Holocaust and Genocide Museum, also made suggestions about potential participants for the research.

FIGURE. 3. Don Krause proudly holding his personal copy of my PhD upon which our book is based.

Criteria for Inclusion in the Study

The participants of the research included five female and four male child Holocaust survivors, nine participants in total, all of whom meet the following criteria.

1. The participants were fourteen years old, or younger, when the Holocaust began in 1939. This ensured that all the participants were children or adolescents when the Holocaust ended in 1945.

2. The participants were interned in concentration camps at some stage during the Holocaust. Since this study focused on trauma, the experience of being imprisoned in a concentration camp meant that all participants were subjected to somewhat similar traumatic conditions.

3. At the time of the interview the participants lived in South Africa and had been living in South Africa since World War II.

4. The participants were psychologically lucid and had good verbal skills, in order to relate their story. (For example, if a person had been diagnosed with dementia, they would have been excluded from the study.) Since the participants were all elderly individuals (generally in their seventies or eighties) it was considered important to ensure that they were lucid enough to provide reliable data.

Biographical details of the nine participants who took part in the study are presented in the table below.

TABLE 1. Biographical information of research participants (pseudonyms are used in each instance) (Farber et al. 2021, p.4)

1. Name	Helene	Dave	Miriam	Lenna	Isaac	Anne	Rina	Shlomo	Menachem
2. Age at interview	72 yrs.	75 yrs.	80 yrs.	77 yrs.	81 yrs.	74 yrs.	71 yrs.	79 yrs.	81 yrs.
3. Gender	F	M	F	F	M	F	F	M	M
4. Country of birth	Germany	Holland	Latvia	Hungary	Germany	Lithuania	Holland	Poland	Poland
5. Age during Holocaust	6–12 yrs.	8–14 yrs.	10–16 yrs.	8–13 yrs.	13–19 yrs.	6–12 yrs.	3–9 yrs.	11–17 yrs.	12–18 yrs.
6. Losses	Mother Father	Father	Father	Mother Father Brother	Father Stepmother Half-brother	Mother Sister	Father	Mother Father Brother Sister	Father Brother Two sisters

Background to the Questionnaire

All participants were interviewed by me and the interviews centered around the set of broad questions. "Participants were seen on a weekly or bi-weekly basis over several weeks. Each interview took between two to three hours, with occasional breaks during each session. The participants' fatigue levels were carefully monitored to ensure that they completed their story to a particular point of closure in each interview session. The interviews were conducted between December 2005 and May 2009 and 74 hours of interview material was generated for analysis" (Farber et al. 2021, p.4).

Interviews were audio-recorded and were transcribed by me and an assistant. Thematic content analysis as outlined by Braun and Clarke (2008) was employed to generate main themes and subthemes. "We (all three authors) first independently extrapolated core themes from the transcripts and subsequently consulted together to determine how best to represent the central, consensus-based findings. Both case specific and across case analyses were generated and a clinical, interpretivist lens informed the theoretical elaboration of themes" (Farber et al. 2021, p.3).

The case study headings were derived out of considered discussion with both supervisors with the aim of doing justice to the most relevant content pertaining to child Holocaust survivors' experiences and life trajectories.

Psychodynamic Research Constructs Used for This Research

Hillel Klein (1983) suggests that the psychodynamics that give rise to the emotional characteristics of survivors are historically and psychologically unique and argues that any effort to compare them to other population groups can only serve to blur distinctions and what may be unique to each group. Klein (1983/2012) argues that it is essential to explore individual survivor's memories and experiences of their pre-Holocaust past, family, and personality, as well as their subsequent experiences. The period of early history, as emphasized in psychodynamic formulations, is crucial in shaping later development, adjustment, and individual ways of functioning. The research with Holocaust survivors should seek to do justice with regard to offering credible interpretations of life events and experiences. However, it is also recognized that there may be some commonalities of experience, and in this respect cross-case analyses may also be usefully undertaken to complement within-case analysis.

Concepts articulated in Erikson's' life cycle approach (1982) were drawn upon to examine the developmental disruption that took place in each of the participant's lives as a result of the Holocaust, as well as to elaborate some of the long-term effects of the trauma. However, it will be apparent that psychoanalytic and psychodynamic analyses of the interview data drew upon theory beyond that advanced by Erikson (1982).

Ethical Considerations

Ethical clearance was obtained from the relevant institutional committee of the University of the Witwatersrand to ensure that all relevant concerns had been addressed in conducting the research study (Ethic Clearance Number M050729). It was recognized that even if participants wished for their interviews to provide some form of testimony to their experiences, participation was likely to be taxing and emotionally demanding. For those who elected to take part it was emphasized that withdrawal from the study was optional: Pseudonyms and disguise of certain personally identifying information were utilized to ensure confidentiality (Winship 2007). Interviews were conducted by me, an experienced clinical psychologist and trauma specialist, who was able to contain any distress arising during the course of the interviews, as manifest in several instances. Follow-up in the form of a brief interview at one week and a phone call at one-month with post-research interviews was carried out. Some of the participants chose to be referred to a caseworker at Johannesburg Jewish Community Services on the basis of these follow-ups, for various forms of support. "None of the participants reported any enduring concerns related to the research process and several reported that they had benefitted from the opportunity to share their life stories. In response to some of the overarching findings of this study a dedicated psycho-social service to address the needs of child survivors was successfully implemented within Johannesburg Jewish Community Services" (Farber et al. 2021, p. 4–5).

Preparation for the Research in Terms of Ethical Considerations

During the research we noted that no social work services were available in South Africa that were specifically designed for Holocaust survivors. I approached Jewish Social Services about this gap in the system and was sent to AMCHA in Israel for a week of training. AMCHA is an organization with offices throughout Israel, which offers psychosocial services to Holocaust survivors and the second generation. I met Holocaust survivor and psychologist Dr Natan Durst, Israeli psychologists, and social workers and received input and training on how to work therapeutically with survivors. This training helped to prepare me for interviewing survivors in the present study and in providing optimal containment where possible.

When I returned from Israel, I offered training seminars to psychologists and social workers, working within the Jewish Social Services in both Johannesburg and Cape Town. This training focused on working therapeutically with survivors and second-generation individuals. In addition, I helped to set up the "Friendship Forum," which was a monthly social club intended for survivors to be run by Jewish Social Services. This project was taken over by the Holocaust and Genocide Museum and their dedicated volunteers who offer support to survivors in the community. From the outset of the research I (with the support of my coauthors) aimed to set up ongoing support structures for survivors beyond the supports provided during the interview process.

One of the benefits of this study is that it focuses on the long-term effects of trauma on children with some emphasis on resilience, through this elaborating on aspects of the developmental negotiation of tasks of old age. Thus, the study aimed to present the participants as survivors rather than as purely victims and may contribute to other research and interventions with aging populations who have suffered mass trauma.

3

Experiences and Testimonies of Child Concentration Camp Survivors

Tracey Farber

This chapter will discuss the findings of the present research and link them to relevant theory concerning trauma and aspects of aging in child Holocaust survivors. Initially, each participant will be introduced within the context of a case history and a *within-case* analysis will be offered. Each case history will be formulated within a psychodynamic framework and will be discussed with reference to Holocaust trauma and developmental disruption within childhood and adolescence. Each participant's life trajectory after the Holocaust will be traced and the specific impact of the Holocaust trauma on each case will be extrapolated as far as is possible from the material available. Since this research concerns itself with the impact of the Holocaust on aging child survivors, special focus is given to the long-term consequences of trauma and loss, as well as its impact on the negotiation of Erikson's (1965) stage of "integrity versus despair." The focus will subsequently move to discussing themes of trauma that were extrapolated from the testimony, which represent *across-case* commonalities and differences. The discussion will move to exploring and explaining the findings as they appeared to emerge as significant in the data related to trauma in aging child survivors in relation to core theoretical constructs including complex traumatic stress, resilience, coping-related defenses, and traumatic bereavement. The conducting of interviews and analysis of material pertaining to each case was colored by traumatic transference and countertransference, and this will be explored and explained as part of the dimension of reflexivity as it is relevant in this qualitative research project dealing with sensitive and compelling life histories. Finally, key conclusions and interpretation of the findings will be distilled and discussed.

Each child survivor was interviewed over an extended period and conveyed life history material that was of significance to them. Each case is summarized against a common set of subheadings that includes general background information, early parenting and attachment experiences, traumatic experiences and recollections, developmental disruptions, and features or symptoms of complex traumatic stress. All the material in italics represents directly quoted material from the interviews with research participants. In addition, each person's apparent functioning within the stage of "integrity versus despair" (Erikson 1965) is discussed.

Helene

Helene: *I cannot bear to think of my parents as walking skeletons or fighting for their last breath in the gas chambers.*

Helene, a child survivor from Germany, was seventy-two years old at the time of being interviewed. She was born in 1933 in Germany in a town near to the French border. Her family spoke German at home and they identified themselves as proud Germans. Although they were observant Jews, they did not speak Yiddish. Helene was six years old when the Holocaust began and twelve when it ended. She and her family were captured by the Nazis and sent to concentration camps in France. She spent three and a half months in Gurs concentration camp and six months in Rivesaltes concentration camp together with her parents. The camp commander at Rivesaltes agreed that some Jewish children were to be released to French and Jewish authorities. In an attempt to save Helene's life, her parents sent her away. Helene left with a group of Jewish children and spent time at two children's homes that were established to look after Jewish refugee children in France.

Helene's extended family in France collected her from the children's home after a period. However, when conditions became dangerous for Jews, they arranged for her to go into hiding in a Catholic convent in Brive. She spent two years at the convent until the end of the war. The nuns taught her catechism every night and she lived as a Catholic child under a false identity. After liberation, her French relatives collected her and she lived with them for six months. After the

Holocaust, she was reunited with her grandmother. They immigrated to South Africa where she lived with her aunt, uncle, and cousins. Helene's parents were killed in Auschwitz; however, she was not told about this until years later. She reported that her South African family was very kind to her and she adjusted well to her environment at school. In addition, she had managed to develop friendships. As such, her environment post-liberation was supportive, and this proved to be a mitigating factor in ameliorating the impact of the losses and trauma-related experiences in keeping with Keilson's (1979) observations. She got married at eighteen years old and gave birth to her first child when she turned nineteen.

At the time of the interview, Helene was widowed after fifty years of marriage. She had two children and lived in Cape Town. She reported that she suffered from osteoporosis, which according to her doctors was a result of malnutrition in her early years during the Holocaust. She described herself as a person who was socially active and enjoyed her hobbies. Helene was involved in volunteer work in her community and reported that she had never suffered from anxiety or depression. She was interviewed on two occasions and five and a half hours of material were recorded.

Memories of Early Parenting

Helene reported that she was an only child and felt loved and cherished by her parents, who were a happily married couple. She described that she was very spoiled and indulged by her mother who did everything for her. Helene described her parents as *wonderful people and devoted parents*. Her memory of her father was that he created a sense of security, and this left her feeling *looked after and cared for. Life before the Holocaust was filled with happy memories . . . that being loved and indulged gave me great strength, which allowed me to be down to earth. It gave me the strength to face life and not focus on negatives.* This latter comment indicated that Helene had some awareness that her history of secure early attachments was instrumental in building her resilience. The importance of secure and positive early attachment for managing subsequent stressors is discussed in research literature (Isserman 2013; Klein 2012).

Helene said she felt *adored* by her grandparents and extended family. Her older cousin Maud was an important role model for her. Although Maud was eleven years older than her, Helene described her as *her best friend*. It was Maud who fetched her from the children's home in France, and it was Maud's family with whom she lived for six months after the war ended. Helene said she was devastated when Maud passed away years later. She explained that Maud was the only person who made her feel loved and special in the same manner that her mother had loved her. Her relationship with this older cousin seemed to be a further protective factor in building her resilience.

Traumatic Experiences and Recollections

Helene remembered Kristallnacht, in November 1939, as her first experience of terror. Her father and grandfather were captured by the Nazis and taken to Dachau concentration camp along with the other men from her town. After her father's release, he was not permitted to work, and she was not sure how the family coped financially. In 1940 the Jews of her province were ordered to gather in a hall. She reported that she and her parents were sent to Gurs camp in the French Pyrenees Mountains. She remembered being cold, hungry, and sick with diphtheria. Many young children died of diphtheria at that time and she felt that she was *lucky to survive*. She and her young cousin helped to take care of his baby brother who died, and she reported that she was very upset by this incident. Helene explained that because of the cold and the hunger many babies and children died. She remembered a woman whose baby had died: *This woman lost her mind, and I remember her running from barrack to barrack, and digging in the mud, looking for her baby.* Helene said that this image remained with her and left her feeling disturbed and very sad for this woman whom she saw as *mad with grief.*

Helene reported that after a period in Gurs she and her parents were sent to Rivesaltes camp, in France. She remembered that, when she arrived there, she and her cousin walked into a barrack that was filled with corpses. She remembered feeling horrified and afraid and running from this sight. She said the food was inedible, and she had to go to the infirmary as a result of stomach problems. Thus, part of Helene's early memory of trauma impact was of somatic or physical problems. Her encounters with death at a young age also clearly stood out for her.

At some point a concession was made for Jewish children who were released from the camp and Helene was subsequently handed over to French Jewish authorities. When she said goodbye to her parents, she remembered her mother giving her a purse that she had made for her. *I remember my father saying, "Always pray, and everything will be ok." I don't remember my mother saying a word. As an adult now, I think she was incapable of speaking because it was so hard for her to say goodbye. What can a mother say if she knows that there is a good chance, she will not see her child again? My grandmother told my aunt that it took a lot of persuasion from everybody for my mother to give permission for me to go. I remember my father waving his handkerchief as far as he could see me. I didn't cry. I didn't know I would never see them again.* Helene was seven years old at that time.

Helene remembered that a twelve-year-old girl named Claire became *like a surrogate mother* to her when she was sent to a children's rehabilitation home near Marseilles. She remembered collecting crusts of bread to send to her parents. This indicated that she "held her parents in mind" and attempted to take care of them by saving her bread to feed them at a later date. She said that she received a letter from her parents to say they were being sent to another place. The place they were sent to was Auschwitz, where they died.

Helene said that being in the children's home was very difficult emotionally for the following reasons: *My parents made me feel that nobody was as wonderful as I was, nobody was prettier or more intelligent than I was. In the children's home, there were children who were prettier and cleverer than me, and it gave me a dreadful complex . . . being one of forty children made me feel that I was nobody special and actually not good enough . . . this was a big complex I carried to my fifties and sixties. That my parents made a mistake, that I was just ordinary, so I lost a lot of confidence, and after that, I never felt special.* This comment suggests that Helene experienced the separation from her parents as injurious to her identity and sense of self, in part because of some apparent idealization on their part that did not have time to transform into a more realistic form of relating and also because the transition away from them to a world of peers was forced rather than scaffolded. The sudden absence of previously available parental mirroring left her feeling dislocated and negatively affected her self-esteem. Her parents did not explain why she was being sent away, nor did they come and collect her. This worsened her sense of abandonment and her feeling of being unworthy. This absence of a "good enough mother" (Winnicott 1965), despite positive early attachment, makes it difficult for a child to hold onto a positive sense of self. The rupture of the attachment broke Helene's sense of self-other continuity and she struggled to hold onto her parents as good internal objects. This is consistent with what is described in trauma survivors who experience a traumatic loss as a rupture in relation to their attachment objects leading to a lack of trust and a fragmentation of a cohesive sense of self (Auerhahn and Laub 1993; Eagle 2013; Herman 1992). It seems that parental attempts to protect Helene from the magnitude of terror and threats the family faced left her vulnerable to interpreting events in terms of her own more personal developmental issues and crises.

Helene, who had never undergone therapy, had the insight to realize that this dynamic related to her early experiences had affected her self-esteem and sense of worth. As described by Dasberg (2001), Helene had aspects of child survivor syndrome. She had experienced a multitude of traumas. For example, she was deprived of her childhood, uprooted from her community, permanently separated from her loving parents, and felt alone and afraid at seven years old. It is possible that Helene felt an unconscious sense of anger at her parents for sending her away as she had no idea why or how they failed to fetch her. This may have caused her to feel rejected by them and perhaps she assumed that it was because she was not good enough or not loved enough. Fraiberg (1959) suggests that early to middle childhood is a magical age where children feel all powerful and blame themselves when they are faced with difficulties. We could also argue that Helene demonstrated Fairbairn's (1952) "moral defence." This is a tendency for abused, neglected, or abandoned children to internalize a sense of badness in order to keep pristine the objects to whom they are attached. This defense might have been operative in allowing the abandoned Helene to retain a sense of attachment to her absent parents.

Helene reported that her feeling of not being "good enough" was prevalent in her relationship with her husband and her children. This suggests that the psychological injury sustained in relation to her separation and loss of her parents may have affected all her subsequent relationships. She continuously questioned her worth and her lovability despite her adult awareness of what had transpired. The feeling of not being special enough persisted into her sixties, demonstrating that her sense of not being worthy was a theme that colored her sense of worth throughout her life.

When Helene's cousin Maud fetched her from the children's home her family arranged for her to be taken into a Catholic convent where she lived in hiding with nuns for a year and a half. *My friend Claire was no longer with me, and I was truly alone and felt I didn't belong anywhere . . . As an adult, I did a writing course and was asked to describe myself as a child . . . I saw myself all alone in a grey garden shed, and I was dreadfully sad.* This quote demonstrates how abandoned, alone, and desolate Helene felt as she had to cope as a young child in a strange place without family or friends. However, unlike many others, Helene received a formal education and was taught catechism in secret every night so that she would be word-perfect the next day. She said that the nuns saved her life. She enjoyed mass and felt comforted in the church. The routines of the environment created some sense of containment for her with recognition that this required conforming to the expectations of others. *I am fearful of authority, I listen, I do, I follow the rules, and I'm obedient. I have learned to merge into a crowd and never stand out. This was how I survived in the convent. I had to fit in.* This reflective observation demonstrates what Kellermann (2001) meant when he said that child survivors became compliant. Helen's identity development appears to have been foreclosed in important respects in the name of adaptation.

When the war ended, Helene's cousin Maud fetched her from the convent, and she lived with her aunt, uncle, and cousins for two years. She said that she used to go to the train station and wait in hope that her parents would return. Her uncles in South Africa offered to take care of her and she consequently travelled to Cape Town with her grandmother. She was told of her parents' death years after she arrived in South Africa, as the Red Cross notified her family that they had died in Auschwitz. *I could never bear to think about it. If I saw pictures of skeletal people in Auschwitz, I looked away. I avoided all books and films about the Holocaust and, as a teenager, I never got depressed and tried to fit in and be normal. If I got sad, I would read or listen to music. Reading was my refuge. I never considered myself an orphan because I regarded my aunt and uncle as surrogate parents ... I never mourned my parents; the pain was unbearable ... I had friends, but I always felt lonely, I always smiled, but the smile was a mask that hid my pain.* This set of comments demonstrates how Helene used suppression and avoidance to bury her grief and conceal her feelings of loss and abandonment from her new caretakers and points to an underlying sense of pain and anxiety that had to be kept at bay at all costs, both for the sake of her sanity and for the sake of those who had taken her in. As she describes it, Helene lived with an inner sense of loneliness, diminished self-esteem, and identity problems, despite her reparative environment. This is consistent with Dasberg's (2001) description of survivors hiding their vulnerability in an attempt to appear normal.

During the interviews for the research Helene became very tearful and sobbed inconsolably as she described her grief surrounding the loss of her parents. She also sobbed when she spoke of their suffering in Auschwitz: *I have never allowed myself to think about it until now! They must have been hungry and cold, living in that hell hole. I cannot bear to think of them as walking skeletons or fighting for their last breath in the gas chambers ... I cannot come to terms with their suffering. They must have felt pain! I feel so sad and angry that they died in Auschwitz!*

Helene spoke in detail about her sense of loss and how much she had loved and missed her parents. She said that she had never allowed herself to mourn them. While she felt slightly detached in her relationship with her children as a result of her trauma, she said that being a mother was *sometimes a rewarding but also a boring experience that left me feeling empty.* She said she was the happiest reading a book. It seemed that she struggled to attach securely to her children. Perhaps her attachment was muted because she held back, fearing that, if she allowed herself to be too close, she would not cope with any future separation or loss. This perhaps was a result of her childhood loss and trauma and the development of a somewhat "false self" persona who adapted at the cost of emotional authenticity. Initially she felt abandoned by her parents and behaved as if her aunt and uncle had become her (substitute) parents. Her "loving memory" of her mother and father only came later with her adult understanding of their situation. In addition, she felt a sense of survivor guilt that she had been rescued while her parents had perished at Auschwitz.

Developmental Disruption

Helene described an early history where she established strong, loving attachments with her parent figures. Her early experiences of feeling loved suggest that her object relationships were secure and her parents met her need for positive mirroring. She has demonstrated resilience and resourcefulness in many respects throughout her life, and this can perhaps be accounted for by the early sense of trust that was established in relation to her parents.

Helene described her parents in idealized terms, which is consistent with her developmental age at the time. In separating from them at the age of seven, she held onto this idealized view despite feeling they had let her go. Subsequently, she was unable to separate and individuate from them and achieve a more integrated view of her parents with some ambivalence, as is typical for an older child. Her separation from her parents came at the latency stage related to what Erikson referred to as requiring resolution of "industry versus inferiority" (Erikson 1982). Helene was affected in many ways. Her sudden loss of positive mirroring from her parents made her feel inadequate and inferior and, as a result, she felt that she had lost confidence in herself and her sense of a solid self or identity became compromised. Her experience of separation and her difference at the convent, coupled with her fear for her survival, led to her attempt to fit in and become unobtrusive as a means of survival. Kellermann (2001) has described that child survivors did their best to fit in and placate new caretakers, in the process perhaps relinquishing aspects of drive and individuality. The cost of survival meant the relinquishing of authentic experiences of the self.

When Helene moved to South Africa, she had to adjust to a new family, learn English, and adapt to a new culture at thirteen years old. She reported that she adapted successfully. Her aunt and uncle were very warm and she coped well at school. She found that she could make friends easily. Helene described her environment post-liberation as supportive. However, the changes and adjustments left restricted opportunity for her to mourn. Helene said that she never cried during or after the Holocaust and her grandmother never wanted to discuss the war with her. She said that the first time she cried was when she had her first child. Her ego defenses helped her to avoid thinking about her parents and she stated that her resilience and resourcefulness helped her to adapt. However, a close examination of her narrative account reveals that, while she had friends, she felt lonely. This suggests that because of her unresolved mourning she was unable to fully bond with her peer group, an essential developmental task of adolescence (Erikson 1982). In addition, owing to the loss and dislocation she endured, her choice to marry and have a baby in her late adolescence was perhaps related to a wish to recreate a family for herself. This is reflected by Laub (1998) who explained that often survivors married and had children in an attempt to reestablish their lost self in the context of a family. However, this early leap into adulthood left Helene with limited time to develop a stable sense of self and may have left her with a foreclosed identity. She spoke of her struggle with post-natal depression and her difficulty in bonding with her baby, perhaps also in part a result of her unresolved grief. It seemed that in becoming a parent the absence of her biological parents became more salient and real to her.

In her description of her husband, she said that, although they had a peaceful relationship, she often wondered if he loved her. From an Eriksonian (1965) perspective, developmental disruption as a child and teenager appears to have affected her sense of identity development and her capacity to develop intimate relationships. Helene openly admitted that insecurity plagued her relationships with her family. Most significantly, her avoidance of the mourning of her parents in adolescence and adulthood meant that it appeared that considerable psychic energy was invested in defending and protecting her from unbearable pain and repressing her grief. This is likely to have restricted her range of affect more generally. It appears that this had consequences for her attachments. It is possible that the defenses that protected her from her emotional pain regarding mourning also prevented her from establishing deep attachments to her children. Her issues of loss and post-natal depression will receive further attention in the discussion chapter of across case themes.

Mental Health Impacts

In the process of the research interview, Helene identified the following features as characteristic of herself, several of which could be viewed as indicative of complex traumatic stress. Helene described a sense of helplessness and survivor guilt. She described her frequent experience of feeling utterly alone. She said that her relationships were disrupted as a result of her Holocaust trauma and she felt isolated and distrustful of others. Her alteration in meaning was seen in her loss of sustained faith. She expressed a deep sense of despair in her unresolved grief regarding her parent's death in Auschwitz. However, Helene reported that she had not suffered from clinical depression, other than a brief period of post-natal depression with her first child. Although her functioning was good, she presented with features of PTSD symptoms, however, she did not qualify for a full diagnosis. In spite of these symptoms Helene appeared able to self-regulate her emotional states and she demonstrated solid levels of resilience.

Experience of Aging: Integrity versus Despair

Helene was in good health at the time of the interview. She walked and meditated, which she reported calmed her, indicating that she had some capacity to self-soothe and self-regulate. She reported that reading had been a haven for her all her life. It is a "place" where she said she could escape her thoughts and feelings, indicating some effective avoidance defense mechanisms. It seemed that reading became her primary refuge or flight into fantasy as a retreat from an overly burdensome world.

Helene indicated that she struggled with her first child as a result of her Holocaust experiences, and she said that she *was not a perfect mother*. However, she felt she taught her children to *have integrity . . . I always believed in making love, not war*. She acknowledged that, although her marriage was stable, she had insecurities in relation to her marriage. Her testimony indicated that she had a capacity to self-reflect and the theme of her yearning for mirroring seemed to influence the way that she related to her husband. She nursed him after he had a stroke and her devotion to looking after him indicated that she had a capacity to express her caring in instrumental ways.

As a widow, Helene was socially active and had good relationships with her friends. She did the Lifeline training course to qualify as a lay counsellor and was the leader of the Jewish Woman's Charity Group. She also volunteered at a local library twice a week. She said that she was proud of her marriage and proud of her children. Helene said: *I have had a full life, I have my children and my friends around me, this wonderful flat to live in, I have been treated well by life, even in difficult times*. She said that she was grateful for her health and that as she aged her memories of the Holocaust did not intrude into her daily life. She was able to *block* them. When asked about her feelings about dying she said that she looked forward to seeing her parents and her late husband in the afterlife. She stated that she was *ambivalent about God* and that she rarely prayed. Of her Holocaust experience, she said: *I found good people wherever I went. It gave me hope for humanity that there were more good people than bad.* She said she never discussed the Holocaust with her children as she was afraid to upset them.

Helene seemed to have attained a good level of ego integrity as she was able to reflect on both the positive and the negative parts of her life's journey with a level of acceptance and appreciation for "a life well lived" (Erikson 1973). In addition, she had reinvigorated, in her adult years, her sense of self that had been foreclosed owing to the trauma she experienced. One could argue that she coped well by compartmentalizing her grief and mourning. She had the ego strength to do this and was able to live an enjoyable life holding onto what was good. *As one gets older one becomes more as they were. If you were a misery when you were younger, then you become more of a misery when you get older. Everything is magnified. I get irritable quicker. As I have matured, I am less afraid to say what I think. I always wanted to fit in and be the same as others. As an old lady* (smiling) *this is not so important to me anymore.* It seemed that in her old age Helene was able to individuate and form a sense of self and no longer needed to placate others.

Process Observations

The research interview was conducted over a two-day period in Helene's apartment. During the first interview she cried continuously for hours. Loud, inconsolable sobs emerged when she began to speak about her parents. I felt that I was sitting with a seven-year-old child who was crying for her father and mother. I was aware that this was an outpouring of grief and mourning that Helene had avoided and repressed for sixty years. Eagle and Long (2009) mention the tension between the researcher and clinician's roles within particular kinds of research. In this instance it helped me to be informed by my clinical knowledge of working with trauma and grief. Although I adopted an empathic stance and reflected how difficult it was for Helene to be in so much evident pain I did not try to reassure or shut down the ongoing crying by distracting her or offering physical comfort. After some time, Helene became more composed and made it clear that she was prepared to continue and she did not want to stop the interview process.

As I listened to and watched the sobbing that continued for most of the initial three-hour interview, I remembered the words of Herman (1992) who said that trauma work involves bearing witness to unbearable grief and trauma. I realized that Helene needed to experience a containing presence to bear her grief with her. This experience was reminiscent of what Eagle (2013) described as a reverie, whereby Helene needed me to hear her distress and understand that it was the outpouring of a child and adult's grief that had been repressed for several decades. The following day she cried much less and expressed gratitude for my having given her the space to cry. She said it was a great relief to begin to finally mourn her parents. I offered to refer Helene for follow-up therapy. Helene declined, saying she had no need as she felt a great sense of relief that she could finally experience her grief. By the end of the interview process, she had stopped crying and chose to read her own poem about the coming of age of an older woman *who lives by her own rules,* instead of feeling like she is obliged to conform to conventional norms. Perhaps this was Helene's way of laying claim to her sense of individuation at this stage of ego integration.

> Helene: *Yesterday I cried in front of you because the whole thing about my parents hit hard. I cried when my husband died but never like I cried with you, yesterday. I have never told anyone but you. I could never bear to think of it, and I am not strong enough to face it, so what I am saying is that you helped me tremendously. I had to face it one day, I faced it, and it's dreadfully painful* (crying).

> Tracey: *I can see.*

> Helene: *I have never cried the way I am crying now, to think that a woman like my mother had to live in such horrible conditions, and my father who was a businessman had to be reduced to that. They were stripped of their dignity, the thought of that is unbearable* (crying)!

In these words, Helene explained her pain around viewing her caretakers as helpless and humiliated. Her difficulty in facing this was perhaps because she needed to preserve them as undamaged introjects in order to protect her internal world, as well as her view of them. By preserving her parents as undamaged internal objects, and repressing her grief, Helene was able to survive psychologically. It was also likely that she no longer needed to retain her parental introjects in the same way as she moved in the phase of her later life.

At the end of the interview Helene asked if she could read me her favorite poem, called "The Lady with the Purple Hat." It seemed to be a poem that represented her own individuation, where she was claiming her sense of self without being afraid of what others thought of her. She said that finally as an older person she felt freer to express herself. I contacted Helene in the week following the interviews to check in with her. She said that she was feeling relieved and was still happy to have spoken to me. Contact was made three weeks later. Helene said she was able to cry on her own and that this did not overwhelm or scare her. A few months later she wrote me a note to say thank you, writing that she was finally free to mourn her parents.

Over the two long sessions, one can perhaps argue that a positive transference had developed. In keeping with what Eagle (2013) suggests, the establishment of a positive transference may enable the patient to recreate an inner container that was broken by traumatic experiences. The process of giving testimony seemed to have developed Helene's ego strength, where she was subsequently better able to experience her grief without feeling overwhelmed and fragmented. From Laub's (1992) perspective, Helene appeared to have had an experience of being empathically held in the interview process. It is also likely that Helene agreed to be interviewed in part because she was seeking an opportunity to better resolve the issues from her past and that this, together with her increasing capacity to reflect back on life, made her more receptive of me as a helpful "object" in this respect.

Dave

Dave: *The gypsies launched a "revenge attack," and twelve of them beat me up with a spade and I was very afraid.*

Dave was a child survivor from Holland who was seventy-five years old at the time of the research interview. He was nine years old when the Holocaust began and fourteen when it ended. After the Germans had invaded Holland, as a member of a Jewish family, he was captured and moved with his parents and younger sister to Westerbork transit camp. After a period of time, his father was sent to Buchenwald concentration camp, where he died. Dave, his mother, and sister were sent to Ravensbruck women's concentration camp. At the age of thirteen Dave was separated from his mother and sister and sent to Ravensbruck men's camp. Finally, he was sent to Sachsenhausen concentration camp from where he was liberated. During the Holocaust he spent a total of two and a half years in four different concentration camps. When he returned alone to Holland, he heard that his mother and younger sister had survived the

Holocaust. After the family had been reunited, they immigrated to South Africa as he had relatives living in the country.

At the time of the interview Dave lived with his wife to whom he had been married for forty-four years. Although he was retired, he worked part-time and was in good physical health. He had previously been diagnosed with both depression and PTSD by a psychiatrist and had been medicated with antidepressants for the previous twenty years. Fifteen years before the interviews took place, he attended weekly therapy for a period of six months.

Dave began by saying, *when I tell my story I am not speaking for myself, I am speaking for one and a half million children who died,* suggesting that he identified with others who perished. He spent his free time giving talks at schools and working in Holocaust education. The interviews took place at Dave's home. He was interviewed twice a week over a period of a month and thirty hours of material were recorded.

Memories of Early Parenting

Dave reported that he came from a happy family and that his parents were loving and supportive of one another. He said he was closely attached to his mother, however, he remembered being a somewhat *difficult child* who gave his mother a *hard time*. He remembered that sometimes he was naughty and she would shout at him. He reported that he was not bonded to his father: *I didn't love him and I didn't hate him.* However, he remembered his father as being *honest, charitable, and having integrity.* He said that he had a caring relationship with his sister who was six years younger. He described himself as an adventurous boy who rode his bicycle and had both Jewish and non-Jewish friends. Dave reported that he had not experienced any antisemitism prior to the war.

Traumatic Experiences and Recollections

Dave said that his first traumatic memory was of his town burning: *The fire was coming towards us, and we had to evacuate as the houses could go up in flames.* After the family had left the house, it was burnt completely. He remembered seeing his whole city burning. He remembered being horrified when he saw the Nazis beating Jews in the streets and he was frightened by the air raid bombardments. These happened nightly and made a very loud noise. He reported that his family moved to a new house and one evening when they were having dinner a

Dutch policeman broke a window and opened the kitchen door. He proceeded to march through the house and told his father to open the front door for a German soldier. The German soldier told them that they had fifteen minutes to pack a suitcase and get out of the house. Dave said that he and his family were shocked and afraid but followed the orders. They were put on a train and sent to Westerbork transit camp. Dave described his experience as a nine-year-old boy, witnessing his parents as fearful and helpless and as impotent to protect him or themselves.

Dave lived in Westerbork transit camp with his family and many hundreds of Jewish people who had been captured by the Nazis. He said that every Thursday morning a train filled with one thousand people would leave Westerbork for the Auschwitz or Sobibor death camps. He had his *bar mitzvah* in Westerbork and his father gave him his watch as a present. When he was told that his father was going to be sent to Buchenwald concentration camp, he slipped the watch into his father's back pocket as a gesture of goodwill. For years afterwards, up to the time of the interview, he reported that he was tormented by guilt, wondering whether his father had been upset or angry when he found it. He wanted his father to understand that it was a *gift of love* and hoped that his father would not have felt that Dave had rejected his gift. Dave explained that until the present he had no closure on this issue and said that he always became very sad when telling this story. This indicates unresolved mourning and guilt, as described in research literature as common amongst Holocaust survivors (Dasberg 2001; Durst 1995; Kellermann 2001; Wardi 1992).

Dave's uncle told him that his father died a *Muselmann* (this was a concentration camp term used to describe a prisoner on the verge of death) in Buchenwald. *I was told that my father was so thin that he had so little flesh on his body, and he was so weak that the Germans did not bother to take him to work anymore.* He reported that he felt very sad and angry that his father had died in this manner, stripped of his dignity. As an adult, looking back retrospectively, he said he had a deep empathy for his father's pain and helplessness regarding not being able to protect his wife and children.

Dave was thirteen years old when he arrived at Ravensbruck women's camp. A group of European non-Jewish women prisoners saw him and the group of twenty children who were with him, and the women started to cry. The women said: *"You are not the first children here. They were sent to Auschwitz." I realized then that I am a Jew and am headed for a gas chamber.* He explained that he empathized with his mother's pain as she watched helplessly as her children starved and suffered from cold during the Holocaust years. He said his mother was a very loving woman and he was constantly with her as she was responsible for looking after a group of twenty children in the camp, including him. She would tell them stories and teach them poetry, and he admired her creativity and her compassion. She taught him *stone walls do not a prison make* and to resist becoming demoralized, instilling that he was in control of how he reacted to his circumstances. Dave's attachment to his mother appears to have been a source of comfort, despite the adverse circumstances, and was a protective factor for him, as described in the literature review was often the case (Klein 2012; McFarlane 1988/2007; Rutter 1985; Valent 1998).

Dave said that the non-Jewish Polish women prisoners were particularly cruel and antisemitic. They used to swear at him and the other children, calling them *cursed Jews*. He said that many women died of sickness and starvation and he was surrounded by death. He described that he had vivid recollections of the sounds and sight of women screaming as they were beaten with sticks. Weakened, cold, and starving, women often got sick with typhus and dysentery. He himself became gravely ill, and a German SS woman, who was in charge of his barrack, fed him extra food that saved his life. It was apparent that he experienced both prejudice and compassion from the adults around him and also that he was prematurely exposed to witnessing intense suffering and death.

When he turned fourteen, Dave was separated from his mother and sent to the men's camp. He remembered that this separation was very difficult for him as he was not certain he would see his mother and sister again. At the men's camp he was beaten daily and forced to work. His mother arranged to visit him two months after his departure and, when she saw him, she hugged and kissed him. He said, *Seeing her, after being separated for a month or two was devastating, it felt like a wound had been torn open! The separation meant I had to break the dependence of a child on his mother. I did not see her again until after the war ended.* This comment clearly demonstrates how painfully Dave experienced the separation from his mother and how he anticipated her loss as he was surrounded by people who were dying or dead. It appears that he attempted to cope with the awareness of the possibility of permanent separation and absence by "forgetting" his attachments or mentally detaching. Seeing his mother in person ruptured this defense temporarily but it seems he returned to a defense of treating his loss as if it has already taken place in anticipation of this likelihood.

The transition to the men's camp represented the loss of his childhood as Dave found himself alone and unprotected at fourteen. The loss of childhood is a theme described by Dasberg (2001) in his conceptualization of child survivor syndrome. Dave described ongoing PTSD after the trauma he endured during this period. He stayed at Ravensbruck men's camp for six months where he received violent beatings daily: *There were thirteen Jewish boys, including myself, and eighty gypsy boys and men. The gypsies beat and humiliated me and the other Jewish boys daily.* He reported that the older (Roma) gypsies encouraged the younger ones to attack the Jewish boys and that the gypsies swore at and stole from them. Consequently, his experiences were persecutory and humiliating. *After reporting this to the camp guard the gypsies launched a "revenge attack," and twelve of them beat me up with a spade and I was very afraid and was knocked unconscious.* It is clear that Dave was the victim of abuse and humiliation at the hands of fellow inmates and this experience had a long-term impact as the trauma disrupted the development of trust and engagement with others in adolescence (Herman 1992). He said that, according to a neuropsychological assessment, he had a short-term memory problem due to the blows he sustained to the head. The frequency with which he was knocked unconscious, both by the gypsies and by barrack leaders in the concentration camps, clearly had contributed to this problem. Not only did Dave use the defense of dissociation to cope with the level of inescapable trauma he was exposed to, but also the physical trauma he sustained was so severe that it caused some permanent neurological damage.

In addition to being severely beaten Dave reported that he was deeply traumatized as a result of witnessing the floggings and torture of other inmates. *There was a flogging block to which the victim was tied, and I remember seeing the victims writhe in pain and scream horribly. We were surrounded by sadists; the guards, the gypsies, and the "Kapos" were all bent on inflicting pain and humiliation.* He reported that, when seeing a guard beat up a child, he realized that he and other children were viewed as vermin, that Nazis had no compassion and were determined to destroy them. One can well appreciate that Dave felt dehumanized and feared for his life and that dissociation was an understandable defense, although it is apparent that he retained some capacity for empathy in his description of being disturbed by others' distress.

Dave said that at Sachsenhausen concentration camp it was so cold that inmates held onto each other in a *spoon position* during the night for warmth and sometimes he woke up holding a corpse. He explained that he became emotionally numb as a result of this trauma and a dead body became *like a sack of potatoes* to him. Dave's description of emotional numbness is similar to the descriptions of the dissociation of the *Sonderkommando* that was highlighted by Greif (2005). Both Dave and the men who were described by Greif (2005) became so disconnected from the horror of managing dead bodies that emotional numbness, as described by Herman (1992) and Wardi (1992), was a means of surviving this form of daily life.

As the Allies approached, Dave was taken out of the camp on a forced evacuation or "death march" that lasted for two weeks. He said that the hunger and the cold were unbearable. The Germans shot a man next to him and he knew that, if he protested, he would be shot too. He said that the death march was his worst experience during the Holocaust because he witnessed so many executions. He felt horrified by them. In addition, he was weak, starving, and constantly under threat of being shot. Of the hundred men on the death march, only fifty survived. After they had been liberated, the Allies gave him and his nine young friends potatoes. They got oil and made fried chips. Eight of these ten boys died as their starved bodies could not tolerate the food. These kinds of descriptions brought home the reality of the level of life threat experienced and it was apparent that Dave had anticipated and almost accepted the likelihood of his own death.

As an early adolescent Dave was forced to fend for himself in an environment characterized by harrowing cruelty. During this time in his life, he reported that he became detached from people and had remained that way until the present time. Dave's description of his forced "independence and detachment" suggests he used the narcissistically oriented defense of complete self-reliance to cope with the painful loss of parental care and environmental attack. The detachment he described seems to be concordant with a form of dissociation, as described in research literature to be common amongst survivors (Herman 1992; Laub and Auerhahn 1983; Wardi 1992). When Dave returned to the Netherlands after the war, he was surprised to hear from family friends that his mother and sister had survived and were living in England.

Dave was pained about the loss not only of his father, but also of the sixteen members of his extended family who were gassed at Auschwitz and Sobibor. He described his horror and fear regarding the death in the gas chambers in great detail during the interviews. He cried as he described how *Lithuanian and Latvian Jews were stripped and shot dead en masse by the German Einsatzgruppen* (mobile killing units) *in forests* and identified strongly with these victims. He said that if he had been a father at that time, he would have held his wife and his child so that they could have died at the same time so as to spare them the anguish of witnessing each other's deaths. Although Dave spoke in a largely detached tone throughout most of the interviews, this was the first time during interviewing that he expressed visible sadness. In a sense, he seemed able to empathize more easily with these somewhat once removed atrocities than to engage with the affect associated with his own direct experiences.

Dave spent a long time giving a detailed description of the gas chambers at Auschwitz. For the past decade, he had visited schools where he showed slides and spoke about the gas chambers. He brought his pictures of Auschwitz and explained the death process in great detail in his interviews. *Just think of the horror and terror of these poor people, standing there naked with their children and suddenly realizing this is not a shower, it's a gas chamber!* Dave constantly perseverated about the deaths at Auschwitz, which could be understood to be one indication of his PTSD. It was apparent that he was very invested in others' appreciating the full horror of the Holocaust and bearing witness to this.

Developmental Disruption

Dave reported that in early childhood he came from a stable and loving home where he was closely attached to his mother. His lack of attachment to his father was noted; however, he described his father with respect and admiration. When the Holocaust began, he was in the latency stage, described by Erikson (1977) as the "industry versus inferiority" stage. His primary school years were disrupted with the burning of his home at the beginning of the war. The family's eviction from their home was his first experience of his parents' inability to protect him.

Erikson (1977) indicates that the core developmental task during adolescence is "identity versus role confusion." Dave's adolescent years were fraught with loss and trauma. Part of adolescent male identity includes developing a sense of physical strength, autonomy, and the capacity to be competent. He was constantly humiliated with being weak, defeated, and a "masculine failure." It is possible that his experience of severe beatings and humiliation, in addition to catastrophic loss at that time, led to the construction of a detached-style defense mechanism. This could have contributed to the manifestation of depression later in his life. During the war, Dave was developing his identity as a boy or young man. He was the victim of continual, violent beatings and reported that he felt humiliated and violated. In addition, hunger, illness, and degradation added to his sense of helplessness and impotent rage. He witnessed executions and feared for his life. These experiences led to the development of PTSD (Herman 1992; Van der Kolk 2007) and disrupted his capacity to form a stable adolescent identity (Erikson 1982). He seems to have experienced himself as "already dead" at times, even though he fought to survive.

Dave said that, when he arrived in South Africa at fourteen years of age, nobody asked him about his experiences during the Holocaust and he did not discuss his experiences even with his mother. His extended family was not supportive of his mother or himself. School was difficult as he did not relate well to his peer group. When he tried to discuss his Holocaust experiences at school the other Jewish boys *shut him up.* Consequently, he became angry and socially isolated. He said that he involved himself in solitary activities such as hiking outdoors, which he enjoyed. Another severe trauma occurred when he visited Israel during the early fifties. He became involved in a fight with a group of young men who beat him to the point of being hospitalized for a couple of days. He reported that this experience was particularly traumatic as he had been beaten up in Israel, by Jews, which left him feeling betrayed and enraged. It is possible that this experience brought back memories of prior beatings and exacerbated his PTSD.

Despite Dave's difficulties with adjusting in South Africa, his resilience prevailed. He was able to work and marry. His capacity to reattach was activated, and he reported that he shared a loving and fulfilling relationship with his wife. However, Dave said that she was the only person to whom he was attached. This positive, nurturing relationship indicated that, despite his PTSD, he was able to make a good object choice, probably based on his secure early attachment to his mother (Klein 2012).

Mental Health Impacts

Dave reported that he suffered from chronic PTSD and depression over several decades. Periodic alterations in consciousness included preoccupation with his traumatic experiences, and he spoke incessantly about his experiences and the death of his family at Auschwitz. He described dissociative episodes including depersonalization and derealization. In addition, Dave ruminatively focused on his Holocaust trauma and had chronic PTSD, demonstrating reexperiencing and mood instability some seventy years after his liberation. He described a sense of survivor guilt, and the sense of stigma associated with his identity during adolescence appeared to have stayed with him. He remained preoccupied with understanding why the Holocaust happened and the Nazi motivation for killing Jews. As a consequence of his traumatic experiences, Dave withdrew socially and was persistently distrustful of people over the course of his lifetime. His lack of faith in God and humankind suggested that his Holocaust trauma had permanently altered his system of meaning. In addition, he expressed a sense of despair regarding his lost childhood and his unresolved grief regarding the loss of his father and the manner of his dying. A psychiatrist had prescribed both medication and psychotherapy for his depression and his PTSD and he had been taking psychiatric medication from his early thirties until the time of the interview.

Experience of Aging: Integrity versus Despair

At the time of the interview, Dave was in excellent health and was fit and active; however, he continued to take antidepressant medication. Dave represents the kind of survivor described by Kellermann (2001), who observes that survivors often have a dual diagnosis of PTSD and depression. Dave worked part-time and volunteered to speak about his Holocaust experiences at schools. He also read extensively about the Holocaust. He told me that in the years following the Holocaust he took up shooting and martial arts to gain a sense of masculine competence. He admitted to placing himself in dangerous situations where he walked around in unsafe areas at unsafe times carrying a loaded gun. He explained that he would rather die than be humiliated again. Dave seemed to be attempting to gain a sense of retrospective mastery over the victimization he endured during the Holocaust. His risk-taking behavior indicated that over sixty years later he remained deeply scarred by his experiences. Dave was still *fighting* as an old man.

Dave was insightful and had a deeply philosophical worldview. He said that as he aged, he became more appreciative of what life offers. He explained that, although he still suffered and was angry at times, *there is more joy than anger, I enjoy life.* He spoke of the deep love that he felt for his wife and said that the love had grown and developed over time. From this perspective, it appeared that Dave had elements of ego integration, such as appreciation for his present life and marital bond; however, he was consumed with despair regarding his trauma and loss as a result of the Holocaust.

Towards the end of the interview, Dave asked if he could sing a song. He chose to sing *Ani Ma'amin*, which means "I believe." That Dave chose to sing this specific song was significant in that he defines himself as an atheist. Despite his atheism, he marked the conclusion of his final interview with a song about faith and God.

Process Observations

After thirty hours of recorded interviews, Dave was keen to continue. When I asked him to reflect on the interviews it was apparent that Dave perhaps held me in an idealized transference relation, as both a listener and someone whom he implored to hear his story.

Tracey: *Dave, what has your experience talking about the Holocaust been like?*

Dave: *Good. If it adds value, it's worthwhile. I enjoy discussing this thing with you.*

Tracey: *What has been beneficial for you?*

Dave: *Have you heard about the ancient mariner syndrome?*

Tracey: *No.*

Dave: *It's a story about a sailor who survives a lot of horrific experiences and eventually he is the only one who survives from the whole crew. As an old man, he looks around a table until he can find someone who can listen to his story, and by hook or by crook he must tell the story; he practically forces the other person to listen to his story. I hope you didn't feel forced.*

Tracey: *No.*

Dave: *He had this compulsion and obsession to talk. I have been inflicting my story on you.*

It seemed that, while Dave was aware that his trauma narrative had been a burden on me, he was also powerfully in need of a validating audience and appreciative of the research time devoted to him.

He continued to say that, because I was a professional, he could tell his story to me without worrying that he would upset me. At points during the interview process, I became anxious about Dave's wellbeing and worried that his reported behavior might be dangerous to him. I felt confronted with an ethical dilemma as I understood that Dave was putting his life in danger apparently in a form of repetition compulsion related to camp trauma but it was not necessarily my role as researcher to take up this issue. He had not asked me to engage him as a clinical professional or therapist. Nevertheless, my clinical understanding became ethically more important to me than adopting a non-interventionist stance as a researcher. In addition, his wife approached me in Dave's presence and spoke of her fear for his safety. I consulted with one of my research supervisors, who is also a clinician, and after this challenged

Dave about his potentially self-destructive behavior, offering an interpretation concerning his compulsion to repeat the trauma. I explained that his actions had potentially dangerous consequences for himself and his wife. After initially resisting the interpretation, Dave acknowledged that he knew that his actions were dangerous. The recognition that his wife would be heartbroken should something happen to him appeared to shift his self-endangering stance.

I offered to refer Dave for therapy, which he refused. I stayed in touch with him and we met eight months after the interview process was completed. The plan was to see how he was coping and reopen the possibility of referring him for therapy. When I asked how he had been since the interviews, he reported that he had stopped his dangerous behavior, much to his wife's relief. I think Dave was so unconsciously trapped in this act of repetition compulsion that it did not occur to him that it could also hurt his wife. He said that the interviews had helped, that he was feeling good and that he would be prepared to receive therapy if it would help the research. I explained that although he had helped with the research the therapy was not for my benefit but rather for his own benefit. He said that he was coping well and did not feel he needed therapy at this point. I observed that he appeared to be doing well and that therefore referring him for therapy was perhaps not necessary. I have retained contact with Dave through various forums as will be further elaborated in the reflexivity section.

Miriam

Miriam: *At one point, when my mother did not return for three nights, I was terrified that I would not see her again.*

Miriam was born in Latvia. She was eighty years old at the time of the research interview. Miriam was twelve years old when the Holocaust started and sixteen when it ended. Soon after the Holocaust began, her father was taken to prison and killed by the Germans. Miriam and her mother were initially moved to the Dvinsk Ghetto and later to Kaiserwald concentration camp, near Riga. After their time in Kaiserwald she and her mother were imprisoned in Stutthof concentration camp for three months. They then moved to Sophienwalde labor camp, a subcamp of Stutthof. After a treacherous death march, the Russian Army finally liberated them. At the end of the war Miriam and her mother worked for a year for the Russians who liberated the camps, after which they then spent a year in Paris. They then emigrated to South Africa, moving to Johannesburg because her mother had family who lived there.

Miriam reported that her extended family was very supportive of her and her mother; however, no one asked about or discussed the Holocaust. Although she and her mother remained close, she stated that they never discussed what they had endured. Miriam studied and obtained a school leaving qualification. After this she got married and had four children.

Miriam was interviewed once a week at her home over a period of five weeks. She was interviewed for a total of eight hours and was very engaging and seemed ready and willing to tell her story. On closer examination she presented as having very strong psychological defenses. She did not become visibly sad or anxious during her interviews and said that she had never suffered from depression. She told her story in a detached manner as if she was a storyteller describing the narrative of another person. This indicated that perhaps Miriam had developed and sustained rigid defenses in relation to managing the impact of the Holocaust period in her life. Her flat affect suggested that there was evidence of her using dissociation as a way of coping with catastrophic trauma and loss, in accordance with Herman's (1992) observations about coping with extreme and prolonged trauma exposure.

Memories of Early Parenting

Miriam said that she had memories of a very happy childhood. She was the only child born into an affluent family and described both parents in glowing terms as educated and culturally sophisticated. Her father worked in his business and he remained at home with her while her mother, who was involved in arts and culture, frequently travelled around Europe. Her father was said to be *a very kind man*, and she described her mother as *a very cultured and dynamic woman*. She was very proud of her mother. She had clear memories of her early childhood and spoke of ballet lessons, which she loved. She enthusiastically showed me pictures of her ballet class when she was six years old. She reported that from the age of two her beloved Latvian nanny Natasha looked after her. Natasha was a devoted nanny who slept in Miriam's room and taught her how to sew and knit. She reported that her nanny was *like a mother to me*. Miriam used to accompany her to church and spent many hours with her. She reported that her nanny risked her life for her during the Holocaust, keeping her in hiding for two months and bringing Miriam and her mother food. Miriam describes her childhood as happy and secure. On closer observation it seems that her nanny was a very important nurturing object and cared for her in place of her mother, who was somewhat absent owing to her travelling. It was evident that Miriam had felt well supported and loved and had introjected primarily positive object relations with all three significant caregivers.

Traumatic Experiences and Recollections

Miriam reported that her first traumatic memory was of running away from the fires caused by bombings. Houses were ablaze, and Miriam and her family ran frightened through a tunnel of fire. She described how sick patients from the nearby hospital were begging for help, shouting and crawling on all fours. As they were also running from the fire themselves, she and her mother were unable to help them. She reported that this image profoundly distressed her throughout her life. Miriam's father and uncle were sent to prison. Her mother had gone to visit her father and found that the prison was empty aside from a large pile of men's clothes. She remembered that her mother had returned home shaken and whispered: *they are all gone, murdered in cold blood!* She reported that she and her mother were so afraid for their survival that they were unable to process their loss and mourn properly for her father. Ghetto selections took place frequently and people were shot and buried in mass graves by the *Einsatzgruppen* (mobile killing units). Miriam said she constantly lived with the threat of death. She reported that she had witnessed the hanging of an older girl whom she knew well. Her crime was that she had hidden her yellow star from view. Her dead body was left to stay for a week and this image was a fearful warning for all to see.

Miriam said that during the time they lived in the ghetto she was constantly afraid of being separated from her mother who she depended upon for survival. *I was covered in boils, and I would scratch the lice, my burning skin hung from my bones. When my mother was taken from the ghetto to town to work, I was left alone and sick, a child of twelve years old. I spent the days without her, and she returned to sleep in the ghetto at night. I lived in fear that my mother would not return.* At one point, when her mother did not return for three nights, she was terrified that she would not see her again. She said that, when her mother returned, she was beaten up and bruised: *Her face was so swollen I didn't recognize her! She said, "Miriam, it's me, your mother!" My mother reported that the Germans took a book and put it on her head and beat her. They kept her in a dungeon and tortured her for three days. A German soldier kicked and humiliated her and made her kiss his feet!* Miriam said that she was constantly afraid that her mother would not survive, and this incident was particularly terrifying.

Miriam reported that her nanny made continuous efforts to help them during the Holocaust period: *My nanny risked her life to bring us bread and got my mother's permission to christen me with holy water in the hope that it would save me. Although I didn't pray, I believe that I survived the Holocaust because my nanny, who was a religious Catholic, prayed for me.* Miriam went to hide at her nanny's home as her mother feared that she would be killed in the ghetto during the day while she was at work. Miriam reported that after two months she returned to the ghetto because people were suspicious that her nanny was hiding her and it became unsafe. When Miriam returned, the ghetto had been "liquidated," and she said that she witnessed a horrific scene of carnage that never left her memory.

Miriam and her mother were then transferred to Citadel, a military camp across the town in Dvinsk. Miriam reported that she used to sew dolls and clothing for the Germans, a skill she had learned from her nanny. She and her mother spent nine months in Citadel. She reported that they were later moved to Kaiserwald concentration camp, in Riga, where Miriam became very sick and weak. Her mother and other inmates helped to nurse her. The hunger and the cold were extreme, yet she was made to work very hard in the rain and cold. She reported that she and her mother were then taken to Stutthof concentration camp. Miriam said that this was a *terrifying experience* as will be described in more detail later in this discussion.

Miriam said that every day someone would commit suicide by touching the electric fence, which became a normal way of life. Miriam described her concentration camp experience in the following way: *The cruelty was in the way they gathered us and counted us, you stood there in the cold, hungry, and it's raining, and they kept you standing for no reason and counted you for no reason, you had nowhere to run too, there was no reason to keep counting! Cruelty was there all; the time the whole thing was cruel! Then someone grabbed a potato from your soup!*

Miriam said that, because she was small and weak, she was constantly afraid of being *selected for death.* She reported that her mother often stuffed her bra in order to make Miriam look older and nourished. At Sophienwalde camp Miriam witnessed a woman being shot as she grabbed a potato from a nearby cart. She reported that she was constantly afraid and traumatized by severe hunger, cold, and lice. Towards the end of the war, she and her mother were taken on a death march overnight for twenty kilometers in the snow, without food or water. When morning came, they could barely move as the Germans drove them into a barn. The next morning the Russians liberated them. She said, *My mother was an amazing, outstanding woman, she constantly looked after me, and she saved my life. I was lucky I had her with me.*

Miriam lost her father in the first months of the war, as well as her cousin Lenna, who was like a sister to her. In addition, her aunts, uncles, and extended family were also murdered. She reported feeling devastated as a result of her separation from her nanny, Natasha, who was *a second mother*. This woman did not have children of her own and was devoted to caring for Miriam. In recent years, Miriam and her family honored Natasha at Yad Vashem, in Israel, as a righteous gentile who put her life at risk to save Miriam.

Developmental Disruption

Miriam said her childhood was very happy, and her parents were described in positive and perhaps even idealized ways. It is significant that she commented on being very attached to her nanny. She seems to have internalized Natasha as an alternative nurturing object. Her frequent separations from her mother from the age of two may have left Miriam anxiously attached; however, her nanny was constantly with her and seemed to be a secure maternal substitute. The sharp contrast between her privileged and protected life before the war and the extent to which she was overwhelmed by trauma, deprivation, and physical suffering during the Holocaust was apparent in her narrative.

Miriam was an adolescent in the stage of "identity versus role confusion" during the time of the Holocaust. In early adolescence, Miriam lost her father and experienced fear and suffering. Both she and her mother were unable to properly mourn his loss as their survival was at risk. Miriam reported that for a period of five years she was constantly fearful of her own death and experienced extreme fear of losing her mother. Her mother cared for and protected her, which was a significant factor in building her resilience. However, she was frequently sick and depended on her mother for survival. Living under the constant threat of this loss may have exacerbated her anxious attachment to her mother. Miriam had to struggle for survival and had no time to form an identity or bond with her peer group, instead she remained with her mother whom she retained as a primary attachment object in the camps. While being with her mother added to her resilience, she remained intensely overattached to her mother. This enmeshment or traumatic bonding was clearly a result of the trauma they endured together. From her narrative, it is understood that Miriam idealized her mother to a degree and considered her a *savior*. However, she may have sacrificed her own identity formation in the service of this intense attachment. The loss of her nanny was very traumatic, as she had been a stable caretaker who had devoted her life to looking after Miriam. As with her father's loss, Miriam was unable to process the separation from and loss of this primary caretaker, as she was focused on her own survival.

During adolescence, Miriam endured humiliation and intrusive bodily attacks, such as injections to the breast and pubic hair examinations for lice, with a stick. She described her initial feeling of humiliation but reported that she later disassociated as a way of coping. Her intense suffering from lice, eczema, cold, and hunger was described in great detail. This seemed to have been experienced as a powerful visceral/physical trauma. It is possible that Miriam's extreme anxiety about losing her mother and dying herself, in combination with her physical suffering, led to dissociation as a way of coping. She reported as an adult that she never became depressed and is not *emotional*. It is likely that she used powerful psychological defenses to disconnect from her loss, humiliation, and sense of imminent life threat.

Miriam reported that she had good familial and social support when she arrived in South Africa and this helped her to adjust to life in a new country. As explained by Keilson (1979), a facilitating environment after the Holocaust was a mitigating factor. She married in her early twenties. Miriam reported that she suffered from nightmares for many decades. The themes of her nightmares always involved running away from the Germans. It is interesting that, despite her conscious attempts to move on from or repress her traumatic experiences, they emerged in this intrusive form.

Mental Health Impacts

Miriam suffered from severe nightmares for decades after the Holocaust ended, a symptom that would be seen as falling under the intrusion cluster of PTSD, and it is evident that this symptom was chronic. Additionally, during her time in the camps she coped by using depersonalization and derealization and there was some indication that these defenses may have become somewhat entrenched. Her flat affect was remarkable, and she avoided expression of any emotional vulnerability. She told me in a hostile tone of voice that no one could understand the Holocaust unless he or she had been there. This suggested her experience of feeling different from others and of having been indelibly changed or marked in some way. Extending upon this, she described her alienation from religion and her loss of faith in people and God. She was prone to irritability and said it was difficult for her to emotionally self-regulate at times. She lived with PTSD and functioned well, as did many of the survivors in the study.

Experience of Aging: Integrity versus Despair

At the time of the interview Miriam was in good health and said she was content with her life. She said that her husband, to whom she had been married for over fifty years, was very kind to her, and her children were a source of pride. She was proud that her children were supportive of one another and did not fight. In this respect she seemed to find it important that her children had not been contaminated by her experience and were generative in their own right.

She said that she never got depressed and kept herself busy with sewing, reading, making jeweler, gardening, and baking. Clearly, her capacity to engage productively and to distract herself with activities and channeling her creativity was her way of coping. She spoke publicly about her story fairly frequently and was acknowledged by her community for her bravery in this respect. When asked whether her memories of the Holocaust became worse as she aged, she said that they were always with her but did not get worse. It seems that her defense mechanism of dissociation, which appeared to largely successfully block her emotional engagement with her trauma, continued to function well in her old age. In addition to dissociation, Miriam seemed to use compartmentalization as a defense mechanism to cope with her trauma as she was able to talk about her experiences without this apparently intruding into her everyday functionality. She seemed to idealize her mother who had saved her life and said many times that her mother was an outstanding woman. It appeared that she had successfully repressed all her negative emotions in the service of survival. Dasberg (2001) indicates that this level of repressing unmanageable trauma is commonly found in child survivors. It was evident that Miriam had underlying hostility towards religious leaders and her hostility also emerged in relation to me, indicating that at particular times she used hostility to cope with her vulnerability.

During the interviews at her house, Miriam would offer tea and an elaborate assortment of biscuits that she had baked, of which she was very proud. She said that all her clothes were handmade as her nanny had taught her to sew. Keeping busy helped her to cope, and the skills she had in this regard were thanks to her nanny. At the end of her interview, Miriam asked if she could show me her jewellery and explained that she had made a living for many years designing handmade jewellery. Miriam was very proud of her work and recounted that she had used her creativity as a way of coping. It seemed that not only had Miriam used creativity as a way of distracting herself from her pain but also that this was perhaps a concrete means of holding onto her internalized good object, as it was her nanny who had fostered her creative skills. Although Miriam was able to express gratitude and pride about her achievements, as well as attain a great level of satisfaction from her life, it was clear that she blocked aspects of her emotional life associated with traumatic experiences. She struggled to process her Holocaust trauma because of her rather rigid defensive style (Herman 1992; Dasberg 2001). Nevertheless, it is important to acknowledge her generative capacity and her retention of good object introjects from her childhood throughout her life.

Process Observations

Despite being apparently comfortable to take part in the research, the interview process with Miriam was rather complex, as illustrated, for example, by the following exchange.

> Miriam: *No one can understand the horror unless they have been there. Even you can never understand!* (Said with apparent aggression.)

> Tracey: *I agree, Miriam, I cannot understand, I was not there.*

During the interview process I felt Miriam's anger and recognized her communication to perhaps be a projection or displacement of hostile feelings. My psychological training helped me to decide that it was best to acknowledge rather than explore her communication, particularly given the context. In addition, I thought it was important to validate that no one could understand Miriam's experience. She was an adult who had been very wounded by her reality.

Miriam continued to invite me for tea after the interviews were over. She also showed curiosity about my life and attempted to befriend me, becoming angry if a long period of time elapsed without hearing from me. She would call me and say in an aggressive tone of voice, *where have you been? Come for tea!* I tried to be as sensitive and tactful as possible in responding to her need but also in setting boundaries. I wondered if in some respects I had become a replica transference object of the nanny that Miriam was so fond of. This impression was to some extent reinforced as Miriam treated me as if I were at her beck and call and as if she was somehow entitled to my attention (as a child might feel towards a caretaker). Perhaps as a result of her distrust she became very controlling of her objects. It felt as if having told me her story, Miriam needed to hold onto the relationship. I felt guilty about setting what I perceived to be a necessary boundary in terms of ongoing extra-research contact and tried to do so as gently as possible. However, Miriam's anger was an indication of her dissatisfaction suggestive of unmet need for a mirror and a listener in the present. It seemed that Miriam had invested herself in the research by telling her story in detail and this meant that perhaps it was difficult for her to let go of the gratifying contact with someone who was empathically engaged. Despite raising this possibility Miriam said she did not want to see a therapist. She kept in touch with me telephonically for over a year but this contact ceased after she suffered a stroke.

Lenna

Lenna: *I have never spoken about what I went through or what happened in the camps, I am not sure I will be able to cope, the difficulty is in expressing it verbally, and then hearing it out loud is too traumatic.*

Lenna was a child survivor born in Hungary. The Nazis invaded Hungary in 1944 when she was eleven years old, and she was twelve years old at the end of the war. She was imprisoned at Auschwitz for a year and then moved to Bergen-Belsen where she was captive for three months before liberation. Her entire family was killed, except for her aunt. After the war ended, she went to live in a *kibbutz* in Israel. After meeting her husband in her early twenties, she immigrated to South Africa and had two children. She worked as a teacher for many years before starting her own business, which became a very successful company.

At the time of the interview Lenna was in good health and was a healthy seventy-four-year-old woman. She worked full-time and lived with her husband. Both of her daughters lived overseas, and she was planning to emigrate from South Africa so that she could be close to them and her grandchildren. Lenna agreed to meet me but warned me that she had struggled to tell her story and had almost never spoken about her Holocaust experiences. Despite her anxiety, Lenna nevertheless chose to go ahead with the interviews with the mutual understanding that she could terminate the process at any point.

She met with me for three sessions that lasted over an hour each and spoke about her early history. She said that the dread of discussing her Holocaust experiences had activated nightmares and she felt unable to continue the interview process. I thanked her for her willingness to make herself available for the research project despite her initial misgivings and she indicated that she was comfortable for her data to be included in the research thesis.

Memories of Early Parenting

Lenna reported that her parents were married for many years before she was born. When she was ten months old, her mother gave birth to her younger brother. Her father contracted tuberculosis shortly before she was born. Later, her father her became very ill, and as a result, she and her younger brother went to live with their grand-aunt when she was four years old. This aunt was her grandfather's sister and she and her husband did not have children of their own. Lenna described them as kind and loving people. She and her brother lived with the couple during the week and returned to their parents' house on the weekend. This living arrangement minimized the risk of the children contracting their father's disease. In addition, their mother worked full-time as the family struggled financially and the mother looked after her sick husband at night. Lenna did not have any memories before the age of four and said she did not recollect ever having felt sad to say goodbye to her mother as her great-aunt was a good parent figure. She said that she did not remember receiving affection from her parent figures and sometimes this left her doubting her lovability. She has memories of being nurtured and cared for by her aunt: *I don't remember being hugged by my parents, it upsets me, but I don't remember . . . I remember everything about my aunt, she was very kind and nice . . . I remember the food she would pack in my lunch and that she would walk me to school.*

Lenna reported that her father's illness was traumatic for her and her brother as they were not allowed to approach him or touch him for fear that he was contagious: *We used to have a board between the kitchen and the bedroom. We would stand on a chair and look over the board and talk to him like that; we would never go in the room. I used to stand outside the door and talk to him.* Lenna said that her father was a refined man who loved poetry and music and she felt attached to him despite the physical separation. When he was in the hospital, they were allowed closer contact although she and her brother had to wear masks for protection. She reported that her father died when she was seven years old. A week before he died, she remembered that he did not speak much, but he blessed Lenna and her brother. No one told Lenna directly that he had died. She remembered that her aunt said it was time to go and, when she walked outside and saw her father's coffin, she then realized that he had died. *It's difficult to say how I felt as a child. I would imagine that his death traumatized me. I used to imagine that my father was talking to me after he died.* After her father's death, she and her brother returned home to live with their mother and it is likely that the renewed separation, this time from her great-aunt, may have been difficult. She reported that she and her brother were always very close. It is interesting that Lenna chose to spend a considerable portion of the interview time talking about this pre-war period. This may have been in part because this early period in her life also held difficult or traumatic memories and was illustrative of a childhood that may have left her vulnerable, even prior to the Holocaust period. However, it may also be that it was easier to talk about this time than her camp experiences, as she suggested.

Traumatic Experiences and Recollections

A year after her father died, the Holocaust began. Thereafter, she was captured and sent to Auschwitz and then moved to Bergen-Belsen where she spent three months before being liberated. At this time, she was very sick and was taken to Sweden by the Red Cross. She said: *I don't think anyone who went through the camps like Auschwitz, Bergen-Belsen, or Majdanek is normal. I don't believe you can be normal! You live with the memories and the people you lost, and what you experienced, it's there with you all the time, so how can you be normal? It's not something that is finished and gone, and you get on with your life. So, you build yourself a way of life; you try to act normal, you laugh, you dance, you go to movies and theatre. I have it all in front of my eyes, and it's hard to forget!* This comment illustrates rather vividly what Dasberg (2001) says is the parallel existence that many survivors experience. Part of them is stuck in their camp experience, whilst they function as if "untouched" in their present lives. Unlike some of the other participants, Lenna would not describe her experiences in the camps in any detail; however, it is evident from the statement just cited that she experienced death and horror of a magnitude similar to that described by others and her reference to her sickness indicates that she also suffered physically.

Despite her lack of elaboration of her camp experiences, Lenna mentioned that she had visited Auschwitz three times after the Holocaust ended and felt a sense of comfort there. She expressed intense feelings of survivor guilt in relation to her younger brother who died in Auschwitz. As indicated previously, she also lost multiple other family members, including her mother and the grand-aunt who had looked after her as a child. Unlike some of the other survivors interviewed, it was evident that Lenna had no sustained relationship with anyone in the camps, before, or after the Holocaust. *I was liberated from Auschwitz. I was twelve and alone.* This isolation may have contributed to her fragility in approaching Holocaust-related recollections as it is apparent that she did not have anyone to share the burden of the experience at the time or subsequently.

Developmental Disruption

Lenna's capacity to have developed basic trust in the first year of life is questionable. Her father was sick with tuberculosis before she was born, and so it is possible that her mother's anxiety regarding her father's illness distracted her from bonding with Lenna as a baby. In addition, Lenna was displaced by the birth of her brother born ten months after her. By the time she was four years old, there was anxiety that the children could contract tuberculosis from their father. For this reason, the children were sent to live with their great-aunt and uncle, returning home only on weekends. This was a major developmental disruption at Erikson's (1982) stage of "guilt versus initiative." Fraiberg (1959) has suggested that children are renowned for "magical thinking" at this age and are egocentric. During this stage, children often feel guilty and blame themselves for difficulties in their environment. It is possible that Lenna unconsciously blamed herself for her father's illness and that she understood the move to her aunt as a rejection and punishment by her mother, despite her positive experience of care in her new home. Her capacity for resilience is demonstrated by how she adjusted to her environment. She also, fortunately, was able to bond with her aunt. Lenna seemed to develop a self-reliant defense as a way of coping, as she knew she could not rely on her heavily burdened mother or her sick father. This self-reliance seemed to continue after the Holocaust as she reported that she never discussed her feelings or her Holocaust experiences with anyone.

Lenna's father's death was remembered traumatically, as there appeared to have been little or no preparation for or mediation of the experience from the adults around her. While she had no memory of affection from her parents and sometimes wondered if she was loved, she remembers that her aunt cared about her. It seemed the separation from her parents at an early age compromised her capacity to form a secure bond with them. One could argue that her sense of being burdensome and her susceptibility to loss was established before the Holocaust in relation to her father's death and her mother's preoccupation with caring for her father. The Holocaust trauma seemed to exacerbate this and translated into an intense experience of survivor guilt in relation to her younger brother and cousins who perished.

During the Holocaust, Lenna missed out on a primary school education and never completed her education thereafter. Erikson (1982) reports that the latency stage involves the core negotiation of "industry versus inferiority." Despite her successful business, Lenna felt she had missed out on her education and reported that she had low self-esteem in this regard. *As far as education is concerned, I never had the chance or the opportunity. I am very sensitive about people saying to me, "What do you know, you never had an education, you think you know everything, you are stupid." That affects me very badly.* This comment illustrates Lenna's sense of inferiority, even though she was able to build a large and successful business. She demonstrates that developmental disruption at this stage of life may well leave its mark on personality development in later life.

Lenna was thirteen when the war ended. Her entrance into adolescence was heralded by experiences of being orphaned and sick. Her entire family had been killed. Her search for an identity was eclipsed by her intense grief for her mother, brother, and extended family. She reported that going to a *kibbutz* in Israel helped to provide a peer group that became important for her. Klein (2012) demonstrated in his research that the close-knit community of a *kibbutz* seemed to provide survivors with a "safe haven," where they had a sense of belonging. It mitigated against the sense of isolation experienced by survivors, especially those who had lost immediate and extended family. This mirrored Lenna's experience, and she said that her life in the *kibbutz* helped her to cope after the Holocaust.

Mental Health Impacts

Although Lenna was unable to complete the interview process, it was clear from what she had said that she was suffering from both complex traumatic stress and PTSD with avoidant and intrusive symptoms such as disturbing nightmares and disturbing recollections. It was evident that she had persistent dysphoria and she described her difficulty in expressing conflict. It was also evident that, despite a motivation to participate, Lenna could not modulate or regulate the powerful affects evoked in talking about her experience of the Holocaust. Alterations in consciousness were evident in her description of dissociative states and avoidant PTSD symptoms. She described a sense of shame and survival guilt in relation to her dead family members. Isolation and withdrawal seemed to characterize her relationships with her present family. This was manifested in her description of disrupted relationships and persistent distrust. An alteration of meaning systems was identified in Lenna's account of her loss of faith and her ongoing sense of hopelessness and despair about the loss of her family during the Holocaust. She described her mood swings and difficulty with self-regulation. Lenna had hidden her vulnerability and coped by being self-reliant. It is possible that her withdrawal from the interview process was a final act of self-reliance and avoidance of the situation where she exposed her vulnerability with another.

Experience of Aging: Integrity versus Despair

Lenna did not fully share her traumatic experiences, and the interview process was discontinued as she was too traumatized to speak further about this period of her life. Some of the information she shared was indicative of her state of mind. She said that she had intense survivor guilt and often asked herself why she had survived as opposed to her brother or members of her extended family. As a result, she said she struggled to enjoy her accomplishments as well as the luxurious standard of living that she had achieved. She was plagued by a sense of inadequacy about her lack of education. She reported that she struggled to speak up for herself when she felt victimized. Although she coped outwardly, on the inside she felt a deep despair and she carried this alone, experiencing enduring inner turmoil. This presentation is consistent with how Dasberg (2001) describes child survivors carrying their pain by creating a "split" between their inner emotional life and their everyday functioning in the outside world.

As previously mentioned, Lenna was likely to have experienced disrupted bonding and early grief as a result of her father's illness and death before the Holocaust. It seemed she used a defense of self-sufficiency and self-reliance, as well as well as compartmentalization, in order to cope. She said that she struggled to enjoy her wealth and success and it was almost as if she did not fully identify with the person who had achieved in this way and was unable to own her sense of mastery.

It seemed Lenna had an inner sense of despair and turmoil as well as repressed anger and survivor guilt, the latter powerfully affecting her sense of legitimacy to a fulfilling life. Despite her outer success and resilience in coping, she clearly coped by compartmentalizing her Holocaust experiences. The possibility of discussing her experiences proved to be too much of a threat to her defenses, and it seemed that she needed to keep her trauma largely unspoken. It is interesting that although Lenna would not share her experiences at Auschwitz, she did share her difficulties in coping with her present life. She mentioned that she loved her grandchildren. She also proudly showed me around her exquisite townhouse and gave a detailed tour of her art collection. The art provided her with a sense of escape, and it was clearly also a hallmark of her great financial success.

Process Observations

At the time of the interviews, I felt great compassion for Lenna in her very evident ambivalence about sharing her traumatic experiences. It appeared that she was able to describe her early history but became overwhelmed when the time came to share her traumatic experiences in the camps. I realized that Lenna's experience of not being able to share her story was typical of many Holocaust survivors who view their traumas as "unspeakable." I felt traumatized upon hearing Lenna describe the *screaming and wailing* at Auschwitz. Since the interview, I have visited Auschwitz, and thought about the horror she endured.

Lenna was friendly and engaging and very apologetic that she was unable to continue the interview process. Although pleasant interpersonally, Lenna did not appear to attach to me in the manner that many other participants did, and in some respects, it seemed that she reenacted avoidance and distrust with me, defenses that she had developed to manage prior trials in her life. However, Lenna retained intermittent contact by telephone and requested to be my friend on Facebook. She remains in touch from Israel, suggesting that she was invested in the research process and that some meaningful connection was made between us.

Isaac

Isaac: *I was forced to hang other Jews in the ghetto—it left me feeling very angry.*

Isaac was born in Germany and was eighty-one years old at the time of the research interview. He had an older sister; his biological mother died of cancer when he was three years old. His father remarried when he was four years old, and the couple had a son who was six years younger than him. He was fourteen years old when the Holocaust began and nineteen when it ended. He reported that in 1941 the Gestapo beat his father up and then his family was rounded up and sent by train to the Riga Ghetto, in Latvia. Isaac said: *They took the Latvian Jews and killed them to make room for us, it was as if their food was still warm on the table.*

Isaac lived in the Riga Ghetto with his family from 1941 to 1943. Soon after he and his family arrived in Riga, his father was sent to a work camp. He was told that his father was shot en route to the camp. He reported that while in the Riga Ghetto he was forced by the Nazis to hang other Jews. When Isaac was seventeen, he arrived home from work in the Riga Ghetto to find that the family home was empty. He was then told that his stepmother, sister, and younger half-brother had been sent to Auschwitz, where, he later established, they were killed. The Germans took him to Niewals to work at the harbor. Thereafter, he was moved to a Hamburg jail where he worked on the railways. Isaac was then sent to Bergen-Belsen concentration camp where he stayed for three months until the British liberated the camp in 1945.

After the war, Isaac worked for the Red Cross at Bergen-Belsen as well as at different displaced person (DP) camps. He was the only survivor of his nuclear and extended family in Europe. After the war he came to live with an uncle and aunt in South Africa. He trained and worked as a pharmacist and joined his older cousin's business. At twenty-five years old he married, and had three sons. At the time of the interview Isaac was physically strong and in good health—he reported that he kept fit and loved cycling. In addition, he reported that his business was financially successful and he was proud of the financial success that he had achieved. I saw Isaac on four occasions at his home in and recorded six hours of material.

Memories of Early Parenting

Although Isaac had no memory of his mother, the loss of a primary caretaker at such an early age would inevitably have been traumatic as he would not have had verbal skills to express grief related to the loss or the cognitive ability to grasp the reality of his mother's death. Isaac was cared for by his maternal aunt for a year and then he lived with his father and stepmother. His relationship with his attachment figures appears to have been inconsistent and fragmented. His attachment was further disrupted as he was placed with his aunt for a year and then relocated to the care of his father and stepmother. It is important to note that Isaac reported that he experienced both his father and aunt as *strict* and that his father was physically violent. This suggests that he had aggressive role modelling from his father and that he may have internalized a punitive super-ego as a result of caretaker inputs. His fragmented bonding is likely to have disrupted the establishment of basic trust (Erikson 1982). Thus, it is apparent that Isaac entered the period of the Holocaust possibly already at some disadvantage in terms of psychological and interpersonal strengths.

Traumatic Experiences and Recollections

Isaac said he felt helpless and angry about the murder of his father who was shot by the Germans and he felt the same way about his stepmother, sister, and half-brother being sent to Auschwitz. Isaac had no closure regarding these deaths and was unable to say goodbye. The family were uprooted and sent to the Riga Ghetto, where the surviving Jews told them that the Latvian Jews had been shot at the edges of mass graves in the forests. Isaac also recalled seeing a German soldier shoot and kill a baby in its mother's arms, as the mother had come too close to the ghetto fence.

Isaac reported that he and some other young Jewish men were rounded up in the Riga Ghetto and forced to hang other Jews. The Jews that were hung stood accused of petty crimes, such as stealing a piece of bread. He was forced to carry out six or seven executions during this time. (This element of Holocaust experience will receive further elaboration later in this discussion.) Isaac stated that, had he not carried out or cooperated with the executions, he would almost inevitably have been killed himself. He said that this experience of being forced to be complicit in the killings of fellow Jewish inmates had left him with hatred towards the Germans and he still wished for revenge. Ever since the Holocaust he was an angry person, noting that he often shouted at his wife and sons. According to him, it was his past traumatic experiences that had left him very angry, and, although he ran a successful business, he fought a lot with his partners, his cousins, and his sons who worked for him.

In Bergen-Belsen, the conditions were terrible. There was a shortage of water and food. The crematorium was small and they could not cope with the number of dead bodies that needed to be burned, so the bodies were piled up. Isaac remembered the horror of the smell of the burning and rotting bodies. At night he shared a blanket with six other men and said that he was full of lice and so thin that he was a walking skeleton. He would help to move dead bodies to the crematorium and it would take four men to lift a body as they were so weak from starvation. In addition, Isaac worked for the Red Cross at Bergen-Belsen after it was liberated. At that time, he encountered thousands of scattered, rotting bodies as there was no place to bury or burn them. Isaac said that he would never forget the repulsive smell of human decay. He also told me that I should include the observation that there were so many dead bodies lying around in different stages of decomposition that the English army reported that they could smell the camp from several miles away. It is thus apparent that Isaac was exposed to terrible experiences of deprivation, death, and degradation and was also compelled to become involved in complicit aggressive acts himself. This left him with many intrusive memories and palpable anger.

Developmental Disruption

The death of Isaac's mother at the age of three was the first trauma in his life. The disruption of the mother-child attachment, at the rapprochement phase in this instance, is likely to lead to the child becoming anxious and fearful (Mahler,

Pines, and Bergman 2000). Erikson (1982) says that trauma during this phase leads to shame and self-doubt, as the child often tends to blame him/herself for the trauma. Early loss predisposed Isaac to sadness and depression. His maternal aunt was mourning for her own sister at the time that she was taking care of Isaac, so it was likely that she was somewhat emotionally preoccupied. At age four he was separated from his aunt and returned to live with his father and stepmother, further interrupting his bonding. It is also possible that he felt displaced by his younger half-brother who was born when he was eight years old, and he reported that he was not particularly close to his older sister.

Because of traumatic circumstances, Isaac was forced to grow up before his time and had a sense of foreclosed identity. In Dasberg's (2001) terms he was deprived of a normal adolescence. At the start of the war, he was an adolescent of fourteen, which marked the beginning of the formation of his masculine and adult identity. Being unable to save his parents, sister, and younger half-brother from death left him feeling impotent and hopeless. Being forced to execute other Jews worsened his helplessness and contributed to a kind of impotent rage and a need for revenge. The experience of the rage and its correlate of underlying helplessness has left its mark on Isaac's personality, as he admitted that he was an irascible and argumentative husband and father. At the time of the interview, he was married for fifty-one years and although he said he enjoyed being a father, he admitted that he was easily annoyed and shouted at his family. It is clear that Isaac felt unable to contain his aggressive outbursts. He reported feeling full of rage and bitterness and disappointed in his close relationships. Isaac's rage and his sense of being let down and attacked by family members and work partners created the sense that he could be stuck in primarily paranoid-schizoid position functioning (Klein 1935).

Mental Health Impacts

Isaac said that a psychiatrist had diagnosed him with PTSD and depression; however, he refused to take medication as he felt that he didn't need it. Isaac described persistent difficulties in affect regulation, including dysphoria and explosive anger. In addition, alteration in consciousness was described, including transient dissociative episodes and depersonalization and a full diagnostic picture of PTSD and CTSD.

He had kept aspects of his Holocaust experiences secret for fear of being stigmatized and appeared to carry internalized guilt for his actions, even if these were defended. In many respects he was completely isolated from others.

It emerged from his testimony that decades later he was still preoccupied with fantasies of revenge against the Nazi perpetrators. Owing to his persistent distrust of others, his family relationships were disrupted, and he felt very alone. He also clearly had unresolved distress regarding the horror he endured during the Holocaust, and the deaths of his father, sister, stepmother, and half-brother.

Experience of Aging: Integrity versus Despair

Within the framework of "integrity versus despair," Isaac's emotional experience was colored by rage and helplessness as a result of his Holocaust experiences as well as by anger. When listening to his narrative, it seemed that his inner world was filled with persecutory objects. He stated that he had no empathy and generally perceived others as antagonists. He reported that he was *hard* when he heard about other people's difficulties and he had a *tough luck* approach. He also carried feelings of anger and resentment towards his family members and in response to this tended to project blame or responsibility onto others. It was apparent that Isaac was a deeply unhappy person with considerable self-doubt. His rage and lack of empathy highlighted the way in which he appeared to be stuck in Klein's paranoid-schizoid position. His survival of the Holocaust horror appeared to have translated into functioning via the employment of the defenses of "splitting" and projection for much of his life.

Isaac also reported that he felt somewhat emotionally blunted, indicating that he perhaps used dissociation as a defense against his vulnerability. The experience of wisdom and despair can be understood as a continuum and it appears that most people have experiences of both aspects of the continuum to a lesser or greater extent. Isaac's preponderance of negative emotion and cognition indicated that he predominantly experienced despair and was generally pulled towards this pole of the continuum. It seemed he used his anger as a defense mechanism to avoid dealing with his vulnerability, helplessness, and shame about his concentration camp experiences.

Nevertheless, Isaac said that for a long time after the Holocaust life was good. He felt blessed that he had survived and was grateful that his aunt and uncle took care of him when he came to South Africa after the Holocaust. He was able to earn a good living and build a successful business and financially support his wife and children. However, later he felt that a range of difficulties hampered him. He felt remorse due to his fairly constant irritability with his family, although he also appeared to want to justify this. He said that his relationship with his wife was highly problematic and they fought continuously. He said that his sons were disrespectful and he fought with them. It was thus evident that Isaac's relationships did not feel supportive and he felt misunderstood, disrespected, and alone.

Despite difficulties in many areas, Isaac's relationship with God seemed to be intact as he mentioned that he frequently attended synagogue and he often referred to how God saved his life during the Holocaust. This perspective changed when he became sick with cancer many years later—he asked to see me and said that he felt that he was finally being punished for what he had done in the ghetto.

Process Observations

Despite his description of himself as irascible, Isaac was very friendly and cooperative and spoke in a coherent and engaging manner during the interviews. He had never spoken about his Holocaust experiences however; it was only in his interviews for this research that for the first time he divulged his experience of being forced to execute other Jews. I was aware of feeling deeply sad and disturbed that he had had to keep such a heavy secret for so long alone and also had to process my own feelings in response to his "confession."

Isaac appeared to use primitive defenses of splitting and projection in engaging with the world, and this was evident in the way he came to idealize me and the research process but remained devaluing of his family. He was needy and dependent and initially became aggressive when I had to cancel an appointment

FIGURE 4A. Isaac's pictures of Bergen-Belsen, photographed by British soldiers who liberated the camp. Piles of dead bodies.

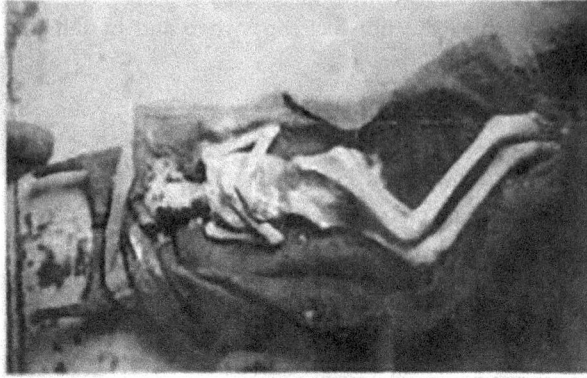

FIGURE 4B. An emaciated dead inmate.

FIGURE 4C. Dead bodies on the side of the road.

FIGURE 4D. More dead bodies.

due to being sick. However, thereafter Isaac was both respectful and needy of attention, appearing to treat me as somewhat of a rescuer. As a parting gift Isaac gave me original pictures taken by the British when they arrived in Bergen-Belsen. He said that the British soldiers had distributed their photographs to many of the young prisoners. The pictures were horrifying and depicted piles of rotting, emaciated bodies. He said that I could use the pictures in my research. It seemed that the sharing of the photographs represented a wish for me to grasp the full horror of his experiences and to bear witness beyond words.

Given my concerns about Isaac and what I perceived to be a level of depression, with his agreement I referred him to a social worker who subsequently visited him.

Anne

Anne: *We heard their screams and gunshots like an echo in the night when we were in hiding outside in the barn, and we were so scared. They were shooting Jews in the forest.*

Anne was a child survivor from Lithuania and was seventy-four years old at the time of the interview. She was born in Subačius, a small town in Lithuania. The Russians took over Lithuania a year before the Germans invaded. She described that many of the bourgeoisie were sent to Siberia. The Russians threatened to send her father to Siberia two weeks before the Germans invaded Lithuania. Anne was six years old at the beginning of the war and twelve when it ended. She reported that, when the Germans threatened to liquidate the ghetto where they lived, there was chaos and panic. Anne's mother left her and her younger brother in the house and ran to her father's factory outside the ghetto to warn him about the liquidation of the ghetto. As her mother returned home to fetch her children, she was shot dead. Ann recalled that a witness told her father that a German soldier cut a finger off her mother's dead body in order to take her wedding ring.

Anne indicated that the Germans and the Lithuanian police knew that her family had escaped the ghetto. She recognized that she and her brother were in danger. Anne reportedly took him and ran outside the barbed wire to her father's factory but found that he was not there. A woman they knew took them to hide in a barn where her father and older sister were hiding. Subsequently, Anne, her father, brother, and older sister hid in a tunnel in a hay barn where they could only sit or lie down. Anne said that, in the chaos, her other sister Miri, who was eleven years old, went into hiding alone. The Germans discovered her hiding place and shot her. Anne had been very close to this sister. Anne described how her family survived living in the hay barn for a year. The farmer used to bring them food and they had to whisper in order not to create suspicion. Eventually, owing to the lice, cold, and hunger, her father decided to take them to a temporary labor camp in the hope of better living conditions. A Jewish guard allowed them to stay as long as the children remained hidden when the Germans came to fetch the Jews in the morning for work. Apparently, the Germans later threatened to kill the Jews in the labor camp and Anne and her family escaped.

Anne described that she went into hiding with a Russian family and that they converted her to Catholicism. She worked as a *herd girl* looking after cattle. The mother of this family did not know that she was Jewish and was told that the priest had asked the family to take the child in. Anne had no idea where her family was or if they were dead or alive. She reported that her father later unexpectedly arrived to fetch her, having managed to get false papers to get them out of Lithuania. They crossed the Alps and stayed in a displaced persons camp in Italy. Later, Anne's oldest sister made the decision to move to Israel, while her father decided to move the family to South Africa to be with their extended family.

When they arrived in South Africa, Anne met her childless married aunt, whom she became close to and moved in with in Durban. Anne said that after the war she was like a *lost sheep* who could not speak English or integrate socially. She did not want to return to school and eventually got a secretarial diploma. She moved to Johannesburg at the age of seventeen and lived with her father's relatives. She married in her early twenties and had four sons. She reported that her first husband was emotionally abusive and she divorced him after several years of marriage. She said that, fortunately, her second marriage was more peaceful. I interviewed Anne at her home on four occasions and recorded eight hours of material.

Memories of Early Parenting

Anne came from a financially prosperous family. Her father had a wood factory. She was the third of four children, having two older sisters and a younger brother. She describes her father as a wonderful man who managed to save three of his children. Anne, her oldest sister, and younger brother survived the war together. Her mother and the other sister, Miri, were murdered soon after the war started. She described happy memories of playing in the street with her friends, doing well at school, and riding on her father's motorbike with him, prior to the war. She described her mother as a very good parent who *looked after her children and took interest.* She says that she was attached to both her parents and she remembered that they had a *very happy marital relationship.* The family went to the river in the forest during the summer time and for summer holidays in Russia. She said, *Life before the war was very happy.* It appeared that Ann had a secure attachment to both her parents as well as to her siblings.

Traumatic Experiences and Recollections

Anne reported that at the beginning of the war German soldiers came to her house for supper. One soldier took her mother to the bedroom in the middle of the meal. Her father remained with his four children. After a period of time her mother and the soldier returned. Anne said that with hindsight she thought that the German soldier threatened her parents and raped her mother during this event. As a child, she remembered being confused as to why this man took her mother to the bedroom, and when she thought about it later it filled her with *disgust.* She felt uncomfortable about an incident that she did not understand and sensed that something was discordant. However, she felt that neither she nor her father could protect her mother. She remembers feeling that something *bad* had happened.

When news broke that the ghetto was being liquidated, Anne said there was chaos and panic. Anne was told by her mother *to stay home and wait.* She took her brother and ran to the next-door house. When she attempted to get back to her home, a German officer kicked her and told her to *go inside.* She was afraid, yet she had the good sense to take her brother and run away to her father's factory. She said that the death of her mother was the worst traumatic experience of her life. As was explained above, her mother was shot returning to fetch her children. Anne said she heard a shot and was sure that it was the shot that killed her mother. The violation of her mother's dead body by the German soldier who cut her finger off deeply traumatized Anne. As a child Anne may have felt somewhat responsible for her mother's brutal death as she was returning in the interests of her children. Anne was also deeply affected by the callous murder of her sister that took place shortly after her mother's death. Anne was told that her eleven-year-old sister had begged for her life saying, *please don't kill me! I will work. I will do anything!*

Anne reported that she was constantly afraid while living in the hay barn with her father and sister. The family knew that German soldiers were looking for them. The living conditions were terrible and they were hungry and cold. Anne's toes froze and her father was afraid that they might have to have them amputated. However, the farmer who was hiding them used goose fat to treat and heal her feet. *The terrible thing was the screaming and shouting we heard. The mobile killing units used to march them* [the Jews] *into the forest, get them to dig a grave and shoot them. We heard their screams and gunshots like an echo in the night when we were in hiding, and we were so scared.* Another terrifying incident reported was when she and her brother were hiding illegally in the labor camp. One morning, a German soldier and his Alsatian dog came to inspect the camp. Anne and her brother were hiding under the bed. The dog came up to the bed and smelled them, then moved away. Anne viewed this as *a miracle from heaven.*

Anne attributes her intermittent depression throughout her life to never having recovered from her mother's and sister's deaths. At the time of the interview, she was on antidepressants but was non-compliant. She told me that, although they were prescribed, she was afraid to become *addicted.* She reported that she cried a lot, as did her sister who lived in Israel.

Developmental Disruption

Anne's trauma and loss seemed to have caused her difficulties throughout her life. Although she was attached to her father and her aunt in South Africa, she reported that for years she cried alone over the death of her mother and sister. Her description of herself as a *lost sheep* in adolescence shows how difficult it was for her to bond with her peer group, probably because she was too preoccupied with her grief and trauma. The importance of a supportive environment has been emphasized as crucial in ameliorating some of the effects of trauma (Herman 1992; Keilson 1979). In Anne's case, it was clear that her post-Holocaust environment was not sufficiently supportive and she struggled to adjust in South Africa. She reported that her short marriage ended in a difficult and traumatic divorce and that her four sons were in boarding school. Her life settled in her later years when she married her second husband. As an older person, Anne's ongoing sense of helplessness due to her health problems and difficulty in walking seemed to have precipitated a deep depression. Her current frailty may have triggered memories of being helpless and trapped in the hay barn and later in the camp, occasions in which she was afraid and endured prolonged suffering.

Mental Health Impacts

Anne suffered from severe depression over many decades but reported that she was unwilling to take her prescribed medication. She reported difficulty with emotional regulation, which was evident in her persistent dysphoria and extremely inhibited anger. Her alterations in consciousness include reported intrusive PTSD symptoms such as flashbacks and intrusive thoughts. Anne also reported a sense of hopelessness and paralysis of initiative that appeared to be part of her depression. As a result, she felt isolated and rather impotent in her world. As indicated previously, Anne had unresolved grief surrounding the death of her mother and sister. It was clear that she suffered from full blown PTSD, CTSD, and depression, and she was emotionally overwhelmed and unable to self-regulate.

Experience of Aging: Integrity versus Despair

Anne experienced sadness and depression related to unresolved mourning, which was complicated by her poor health, contributing to hopelessness and despair. Anne was relatively in touch with her feelings of grief and despondency and able to express these in the interviews. She did not appear to use compartmentalization or dissociation in the same way that other participants evidenced and was unable to block out or escape the persistent mourning and despondency that she experienced in old age.

Anne said that as she looked back on her life she saw good things, like having children, and she stated at times that the Holocaust seemed like a *bad dream*. She also noted that being a survivor had prepared her to deal with later hardships. She said she could not forget about the Holocaust and she was most affected by her sadness regarding the loss of her mother and sister. At the end of the interview Anne asked to show me pictures of jewellery that she had made. The jewellery was constructed of handmade silver presented in a unique and beautiful style. It thus appeared that Anne had found an outlet for personal expression and creativity and had brought objects of beauty into the world. It was also apparent that in her jewellery-making she had been able to persevere with tasks and to be productive. It would seem that in showing me her pictures Anne was demonstrating some level of mastery that she had been able to achieve despite her ongoing depression.

Process Observations

Anne was very kind, warm, and cooperative in her interactions with me and she seemed keen to relate her story in a detailed and cohesive manner. I felt an incredible heaviness when I was with her and was often left feeling very depressed after the interviews. I wondered whether this may have been related to a powerful projective identification that occurred in the context of the research interviews, in which I became the unwitting container of aspects of her profound sadness and helplessness in addition to being a witness to her tragic story.

Towards the end of the interview process, I expressed my admiration for her jewellery craft when she shared pictures of this with me. It was the first time during the process that I was able to see a sense of animation and pleasure in her, which seemed to contrast with the heaviness of her depression.

After the research interviews were completed, I was able to refer Anne to a social worker and she was able to terminate the relationship with me. Anne adjusted to her caseworker and formed a warm relationship with her. The social worker was alerted to Anne's resistance in taking the antidepressants and appears to have encouraged Anne to reconsider her rejection of the medication. When I followed up some months after the interviews had taken place, Anne reported that she had begun to take her medication and was seeing her caseworker regularly.

Shlomo Pieprs

Shlomo: *My mother was sent to Auschwitz where she eventually died. We had no time to say goodbye . . . no time to say anything.*

Shlomo was a child survivor from Poland who was seventy-nine at the time of the research interviews. He was born in 1928 in Poland. Shlomo was eleven years old when the Holocaust began and seventeen years old when it ended. His family was very religious, and they spoke Yiddish at home. During the Holocaust, he was sent to a labor camp for six months; thereafter he was sent to Blechammer (Auschwitz 4) labor camp. He reported that he was taken on a death march to Gross-Rosen concentration camp for ten days. Finally, he was marched to Buchenwald where he remained for a short period before liberation. After the war Shlomo went with a group of child survivors from Buchenwald to Israel, where he lived in a *kibbutz*. He became an officer in the Israeli Army and joined the Haganah (early Zionist military organization) as a fighter. At the time of the interview, he lived in Johannesburg with his wife of fifty-three years. They have two sons and three grandchildren. Their older son had emigrated from South Africa, and their younger son was a resident in Johannesburg. At the time of the interview Shlomo's health was good, and he was still working full-time in his own business. He was interviewed on three occasions and four hours of material was recorded. Shlomo requested many times that I write a book about his story. I told him that I could not at the time, as I had to complete the research. I referred him to authors; however, this did not work out. Finally, on writing this book, we got a chance to do so—he had since died and I was given signed permission from his wife Mrs. Pieprs who was pleased that his story would finally be told.

Memories of Early Parenting

Shlomo spoke of his mother with love and admiration. He described her as a nurturer, to whom he felt very close. *She made wonderful Shabbos* (Friday night) *meals. I remember her food, for example, she made "challah"* (Jewish blessed bread) *as well as fish cutlets and "cholent"* (stew). *She was a "model mother" who was good to me. She cleaned and cooked and prayed and said "Tehillim"* (Psalms). He described his father as a good man, to whom he was also attached. His father was religious and he owned a grocery shop. The family lived in a two-bedroom flat. *My father prayed every morning, and he had a "shtiebel"* (a small room used for communal Jewish prayer). *Most of the people in his "shtiebel" were family because we had a big extended family—my mother had six siblings and my father had five.* Shlomo said that he was close to both his parents, particularly his mother, and was the youngest of five siblings. Shlomo described his relationships to his older brothers and sister as very warm and caring. He felt particularly close to his oldest brother who was his only sibling to survive the Holocaust. He said that his parents were happily married and there was order and structure in the family. For example, Shlomo would not leave the table until his father had finished eating. Shlomo's family were very close to his extended family and they would all gather together on a Friday night. He spoke nostalgically about his life before the Holocaust and said that he was very happy. There were sixty thousand Jews in his town, all of whom spoke Yiddish. He reported that he went to *cheder*, a strict religious school, where he had *payes* (ringlets hanging from the sides of the head, worn by very religious Jews). He said that he *studied the Torah* (Bible) at school from beginning to end.

Traumatic Experiences and Recollections

Shlomo explained that he was eleven when the war started and clearly remembered when the German troops marched through his hometown. There was a curfew and they kept indoors with their doors locked after 6 p.m. He remembered how frightened he was. He knew that Jews were being hurt in Germany, as there were rumors about this in Poland. The Germans publicly executed a baker and a butcher to frighten the community; however, he was not present to witness this. He had heard his parents discussing the event and he realized that they were also frightened. Shlomo described how the Germans closed his religious school and how he had to work in a factory. He remembered his mother crying when his two older brothers were taken away to concentration camps. He said that his separation from his mother was particularly traumatic. Shlomo, his parents, and his sister were taken to a soccer field for selection with other Jews in 1942. The Germans kept them captive for three days and three nights without food. It rained continuously and there was no shelter. He said that the intention was to weaken them. There were three points of selection: he, his sister, and their father were allowed to pass through. However, his mother was stopped at the gate and sent to Auschwitz. He was told that she was going to a work camp and he recalled that they had *no time to say goodbye . . . no time to say anything*. He never saw her again because she was killed at Auschwitz.

Shlomo was fourteen years old when he received a letter from the Germans to report for further selection. Both his father and his sister came to say goodbye at the train station. They kissed him and cried. It was the last time he saw them as they too were sent to Auschwitz where they were killed. He said that he was sent to Erfurt near the German border. It was a labor camp of three to four thousand people. He said he was hungry and frightened and stayed there for seven months, where he again worked in a factory. Thereafter, he was sent to Blechammer where his arm was tattooed with the number 184738. Shlomo indicated that he thought that Blechammer was cleaner and had more food than at other camps because the Red Cross did inspections of the camp. However, many Jews were beaten to death and there were public hangings. He reported that every two to three weeks everyone was forced to stand and watch as Jews were hanged. These hangings were conducted in response to petty offenses such as stealing a piece of bread or having a wire shoe lace that could be used for *sabotage*. The offence was announced before the hanging took place.

Shlomo explained that he and his fellow inmates *never knew what tomorrow would bring*. There was always fear that they would be hanged next. He reported that during his two years at Blechammer a Jewish *Kapo* who was kind to him assigned him to assist a German engineer who taught him to weld iron. This man did not agree with Hitler's politics regarding Jews and did not persecute Shlomo. He taught him welding skills that he was able to use successfully at a later date. He remembered that the *Kapos* were sometimes good and sometimes cruel. *The "Kapos" worked for the Germans; therefore, to impress the Germans, the cruel "Kapos" would hit the Jews for no reason.* He reported that the Germans liquidated Blechammer as the Russians were approaching and he was taken on a three-month death march in the middle of winter, where they walked for twenty-five kilometers daily. He said, *You did not think about your parents or your family or being burnt alive, you only thought about food because it was freezing and you were starving, hungry!* They arrived at Gross-Rosen concentration camp. He said that it was such a terrible camp that prisoners ran into the electric fences to commit suicide. He reported that he witnessed a stampede where people choked in the mud. He said he was lucky to survive this camp and he lived in fear of his life. He stayed at Gross-Rosen for two weeks. It was reported that the Americans were coming and so prisoners were taken to Buchenwald where he was held captive for a short time before liberation.

When speaking about the loss of his mother, Shlomo explained that he continued to feel grief and sadness until the present time because he was so close to her. Shlomo felt that he had no closure as he had no time to prepare to separate or to say goodbye to her. During the interview he became very emotional whenever he mentioned his mother. His father, mother, sister, and two older brothers were killed at Auschwitz. In addition, Shlomo's extended family, friends, and community were all killed in the Holocaust. He said that very few people from his hometown survived. His oldest brother survived and moved to the United States. He was told that a cruel Jewish *Kapo* in the camps beat his one older brother to death and he felt enraged by this. He said that when he dreamed about his family, he woke up happy and looked forward to being reunited with them after his death.

Developmental Disruptions

Shlomo explained that he was deeply attached to his mother and came from a very close family. He described his mother as an archetypal *yiddishe mamma*, a loving nurturer who was focused on caring for her family. His description of her indicated that he had introjected a very positive image. His closeness to his family and nostalgic description of his happy life before the Holocaust sharply contrasted with his later catastrophic loss of parents, family, and community.

In relation to Erikson's (1965) theory, Shlomo's Holocaust experience fell into two stages. First, he was at the end stage of "industry versus inferiority" (ibid.) when the Germans invaded his town. At the same time his religious school was closed and he was sent to work in a factory. Thus, it appears that the stage of "industry versus inferiority" (ibid.) was disrupted as Shlomo was forced to drop his academic studies and became aware of being vulnerable and discriminated against, in part through his parents' anxiety. As conditions worsened, he moved into early adolescence where he was traumatically separated from his mother at fourteen years old. He was then separated from his father and sister and sent off alone to a concentration camp. In accordance with Erikson (ibid.), the time of identity formation takes place when the adolescent moves away from his family towards his peer group. In Shlomo's case this separation was forced and he had no known peer group to bond with as he was sent off with a group of strangers to the concentration camps. His identity was also compromised by the attack on many aspects of family and cultural identity he held dear—that which he cherished also became that which placed him at risk, adding complexity to his identity formation. It is also evident that he had to place survival above all other needs for an extended period in his adolescence.

Shlomo's resilience and fortitude were evident in the manner with which he accepted the German engineer as a mentor and was able to learn to weld steel despite his terrible trauma and physical suffering in the camps. In addition, he was able to use this knowledge creatively at a later stage, namely, building machine guns in the Israeli Army and making a living out of welding. He said, *I had to grow up and do what I had to do*. It seems he built his identity around work and this was useful to him during and after the Holocaust. He lived in fear and witnessed death, cruelty, and starvation, yet what seemed to be the hardest was his loss of his mother and immediate and extended family. Shlomo described a lack of closure regarding the loss of his beloved family and observed that he has lived with the sadness all of his subsequent life. At sixteen years old, he immigrated to Israel as an orphan and lived in a *kibbutz*. He described a sense of belonging in this *kibbutz*, and perhaps this was his first point of healing after the Holocaust. With great pride Shlomo told me that he was a soldier in the Israeli Army and he showed me his pictures on the wall of himself as a soldier. He said that he used his welding skills to build weapons and he fought in the Israeli war of independence in 1948. Significantly, Shlomo went from being a camp prisoner and orphan to an officer in the Israeli Army. This indicated his capacity for some mastery over his trauma. In addition, this experience of mastery may have restored his sense of being emasculated as a camp prisoner during his adolescence.

Mental Health Impacts

Shlomo reported that he had enduring features of PTSD. During the Holocaust he was interned at Auschwitz, Bergen-Belsen, and Gross-Rosen concentration camps, and after that he was troubled by many intrusive memories. For example, he had an intrusive memory of witnessing a hanging of a young Jewish boy in the camp. In addition, he had a horrific intrusive memory of fellow Jewish inmates chocking to death in the mud during a stampede after they were attacked by Nazi guards and their dogs. His capacity to emotionally self-regulate was good and he seemed resilient.

Shlomo described alterations in consciousness such as dissociation and derealization. In addition, he described intrusive memories and reliving of events in the form of PTSD symptoms. He spoke of a sense of isolation and a persistent distrust of others. Although he spoke of being attached to his wife and children, he had never discussed the details of his Holocaust experience with them. Despite his success Shlomo carried a sense of despair regarding the loss of his parents and siblings and appeared to have aspects of complicated bereavement. As a consequence, he struggled with his sense of loss of faith in a God who had failed to save his family and to protect the Jews during the Holocaust.

Experience of Aging: Integrity versus Despair

Shlomo explained that his business had been very successful and he was financially affluent. He worked full-time and demonstrated that he was proud of his achievements. He was very active in his community and had built gates for the building in which he lived. He played golf and had a socially active lifestyle. His resilience was seen in his creativity and his ability to make a continued contribution to his community.

Despite Shlomo's deep sadness, he functioned very well and did not suffer from depression. He was able to establish a family and had been married for over fifty years. He was attached to his wife, who he said had taken away his sense of aloneness: *Otherwise, I would have been alone in the world; my wife took the feeling of being alone away from me. And my children, my own flesh, and blood.* He said that looking back his wife and sons had been a great solace to him.

Shlomo said: *I have clear memories of some things and have forgotten a lot, like how my parents looked—no pictures. I am still sad about losing them because I was so young and alone in the world from fifteen.* Despite his positive experiences within his current family, Shlomo remained deeply disillusioned with God and religion.

He followed cultural rituals related to Judaism such as going to synagogue and giving money to charity, but continued to feel disappointed that God did not help the Jews during the Holocaust. Shlomo explained that he thought more about his parents as he got older and hoped to meet them after he died. He added that he frequently saw them in his dreams and he woke up feeling happy for this fantasy contact.

Shlomo said, *It would be better to get old and get younger so we could enjoy our lives better. As you get older it's harder to enjoy life, you get sick, and you don't know when you're going to die.* He said that he thought more about the Holocaust with time because he had fewer current worries, such as concerns about money. He said that as he got older, he got sadder as opposed to angrier.

Shlomo seemed to express a parallel experience of both integrity and despair. He was proud of his achievements, grateful for his wife and family, enjoyed his work, and generally functioned well. However, he said that he got very sad that he had no siblings together with whom he could grow old. His disappointment and sadness regarding God also intensified as he aged and this was difficult for him. Given these polarities, Shlomo seemed to have a good measure of ego integrity but this was coupled with an experience of, perhaps appropriate, despair. Initially Shlomo appeared to be very aloof but as the interview process developed and a rapport was formed, he seemed less guarded and spoke of his grief related to the loss of his parents. Shlomo's presentation was perhaps in keeping with Dasberg's (2001) observation that many survivors embody a parallel existence where they may have outer success but still feel inner despair that was compartmentalized.

Process Observations

Shlomo initially interacted in a business-like manner and appeared to be somewhat of an intimidating and preoccupied businessman. As the interviews progressed and his defenses dropped, he shared a narrative that was fraught with traumatic loss. During the interviewing process I was aware of my role as interviewer and worked at fielding my way through Shlomo's defenses. I was somewhat surprised by the sadness and deep despair that emerged. At the completion of the interview process, Shlomo said that he wanted to show me the gates he had made outside his building. The gates were very artistic and solid. They were the main gates of his apartment block that was situated in a very affluent area. Shlomo's need to show me the gates seemed significant in that he demonstrated the level of mastery that he had achieved in acquiring a skill in Auschwitz that he had been able to use for the benefit of the Israeli Army as well as in his business in South Africa. He was also able to contribute to the community in which he lived. This was his concrete proof of his mastery over his trauma. In addition, Shlomo showed me pictures of himself as a young man in his soldier uniform. This picture hung on his wall and was a testimony to his trajectory from a child/teenager who lived in captivity to a soldier who rose to the rank of officer and fought as a free Jew in the Israeli Army.

FIGURE 5A. Shlomo Pieprs aged eighty.

FIGURE 5B. Shlomo Pieprs as a new immigrant in 1945.

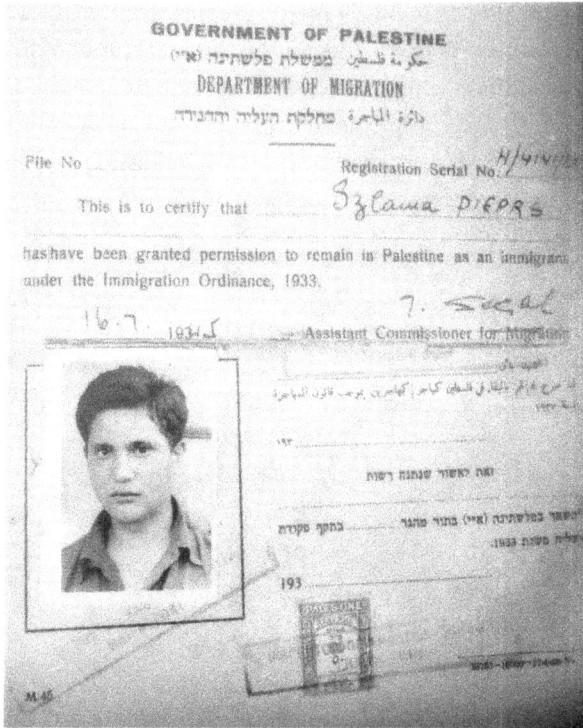

FIGURE 5C. Shlomo Pieprs's documents to enter Palestine.

FIGURE 5D. Shlomo Pieprs in the Israeli
Army, 1948. He showed me this picture with
a great sense of pride.

FIGURE 5E. A collage of pictures of Shlomo in the Israeli Army around 1948. His journey from camp inmate to officer was a source of immeasurable pride for him.

FIGURE 5F. Shlomo Pieprs, from child concentration camp survivor to soldier in the Israeli Army.

Upon reading the case history and transcripts, I felt a terrible sense of sadness for Shlomo's loss of his *yiddishe mamma*. I also felt a deep sense of mourning for his description of an idyllic *shtetl* lifestyle that was destroyed by the Holocaust. After the interview process had ended, Shlomo phoned me and said: *Please, will you write my story. I want you to write a book about me.* I said I was unable to do so as I was busy with the research and referred him to an author. He reported that he had an argument with the author and his book was never written. Shlomo said he enjoyed speaking to me as part of the research process: *No one has ever asked me those kinds of questions because they don't want to hear the answers.* A week after the interviews were over, I phoned to see how Shlomo was. He said he was fine and again asked if I would write his story. Here finally his story is told.

Rina

Rina: *I wished that I could grow wings and fly over the walls of the camp to escape from the horror and misery.*

Rina was a child survivor born in Holland in 1936 and was seventy-one at the time of the interviews. She was three years old when the Holocaust began and nine years old when it ended. In 1942 the Germans invaded Holland. She was five and a half at that time and she lived with her parents and her older brother. After the German invasion she and her family were taken to Westerbork, a transit camp where Jews were kept captive before being transferred to Auschwitz or Sobibor death camps. The family remained there for sixteen months. Rina had no memories of her father at Westerbork and this loss of memory surrounding him has been distressing for her, leaving a disturbing absence in her mind. She reported that she knew that her father was taken to Buchenwald concentration camp where he died. He was badly beaten and as a result was weakened, which led to his death. Rina, her mother, and brother were sent to Ravensbruck women's camp for sixteen months. Her older brother was moved to Ravensbruck men's camp when he turned fourteen. Since Rina's mother held an English national passport, they managed to leave Ravensbruck for Sweden as part of an international agreement. After spending six weeks in quarantine in Sweden, they were allowed to join their extended family in England. Rina's older brother also survived the war and he managed to meet up with them in England. In 1946, Rina and her family moved to South Africa.

After finishing high school, Rina studied and became a librarian. She had been married for fifty years and had four children at the time of the interview. Her daughter and one of her sons emigrated, and the other two children remained in Johannesburg. She was interviewed for a total of six hours at my practice office, over a three-week period, twice a week. She requested that the interviews take place at my office to allow for privacy and to be free of disturbances.

Memory of Early Parenting

Rina reported that she had positive memories of both parents, who she said were loving and affectionate. She said she was more attached to her father in her early childhood. He used to read her stories, tuck her into bed, and comfort her when she was afraid of the dark. When she became sick with measles at the age of five, she remembered him saying, *If you wake up in the middle of the night, wake me, not your mother; she is tired.* She remembered her mother sewing and making dresses for her as well as clothing for her doll. Rina described her mother as affectionate, *very caring, but strict and reserved.* She remembered her father as more affectionate than her mother, however, she said that she felt loved by both parents.

Traumatic Experience and Recollection

Rina was five and a half years old when the Germans ordered the family to leave their home. She reported that as they were packing, she grabbed her favorite doll. *My father said, "Rina, you can't take that doll!" and I said "Why?" and he said, "I promise we will come back for it" … and we never did … I never forgot that* (with tears in her eyes). *I see his point of view now, we could carry so little, and they were banging down the doors, he wanted me to rather carry a warm jersey … Why do I mention it? Because I never remember seeing him after that, even though we were with him for sixteen months at Westerbork transit camp.* Rina spoke continually about her difficulty in remembering her father. Rina said she had no memory of the traumatized people at Westerbork transit camp and no memory of her brother's *bar mitzvah.* She also did not remember saying goodbye to her father before he went to Buchenwald concentration camp where he died. Her only memory during that period was of singing Hebrew and Yiddish songs with the other young children.

Rina arrived at Ravensbruck concentration camp at the age of seven with her mother and her older brother. She said that she was scared and horrified on her arrival there when she saw the emaciated women prisoners whose hair had been shaved off. She said that thanks to her mother, who cleaned her hair, she did not have lice and never had to have her hair removed. Rina reported that her mother was very protective and always covered her eyes with her hands to shield her from traumatic incidents and did not answer her questions about what she was seeing around her. She mentioned many times that she felt her mother was overprotective because she constantly covered Rina's eyes and refused to discuss or explain what Rina was seeing or hearing.

Rina reported that she felt empathy for her mother's sense of shame and humiliation when her mother was forced to parade naked in front of the German guards. She remembered the smell of unwashed bodies and the dirty barracks at Ravensbruck. She described life in the camp in the following way: *You never saw a flower, you never saw a tree, you saw nothing but stone walls and the electric fence. You didn't see kindness or niceness, people screamed and cursed, it was dirty. You were always hungry and cold, it was horrible, but you had to adapt.*

Although she was hungry, Rina remembered the bad taste and disgusting smell of the food. *They gave us a piece of bread in the morning, it wasn't proper bread, it was mixed with sawdust, but it was something to eat. Nobody got lunch, and at night there was this ghastly soup.* Rina reported that she was so malnourished that she did not grow in three years. She was considered very small for her age after the war. *It must have been terrible for my mother to see her children hungry and worry about us all the time . . . We were forced to go on parade and stand for hours in the cold at twenty-eight degrees below zero, and they counted us, nobody had a jacket. We were always cold and always hungry.* During the day, Rina's mother went to work and she spent time in the barracks with other children. She always worried that her mother would not return and she suffered terrible fears of abandonment throughout the Holocaust: *Worse than the screams or anything was not knowing if my mom would come back or not.*

With tears in her eyes, Rina said that as a child in the camp, *I wished that I could grow wings and fly over the walls of the camp to escape from the horror and misery.* She said that once a day the prisoners had to stand in line for roll-call and the German soldiers would bring their dogs who would often attack the emaciated inmates. Despite her mother covering her eyes, she had ongoing recollections of the screams that she heard, taking in information in an auditory way. The sound of the screams made her fearful. As an adult, she read about Ravensbruck and realized that the screams she remembered hearing were from victims undergoing medical experiments or being tortured. Rina's worst traumatic memory was of a Gentile Polish woman prisoner who burnt her on the neck with a hot iron, at Ravensbruck. She was seven years old at the time and was left with a big scar that was surgically removed after the Holocaust.

After some time, the Ravensbruck staff built a gas chamber and crematorium. *There was black smoke belching out, and the smell and the screams were terrible. The smell was of burning flesh. I could never forget the smell! I would say to my mom, "What's that?" and she would cover my eyes and say, "Don't look, I don't ever want you to look!" and she never told me what it was. It would have been better if she had not covered my eyes because I had many empty patches in my memory and I had nightmares for thirty-five years!* Rina mentioned that a German guard saved the family, who were on a list of inmates to be sent to Auschwitz. This woman called her and her mother and showed them their names on the list. She crossed out their names and added three other names instead: *Whom she picked we don't know, but the poor souls went and never came back. This woman gave me a green ribbon for my birthday and saved us, yet afterwards we heard she was a war criminal and beat a few Jewish women to death.* It was evident that Rina had recollections of several contradictory experiences with adults in the camp that left her confused and not knowing whom to trust. It was also apparent that she had done mental work (perhaps in her therapy) to attempt to retrospectively comprehend aspects of her experience and what transpired during the Holocaust.

Rina said that her father had died in Buchenwald. Owing to her deep attachment as a young girl, his death was heartbreaking for her. She engaged in a search to find out what had killed him and she found her answer from her uncle who was at Buchenwald with her father. To her horror and devastation, she found out that he died a *Muselmann*. He had been beaten so badly that he was unable to work and he ate very little. He became like the *walking dead*. According to her uncle, her father *died in the mud, he collapsed, and that was that!* When she described this incident, she cried both for the loss of her father and because of the degrading death he suffered. During the research interviews Rina would cry whenever she spoke about the loss of her father and her lack of closure regarding his death. As described by Durst (1995), Rina experienced her father as impotent and unable to protect her or himself, a particularly poignant image considering her prior image of him as a comforting, protective, and capable person.

In addition to her practical search for information regarding her father's death, Rina had tried to see if she could remember relating to her father in Westerbork. However, she had no memory of saying goodbye to him. To attempt to recall memories of her father, she searched her memory for decades, including undergoing hypnosis twice under a psychiatrist and returning to the camps as an adult. These attempts did not help, and the lack of memory remained a source of great regret and discomfort for Rina. The gaps in her memory appear to be suggestive of a degree of dissociation and lack of full engagement with the external environment as a self-protective measure, as has been observed in other child survivors (Herman 1992). Rina reported that in her old age she continued looking for closure regarding her father's death and that parting from those she loved remained a difficult, painful, and somewhat dreaded experience.

Developmental Disruption

Rina reported that she was securely attached to both her parents as a young child. However, she remembered her father as the more nurturing caretaker. It is clear from her description of her early childhood experience that she felt she was the focus of her parent's attention. From age five and a half to eight and a half years, Rina was in the camps. These would have been her school years, and consequently the negotiation of the stage of "industry versus inferiority" was disrupted. She did not receive a formal education, even though her mother taught Rina to read and write. At school in England after the war she reacted badly to antisemitic remarks from another child. She reported that she beat this child so badly that she was asked to leave the school. It is apparent that in this context Rina felt able to express some aggression derived from her frightening and complicated experiences in the camps.

The extent of the efforts Rina has made to retrieve further tangible memories of her past, including having hypnosis and returning to the camps, illustrated her desperation to hold onto something of her father as a positive introject. Her traumatic separation from him seemed to have precipitated a preoccupation with his death. Her crying and lack of closure regarding this loss demonstrated that she still felt this pain many decades after the Holocaust. Her relationship with her mother was ambivalent, both appreciative and critical. On the one hand, she was grateful for her mother's caring, while on the other hand she resented her mother's *overprotection*. For example, her mother's refusal to explain the screaming Rina could hear around her but could not see reportedly left her with gaps in her memory and led to the experience of nightmares for over thirty-five years. It seems that her mother was so deeply traumatized that she was unable to mediate the trauma for Rina and attempted to protect her by encouraging a defense of denial—what one does not see cannot be real and should not affect one. Although Rina's mother's motives were to reduce the harm her daughter was exposed to, this left her feeling anxious and unable to process what she knew to be true in the camp. Consequently, she was left with violent fantasies, which manifested in her nightmares. In addition, she reported that after the Holocaust she would run out of the room and cry if her brother discussed the Holocaust. She was unable to read books or to see films about the Holocaust.

When Rina met Holocaust survivors shortly after the war in Israel, she did not disclose that she too was a survivor. She enjoyed the fact that people thought she was not Jewish, owing to her blonde hair and blue eyes. This suggests that Rina was unable to absorb and process her Holocaust experience at that time and avoided thoughts and feelings about her life in the camps, as originally encouraged by her mother. It seems that her traumatic nightmares drove her to seek psychotherapy and the therapeutic experience helped her to deal with some aspects of her trauma.

During her childhood she was aware of her mother's humiliation and powerlessness in the camps and remained deeply anxious that her mother would not return from work. She was terrified that she would be abandoned, helpless, and unable to survive alone. The vicious burn attack she experienced at seven years old may have exacerbated her fear for her survival without the protection of her mother. She was overwhelmed by fear, owing to the cruelty she witnessed and experienced. The German guard who saved their lives presented her with an anomaly as this was a person capable of both kindness and cruelty. Her aggressive outburst at a child, soon after the war, as well as her sense of glee about the destruction of Berlin, indicated that she was extremely angry regarding the cruelty, degradation, and loss that she had endured. Rina's raging outburst is also a good example of the way trauma shatters the child's ability to self-regulate, as described by Cook et al. (2017).

Rina reported that she did not suffer from any depression or anxiety in adulthood, however, she indicated that after the Holocaust she suffered from unremitting nightmares for which she sought treatment. As an adult, Rina had surgery on her eyes to correct her vision. Under the local anesthetic, the smell of her burning flesh triggered an olfactory flashback of the smell of burning flesh from the crematorium at Ravensbruck. She reported that her therapy experience helped her to integrate and accept her Holocaust experiences and after thirty-five years the nightmares finally abated. Rina's willingness to seek and utilize therapy suggested a capacity to trust others to assist her.

Rina's resilience could perhaps be largely attributed to her secure attachment to her parents in early years and the development of a deep sense of trust, autonomy, and initiative. In addition, Rina survived the Holocaust because her mother loved and protected her at all times. This was a major factor in building her resilience. Although she was an angry child who lacked confidence, she completed her education and worked as a librarian. She reported that she was not afraid of close attachment and was very demonstrative with her children and grandchildren.

Mental Health Impacts

Rina described alterations in consciousness such as her amnesia regarding traumatic events. This was evidenced by her difficulty in remembering her father. In addition, her trauma was triggered by flashbacks, intrusive thoughts, and nightmares. She also reported having suffered from PTSD and CTSD, even though she was high-functioning and resilient. She endured the concentration camp experiences with her mother who covered Rina's eyes to protect her from seeing horrific imagery. She reported that she suffered from intrusive memories of people screaming—sounds that her mother was unable to protect her from. Rina reported feeling a sense of stigma regarding being a Holocaust survivor and a sense of survival guilt. In addition, her meaning system was disrupted by her ongoing sense of despair regarding the loss of her father and her unresolved grief. Rina was able to function and self-regulate and she was resilient. After suffering from nightmares in her thirties, she consulted a psychiatrist. In addition to psychiatric treatment, she also received psychotherapy twice a week for six months. This experience was very helpful in allowing her to work through her Holocaust trauma, and she reported that the nightmares abated (Farber et al. 2021).

Experience of Aging: Integrity versus Despair

Rina was able to have an intimate relationship with her husband and she reported that they grew closer over time. She thrived in generativity, largely from the experience of being a mother. She said that having her four children was the *best thing I ever did*. This was a source of mastery and self-healing where she was able to give her children the childhood she missed. She realized that she had made mistakes as a mother and acknowledged that she was overprotective of her own children but they enjoyed loving attached relationships.

Rina survived cancer twice as an adult. A few years prior to the interviews she had a partial mastectomy and radiation treatment. She reported that she had also survived two vehicle hijackings. Despite these later traumatic experiences, Rina appeared to be functional and well adjusted. She described her coping skills as follows: *I don't dwell on the past, I move forward*. This appeared typical of Rina's coping style. When asked how she had experienced the interview process, Rina said:

> Rina: *You asked if me going through the Holocaust had made me stronger, I have had eighteen operations, I've been hijacked, twice had cancer twice, yes it has made me stronger, but I have never verbalized it.*

> Tracey: *How has this "strength" helped you?*

> Rina: *I don't panic in a crisis and also as a child I remember that you never make eye contact with an attacker.*

These comments demonstrated that Rina had a level of mastery and resilience that was part of her repertoire of coping skills. She observed that surviving the Holocaust had strengthened her capacity to adapt and to recover from trauma: *As I get older, the memories of the Holocaust do not get clearer, and I am not depressed. Since I have had cancer, I am grateful for every day, every day is a gift, the skies are blue, the grass is green, and I have my family and thank God we are healthy.* It is clear that Rina has a good sense of ego integrity regarding her aging process.

Rina had been for twice weekly in-depth psychotherapy for six months, which seemed to have helped her to deconstruct her defenses and work through her Holocaust trauma. *At my age, I have survived so many things including cancer and hijacks. It's no good saying "Woe is me" or "Why did this happen?"* She acknowledged that she had made mistakes in perhaps being overprotective as a mother and had clashed with her daughter over certain issues. However, she remained committed to her children and she was very involved in caring for her grandchildren. This was deeply rewarding, she said. Rina had a deep sense of gratitude for and acceptance of her life, both good and bad parts, and a stable sense of ego integrity.

Process Observations

Rina was very cooperative and engaging. Although she frequently became emotional, she demonstrated insight into her experiences. It was extremely useful for the purpose of the research that Rina was able to convey what it meant for her to experience a concentration camp through the lens of her childhood memory. I felt deeply moved by her story and was grateful that she was able to portray her experiences as a child with such clarity. She arrived at the final interview with a gift, saying: *I want you to have this perfume, it's special, and I want to thank you, I just feel good when I leave here, it's like having a comfort blanket it's nice*. I was quite embarrassed and overwhelmed by the gift—I realized that it was a token of her appreciation and to reject it would be hurtful. I thanked her. Rina thus appeared to experience the interview process as not only respectful but also nurturing and gratifying. It is possible that her positive experience of the psychotherapy and her early secure attachment was transferred to me in the engaged listening process of the data collection.

I phoned a week after the final interview to ask how Rina was. She reported that she was well and asked to meet at a public place for lunch, where she engaged socially and did not mention the Holocaust. Significantly, Rina did not appear to form a dependent transference and, unlike several other participants, did not appear to prolong contact. She is still in touch infrequently and continues to attend group functions for Holocaust survivors.

Menachem

Menachem: *Never in my life have I seen such a thing! Babies being thrown from the third floor of a building!*

Menachem was eighty-one years old at the time of the interview. He was born in a town in Poland, near Krakow. He was thirteen years old when the Holocaust began and eighteen when it ended. In 1943 the Germans took over his town and he started working for the Judenrat (the Jewish council who supervised, among other things, the deportation of Jews to the concentration camps). As such, he received temporary protection from deportation. Eventually, Menachem was himself captured and interned at a labor camp, Pustkow, for six months. At a later stage he was sent to Blechammer, a labor subcamp of Auschwitz, where he remained for two years until the end of the war. Menachem's mother died of typhus in 1941 when he was thirteen, just before the advent of the Holocaust. He lost his whole family during the Holocaust. In 1948 he met his wife and her family. They took him in and he married at the age of twenty-one. Initially he and his wife moved to Israel where they lived for three years. Due to scarce work opportunities they decided to immigrate to Rhodesia and then to South Africa during the 1980s.

Menachem said his memories of the war years were sound; however, it must be noted that he suffered a mild stroke some twenty years ago. Since then, he has held a full-time position of employment as a manager in a large retail chain. As described by his wife, he had made a good recovery from his stroke. At the time of the interviews Menachem had retired from his job and did sewing alterations to earn extra money as he and his wife struggled financially. He had been married for sixty-one years and had two sons. One son lived in Canada and the other in South Africa. He had four grandchildren and five great-grandchildren. I saw him weekly over a three-week period, and three hours of material were recorded.

Memories of Early Parenting

Menachem was the second-born of four children. He had an older sister and a younger brother and sister. His father was a kosher butcher, and his mother worked as a seamstress. He remembered helping his mother thread her needles and fixing her sewing machine. The family was religious and kosher, and Menachem wore a *kippa* (skullcap). He described his mother as *not having time for us as she was either busy working, cooking, or cleaning*. In addition, she was described as *strict*. Menachem reported that he was very attached to his father, who was a loving parent. He spent time helping him in his butchery. He described his father as a warm and charitable man who would give food to the poor and he had happy memories of spending time with him. He was closely bonded to both sets of grandparents and he had joyful memories of playing with his friends in the woods before the Holocaust.

Traumatic Experiences and Recollections

When the Germans first took over Menachem's town, there was a strict curfew. *We were only allowed out from eight in the morning until five in the evening, you could not walk from place to place after five, and we were forced to wear yellow armbands. Jews who walked in the street after 5 p.m. were shot.* The Polish police shot Menachem in the leg while he ran away in the Ghetto on one occasion. Fortunately for him, it was a flesh wound. He said that he often had nightmares relating to this incident where he was running and was shot at. As a result, he often woke up startled and afraid during the night.

In 1943, the ghetto was liquidated. He remembered how the Germans surrounded the town so that nobody could leave. They ordered them to each pack a suitcase and wait in the street until 9 a.m. the next morning. He was fifteen years old when he got a job working for the Judenrat. His job was to go to houses to warn Jews that if they did not obey orders they would be shot. This meant that he had some authority and protection from being persecuted and relocated to a concentration camp. He reported that many Jews were taken to the cemetery, forced to dig a hole and undress. Once their valuables were confiscated, they were shot. He said he was forced to work together with a Polish policeman. This man would shoot Jews in front of him and Menachem was then forced to remove their wallets and hand over their money to him. He said that after the Holocaust he bought a gun with the intention of killing this policeman; however, he was never able to trace him.

Menachem's two sisters were sent away to Majdanek concentration camp. As they left, they gave him a piece of bread. Both his sisters died at Majdanek.

When his ghetto was liquidated, Menachem described how the Germans would search the houses. He said that he witnessed babies and children being thrown out of the windows of three-story buildings. *Sometimes they were seven days old, or between two and three years, it was unbelievable. Mothers who had given birth that day and were not able to move were shot by the Germans and had their babies thrown from the windows.* Since he was working for the Judenrat, one of his responsibilities was picking up dead bodies from the floor and taking them to the cemetery. Having witnessed the inhumanity just described left him deeply troubled with spiritual issues. *In the beginning, I could not believe it. Never in my life have I seen such a thing! Babies being thrown from the third floor of a building, so how could I believe in God at all?* Menachem reported that at the time of the interview, when he lay in bed at night, he had flashbacks of these experiences, even though it was over sixty years since the Holocaust.

Menachem said that eventually he became accustomed to seeing dead bodies: *Eventually, you get used to it; I have seen hundreds of dead bodies.* In addition, he lived with fear each day and expected to be killed. His younger brother, aged seven, was in hiding on a farm in Poland and Polish people from a nearby village informed the Gestapo that he was Jewish. The Gestapo tied him up and shot him. This incident continued to be a source of rage for Menachem. He reported that the Polish police shot his cousins and extended family. His father was shot in the woods while building bunkers to hide Jews. He said that he was deeply saddened that his father died at the young age of thirty-eight. Menachem was taken to Blechammer labor camp for nearly two years. He remembered seeing Jews kicked and beaten by Germans.

After the camp was liberated, Menachem returned to his hometown. He found out that his whole family had died during the Holocaust and that the entire town was burned down. He felt completely alone and robbed of any anchoring points in his life. There were fifteen survivors out of 500 Jews from his town.

Developmental Disruption

Menachem described his mother as somewhat absent, unavailable, and preoccupied with household chores. He described his attachment to his father as warm, loving, and close and he saw his father as an enlivening and generous man. He was in his early adolescent years when the Holocaust began and it was apparent that he was unable to fully negotiate the phase of "identity versus confusion." The Holocaust-related experiences disrupted his personal social and educational development. In addition to witnessing ongoing violence, the catastrophic loss of every family member focused his attention on survival. The trauma and loss he experienced had a shattering effect, compromising the negotiation of a coherent and positive identity. Up until the time of the interview Menachem continued to feel guilt, helplessness, and rage about the loss of his father and siblings. His spiritual conflict regarding God presented him with a dilemma as he had been raised in a religious home. This further contributed to problems in achieving a sense of self that felt wholesome or whole. His early marriage was linked to his focus on survival as his wife's family *took him in* and he was perhaps plunged into adult responsibilities before he had a chance to properly recover from the trauma and loss associated with the Holocaust. In addition, he was forced to be complicit in the harming and destruction of other people at a critical time during the formation of his masculine identity. This experience seems to have left him with a sense of helpless rage and a need for vengeance indicating a developmental rupture.

Mental Health Impacts

Menachem reported that he had been diagnosed with chronic depression and PTSD and was on psychiatric medication for a decade before the interview. He described alterations in affect regulation such as persistent dysphoria. In addition, he described dissociative episodes and intrusive symptoms of PTSD such as ruminative preoccupation, nightmares, and flashbacks, continuing many decades after the Holocaust ended. Although his health was good, he was often overwhelmed with sadness and his capacity to self-regulate his emotions was impaired. He had recurrent distressing memories of watching Jews being murdered in the ghetto. The flashback that haunted him over the course of his lifetime was when he witnessed babies being murdered in brutal ways. In addition, he relived his experiences of being shot in his leg by a German during his nightmares. These persisted until the present time, and Menachem's reports of his intrusive symptoms suggested that he has remained fixated on the trauma he experienced (Farber et al. 2021). Alterations in self-perception were described, as well as a sense of paralysis of initiative, which formed part of Menachem's depressive picture. He expressed a sense of shame about his financial struggle during his life and felt very alone. He had been and still was to some extent preoccupied with a need to take revenge against the Nazis. He was withdrawn and distrusted others. He expressed a lack of faith in God and a sense of continued grief regarding the loss of his parents and siblings. Menachem reported that he frequently felt tearful and negative regarding the meaning of life.

Experience of Aging: Integrity versus Despair

Menachem married at the age of twenty-one and was in a stable marriage for sixty-one years. When asked what it was like to get married so young, he answered, *we just worked on survival matters, there were no emotions involved.* Despite his struggles, he was able to parent his children and recognized that he was attached to both his sons.

In his old age Menachem suffered from lung problems as a long-term health consequence of having had tuberculosis in the concentration camps. He said that aging was difficult as he had lost his independence and had debilitating health issues. *It's not so nice getting older, as a young person I was so independent. I recently broke my knee.*

He said that the Holocaust interrupted his education and prevented him from obtaining qualifications that might have prepared him to engage in a lucrative profession. He regretted that he was unable to make a consistent living and described himself as a *Jack of all trades, but never completed anything,* indicating an apparently low self-evaluation. Menachem reported that the pain of the impact of the Holocaust has intensified as he has aged. Not having his siblings around him was a constant source of sadness: *I lost everybody.* As he got older, Menachem reported being less busy, which allowed more mental space for his Holocaust-related memories to return and retraumatize him. He said he would never have closure because of the gravity of his losses and retained frustration in relation to not having been able to personally avenge the harm individuals had committed against his family and community. He seemed deeply depressed and despondent about his life. Menachem appeared to be the most compromised of all the participants in terms of his current functioning and it was evident that he leaned strongly towards the polarity of despair.

Process Observations

I struggled to establish rapport with Menachem as his English was poor and his concentration fluctuated. This could be owing to his post-traumatic stress, his health difficulties, and the stroke he had suffered. In spite of this limitation, he was able to convey his traumatic experiences and I was profoundly affected by hearing about his experiences. The detailed account of the harming of infants was particularly troubling for me. In addition, I was distressed by Menachem's conviction that he had been abandoned by God. I phoned Menachem after the interview to see how he was and he reported that he had already been seen by a social services representative, an intervention that I had recommended. I gave feedback to the social worker that he appeared to be deeply depressed and needed ongoing care and management. I understand that he remained in the care of Jewish Social Services for Holocaust survivors, a service that was initiated as a result of this research.

Summary

Given the detail and extent of narrative material that emerged from the interviews, this chapter presentation has attempted to capture core aspects of the life trajectory of each participant in a case study orientated manner. Observations about developmental disruptions, mental health impacts, and the negotiation of the aging life conflicts associated with "integrity versus despair" have been extrapolated. It will be evident that in each instance prior life experiences and extra-Holocaust events played a significant role in the participants' lives and contributed to their adjustment as children in internment camps. It is also evident that all of the participants were exposed to traumatic events of great severity both as direct victims and as witnesses to the suffering of others. Such exposure appeared to have had chronic effects of various kinds almost without exception. Nevertheless, all of the participants had married and the majority had established productive careers and had borne children of their own. As elderly people they were coming to terms with the impact of the Holocaust on their lives in varied ways as they reflected upon in the course of the interviews. It is impossible to do justice to the entire body of material that was shared with me but it is intended that the more longitudinal and individually focused analyses will serve to underpin and inform the across case analysis presented in the following chapter. Within this subsequent chapter many of the issues highlighted in relation to individual cases will be elaborated and engaged in greater depth. It is intended that the across-case analysis will deepen appreciation of the complexity of integrating experiences of this kind of magnitude into one's life trajectory from childhood onwards.

4

Findings and Discussion: Themes of Trauma and Devastating Loss that Emerged from Testimony of Child Concentration Camp Survivors

Tracey Farber

In the previous chapter, each case was described in detail. In this section, themes that emerged across the participants relating specifically to the negotiation of aging and the life crisis of "integrity versus despair" will be emphasized as this was the main focus of the study. Since it is accepted that this final life stage is predicated upon earlier life experiences and negotiation of core conflicts the discussion includes elaboration of a range of areas that emerged as salient across the interviews. Examples from the cases and verbatim testimony will be used to elaborate the developmental disruption, traumatic experiences and the apparent mental health and psychological impacts of living through the Holocaust as a child or adolescent. Coping capacity and defensive style will be described and examples of different defense mechanisms will be explored in relation to the different cases. The description and exploration of defense mechanisms are relevant as described in the literature review. The last section of this chapter will examine aspects of "integrity versus despair" in more depth.

Developmental Disruption and Child Survivor Syndrome

Dave: *I lost my childhood, my father, and sixteen members of my family.*

In the cases discussed previously it is evident that each participant was denied a normal childhood or adolescence as a result of the traumatic impact of the Holocaust. Child survivors in the present study suffered the physical loss of parents and close family members as well as the losses associated with being interned in concentration camps. The present research tends to substantiate the prevalence of what Dasberg (2001) described as "child survivor syndrome" in child Holocaust survivors, where the combination of trauma, fear, and loss in child survivors resulted in the loss of a childhood. In accordance with Dasberg's description of "child survivor syndrome," all of the participants in this study were subjected to hunger, conditions of inadequate hygiene, vulnerability to infectious diseases, cold, and the lack of a stable home environment. This was particularly relevant for those who were subjected to these extreme conditions in the concentration camps and in hiding. All of the participants in this study were exposed to severe traumatic stress, both in ghettos and in concentration camps, where they felt terrorized and helpless. This had a long-term impact on the development of PTSD symptoms, their capacity to self-regulate, and alterations in their relationships, and contributed to alterations in self-perception and the development and consolidation of meaning systems that needed to take account of what they had experienced and witnessed.

The child survivors in this study were all victims of traumatic loss, both in respect of the *circumstances of the loss* and in respect of the magnitude of the losses they suffered. They lost their families and communities and many found themselves very alone after the Holocaust, needing to build relationships with those who were available but unfamiliar to them. Dasberg (2001) emphasizes unresolved grief and mourning as part of "child survivor syndrome," which was seen clearly in all the survivors mentioned above.

Age-Related Developmental Disruption

In the present study, the child survivors were clustered in different age groups in terms of the period of their lives during which they endured the war. Helene and Rina were both around five when the Holocaust began, and Lenna and Anne were in the latency stage. These children were particularly young when they lost their parents. Their education was disrupted and they were uprooted from their familiar environments. Miriam, Shlomo, Dave, Isaac, and Menachem were all in early adolescence during the Holocaust. From Erikson's (1982) perspective, their capacity to form a stable identity was disrupted. Miriam spoke of sexual humiliations in the camp as an adolescent girl and all the males struggled with a sense of helplessness that was damaging to their developing masculine identities.

There may be different emphases in the impact of trauma at different developmental stages based on developmental capacities to absorb and manage what the environment is demanding. It seemed that younger children experienced the horror and perhaps processed the trauma in more sensory ways but did not necessarily fully comprehend some of the meaning-related aspects of what they endured, whereas older children could better grasp some of the enormity of the threat and perversion exemplified in certain incidents. For younger children there was also greater reliance on adults to mediate trauma impacts, whereas older children were often removed from care as they came of a certain age and were compelled to become prematurely resilient and self-sufficient. This was evident in some of the differences in coping styles adopted by participants. Early exposure to trauma altered their sense of identity and self-formation as described in the literature review (Cook et al. 2017; Herman 1992; Laub and Auerhahn 1993; Van der Kolk 2007).

Mediators of Trauma

Anne describing her life as a fourteen-year-old in South Africa after the Shoah: *I felt like a lost sheep.*

The purpose of this discussion is to compare and contrast aspects of the case material discussed in the previous chapter, in this instance with specific reference to trauma exposure and developmental disruption. Klein (2012) made the point that each survivor is different based on early developmental history, form of Holocaust trauma, and life circumstances post-liberation. This was true for the survivors described in the present research, where early attachment experiences, traumatic experiences, and life post-liberation were very different.

Klein (2012) spoke of the importance of early attachment in building resilience in Holocaust survivors, which has been substantiated by previous research (Isserman 2013; Lee 1988; Paris 2000). The participants in this study displayed the capacity for secure attachments, with some variation. Shlomo and Helene described the strongest maternal attachments. All the others reported "good enough" attachments to their parents. Isaac lost his mother before the Holocaust, and Menachem reported that he was not attached to his mother. It was also apparent that parental mediation was more significant at a younger age. For example, Rina was very young and depended on her mother, and Anne relied on her father. In both instances the presence of these parents proved directly protective and also appeared to serve some function in allowing the children to retain an image of a caring adult who was to some extent able to minimize threat and to act strategically in the environment, reducing the sense of utter helplessness in the face of annihilating forces.

Before an attempt is made to compare survivors, it is important to outline their differences. For instance, Helene had secure early attachments to her parents and spent a few months with them in the concentration camp before being sent away. In contrast, Isaac lost his mother before the Holocaust and was exposed to extreme cruelty in the Ghetto. This cruelty included being forced to hang fellow Jews as an older adolescent. Anne was in a concentration camp for three days, and then she was in hiding with her father and brother in the fields of Lithuania, while both Miriam and Rina were with their mothers in concentration camps for years. As Keilson (1979) mentions, it is relevant to notice the life trajectories before, during, and after the Holocaust. For example, some of the participants describe the anxiety that was experienced prior to actual internments such as Anne's sense of her mother probably having being raped, Dave's sense of running away from the fire in Rotterdam, and Helene's memory of Kristallnacht. This indicates that many of the child survivors in this study experienced terror in the lead-up to deportation and imprisonment. In accordance with Keilson (1979), the trauma was present in an ongoing way leading up to the Holocaust and disrupted the developmental trajectory of child and adolescent survivors over an extended period of time.

Keilson (1979) emphasized that a supportive environment after liberation was an ameliorating factor. This was reinforced by Herman (1992), Felsen and Brom (2019), and Klein (2012). In the present study, child survivors experienced a great variance in their post-liberation environments. For example, Lenna and Shlomo were the sole survivors of their families and were taken to *kibbutzim* in Israel. Both of them described the sense of comfort and solidarity they felt in the *kibbutzim,* and they remained connected to these environments, visiting their former *kibbutzim* decades after leaving. As outlined in the literature review, Klein (2012) demonstrated in his research that Holocaust survivors experienced *kibbutz* life in Israel as offering a supportive environment, giving survivors a sense of belonging and a sense of home, which was needed after their traumatic loss. It was also an ameliorating factor, post-liberation. Both Lenna and Shlomo demonstrated strong levels of resilience in their coping styles, and it is possible that their supportive experiences in the *kibbutzim* were a factor in building their resilient coping.

Helene, who was sent to live with relatives in South Africa after the Holocaust, described her uncle and aunt as very supportive. However, she never discussed the Holocaust with them and it was years before she was told of her parents' death. Both Helene and Rina described needing to fit in with others, and this to some extent compromised their personal individuation, in keeping with observations offered by Kellermann (2001). Dave described his post-liberation environment in South Africa as critical and unsupportive. He felt marginalized in relation to social groups and the betrayal of being beaten up by fellow Jews in Israel immediately after liberation was devastating for him. From a similar perspective, Anne experienced her post-liberation environment as alienating, as she did not fit in socially. She felt like a *lost sheep*. It is possible that the alienation experienced by Anne and Dave isolated them socially during the period of middle adolescence, a time when peer input is particularly significant. Social isolation is the opposite of what is developmentally required at this stage. Erikson (1982) states that the task of adolescence is to find an emergent identity within a peer group. Menachem struggled to integrate socially living in tents in Israel together with other immigrants. He said he felt traumatized by this experience and after some time left to settle in Rhodesia. The various testimonies demonstrate that, although some of the survivors had environments that were supportive to varying degrees, they carried their memories and were unable to process their traumatic experiences, the most common consequence being an inability to integrate and feel accepted by their peer group. This further lead to an inhibition of feeling and reluctance to speak of these experiences. In addition, they were responsive to signals from others that their Holocaust experiences were not to be revisited in conversation.

Other participants such as Miriam, Helene, and Rina experienced their post-liberation environments as supportive and were able to make friends and integrate socially. It would seem that both previous theory and research, as well as the present study, support Keilson's (1979) findings that a supportive environment after liberation was an important protective factor for child survivors in the amelioration of their traumatic loss and trauma. Conversely, negative post-liberation experiences further exacerbated the trauma and sense of loss of all significant connections amongst child survivors. All of the participants in this study who coped well and displayed resilience reported a supportive post-liberation environment. On the other hand, all of the participants who struggled to adjust to hostile, unsupportive environments, described a continual struggle with PTSD, depression, and a sense of social isolation. As such, Keilson's (1979) theory regarding the importance of a supportive post-liberation environment in ameliorating trauma is substantiated by the present findings.

The presence of a parent during the concentration camp experience was a mitigating or protective factor in the face of trauma (Klein 2012); however, it presented complicated dynamics. This was explained by both Rina and Miriam, who survived with their mothers. Both participants said that they were constantly afraid of being separated from their mothers, as this was a threat to their survival. A difference did become apparent between the two cases. Miriam, an older child, idealized her mother and expressed ongoing gratitude towards her. Rina, a younger child, was critical of the way in which her mother covered her eyes and later refused to explain or discuss what they had experienced, decades after the Holocaust ended. This left Rina feeling resentful of her mother's perceived overzealous protection of her. Eventually, Rina saw a therapist to help with her ongoing trauma, which allowed her to process some of what had been hidden. Dave stayed with his mother for a period. He stated that he often thought about her pain, having to witness two cold and starving children whom she was unable to nurture and protect, indicating an important capacity to identify with her and to reflect on her experience. He said she fed him emotionally by teaching him about poetry and he appreciated her supreme effort to keep her children alive and as safe as possible.

All the child survivors in this study were traumatized by the impotence of their parents in not being able to protect them (Durst 1995). Rina felt angry, but Miriam, who idealized her mother, was perhaps unconsciously protecting herself against any negative feelings towards her. Some survivors arguably felt unconsciously angry towards their parents for failing to protect them (Hass 1995), in addition to feeling guilt either about their deaths or about any critical feelings they had (Kellermann 2001). This was possibly evident in Miriam's idealization of her mother and inability to even consider any negative thoughts towards her.

Another protective factor, as described by Klein (2012) and Herman (1992), was the significant relationships formed in the concentration camps. Dave mentioned having a younger friend to protect and look after. Anne, Shlomo, Helene, Lenna, and Isaac all described the pure desolation and aloneness they experienced. The world lacked empathy (Laub and Auerhahn 1998) and they felt abandoned by all good objects (Eagle 2013; Garland 1998; Gerson 2009). However, several of the child survivors in the study also made some reference to the kindness of righteous gentiles who helped to save their lives. Miriam spoke at length of her nanny who was both a maternal object and a rescuer and at one stage hid Miriam, risking her life to save her. Dave spoke with great gratitude about an SS woman who saved his life by feeding him extra food when he was sick and weak. Rina mentioned a non-Jewish woman who saved her and her mother. Helene spoke about the nuns in the convent who secretly taught her catechism at night so that she could successfully hide her Jewish identity. Shlomo spoke of the German engineer at Auschwitz who was kind to him and taught him welding, a skill that enabled him to be very successful after the Holocaust. These experiences of humanity were crucial in saving their lives and also symbolized some hope in human goodness. As described by Klein (2012), hope was a crucial aspect of the internal worlds of survivors and these redeeming experiences in the face of so much brutality and inhumanity were significant and well-recollected.

Klein (2012) links the importance of hope to parental attachment, acquiring a sense of agency, surviving trauma, and rebuilding a life after the Holocaust. His observation concerning this was supported by the testimony collected in this study, where the attachment to parental objects appeared to have facilitated creative resilience. This was seen in Shlomo, Rina, Lenna, Dave, Helene, and Miriam, who all reported secure parental attachments and were able to find and access helpful relationships during the Holocaust. Also, they were able to make good object choices and build positive relational connections in their lives after liberation.

Developmental Disruption as a Result of Witnessing Murder and Violence in the Concentration Camps

Miriam: *No one can understand the Holocaust unless they have been there . . .*

All nine survivors were interned in concentration camps for various periods of time. Most of the survivors spent extended periods, several months and years, in the camps. This included Dave, Miriam, Lenna, Isaac, Rina, Menachem, Shlomo, and Helene. In addition, many of the child survivors were in two or three camps and also went on death marches. All the child survivors with the exception of Anne reported seeing piles of dead bodies and witnessing the horror of murder in the camps. Anne spent only a few days in a camp; other than that, she was in hiding with her father and brother where she heard the mass killings at night. Being exposed to death and murder on a large scale and living in the context of danger in the concentration camps meant that normal developmental tasks of childhood and adolescence were disrupted.

The chaos of death and horror was described by Dave, Miriam, Rina, Helene, Menachem, Shlomo, Isaac, and Lenna, who all witnessed it. The developmental disruption of this severe trauma meant that their sense of being protected children was over. They lived in fear of their lives and were in a constant fight for survival as they were part of a group that were marked for death and confronted by humankind's capacity for evil. This witnessing of murder and cruelty in the concentration camps, as described in all the case histories, engendered a primitive fear of death as well as a fear for their own safety, which extended for years beyond their captivity. The ongoing terror created a developmental disruption that changed their lives forever. They were no longer worried about normal developmental tasks of childhood or adolescence—survival became the only task that was of any relevance. As described by Eagle (2013), it forever shattered their trust in people. This is also described by Garland (1998) and Gerson (2009) who concur that the trauma survivor has a sense that the world has no empathy and is impervious to suffering. In addition, they needed to reestablish some of the "illusion of safety and invulnerability" as these had been shattered by their traumatic experiences during the Holocaust. This level of repair seemed to be difficult in cases of such severe trauma (Professor Diana Shmukler, personal communication, February 7, 2019).

Child Survivors Witnessing and Experiencing Cruelty

Rina: *She said, "You are a Jew! And I hate Jews!"*

Children and adolescents were not protected in any way in the concentration camps. Rather, they were targeted for death and cruelty to the same degree as adults. The following description indicates the level of cruelty that child Holocaust survivors were subjected to. At the age of seven, Rina was attacked by a non-Jewish Polish prisoner in the concentration camp. The woman was responsible for washing the SS uniforms, and she offered to wash Rina in the dirty water. She bathed and dried Rina, and while Rina was getting dressed, the woman burnt her on the neck with an iron: *I screamed and said to her, "What are you doing?" The woman replied, "I am doing it because you are a Jew! And I hate Jews!" She burnt me, and I had a big scar. Of course, my mother never allowed me near her again. The scar remained, and I had plastic surgery to remove it after the Holocaust.*

The account demonstrates that child Holocaust survivors were not only witness to trauma and genocide but were also direct victims of cruelty and torture.

To experience pain and cruelty at this level was to face the world with no empathy (Eagle 2013; Garland 1998). In this example, Rina was deliberately tortured by an adult who treated her like an object of hate. This form of treatment shattered her sense of trust in other adults and in the benevolence of the world in general (Gerson 2009). Rina's mother was unable to protect her from general cruelty and stigmatization and in this instance her physical integrity was violated (Pynoos et al. 2007). What is also evident is that it was the betrayal of trust in a situation in which she was ostensibly to be cared for that shocked and alienated her. It is evident that something of this experience of potentially being discriminated against and misled remained with Rina as a kind of psychological scar.

Children and adolescents who witnessed murder were sullied with a sense of horror. For example, Menachem's responsibilities included picking up dead bodies, including infants who were thrown out of windows, while the mothers who had recently delivered them were shot. When Menachem spoke about the infant killing described previously it was evident that the level of inhumanity felt beyond comprehension to him. His preoccupation with this part of his Holocaust experience communicated that some fundamental sense of trust in a meaningful and ethical world had been broken and remained difficult to rebuild. Having witnessed this deliberate level of cruelty in which not even the life of a recently born baby was sacrosanct, he found it impossible not to forget that human nature could take this form. He said that he stopped believing in God after seeing these atrocities being perpetrated, and that his spiritual beliefs were consequently shattered (Greif 2005; Herman 1992; Janoff-Bulman 1985).

Shlomo's experience of horror was at Blechammer labor camp where every week he was forced to watch hangings: *There was a permanent scaffold, three or four people were hung at a time, they stood on a chair then the chair was kicked away … The Germans were cruel to those who could not walk. They were immediately shot, or petrol was thrown onto them, and they were burned alive. They were made to walk in rows of five. If one of the group fell or was missing, the remaining four were shot.* He further recounted similarly sadistic and brutal treatment of inmates at Gross-Rosen concentration camp: *We were put in a building with no roof, and it rained all night, and there was no place to sit. The next day the Germans came with dogs and chased us out. There were holes in the ground, people fell into the holes, on top of each other and they could not stand, so they drowned and suffocated and choked in the mud and the stampede, it was terrible.* Shlomo recalled these traumatic experiences vividly during the interview. It was clear that, like Menachem, he was unable to make sense of this cruelty and inhumanity. Shlomo said that he did not understand how God had allowed this to happen. He too carried these memories throughout his life. As described by Eagle (2013) in relation to extreme forms of interpersonally inflicted trauma and violation, this experience forever shattered his trust in people.

Menachem and Shlomo were not the only participants to describe sadistic and inhumane acts. Participants such as Miriam, Lenna, Rina, and Helene saw deformed and dead bodies in the camps. They spoke with a level of disbelief that such things could have occurred, and yet they were direct witnesses to such atrocities and therefore forced to comprehend that such grotesque acts did indeed take place. The child Holocaust survivors were exposed to a world of horror at an early life stage. The knowledge that existence could become degraded and threatening to the extent that they had experienced stayed with them in some form for the rest of their lives. This kind of damage to meaning systems and assumptive worlds presented by the Holocaust has been well documented by others (Chalmers 2015; Grief 2005; Janoff-Bulman 1985). As described by Garland (1998), Gerson (2009), and Eagle (2013), in these conditions the trauma survivor is left with a sense that the world has no empathy and is impervious to suffering. Worse still, the child survivors reported that they were confronted by humankind's capacity for sadism and cruelty on a daily basis.

As time passed and they grew older, they were able to reflect on what they witnessed. The long-term impact of this cruelty and horror lead to PTSD and CPTSD. In some participants the witnessing of extreme horror caused them to question not only interpersonal relationships but also their subsequent spiritual beliefs. Their belief in a benign God was questioned, which led to a profound sense of spiritual isolation. In some instances, this led to decades of feeling spiritually abandoned and bereft of this form of solace, as will be further elaborated in subsequent discussion.

This discussion will now move to a description of long-term symptoms and mental health-related conditions experienced by child survivors.

Mental Health Symptoms and Long-Term Impacts

Lenna: *No one could be normal after the camps.*

A ubiquitous finding of this study was that all the participants suffered from symptoms of traumatic stress, including aspects of PTSD and CPTSD. The purpose of this section is to elaborate the particular nature of the trauma that was endured and the mental health sequelae of this exposure so that the long-term implications for the aging process can be better appreciated. In the present study all survivors, whether or not they were part of a clinical subgroup suffering from diagnosed or diagnosable depression, reported that they suffered for decades with symptoms or conditions that clinically would be associated with traumatic stress. Eight of the nine participants suffered from of PTSD but did not qualify for the full diagnosis.

Almost half of the participants in this study, Dave, Anne, Menachem, and Isaac, suffered from chronic depression and PTSD. These participants comprised a clinical subgroup in the larger group of participants. Shlomo, Lenna, Miriam, Rina, and Helene employed various defenses to block the overwhelming trauma they had been exposed to, some of which compromised their functioning. These survivors formed part of an apparently resilient subgroup in this study. Rina had suffered from debilitating nightmares and had attended psychotherapy, however, she seemed to be somewhat anxious rather than depressed and her coping skills were generally good. Rina and Dave had both attended in-depth psychotherapy to deal with their Holocaust traumas. Within this resilient group all of them had full-blown PTSD except for Helene who had several symptoms but did not qualify for the diagnosis.

Intrusive Symptoms

Lenna: *The nightmares have been with me since the war.*

In this section, examples of intrusive symptoms will be discussed, including reports of nightmares, flashbacks, and intrusive thoughts and memories. It is interesting to note that each survivor had a unique profile of intrusive symptoms.

Lenna describes an experience with intrusive symptoms related to her dream life: *The nightmares have been with me since after the war. They have been less the last few years. The dread of talking about my experiences to you has brought them back. I am sorry, I cannot discuss my Holocaust experiences.* The interview process reportedly triggered more nightmares for Lenna, who was not able to give testimony as it proved to be too traumatic for her. It was evident that decades after her time in the camps her nightmares were still so vivid as to cause her marked distress.

Miriam's account of her ongoing nightmares indicated that she was persecuted by her intrusive symptoms for decades across her life trajectory: *For many years after the Holocaust, I would wake my husband up as I had been screaming in my sleep from nightmares. I would wake up so stiff from anxiety that I couldn't move. I always dreamt that the Germans were attacking my children, even though at the time of the Holocaust I was a child . . . my children were born twenty years later. My repetitive nightmares continued for many years.* One has a sense that suffering with this ongoing symptom further isolated her from others and, as with Lenna, kept her concentration camp experience vivid in her consciousness. In addition, it is possible that Miriam's nervous system remained in a hyper-aroused state when she awoke from the repetitive nightmares as evidenced in her comment: *I would wake up so stiff from anxiety that I couldn't move.* It is also interesting that her experiences became transformed in her dreams into persecution of her children. It is not uncommon in PTSD for nightmares associated with the traumatic event to represent it in a more symbolic manner. It seems that Miriam identified with both mother and child parts of herself in her dreams. Miriam's description of her debilitating nightmares demonstrated themes of fear and terror as well as a sense of being worn down by their repetitive quality. She reported that they caused significant distress for years. Several of the other participants also described intrusive nightmares.

It is clear that for a child survivor like Lenna unprocessed memories continued to distress her throughout her life despite her best effort of avoidance. Rina also described nightmares that endured for decades:

> Rina: *I had nightmares for thirty-five years. I don't know if I was screaming or making a noise but I would wake my husband, and he would shake me and say, "Rina, are you okay? Wake up!" I would run to my children's bedrooms to check they were ok, make a cup of coffee and go back to sleep . . . and when I went back to sleep, I would carry on the dream where I left off. I am not joking."*

> Tracey: *It sounds as if the dreams persecuted you.*

> Rina: *It persecuted me for years, but it was horrendous! I dreamed I am six or seven years old. I dream in Dutch. It's night, and I am on my own, and the Germans are behind me, and I hear their feet marching, and they are shouting and I know I have to get away because if I don't they will take me back to the camp, and as I am running my feet get heavy like iron and I can't walk and they are getting closer and closer and in my dream they never catch me because I wake up crying . . . and when I get back to sleep it would start all over again from where it left off, and they would get closer, and I would wake up in the morning exhausted and in a cold sweat. When I had children, I dreamed they were alone with me. And the Germans are wanting to take me back to the camps, and I am thinking, "I can't go through this again, how will I protect my children?" And that dream was ten times worse than being chased myself.*

A possible explanation for the persistence of the nightmares is that adrenaline is triggered when there is such a visceral fear response. It is likely that these nightmares triggered a physical "fight or flight" response, which may have kept her Holocaust experience alive at a neurophysiological level as well as at the level of imagery and affect. Clearly it was impossible for Rina to effectively block out her Holocaust experiences as they returned to disturb her at night.

It is important to note how the traumatic experiences of the Holocaust evolved into fearful dreams involving the survivor's own offspring. Their fear of not being able to protect themselves transferred into a fear of not being able to protect their children as mothers in the present. Their trauma had continued in time and through a generation. It is possible that they as adults identified with their mothers' helplessness and empathized with their mothers' struggle. It is significant that both Miriam and Rina, survivors who were in camps with their mothers, have nightmares about protecting their own children. These participants demonstrate that, even on an unconscious level, the trauma ruptured their sense of trust and safety in the world and had become an internalized aspect of their identity (Eagle 2013; Garland 1998; Gerson 2009; Herman 1992). As highlighted in the case analyses in the previous chapters, it was evident that in many instances children were not unexpectedly very attuned to their parents' anxieties and fears, which was later reflected in their traumatic representations of danger in their nightmares.

The intrusive symptom of trauma-related nightmares appeared to persist after the Holocaust for Lenna, Rina, and Miriam, all of whom reported suffering from chronic nightmares in spite of their generally effective functioning. This indicates that post-traumatic symptoms may well endure for decades after the Holocaust as described by previous researchers (Barak 2013; Barak et al. 2005; Barel et al. 2010; Cohen et al. 2003; Joffe et al. 2003; Kellermann 2001; Wardi 1992). Even though survivors found ways to continue engaging productively in life, it is painful to think of aging survivors having had to endure the ongoing levels of anxiety and stress, which emerged in their dream life. It is also apparent that this anxiety was communicated to others such as husbands and children.

Menachem, who was diagnosed with PTSD and depression, also described being affected by nightmares. Menachem said that he had symptoms of post-traumatic stress, including flashbacks and nightmares regarding the babies whom he witnessed being thrown out of windows. He reported that his nightmares were so intense that he would often wake up in the middle of the night in a state of anxiety. He said he would also have a repetitive dream where police were chasing him and he was shot in the leg. He did receive a flesh wound in an actual shooting that took place in later life, and even though he recovered, the trauma continued to torment him in his dreams. His psychiatrist who diagnosed him with PTSD told him that his nightmares were from a lack of closure concerning the loss of his family. It is interesting to note the severe anxiety reflected in his nightmares, and how they continued, unremitting, for decades. Both the horror of the infant killings and the physical injury and life threat related to the shooting (probably mapped onto prior Holocaust trauma) continued to haunt him in the present.

It was evident from the reports of nightmares by four of the participants that the Holocaust continued to play out in their unconscious life but in such a way that their replayed imagery and physiological sensations often broke through into consciousness. All four survivors spoke of this symptomatic feature of their lives as deeply troubling and debilitating, even though they had come to live with the prospect of facing frequent nightmares.

In addition to nightmares, other kinds of intrusive symptoms were also volunteered by participants. Rina described a particular experience when an olfactory flashback from the Holocaust was triggered in her sixties. She had a kerectomy procedure to correct her vision: *They burn off the top layer of your retina to correct your vision. As soon as the doctor lasered my eye, I got the smell of burning flesh, and I thought, "Oh my God!" It was terrible! I couldn't move. I couldn't do anything! I was supposed to go for my astigmatism, but I couldn't go back.* As Rina elaborated, the eye procedure had triggered the olfactory memory of burning flesh from the crematorium at Ravensbruck concentration camp. The above example demonstrates that as a high-functioning resilient survivor Rina experienced flashbacks five decades after the Holocaust. Van der Kolk (2007) and Pynoos et al. (2007) discussed the long-term deep and indelible mark that trauma leaves on the psyche of a child, which is supported by the case material here—the olfactory memory having been unconsciously retained and resurfacing unexpectedly.

Lenna, although one of the more resilient survivors, could not find the words to describe her experiences. She continued to be tormented by her intrusive traumatic memories:

> Lenna: *Visiting Auschwitz is a quiet experience for me now. You don't hear screaming anymore; you don't hear wailing.*

> Tracey: *Did people used to wail?*

> Lenna: *Yes, they knew they were being taken to their deaths, and they used to cry out and beg to be saved.*

She made it clear that the intrusive memories of Auschwitz lived in her mind like a permanent dark cloud that could easily overwhelm her consciousness. Intrusive memories continued to traumatize her: she said that her recollections of Auschwitz and her family's deaths lived with her constantly and continued to interfere with her capacity to enjoy her present life. She reported that her PTSD symptoms were a constant reminder of her past from which she was unable to escape.

Dave described persistent traumatic recollections after the trauma he endured. He remained preoccupied and obsessed with the Holocaust. It seemed he lived a parallel existence where his memories were so intrusive that he struggled to engage with his present life. He spoke of the way in which he was violently beaten by gypsies in the concentration camp, and as a result he was constantly vigilant and fearful of being humiliated and attacked in his present life. Dave described an intrusive memory that continued to trouble him from when he was thirteen at Ravensbruck concentration camp: *I was sent to feed a group of Muselmanner, these were people who were on the brink of death. I was traumatized for the rest of my life after seeing the following image: All these skeletons got up and shuffled towards me, open mouths, staring hollow eyes, their hands stretched out, they never grabbed. I gave them the biscuits as quickly as I could and ran away. It was such a horrifying experience that I was traumatized for the rest of my life! They went on the next transport to Auschwitz.* As an older man, he described his terror as a child upon seeing such a horrifying spectacle. Terror filled his voice and it was clear that he continued to be affected with a sense of horror, decades later. The sense of awfulness of this engagement was palpable in the interview room and brought this image chillingly to life.

Miriam described an intrusive memory that haunted her for decades: *When the ghetto was liquidated there was blood all over the walls. I was horrified. There were pools of blood and dead bodies and broken bottles, most of the ghetto had been burned, and out of thirty thousand, three hundred survived. It happened in 1942 on the day of my thirteenth birthday. I have never been able to celebrate my birthday since; the memories are too horrific.* Miriam said that this memory tormented her until the present time, leaving her unable to experience the joy of her birthday and leaving a cloud over this celebration ever since. Miriam also reported another terrifying memory from her time at Stutthof concentration camp: *Although we were there for only two months, it was the most terrifying time of my life. When we arrived the sight of it was a chilling indication of what was in store for us: on both sides of the entrance were mounds of shoes, spectacles, some artificial limbs and suitcases bearing silent testimony of what had gone before.* Thus, Miriam described the horror of knowing that Jews were being killed at the camp and the imagery of clothes, crematoria, and skeletal corpses filled her with fear that she and her mother might also be killed. Living with this threat of death over a long-term period may have been overwhelming and perhaps have contributed to Miriam's use of dissociation and compartmentalization as a way of coping, as will be discussed later. However, what is evident here is the detail of the recollection, which produced associations that continued to impact her present life.

When he was fourteen, Dave's work in the concentration camp was to collect dead bodies, load them into a wheelbarrow, and drop them off in a room. He described a time when *soldiers took me by my hands and feet and began to swing me over the dead corpses as if they would throw me in, as they did this they laughed. I was terrified that they would drop me on the corpses, and this scene tormented me for years after the Holocaust. My psychiatrist said that that experience was one of my worst traumas.* It would seem that the trauma of this experience was associated not only with being exposed to the dead bodies but primarily with being sadistically taunted by the soldiers. As a fourteen-year-old boy, Dave's horror was not only that he would join the dead but because he was taunted and rendered helpless by two adult men. This incident highlights how cruelty etches itself on the psyche in the form of intrusive PTSD symptoms that torment the survivor. For Dave, it symbolized a persecuting world and the loss of a connection with an empathic other (Eagle 2013; Garland 1998; Gerson 2009; Laub and Auerhahn 1993; Van der Kolk 2007). Cruelty leaves a permanent scar on both the psyche and the nervous system (Herman 1992) and the experience remains an emotionally laden intrusive memory.

From the examples presented it is evident that intrusive symptoms continued to disturb survivors across their life trajectories, including intrusive images and memories, somatic associations, nightmares, and physiological arousal. The level of detail in the accounts speaks to the retention of material in traumatic form. Most of the testimony from the participants had an "unprocessed trauma" feel as the imagery was vivid and the recollections were accompanied by strong affect in many instances. They also had a "present-tense" quality. This conveyed something of the way in which these participants carried unbearable trauma that remained unprocessed and became present in unexpected ways.

Having discussed some of the intrusive features associated with PTSD that were evident in the accounts of the survivors, the following subsection looks at some of the more avoidance-related features.

Avoidant Symptoms

Lenna: *I can't talk about what happened in Auschwitz.*

Avoidant symptoms of PTSD enable the survivor to avoid confronting the painful affects associated with the trauma (Herman 1992). Emotional numbing and dissociation have been described as the severing of the link between thought and feeling as a response to severe trauma. Sometimes, this is the only mechanism to deal with the ongoing paralyzing fear associated with traumatization in captivity (Herman 1992). Wardi (1992) employs the term "robotization" to refer to a similar aspect of impact. All respondents reported in great detail the horror and revulsion they felt upon witnessing degradation, harm, and murder in the camps. However, they explained that after a period of time they became impervious to the horror they witnessed and endured. Dave, Miriam, Isaac, Rina, Shlomo, and Lenna all described how they became emotionally blunted after being repeatedly exposed to horror and trauma. For example, Dave said after being horrified by dead bodies that he came to view them as *potatoes*. Miriam said that after a period she became numbed to the experience of being forced to parade naked before German soldiers—*we didn't care*. Isaac said that he got used to seeing and smelling the piles of rotten bodies in Bergen-Belsen. In addition, most of the survivors in this study came across as emotionally blunted. Both Dave and Isaac were aware that they were emotionally "numb" and spoke about it in their testimony, and Miriam appeared particularly emotionless when discussing her internment. Of all the participants in this study, Lenna had the most extreme avoidant symptoms as she was unable to speak about her experiences in the Holocaust at all.

As will be discussed in greater detail in relation to defensive strategies, the most extreme form of avoidance across cases was represented in the compartmentalization of Holocaust-related recollections and associations. For the greater part of their lives, the survivors appeared to have almost packed away this period of their life history and had avoided talking about their experiences to anyone. Whether this avoidance was a feature of PTSD and their own anxiety about what approaching such material might evoke, or whether it was in response to non-receptiveness from others (or both), is hard to determine. Nevertheless, there did appear to be some cognitive or mental effort expended in ensuring that difficult Holocaust-related contents of their minds was generally kept at bay or locked away.

In conclusion, in relation to PTSD and traumatic stress symptoms the testimony outlined in this subsection demonstrates that these child Holocaust survivors have aspects of post-traumatic stress that have persisted for decades—as has been documented in previous research (Barak 2013; Barak et al. 2005; Barel et al. 2010; Brom 2001; Cohen et al. 2001; Joffe et al. 2003; Kellermann 2001/2009; Wardi 1992). Both the clinical subgroup and the non-clinical "resilient" subgroup experienced intense symptoms of post-traumatic stress, in keeping with what has been documented by Cohen et al. (2001). This indicates that both high-functioning resilient survivors and those diagnosed with PTSD may well suffer from traumatic stress symptoms decades after the Holocaust. Child survivors in this study, not unsurprisingly given the events they were exposed to, reported that they were traumatized by Holocaust events into their old age.

The constellation of traumatic stress symptoms of participants in this study had both differences and similarities. Whilst all of the participants had PTSD symptoms, the clinical subgroup (Dave, Isaac, Anne, Menachem) had a joint diagnosis of PTSD and depression. In addition, they had more intrusive PTSD symptoms such as flashbacks and ruminative symptoms. It is possible that with the exception of Shlomo the males in this group had worse PTSD as they were exposed to particular kinds of traumatization where they were involved in directly handling dead bodies. While almost all of the participants appeared to have some intrusion-related symptoms, it was also evident that many had experienced shattering of core assumptions and continued to struggle to comprehend the kind of world in which these events could have taken place. In addition, those who had either been forced to be complicit in some way or had enjoyed partially helpful relationships with particular perpetrators struggled with feelings of guilt and ambivalence of a kind that might be associated with more complicated forms of traumatic stress.

For the purpose of this study, Herman's (1992) concept of complex traumatic stress is helpful as it describes the long-term characterological changes that take place as a result of trauma in captivity, associated with difficulties in affect regulation, dissociative presentations, and alteration in systems of meaning, amongst other features. When trying to make sense of the impact of years of ongoing trauma it is possible to formulate that for child survivors there was a significant rupture of the self (Benyakar et al. 1989; Dasberg 2001; Gerson 2009; Herman 1992, Kellermann 2001; Laub and Auerhahn 1998), in addition to a rupture in relationships to others and the world. As a result of severe ongoing trauma and loss, survivors' developmental process was disrupted and often perverted in ways that presented both consciously and unconsciously. In spite of this, most of them were able to cohere in some way and then generally were able to live productive and functional lives. The function of defenses in coping with the trauma as well as the impact on the developmental stage of aging will be discussed later in this chapter.

Pervasive Anxiety and Fears of Abandonment

Miriam: *My biggest fear was that my mother would not come back and who would look after me, and what would happen to me?*

For those who had access to caretakers, the participants' fear of being abandoned by their parent in a ghetto or concentration camp was life-threatening as they depended on their parent for survival. The atmosphere of death and violence and fear of losing their parent led to a pervasive sense of anxiety and fear of abandonment that is clearly described by Rina: *I was seven and a half at the time. I was hungry and cold and frightened all the time. I heard screaming and screaming. I was old enough to understand that people were screaming from pain . . . I saw a lot of people being beaten, and I saw people being attacked by dogs, bloodhounds and Alsatians. Thank God, my mother was never beaten. Every day my mother went out to work, and I remained with the children in the barracks. My biggest fear was that she would not come back and who would look after me, and what would happen to me?* In this quote, Rina described her fear that her mother would disappear and that she would be left at the mercy of the camp guards to face the continual horror that she witnessed, as well as the continual threat of death.

Miriam also described her panic when her mother disappeared and then returned so badly beaten that Miriam did not recognize her. Her mother reported that she had been tortured by the Nazis, which left Miriam with a pervasive fear that she would lose her. Both Rina and Miriam were constantly afraid of losing their mothers. They feared the loss of their mothers as primary attachment figures, and they also knew that their chances of survival without their mothers were unlikely in the terrifying atmosphere of the concentration camp. Their sense of safety and security was lost, and this disrupted their negotiation of separation and individuation as might be anticipated in normal childhood development. Van der Kolk (2007) described the vulnerability of a child on a biological level and argued the likelihood that enduring anxiety at this time of life might contribute to later problems with intimacy and productivity of various kinds.

Loss and Mourning

Helene: *I am crying and I can't stop.*

The literature review discussed the centrality of loss for child Holocaust survivors and the case material described the tragic loss and unresolved grief of each child survivor. Within the data of this research, loss emerged as a major theme. Unresolved loss and traumatic bereavement was experienced by all participants even six decades after the Holocaust. It is evident from the testimony that child survivors sustained losses on multiple levels. The extent of the grief and mourning is hard to imagine: all the participants in this study lost at least one parent as well as siblings and extended family. The following were orphaned: Isaac, Lenna, Menachem, Helene, and Shlomo lost both primary attachment figures. Dave, Rina, and Miriam survived with their mothers; however, their mothers were traumatized themselves and compromised in their capacity to perform normal maternal functions. Often the mothers were themselves changed after the Holocaust and unable to process their own loss and trauma. Their compounded losses interfered with their capacity to assist in the healing of their children.

Anne was deeply traumatized by the loss of her mother; however, she survived with her father who she reported never discussed the Holocaust with her. She was deeply traumatized by the loss of her sibling, as were Lenna, Menachem, and Shlomo. The multiple losses of parents, siblings, extended families, and communities were so overwhelming that survivors were unable to mourn in a manner that led to some resolution of grief. The difficulty in mourning may be attributed to the extent and intensity of the loss. In addition, there was no support or opportunity for them to express their grief as they had to focus on survival.

Helene, who, as previously described, cried for hours during her interviews, also described how the grieving for her parents had remained permanently open or unresolved, in part because she had not allowed herself to fully appreciate what had happened to them. *I think I felt the trauma I was hiding, but I never got over the loss, there was no closure.* Helene also referred to a sense of loss with regard to growing up without her parents: *I just think of the way I loved them and the way they loved me. I am crying, and I can't stop because for the first time I am allowing myself to think about how I missed out and I am left with emptiness and incompleteness.*

Helene's comments echo the lack of closure regarding unresolved loss and mourning in relation to Holocaust survivors as described in the literature review (Dasberg 2001; Durst 1995; Krell 1985; Witztum and Malkinson 2009). Frequently grief was delayed as there was a more immediate focus on survival and there was little post-Holocaust containment and support to express grief. The unexpressed grief that lay dormant and was repressed for decades found its expression in the outpourings that continued for hours in the research interview.

Lack of closure regarding loss was observed in the present research and substantiates the findings of previous researchers (Durst 2003; Gampel 1988; Kellermann 2001/2009; Kestenberg and Brenner 1986; Klein 1974/1983/2012; Krell 1985; Wardi 1992; Wiesel 1974; Witztum and Malkinson 2009). Traumatic loss will be discussed under several subheadings to further clarify the nuanced experiences described by participants in this study and to deconstruct the core issues that contribute to the intensity of traumatic bereavement.

The Lack of Opportunity to Anticipate Loss and "Say Goodbye"

Rina: *My father died in Buchenwald concentration camp, and I never got to say goodbye* (crying).

Traumatic bereavement in essence entails a sudden loss where there is no preparation or leave-taking. The sudden severing of primary attachment relationships caused a major distress, trauma, and developmental disruption. Many of the child survivors described how they "lost their childhoods" as they were forced to fend for themselves after losing their parents.

Most of the children in this study described the initial shock of being separated from their parents during the Holocaust. Miriam described her father's arrest and removal from the family. Isaac described how he arrived home to find that his family had been sent to a concentration camp, where they were murdered. Anne described hearing the gunshot that killed her mother and was also devastated by the murder of her older sister, having had no opportunity to say goodbye to either. Menachem and Lenna also spoke of their ongoing grief for their younger brothers who were killed without warning. This sudden and traumatic loss, with no sense of closure, continued to torment child survivors even in their old age. It is possible that the suddenness of the deaths contributed to the ongoing enduring sense of catastrophic grief.

It seems that the moment of loss is frequently engraved on the psyche of child survivors. Rina described the loss of her father and her intense pain at not having anticipated that she would not ever see him again. Rina said, *I don't remember saying goodbye to my father at Westerbork transit camp, I was very close to him, and it has worried me all my life, I went to two psychiatrists for hypnosis, and I got nowhere. My father died in Buchenwald concentration camp, and I never got to say goodbye.* (Crying.) *Until today, I cannot say goodbye I find it very hard because the people you were close to you couldn't say goodbye to them.*

Shlomo became very emotional when he described his final separation from his mother and his brothers, who were all taken to Auschwitz. When he was fourteen years old, he was held captive with his parents and siblings for three days without food and shelter. They were hungry and afraid prior to their traumatic separation, meaning that to some extent they were each preoccupied with survival. Shlomo described how he and his father and sister were allowed through the gates during selection. *As we went out from the gate, they stopped my mother and sent her on a train to Auschwitz. That was 1942, we never saw her again* (his voice cracked). *It happened so quickly there was no time to say goodbye.* Later he was called up for selection by the Germans. His father and sister took him to the train station, they kissed him goodbye, and they all cried. His sister and father were both sent to Auschwitz, where they later died. There is something about the arbitrary nature of the decisions that took his family that left Shlomo still tied to these memories of partings. In the case of his father and sister, it is evident that they may have had some sense of this being a final leave-taking but that the notion of this was too overwhelming to fully entertain and so their sadness was expressed but there was a limited capacity to acknowledge the significance of this moment. He continued to say in a deeply sad tone of voice: *I hate a cemetery. Because my parents are not there and I don't know where their bodies are! I get upset, even though I am nearly eighty it still upsets me.* This statement demonstrates that there is no mourning site to visit and no closure for an unending grief that continues into old age. Shlomo was profoundly sad as he talked of these immediate family losses and being robbed of the opportunity to say goodbye. Because he was unable to physically locate his loved ones somewhere, his grief was left in a kind of limbo. He felt torn from his family without warning, and he was deprived of the opportunity to mourn and achieve closure.

When asked if he got depressed, Shlomo said he never suffered from depression, however, he had *gotten used to being sad*. He said he was always sad that he did not have access to his family, with whom he was so close. He said that worse than the cruelty and torment of the Holocaust was the loss of his family, for whom he continued to grieve. The lack of closure and inability to engage in ritualized mourning practices leaves a gap where memory is the only memorial left for loved ones. Although Shlomo was very resilient and successful, his description of his mourning suggested the presence of an open wound, as described by Amir and Lev-Wiesel (2003). It is clear that traumatic losses left Rina and Shlomo with a sense of unresolved bereavement that continued into old age, similar to other participants in this study.

Scale of Loss of Family and Caretakers and the Loss of Childhood

Lenna: *I lost everyone. I was twelve and alone in the world.*

The loss of parents or caretakers threatens children's survival, and in the case of the participants it made them feel utterly alone and vulnerable in the dangerous world of the Holocaust. Although Lenna would not speak about her trauma, she expressed her experience of being alone as the sole survivor of her immediate family. As a child survivor of the Holocaust, she reported: *I lost everyone—they died in Auschwitz, my whole family, my brother, my mother, my grandparents from both sides. Aunties and uncles. Cousins from both sides.* This quote highlights the impact of loss for Lenna when she found herself completely alone in the world at the age of thirteen. As a result, she was forced to fend for herself, as were many of the participants who lost both parents, experiencing extreme developmental disruptions as they were prematurely catapulted into adulthood. The overwhelming loss is difficult to conceptualize. By listing her losses, Lenna emphasized the scale of her loss and her sense of isolation from her family.

Dave illustrated the way in which compounded loss disrupted his childhood in the following way: *I lost my father and my childhood during the Holocaust, including sixteen members of my family who were murdered at Auschwitz.* Dave also listed his losses as a way of emphasizing his sadness and suffering. He claimed that this was the root cause of his depression as he was unable to come to terms with the magnitude of loss of his family members. The extent of this loss, coupled with the trauma he endured, lead to the depression and PTSD he suffered over the decades of his life.

The experience of being left utterly alone is also expressed in the following testimony from Menachem: *When I went back to Poland, I did not find any of my family alive. My father's side were a big family, and they were all gone, no sign of them.* He said that his whole family was killed and he was the sole survivor. He was particularly grieved about the loss of his father to whom he was very attached. It upset him deeply that his father was shot in the woods by the Germans and lost his life at the young age of forty-eight. Not having his siblings around him was a constant source of sadness: *I lost everybody.* Menachem expressed that the loss of his whole family left him alone and vulnerable in a dangerous world.

Miriam spoke at length about the loss of her father at the beginning of the Holocaust. However, she said she was *devastated about losing my nanny, who was like a mother to me.* Although she said she was never depressed or sad, she described this devastation in a very solemn voice. It was clear that her nanny was a central parental introject that she lost as a result of her Holocaust experience. Her deep sense of mourning regarding the loss of her nanny demonstrates that, although she survived with her mother, the loss of her nanny who had cared for her in her early years, embodying a major maternal figure, was experienced as significant across her life trajectory. It was evident from her constant mentioning of her nanny that Miriam was deeply impacted by the loss of this important mother figure whom she missed for decades.

It is evident that not only was the scale of loss devastating in terms of leaving child survivors dislocated from those who would have assisted them to negotiate both ordinary and extraordinary life demands, but that the loss of anchoring relationships also left them struggling to retain continuity of identity. The kind of mirroring of self that children receive from caretakers and extended family was no longer available to them. These child survivors were uprooted from their communities and geographically dislocated, so continuity of identity was difficult to sustain and they were forced to adjust to cultural changes related to living in a new country and learning new languages. It is difficult to maintain a coherent sense of self after such trauma, loss, and relocation. Dasberg (2001) and Kellermann (2001/2009) describe how child survivors placated their new caretakers as a means of survival. Helene and Rina emphasized how they did their best to fit in and look *normal*. However, the cost to the development of a secure and coherent identity meant they were plagued by insecurity. Dave and Anne spoke of their struggle to adjust to their new communities. Dave became detached, and Anne said she felt like a *lost sheep*. As such, both were aware of the developmental disruption that was caused by their loss and trauma as well as the impact it had on their lives. Many references have been made to Dasberg's (2001) child survivor syndrome. He was specific about the fact that child survivors were deprived of a childhood because of the loss and trauma that they endured.

The testimony above points to how intense the traumatic loss of parent and family was and the way in which these losses had a significant impact on participants' childhood trajectory where they were forced to fend for themselves and also lost the sense of going-on—being tied to familiar people and environments.

Grief Exacerbated by Empathy for the Circumstances of Their Parents' Deaths

Rina (crying): *My father was a "Muselmann"* (weak and emaciated). *I was told he died in the mud!*

Owing to the empathic attachment between children and their parents, it is possible that children felt a deep sense of empathy for the suffering that their parents endured during the Holocaust and this was certainly evident in much of the interview data. It is possible that this was a retrospective process whereby greater empathy occurred with age and adult perspective.

Helene said that she had avoided thinking of how her parents suffered and died in Auschwitz and described how she repressed her associations to the likely circumstances of their deaths until the time of the interviews. *I have never cried the way I'm crying now. To think that my mother had to live in such horrible conditions, and my father who was a businessman was reduced to that. They were stripped of their dignity. That is unbearable . . .*

Rina's testimony also shows how, decades later, her parents' suffering and the circumstances of death hold unbearable pain: *My uncle told me that my father was beaten so badly at Buchenwald camp, that he could not work, he stopped eating and got weaker and weaker, and then he died in the mud!* In this instance, Rina was crying for the loss of her father and the loss of his dignity, as well as her own internal loss of a protective, parental introject. She carried terrible pain knowing that her protector had died in such a defeated way. As a result, she described her lack of closure and unresolved grief for her father who was remembered as a damaged object. With adult perspective came a renewed identification and understanding of her father's suffering.

In both the above cases, Helene and Rina wept about the loss of their parents who died brutally. Anne also described the way her mother's dead body was defiled when a Lithuanian policeman cut a finger off her body as he wanted her ring. In each instance, parents were internalized as damaged objects, which may have intensified their trauma and grief. It may be possible that internalizing dead parents in this way was so devastating that it caused a shattering of the self that led to either severe PTSD and depression, as in Anne and Dave, or the use of defenses such as compartmentalization and repression, as observed in the more resilient survivors, Helene and Rina.

Loss, Melancholia, and Problems with Subsequent Attachment

Dave: *I never really trusted anyone after the Holocaust. I would cry only in front of my dog "Shayna."*

The impact of the deaths previously described appeared in some cases to have led to melancholia as opposed to mourning as described by Freud (1935). For example, Anne described the way her mother was shot dead as she returned to attempt to protect her children from harm. She said, *It was terrible. Too terrible! Before I couldn't talk about it, I would just cry!* She spoke in a shrill tone, and it was evident that she continued to be horrified by the image of her dead and defiled mother. In this instance, her sense of horror (as discussed above) and catastrophic grief were indelibly entwined.

The concept of melancholia is used to describe Anne's deep despair and ongoing grief about the traumatic loss of her mother—in this case, a literal and symbolic loss as her mother's goodness, protectiveness, and capacity to protect her children was also denied Anne through her death and made very evident in Anne's subsequent experiences of danger and deprivation. Although she lost her mother in reality, it was evident that also on a parallel psychic level her good attachment figure was rendered impotent. Her internal container was shattered (Garland 1998). Her sense of the loss of a good internal object was palpable in her sadness. She spoke about the traumatic loss of her mother as if it was a recent event and described the subsequent shootings in the forest with fear in her voice. It seemed that she had internalized a "damaged and violated" good object, an object robbed of agency and the capacity to protect. She expressed that she still carried guilt as it was her mother's tenacity and commitment to her children that placed her in danger and cost her life. It was evident that Anne had internalized an identification with a damaged mother and that she in some way felt complicit in having produced this damage as it was her mother's attachment to her children that led her to be in a position of risk.

Menachem was also deeply depressed about the loss of his family decades later. He was particularly upset by the deaths of his brother and father who were murdered by the Nazis. Dave was preoccupied with the death of his father and the sixteen family members who perished at Auschwitz and spoke incessantly about the Holocaust. Given the way that Anne, Menachem, Isaac, and Dave were engulfed by grief and depression, it was as if a part of them had died too, as they seemed to struggle to reengage with life and they remained cathected to the dead objects that they had lost as described in cases of melancholia. This also led to difficulties in the capacity to attach libido to new relationships in the aftermath of the Holocaust.

After suffering from such extensive loss, it is easy to understand why forming new attachments was associated with the fear of further loss. Helene said: *It took me years to get over the feeling that my children didn't belong to me, because I carried the feeling that nothing belonged to me, too many things had been taken from me. I felt sad very often . . .* She added that the fear of loss held her back as she was afraid to attach and lose again. This dynamic affected her relationship with her first child who, in her own words, *bore the brunt* of her Holocaust experience. In addition, she struggled to believe that her husband loved her.

Helene described her lack of closure in the following way: *To be an orphan—no one can replace the love of a mother and a father. I hoped for years after the Holocaust that my parents would return.* This comment demonstrates how child survivors held onto the hope of their parents' return, thus complicating the grieving process as fantasies that their loved ones were still alive persisted. Helene said that looking back she feels that she is not compassionate and that as a consequence of losing so much she did not attach as strongly as she should have in her adult life. She thinks this perhaps limited her capacity for empathy. This may be linked to her capacity to risk mutual dependency and demonstrates the enduring impact of catastrophic loss on the capacity to form new attachments.

Rina said that she was aware that the traumatic loss of her father had made her overprotective of her children and she mentioned that she particularly struggled to bond with her female child. Although Dave did not have children, he reported that he struggled to attach to others after the Holocaust and preferred to be alone and only felt safe to cry with his dog. Isaac also struggled to form new attachments and complained that he fought continuously with his family, and Lenna complained that she struggled to express herself within her family relationships. This suggests that possibly the impact of traumatic loss may have led to difficulties in forming satisfying attachments after the Holocaust. It is possible that child survivors suffered from melancholia as there was no closure for the sense of loss and there was a difficulty in transferring libido from lost objects to new attachments. Their capacity for intimacy was cauterized in some way.

Most of the survivors said that they did not share the details of their trauma and loss with their spouses as they preferred to compartmentalize their painful emotion, further limiting their capacity for intimacy in interpersonal relationships. In addition, Rina, Lenna, Helene, Anne, and Isaac spoke about difficulties with their children indicating that their traumatic experiences may have compromised their capacity to parent effectively. Although the present research did not cover this topic in detail, a body of research literature has been written on second-generation Holocaust survivors and the difficulties that survivors faced in parenting their children born after the Holocaust (Klein 2012; Wardi 1992).

Depression as a Consequence of Catastrophic Loss

Anne: *My mother died—I did not have a childhood, I grew up with a cloud over my head.*

The research literature demonstrated that depression was a common long-term effect of Holocaust trauma. Within this research, Dave, Anne, Menachem, and Isaac suffered from depression. This was clearly a long-term mental health impact that included a sense of "deadness" and bleakness in their internal worlds—a sense of hopelessness that was a long-term outcome of their extensive loss and trauma. All these participants had been diagnosed with depression by a psychiatrist and were prescribed antidepressant medication.

Anne said that she continues to mourn her mother and sister who died when she was five years old:

> Tracey: *Do you think it had something to do with your depression now?*
>
> Anne: *I am sure!*
>
> Tracey: *In what way?*
>
> Anne: *Because of the way my mother died. She was coming to fetch us* (pause), *and that was the main reason. I loved my mother very much and growing up I did not have a childhood. I grew up with a cloud over my head.*

In this quote, it can be seen that Anne's depression and loss were related to the circumstances of her mother's death, as well as survivor guilt. She said that her depression started soon after she arrived in South Africa when she was fourteen years old. It seemed that her depression resulted from traumatic bereavement, which persisted across her lifespan and remained as a continuing vulnerability in her old age. Her description and use of the metaphor of a cloud to describe her depression gives the sense that her dark feelings and bleak outlook permeated her life.

It is significant how Isaac spoke about the loss of his father, stepmother, and half-brother. After the war, he was the sole survivor of his family. He was the only participant who did not express extreme sadness and mourning. Rather, he expressed a great sense of rage at his father's death and at not being able to say goodbye to his family. Indeed, his rage may have been a defense against his pain. He was clearly deeply depressed and his depression was expressed in an angry and agitated form. Garland (1998) describes this kind of response as a function of being so traumatized that a person may be stuck in the paranoid-schizoid position. Isaac used his anger as a defense against his vulnerability, and it is possible that the traumatic bereavement he endured contributed to his depression in old age.

It seemed that the traumatic grief experienced by child survivors left its mark by causing long-term problems with depression in some of them. Dave had a bleak outlook as a result of the trauma he had suffered. His depressive symptoms took the form of emotional blunting and a bleak perspective, he was fixated on the Holocaust and spoke about it constantly. This may be understood as a symptom of both depression and PTSD. For Menachem, life had a sense of meaninglessness—he was so overwhelmed by his losses and traumatic memories that he was chronically depressed and unable to focus on the present.

Catastrophic Grief and Traumatic Loss

Shlomo: *I am over eighty and I still miss them.*

Each participant mentioned the impact of the traumatic loss of parents and siblings in addition to the losses of extended family and community. Kellermann (2001/2009) noted the significance of this loss on multiple levels and underscored the fact that there was no closure for mourning. This was substantiated in the present research, where the scale and depth of loss was catastrophic. Typically, the term "traumatic bereavement/grief" is used to describe the loss of Holocaust survivors (Witztum and Malkinson 2009). In the trauma literature, traumatic bereavement is considered to be an applicable term when there is a single loss that occurs traumatically, for example, the violent and sudden death of a parent (Pynoos et al. 2007). Witztum and Malkinson (2009) suggest to use a lens of "traumatic grief" in understanding Holocaust survivors for whom trauma and loss coexist. However, it is proposed that the term "catastrophic grief" may be even more apt when describing the nature of the grief expressed by aged child Holocaust survivors. This is because child survivors endured multiple traumatic bereavements, over an extended period of time, in the context of severe ongoing trauma. Their continuing grief stemmed from these facts: who was lost; how many were lost; the circumstances of their dying; the degree of personal life threat associated with their passing; the helpless and dangerous circumstances within which they found themselves while trying to process loss; and the limited psychological tools they had available to make sense of experiences at the early developmental stages of their lives. In addition, there appeared to have been limited opportunities, if at all, to process loss even when in post-Holocaust environments. Their developmental trajectory was disrupted by catastrophic loss that occurred on multiple levels and remained present for decades after the Holocaust. There was an intensity to this dimension of participants' testimony that attested to the primacy of this early exposure to the death of significant others in shaping all subsequent development. Although other researchers have emphasized loss as a core dimension of Holocaust impact, it is argued that the elaboration of loss amongst the child survivors interviewed for this study represents an expansion of prior understandings. The burden of catastrophic grief was a defining theme in the life trajectories of participants, contributing to their sense of despair in this late developmental stage.

The description of "catastrophic grief" also links to the well-recognized catastrophic nature of the Holocaust. Significantly, in Hebrew the Holocaust is known as *Shoah*, which means "catastrophe." Indeed, the term "catastrophic grief" captures the extreme loss and trauma of child genocide survivors given that the losses they experienced were catastrophic in both their volume and intensity.

A critique of Herman's (1992) construct of complex traumatic stress is that, despite applying the construct to Holocaust survivors, she does not include any mention of the grief of those who have been subject to prolonged traumatization. Within the research literature, terrible grief has been described as a core element of their distress by almost all Holocaust survivors (Dasberg 2001; Durst 2003; Malkinson and Tur 2005; Witztum and Malkinson 2009), as well as genocide survivors in general (Gerson 2009). Within Herman's diagnostic model, it would be helpful to specify that unresolved grief and mourning may be a key or added dimension of CPTSD stemming from genocidal-type traumas. Herman (1992) does not cover the complexity of bereavement and loss in relation to genocide survivors. The formulation of CPTSD is helpful in understanding survival-related strategies of victims/survivors in enduring months or years of cruelty, in captivity. However, as a mental health formulation CPTSD does not do justice to capturing the loss and grief dimension of Holocaust trauma. The present research is suggesting that complex traumatic stress as applied to child genocide survivors should incorporate some formulation of alterations in the self-structure and symptom expression that occur as a result of the developmental disruption caused by unresolved bereavement.

It is a significant finding of this study that, while the participants had differing degrees of depression and PTSD symptoms, they all carried intense catastrophic grief regarding the loss of parents, siblings, families, friends, and communities as a result of the Holocaust. This combined with their CPTSD contributed to their experience of despair in old age, as will receive more attention later. At present this discussion will move to an important affective impact of the Holocaust, namely, anger in child survivors.

Anger and Rage

Herman (1992) discusses the experience of rage as a response to the devastation of trauma. Anger has also been reported in Holocaust survivors in their life subsequent to the Holocaust (Gampel 1998; Kestenberg 1984). Within the present study, rage and anger emerged as a major theme in many of the testimonies taken from participants.

Anger as a Response to Catastrophic Grief

Anne: *They killed my mother and my sister. Of course I am angry!*

Many of the participants in this study described their anger towards the Germans because of the loss of their families. Helen, Rina, Lenna, Anne, and Menachem mentioned specifically the rage they felt towards the Germans who had killed their parents and their siblings. It is possible that anger is a defense against catastrophic grief that enables the trauma survivor to feel less helpless and despairing. As children they felt angry about having lost a parent under such traumatic circumstances and it seems that this sense of outrage persisted in the long term.

Lenna expressed her unforgiving rage against the Germans who killed her whole family as follows: *I never buy anything German. People say, "Forgive and forget." To forgive, never. I don't care what the Germans do. I don't care how they try to make up for it. I don't care how many generations come after. A German is always a German, forever.* It is clear that, for Lenna, the loss of her family was so catastrophic that decades later it was still beyond forgiveness and reparation. Her rage was unremitting. Her furious tone conveyed that she refused to be talked out of her position, however unreasonable she knew it to be. Possibly, her position expressed her way of remaining faithful to those she has lost.

Both Menachem and Anne were deeply traumatized by the death of their younger siblings who were hunted down and murdered. Anne said, *The Lithuanians were all murderers, they took the Jews from their homes and took all their possessions. My mother and my sister were killed! Of course I carry a grudge. I don't like the Germans and am still angry.* This sentiment was echoed by Shlomo, who lost his parents and sister: *I don't trust the Germans, I hate them; all Jews hate them. I hate them for what they did to my family.* From these quotes it can be seen that these survivors were unable to let go of their anger because to do so would diminish the injustice of their loved ones' treatment and deaths, and they held on to their anger as a way of remaining loyal to them. In addition, the enduring anger expressed something of the enduring loss and suffering that they carried in their lives because of the irreplaceable loss of family members.

Menachem reported that he was particularly enraged that his nine-year-old brother was hunted by the Germans and reportedly tied up and shot. This was after a Polish man tipped them off about his whereabouts. He said that he remained enraged about this throughout his life: *I hate the Polish more than the Germans because, when the ghetto was liquidated, they stood in the street clapping their hands.*

Miriam's response was different. She said she was not angry towards the Germans and wanted to forgive them, but not forget. She said, *Feeling hatred is destructive, and it spoils one's life.* This was an interesting response because she frequently mentioned her anger at religious Jews and rabbis for not adequately commemorating the Holocaust and the loss of Jews, and she refused to buy German products, thereby displaying her anger towards Germans. Shlomo, Dave, and Menachem said that they were not really angry with the Germans but rather disappointed and angry with God who had allowed the Holocaust to happen.

It is interesting that some participants were angry with the perpetrators, while others held God accountable. Perhaps it is easier to hold the Germans responsible and protect God from ultimate responsibility (Juni 2005). Those who were angry with God, such as Dave, Shlomo, and Menachem, also seemed to have deeper levels of despair. It is possible that the ultimate disappointment and anger in God is a hopeless despairing position to hold.

Most of the survivors expressed their rage at the Germans, whom they held responsible for the murder of their parents, siblings, and extended families. From this perspective, anger is primarily linked to loss and grief, and what is notable is that, as with the sense of loss, the anger remained for decades. Although males had more revenge fantasies, women raged too, although they were less graphic in describing revenge fantasies.

Anger and a Wish for Revenge

Rina: *After the war I was happy they* [the Nazis] *were suffering!*

Anger and a wish for vengeance was expressed by Rina—she was able to explain her anger as a child and her wish for revenge. Rina was eight and a half years old when the Holocaust ended. She remembered driving through Berlin with her mother at the end of the war: *Berlin was devastated, there was hardly anything standing. This was the most beautiful sight I had ever seen, and I said to my mother, "Good! Now they are suffering!" I was happy they were suffering . . . after what we went through because we were Jews! I mean what crime had we committed?* This comment illustrates a young child's anger and wishes for revenge against the Germans. After the war she went to school in England at the age of nine. At this school, a fellow learner called her a "bloody Jew." She said,

> Rina: *I went mad. I pushed her although she was bigger than me; I pushed her head to the ground and banged her head on the stones. I would still be banging if they had not stopped me! I was expelled from the school.*

> Tracey: *I can hear that as a little girl you were angry.*

> Rina: *Sure, I was angry, you can't forgive what happened, if you forget it, they can do it again.*

This is a good example of how traumatized children lash out and struggle to self-regulate, as described by Cook et al. (2017) and Van der Kolk (2007). Her testimony adds a childhood perspective on primitive anger and revenge.

The participants' rage and wish for vengeance occurred in the context of genocide. Laub (1998) makes the point that genocide is resonant of the death instinct. The ongoing cycle of rage and homicidal revenge is understood within a cycle of violence where the death instinct prevails. It would seem from the present research that the themes of rage, retribution and killing in genocide, to some extent support Freud's (1920) idea of the death instinct, and Klein's (1935) concept of the paranoid-schizoid position. It was clear that the wish for vengeance persisted across the lifespan and the rage persisted into old age. While some participants blamed the Germans and others blamed God, anger itself emerged as a predominant theme in the testimony of aging survivors. The presence of anger in the testimony of so many participants suggests that rage is a permanent long-term effect of Holocaust traumatization in many child survivors, pointing to the presence of perhaps another dimension of CPTSD.

Forced Complicity and Rage

Isaac: *I was forced to do the hanging.*

Herman (1992) states that, when trauma survivors are put in a moral dilemma, or forced to do something that is morally questionable, the damage to the self is intensive. For those participants who had been compelled to become complicit in some way with their persecutors (in this study, exclusively male survivors) this tended to represent a profound aspect of their traumatization and subsequent life torment. This is illustrated in the following excerpt from the testimony given by Isaac about his experiences when he was fourteen. Although he appeared dispassionate in the telling, he subsequently told the me that he had never divulged this information to anyone. It seemed that he carried a level of guilt and shame and feared that he would be persecuted for what he had done and therefore chose to keep it a secret from both himself and others.

> Isaac (describing life in the Riga Ghetto): *If a person was caught stealing, they would be hung.*
>
> Tracey: *Did you see the hanging?*
>
> Isaac: *We did the hanging.*
>
> Tracey: *What do you mean?*
>
> Isaac: *You could put eight or ten people to be hung at the same time, and you put a rope around their neck, and they stood on a plank. They take us and give a signal, and we would pull the rope, and you pull the plank away, and these people hung. The aim was to break the neck. If the rope broke, the S.S. would come over and shoot the person in the neck.*
>
> Tracey: *How did you experience this?*
>
> Isaac: *It was just another part of life. I mean it wasn't the right thing to do, and you had to do it, or the Germans would kill you.*
>
> Tracey: *How did this affect you?*

Isaac: *The only way to deal with it is to hate the Germans.*

Tracey: *How many group executions were you forced to do?*

Isaac: *I must have done five, six, or seven.*

Tracey: *If you would have refused, would the Germans have shot you?*

Isaac: *Probably yes, but nobody would have thought to resist them. If that were the case, people would have resisted before they took us to the camps.*

It was striking that Isaac conveyed this significant aspect of his trauma in an apparently matter-of-fact way. He described the way he was forced to murder other Jews in a very dissociated, unemotional manner, with no obvious sense of regret. He appeared to have translated any distress he felt into feelings of intense anger. He explained that this trauma left him with a sense of impotent rage, which, as he later explained, affected every area of his life. In Kleinian terms, it could be argued that he felt paranoid and angry as a result of an attack by a bad internal object that would not forgive him for his own aggression exercised in the service of survival and that he needed to expel his feelings of guilt, even if these were largely unconscious. Possibly, his feelings of internal badness and shame compelled him to attack others. A clear rupture in his sense of self seemed to be evident in the way he devalued others and was unable to self-regulate his rage (Herman 1992). His pervasive feelings of paranoia manifested as an inability to trust in the goodwill of his loved ones. In addition, his sense of guilt, while not admitted, seemed likely as he had never told anyone about his actions, fearing their judgement. This increased his sense of isolation and paranoid-schizoid approach to his world.

Although Menachem was not forced to kill other Jews, he worked for the Judenrat, and he was also forced to work for a policeman who would kill Jews and steal their belongings. He said that this work left him feeling enraged that he was forced to be complicit in the killing of Jews. He, like Isaac, did not express guilt—just rage. It is possible that the shame of taking part in aggressive acts is so overwhelming that it is unbearable and the rage is a defense against the shame. Both men expressed themes suggesting ongoing helplessness in relation to their lives. It was possible that their extreme helplessness at being forced to be complicit in killings had long-term consequences as it challenged their sense of agency and mastery across the trajectory of their lives. Both men remained deeply depressed and angry and both had ongoing symptoms of severe PTSD, indicating that perhaps the forced complicity had severe long-term impacts. This is in line with what Greif (2005) found when he interviewed members of the *Sonderkommando* who were forced to prepare Jews for the gas chambers and were responsible for removing their belongings and disposing of dead bodies. Like the participants of the present research, those who were forced to be complicit in the Nazi death machine showed the severe impact of long-term PTSD and ongoing rage about their forced complicity.

Preoccupation with Revenge as a Result of Forced Complicity and/or Violent Attacks

Isaac in reference to the Nazis: *I could burn them!*

Although all the participants who expressed anger spoke of some feelings of revenge, this section will focus on the participants who were preoccupied with revenge as a result of their forced complicity or involvement in collecting dead bodies. For example, Isaac described his impotent rage after disclosing that he was forced to hang Jews in the ghetto. He described his anger towards the Germans: *I could put them all in a hall and burn them, and I wouldn't care! I could go out for lunch with you afterwards!* Isaac articulated his murderous fantasy that he wanted to be a perpetrator of mass murder and showed no sense of conscience or guilt. The fragmentation of his sense of self resulted in a rage that he unleashed against his wife, sons, and people around him. He admitted to me that he shouted out his anger. He said: *These experiences left their mark of anger and hatred that I will carry with me to the grave.*

Menachem said that for decades he had harbored revenge fantasies about the Germans who had murdered his younger brother and the Poles who had informed the Germans. In addition, he said that for decades he had wanted to kill the policeman who had forced him to help to collect the valuables.

The death instinct, introduced by Freud (1910) and underscored by Laub (1998) as important in the case of genocide, seems relevant here. Isaac was forced to murder other Jews and Menachem was forced to be complicit in helping a policeman to kill Jews and steal their valuables. Both carried shame and a homicidal rage against the Germans for several decades after the Holocaust. Neither expressed guilt as they explained that they were forced to do this. However, both carried a sense of shame and said that they did not disclose these experiences to others. Hass (1995) makes a point that survivors often cope with their sense of personal responsibility by focusing their rage on the Nazis. This may be true for Isaac and Menachem both, as they were trapped in their rage and shame, which led to an embittered worldview as described by Lifton (1967) and Auerhahn and Laub (1984).

Similarly, Dave expressed a wish for revenge. He appeared to be so psychologically damaged from anger and humiliation at being beaten up by the gypsies in the concentration camp and expressed homicidal rage:

> Tracey: *Do you think that as a result of all the humiliations you experienced left you angry after the war?*
>
> Dave: *Ya.*
>
> Tracey: *How did this anger present itself?*
>
> Dave: *If I am attacked, I am prepared to kill rather than relive the humiliation.*

Dave and Isaac's quotes express the homicidal face of rage that is a consequence of violence and humiliation. It is worth mentioning that Isaac, Dave, and Menachem all illustrate how victims of a genocide or Holocaust experience homicidal rage generated from utter impotence. They may have experienced their trauma as teenage boys, as an assault on their developing masculinity, and have harbored this rage for decades after the Holocaust. Impotent rage had led to homicidal rage in all three instances.

The testimony from Isaac, Dave, and Menachem showed a homicidal anger and a wish for vengeance. On a developmental level, during the Holocaust they were young adolescents who felt impotent in protecting their family from death. All three of these participants were involved in the coal face of death, Dave and Menachem in collecting dead bodies, and Isaac in the hangings of Jews. Their involvement in the Nazi killing machine made them prone to anger and also at risk for PTSD, a diagnosis they all shared. It is possible that their anger and wish for revenge in old age was some evidence of complex traumatic stress.

Although fantasies about avenging the wrong perpetrated were only evident in three participants, the feelings were sufficiently strong to comment upon as part of the trauma impact. Menachem and Isaac in particular were preoccupied with a need for revenge on the Nazi perpetrators—Dave was randomly looking for an opportunity to vent his rage. It is perhaps not unexpected that it was the three male participants who presented with this kind of ideation given gender socialization and expectations of men to counter aggression with aggression. Their revenge fantasies seemed to be associated with regaining potency through retribution, both on behalf of themselves and on behalf of other victims, including family members. It is possible that if there had been more men in the participant group, the theme would have emerged more strongly. Still, it should be noted that many of the women participants also carried anger and rage, even if this did not translate into revenge fantasies.

Menachem said that he still he wished he could take revenge on the Germans who hunted down and killed his younger brother. Isaac wished he could seek revenge on the Nazis by killing them. Dave wanted an opportunity to fight a nameless perpetrator. While all recognized that the original perpetrators might not be available for punishment, they nevertheless continued to entertain fantasies of exercising aggression in relation to them. It was noteworthy that these three participants had more intrusive PTSD symptoms, such as flashbacks and ruminative symptoms, than many of the others. It is possible that the males in this group had aggravated PTSD as they were involved in the collection of the dead and other tasks that involved contact with violated human bodies. Significantly, Shlomo—the only male in the present study who was not involved in the collection of dead bodies—had less PTSD symptoms and was not preoccupied with revenge. It is possible that Isaac, Menachem, and Dave had worse PTSD because they worked with dead bodies. They had a mature cognitive awareness of death, and in the face of loss and trauma with no parental support they developed full blown PTSD and depression. The need for revenge may be linked to impotent rage. Their preoccupation with revenge may also have been linked to their shame about forced participation in the Nazi killing machine, as discussed earlier. It is significant that their feelings of vengeance persisted for decades and were still present in their advanced years. This says something about the sense of rage and indignation that they endured, and the sense of outrage that did not appear to diminish with time and persisted across the life trajectory.

It is important to think about what it might mean for an adolescent boy, poised to experience his independence and potency as a young man, to be subjugated and terrorized and how the need to escape this kind of emasculation may have endured for many male child Holocaust survivors. In addition, witnessing the abusive use of aggression in the camps may also have left them with complicated feelings about their own aggression propensity, as discussed to some extent in the individual case analysis chapter. It is possible that part of male adolescent identity development includes the cultivation of physical strength, competence, and the capacity to protect, fight, and win. Their traumatic experiences undermined male development of physical capability. Instead, their adolescent experience was that of weakness, failure, and impotence. This is potentially what sowed the seeds of revenge as feelings of humiliation, impotence, and shame were experienced in a developmental phase of male adolescent development.

Having discussed anger and the preoccupation with revenge, this discussion will now move on to address the issue of guilt and survivor guilt.

Guilt and Survivor Guilt

Primo Levi (in Hass 1995) described the burden of survivor guilt and how survivors had a sense of shame and existential pain that they had survived in place of another. Hass (1995) indicated that survivor guilt usually waned with time. This finding was not supported in the present study where guilt and survivor guilt were strongly represented in several testimonies. Some distinction is made between guilt and survivor guilt.

Guilt about Surviving while Others Suffered or Perished

Helene: *I had people who rescued me. They had no one!*

Throughout Helene's testimony, it was clear that she considered herself fortunate and felt guilty that her parents had suffered terribly while she was protected and rescued.

> Helene: *When I think of my parents dying in Auschwitz I cannot come to terms with their suffering or their pain. What happened to them is much more unbearable than what happened to me. I had people who rescued me and loved me, but they had no one . . . they had to die and go through this terrible thing!*
>
> Tracey: *So, you feel fortunate when compared with your parents?*
>
> Helene: *Yes, look how they had to die, no one rescued them, and this is why I feel so bad for them, I still cannot bear to think of them in the showers being gassed, nor can I see them as walking emaciated skeletons* (sobbing).

It would seem that Helene tried to cope by repressing both her sense of the circumstances of her parents' deaths and her guilt for having been spared from their terrible fate. Klein (2012) states that survivor guilt is linked to loss; and, when person experiences guilt, it signals a beginning of mourning. In Helene's case, both were unbearable affects. In her early life she seems to have felt abandoned by her parents as she was sent away with no explanation. It is evident that feeling angry with her parents and then hearing how badly they suffered would have exacerbated her sense of guilt. From this vantage point, it is understandable that she would use a defense mechanism such as repression to avoid dealing with these unbearable feelings.

Survival in the camps was a complicated process, as everybody was fighting for his or her life. Dave tells the story of how guilt had a lasting impact on him: *The death march was the worst experience. It took two weeks, and you passed dead bodies or stepped over dead people who were shot, and had people executed in front of me! There was a comatose man next to me, he could not move so they warned him, but he didn't move, so they shot him! I looked at him straight in his face as he was shot, no muscle moved, no fear in his eyes was present. I wanted to scream, "Don't shoot him! don't kill him!"* But I was afraid I would get shot. Dave's description of this event implies his guilt surrounding not standing up to protect a fellow Jew and reflects his sense of shame regarding his lack of bravery. Herman (1992) describes the shame of putting one's survival ahead of one's fellow man. Dave's story is reminiscent of how Primo Levi (in Hass 1995) described the shame of survivor guilt, where he felt that he was cowardly in not standing up for a fellow human being as he feared for his own life.

The guilt of surviving while other family members died can become an ongoing, perseverating thought that is disturbing, as explained by Menachem who felt guilty about accepting a piece of bread from his sisters when they left for Majdanek concentration camp, where they died. He said he could not forgive himself for taking it: *They needed it more than I did.* He explained that he was tormented by this thought for decades, and he was left with a sense of guilt and shame. His sense of guilt and shame left him feeling bad that he had allowed his needs to take precedence over theirs and they may have suffered intense starvation before meeting their deaths. This ongoing kind of self-recriminatory rumination may cause a rupture in the self (Herman 1992) where the survivor has a sense of him- or herself as bad and shameful, which in Menachem and Dave's cases intensified their depression. Their guilt endured for decades.

Survivor guilt is different from normal guilt in that survivor guilt is more about the sense of surviving at the expense of the other or that it could equally have been you that died had circumstances been different. Survivor guilt has a specific trauma-related context and meaning.

The following example from Lenna demonstrates how extreme survivor guilt can cast a dark shadow on the potential to have a good life:

> Lenna: *I feel sadness and guilt. I had cousins my age, and they are gone, and you ask yourself, "Why me?"*

> Tracey: *Is that guilt you are speaking about the feeling of "Why me"?*

> Lenna: *Yah, there was ten months' difference between me and my younger brother, why did he go and not me? There are no answers for this; it's like hitting a brick wall. You think about the people you lost, who were close to you and vibrant who had the same right to life as you, they are gone . . .*

Lenna's words suggest that there was an arbitrariness to her survival that makes the existential question as to why some lived and some died unanswerable. The phrase "like hitting a brick wall" is a strong and brutal image and suggests the impenetrability of any meaning around this. Her feeling was that her younger brothers had the same right to life as she did. Their death may have left her feeling that she was not entitled to the life she did end up having, which may have translated into a sense that she was not entitled to pleasure and enjoyment. Somehow, to take one's longevity for granted would represent a denial of the circumstances that made this possible.

Survivor guilt is, in a sense, an ongoing reparative exercise towards those that might have survived instead of you should circumstances have been different. This dynamic is similar for Anne who explained that her mother had been murdered and lost a finger while coming to fetch her. Here we see a child's sense of responsibility and guilt that her mother died violently and this intense survivor guilt contributed to her depression. In some participants such as Lenna and Anne their sense of obligation to the dead "tainted" or "haunted" their whole subsequent life experience.

Humiliation, Shame, and Degradation

Herman (1992) and Wardi (1992) describe the way in which survivors were dehumanized in concentration camps. This was poignantly true for child survivors who were exposed to extreme deprivation, including cold, starvation, lice, dirt, and inhumane treatment, in the ghettos and concentration camps (Dasberg 2001; Wardi 1992). In the present study all child survivors described dehumanizing conditions and humiliating experiences that they endured in the camps and ghettos. In addition, there was a compounded trauma for the children who witnessed their parents suffering humiliation.

Personal Degradation and Humiliation

Dave: *When you come across a rat, you kill it—you don't ask how old it is.*

Personal degradation and humiliation included the deprivations of concentration camp life. This was reported by all the child survivors in this study—including Anne who lived in hiding in a barn and only spent a short amount of time in a camp. Miriam, Rina, Shlomo, Helene, Dave, Menachem, and Isaac, who were all in the concentration camps, spoke about the continual hunger, cold, lice infestation, and meaningless roll-calls. They all said that the extent of the hunger and cold was difficult to accurately explain as it was severe and hard for others to comprehend.

Dave reported that he experienced severe deprivation and illness while he was in both Ravensbruck men's camp and Sachsenhausen camp. He reported that due to the starvation he had suffered from stomach problems, specifically, chronic diarrhea—this symptom persists until the present day.

Dave described his experience of being dehumanized in the following way: *When I saw a guard beat up a nine-year-old boy, I realized that myself and the other Jews were regarded as subhuman, irrespective of our age. When you come across a snake or a rat you kill it; you don't stop to ask how old it is. We were surrounded by sadists; the guards, the gypsies, the barrack leaders, and the "Kapos." They were bent on inflicting pain and humiliation.* Herman (1992) explains how the survivor experiences a sense of shame from being powerless and at the mercy of another person. Here Dave describes what it feels like to be subhuman. As previously discussed by Herman (1992), the methods of dehumanizing people were part of the assault on the identity and dignity of the survivors where their humanity was denied.

Dave reported that the roll-calls were an opportunity for the Germans to count and see if anyone was missing. They were forced to stand outside in freezing temperatures below zero for hours from 3 a.m. in the morning. They were poorly clothed and starved: *We were fed two potatoes a day, and we were emaciated. To keep warm, we held the person in front of us as we slept. Often you woke up in the morning and you were holding a corpse. Sometimes, in the men's camp, the guard would throw the boiled potatoes on the floor and watch the starving boys and men grabbing food from the filthy floor. The man would watch with a smirk on his face.* Dave said that towards the end of the Holocaust he suffered from bad eye infections: *You woke up, and your eyes were glued shut from the puss, you couldn't see, and the puss dripped all over your face.* It is evident how this form of suffering and exposure to disgusting body material became commonplace.

Dave spoke at length about the way in which the Nazis controlled the bowel movements of camp inmates, and the humiliation associated with this. *Of course, diarrhea was a big problem, and you would get beaten for losing control of bowel movements by the guards, as well as the other prisoners.* He went on to elaborate how the physical deprivation contributed to the felt dehumanization and allowed the guards to see and treat prisoners as subhuman, something that was difficult to resist internalizing given the circumstances. *In the camps, you were starving, cold, dirty, and crawling with lice. You were a demoralized dehumanized person; they killed your spirit and then your body. Those who gave in to despair committed suicide or became walking zombies.* It emerged from the interview process that Dave was so disturbed by the humiliation he suffered that it affected his behavior on a long-term basis, indicating that he had both PTSD and complex traumatic stress. Dave spoke constantly about the Holocaust and lived a parallel existence as if he was still "there." He said that he was a vegetarian and was unable to think of eating an animal that had been killed. His disgust at the degradation that he and others were forced to experience and confront was palpable in his descriptions, and this seemed to have been one of the worst aspects of the Holocaust experience for him.

Miriam recalled that she was emaciated: *We were so cold and did not have proper clothes. I remember my hands were frozen; my skin itched from lice and eczema. We were starving and given a piece of bread a day. It's difficult to understand unless you were there. Until today I cannot throw away a piece of bread.* Miriam described the humiliation and dehumanization and how fear of starvation impacts her present consciousness. She focused primarily on the deprivation she suffered and the manner in which it rendered her and others vulnerable to disease. The torment of ongoing hunger was present in her consciousness across her life trajectory and her obsession with not wasting food continued into her old age.

Shlomo showed the researcher the number tattooed on his wrist, from Blechammer (subcamp of Auschwitz). The number was written clearly as 184738, several decades later. He said the number was like his name. When they called his number, he had to say "yes," demonstrating that he accepted his dehumanized role as it was in line with survival. In many respects, survivors got used to being treated as things rather than people and having all individuality stripped away from them. As mentioned previously, it was difficult not to internalize aspects of this dehumanization and "thing" status.

Concentration camp life in Bergen-Belsen was described by Isaac in the following way: *They put six of us in one bunk with one blanket, in winter. The blanket was full of lice. It was terrible, there was no fresh water, just a dam, and we used to drink the water. When the English came, they emptied the dam and found dead bodies. Probably the people who went to fetch the water were so weak they fell in it and drowned.* Isaac said that he and the other inmates were used to the smell of rotting bodies as it was part of their everyday life. Isaac explained further that, when the English found the dead bodies in the dam that they were drinking from, it became clear that even the water was infected, which is part of what had exacerbated the disease and illness in the camp. It was a cruel reality. Isaac indicates that something that was vital to survival was contaminated but that their level of desperation to stay alive meant that they drank from the only source available, one that they subsequently discovered to be terribly polluted and tainted. He said that there were no gas chambers at Bergen-Belsen, however, the poor sanitation and surplus of dead bodies caused a level of contamination and illness that killed thousands of people.

Rina described being publicly shamed and humiliated. The child survivors of the camps were exposed to both physical and psychological cruelty. All these experiences were absorbed and internalized to contribute to the child survivor's sense of a ruptured self. Rina described her humiliation when a Nazi officer, who thought she looked German, singled her out. This was because she had blonde hair and blue eyes and did not look typically Jewish. After examining her in front of thousands of people, he exclaimed, *She has Jewish ears!* She said that she felt publicly humiliated and ugly and it left a mark on her confidence. She said that as a young child she remembered posters in Holland *of Jews with big hooked noses and thick lips, grasping bags of money.* Rina said that this experience left her feeling humiliated as she was singled out in a potentially positive manner and then ridiculed in a prejudicial way. This experience of being publicly denigrated made her feel very unattractive and self-conscious. She said that until the present time she always covered her ears and was very self-conscious about them. She explained that she would never forget how the German officer shamed her in public. This testimony demonstrates how the child survivors internalized the cruelty that they experienced at the hands of the Nazis, and this had an impact on their developmentally fragile sense of self. They were made to feel worthless and inferior.

The experiences of humiliation described in the interviews is linked to what Herman (1992) described as severe dehumanization in captivity. The effect of such cruel and dehumanizing treatment on children and adolescents contributed to developmental disruptions such as the internalization of a fragile or denigrated sense of self (Herman 1992; Laub and Auerhahn 1998; Wardi 1992). The long-term effects of such traumatization can be seen by the way these experiences impacted personality formation as evidenced in compromised positive identity formation and lack of trust in others (Benyakar et al. 1989). The experience of shame as a result of being dehumanized was traumatic for child survivors. This could possibly support the contribution of humiliation in captivity to the development of complex traumatic stress where the personality structures of participants were altered as a result of the cruelty they experienced and witnessed. Their CPTSD included mood instability, depression, anger, loss of meaning, and a sense of despair, linked to the multiple abuses and cruelty they were compelled to suffer in the context of captivity.

As Klein (2012) said, children in the camps were betrayed by an adult world that aimed to humiliate, dehumanize, and finally destroy them. Being the object of hatred and persecution must have had an impact on their developing sense of self that was devastating, not only in some instances affecting their physiological development but also compelling them to take in negative images of their own and others' bodies and bodily functions. In many instances, this seemed to have resulted in splitting defenses to cope with the overwhelming shame, rage, and helplessness. Most of the survivors in the study were extremely well-groomed and appeared to pay particular attention to their appearance. This is perhaps an attempt at compensating for the broken and shamed sense of themselves in the camps where they were dirty and humiliated. H. Gordon (personal communication, February 1989) expressed this compensation in her description of Holocaust survivors wearing "silk bandages"—this was a symbolic attempt to restore the dignity to a damaged and humiliated sense of self.

Sexual Shaming of Child Survivors and Their Mothers

Miriam: *The Germans would then use sticks to check for lice in our pubic hair. They wanted to make fun of us.*

Chalmers (2015) describes how women were sexually humiliated during the Holocaust. This was also noted by Miriam, who was a young adolescent at the time. Miriam said that in the ghetto the Germans took a group of ten women and divided them into two groups. They made them run in rows, dropping soil.

> Miriam: *This was a meaningless task. We were starved and cold, and we had to run up and down. This was torture. The cruelty was in the way they frequently gathered us and counted us for hours, no matter how cold it was. Once a month we were taken for a bath. The Germans would then use sticks to check for lice in our pubic hair. They wanted to make fun of us.*

> Tracey: *Humiliation?*

> Miriam: *Yes, humiliation. I was thirteen, after a while I didn't care anymore. We were so relieved that they didn't kill us . . . I saw a play written by Primo Levi, I knew exactly what he was talking about. I was there, I knew every expression, every cold, every hunger!*

As a young adolescent heightened by a sense of self-consciousness, Miriam would feel humiliated by having her pubic hair prodded by the Germans. However, she described a sense of detachment. It seems that dissociation and detachment was helpful in the service of survival, as described in the research literature (Herman 1992; Laub and Auerhahn 1998; Wardi 1992).

Durst (1995) describes how it was particularly traumatic for child survivors to view their parents as shamed in front of their families. Indeed, there is a compounded trauma when children witness their parents being humiliated. This is described by Rina in the following testimony. Rina said that at Ravensbruck camp her mother and the women were stripped naked and forced to parade in front of the German officers:

> Rina: *My mother was very upset and embarrassed, I could see. She was a reserved person.*

> Tracey: *It was terrible for you to see your mother humiliated?*

> Rina: *Not only my mother but all the naked women—and their heads were shaved, and they were emaciated. You don't expect to see your mother naked. They took her wedding ring and looked all the women up and down to see if they were fit to work.*

Chalmers (2015) notes that this stripping and parading of women was a version of sexual abuse and shaming, that was inflicted on women in the concentration camps. This was mentioned both by Miriam, who was an adolescent child, and by Rina, who was a young latency-age child. Both carried their mothers' sense of shame and helplessness. This brings home what extreme levels of control captors had over their lives—including over their bodies—and that survivors had no rights to privacy of any kind.

Summary

From the above discussion, it is clear that the symptomatic and affective impacts of trauma continued to disturb and torment child survivors for decades. It seems that in the case of the traumatized child survivors interviewed in this study, catastrophic grief, anger and survivor guilt could be viewed as a "trauma trilogy." These affects seem intimately entwined for child survivors and appear central to the experience of the catastrophic loss experienced during the Holocaust. In some cases, survivors became trapped in their anger or survivor guilt as part of an avoidance of processing the pain of catastrophic grief. For example, it is possible that survivors like Dave and Menachem were stuck in their anger and Lenna and Anne were stuck in their survivor guilt as they struggled to process their underlying grief.

The "Trauma Trilogy"

We propose that the "trauma trilogy" experienced by the child survivors interviewed in this study captures the sense that catastrophic grief tended to be intertwined with aspects of survivor guilt and anger. When anger and survivor guilt were deconstructed, what lay beneath was catastrophic grief (Farber et al. 2021).

In the case of most participants, catastrophic grief was accompanied by guilt and/or anger with little hope of closure with respect to these disturbing affects and accompanying fantasies. In relation to guilt, participants were left with no opportunity to ask forgiveness or make reparation, and their survivor guilt was embedded not purely in the fact of their having lived in contrast to those they loved, but also in the kinds of self-recriminating memories described. Anger appeared to serve a protest function but also in some cases seemed to serve a function in keeping grief, pain and, guilt at bay. Participants appeared to experience this "trauma trilogy" set of affects as particularly weighty to have carried throughout their lives.

Helene, Rina, and Shlomo expressed their grief with themes of survivor guilt and anger emerging as secondary in their narratives. Helene, Lenna, Menachem, Anne, Dave, and Rina felt particularly tortured by their experiences of survivor guilt in relation to their parents and siblings. Most participants were aware of carrying feelings of anger and hostility toward those who had deliberately killed their family members and yet felt unable to discharge or target this anger productively. Although males had more revenge fantasies, the women also expressed rage, as is evident in the data. In the cases of Isaac and Menachem their preoccupation with revenge and impotence to actively punish those responsible left them "bitter and irascible" (Farber et al. 2021).

> It is noteworthy that when emotional states were opened up for exploration during the interviews the task of grappling with grief dominated experience, however it was evident that the presence of survivor guilt and anger in survivors complicated mourning and compromised mental wellbeing. It was also evident that when anger could not be translated into action in reality, it could be turned against the self, further compounding survivor guilt for not having avenged or redressed the wrongs done to loved ones (and oneself). What lay beneath survivor guilt and anger tended to be awareness of a rupture to participants' lives and to their intimate bonds that could never be fully comprehended and internalized and that could never be satisfactorily repaired or healed. This awareness of the impossibility of rewriting the past was particularly acute as the life trajectory of child survivors became more attenuated. (ibid.).

Summary of Mental Health Impacts

The participants in this study articulated the way in which their Holocaust experiences traumatized them and altered their lives forever. Their lives have been marked by unresolved grief, anger, and guilt, described by the "trauma trilogy." The experience of cruelty, degradation, humiliation, and extreme dependence on others for survival, together with a compromised sense of agency, emerged in some presentations that were resonant of CTSD. All these experiences and affects have contributed towards the development of PTSD and ongoing complex traumatic stress in several survivors, as well as a propensity towards clinical depression in many. Even for those survivors who appeared relatively resilient in relation to mental health impacts it was still evident that they suffered profound emotional impacts of a range of forms, as elaborated in this first broad set of themes.

Coping Capacity and Defensive Style

Tracey Farber and Gillian Eagle

Kellermann (2001) notes that the debate around the issue of child survivors regarding resilience versus vulnerability is ongoing. To not mention suffering is to betray the survivor, and to ignore any mastery they manifested would be to dismiss their bravery and resilience. Aging requires a retrospective perception of past experiences (Aarts and Op den Velde 2007). This posed a challenge to child survivors who have used a series of coping mechanisms, ranging from repression to splitting, as a means of coping with and blocking overwhelming trauma and loss. As explained by Laub and Auerhahn (1993) in their article, *Knowing and not Knowing*, psychological defenses protect the survivor from the experiences of overwhelming trauma.

The following discussion will elaborate on defense mechanisms used by survivors as evident in this study. As previously argued, the severe trauma caused ruptures in the self that mobilized psychological defenses to repress, split, or block memories associated with overwhelming loss and trauma (Dasberg 2001; Herman 1992; Wardi 1992). This had consequences for the successful integration in the aging process. As argued by Dasberg (2001), Holocaust survivors are at a disadvantage as their defenses block them from integrating all their experiences, depriving them of the capacity to view their lives retrospectively in a fully integrated manner. However, without defenses, they are likely to be overwhelmed with despair. This discussion will firstly look at defenses in more depth before elaborating on their impact on the survivors' capacity to integrate their life trajectories. It is evident that defensive styles carried both adaptive and maladaptive features and that they were strongly linked to the life history experiences of the participants.

Suppression

Helene: *I used to block out all thoughts of my parents' deaths.*

It was evident that many of the survivors had suppressed aspects of their experiences for extended periods. Klein (2012) and Dasberg (2001) speak about the suppression of grief and mourning. The grief of child survivors was overwhelming and in order to focus on survival their grief and associated memories were pushed out of conscious awareness. This was demonstrated by Helene:

> Helene: *I used to block out all pictures in my head of my parents in Auschwitz. I only started mourning them when my husband died. Even now I won't allow pictures of my parents as walking skeletons. I don't want to see them dead. I don't want to see them as people who had to suffer, it makes me angry, and it's unbearable to think about* (holding back the tears). *I have always had a wall around me, and I feel if it's penetrated, I am going to suffer. I think as I am getting older, I am allowing emotions to come to the surface. I think I only started grieving for my parents yesterday when we spoke* (she starts crying). *I only started grieving for my parents yesterday.*

> Tracey: *Do you think that it's because it was so difficult to think of them suffering that you didn't mourn them?*

> Helene: *I think so, for now, it's difficult; it's the most difficult thing I have been through in all my life* (crying). *I am not a sad person; I am always smiling, but my smile covers a lot; it's a mask I want to be seen as normal.*

This testimony demonstrates how Helene used suppression to block her grief out of consciousness for decades. She describes how the images associated with her parents suffering were unbearable and therefore blocking her visceral memories enabled her to cope with her life. Interestingly she said that as she was getting older it was becoming more bearable to engage with the painful memories—the interview process enabled her to begin to grapple with the grief she had kept at bay for decades. In addition, she described a normative mask that enabled her to "fit in" and hide her grief.

In the case of Rina, her mother covered her eyes during the camp years to protect her. In addition, she refused to give her information about their experiences in the camps in the years following the Holocaust. She was resolute in keeping Rina protected from the full implications of what had taken place in the camps. This encouraged Rina to also attempt to suppress her Holocaust experiences: *My mother always taught me to look on the bright side, and not look back, and to be positive. She discouraged me from talking about the Holocaust, and when I asked a question, she would say, "You are lucky that you don't remember, leave it like that"; and would not even discuss my father's death with me! Meanwhile, not that it was her fault, I had nightmares for thirty-five years! I wanted to look like everyone else and talk like everyone else. I never wanted anyone to know that I was a survivor.* With hindsight Rina was frustrated by her mother's unyielding protection of her as it gave her no closure and infantilized her on some level. Rina's mother's attempt to protect her daughter, even as an adult, by not talking about their experiences, also communicated to Rina that speaking about the Holocaust was shameful in itself.

Rina said: *as a teenager and young adult I didn't want anyone to think that I was different, and I avoided discussing the Holocaust. In 1955, I went to Israel, and when I saw so many survivors with numbers on their arms, I nearly died! And I never said a word, and never admitted that I was one of them.* Rina said that she enjoyed the fact that she had blonde hair and blue eyes and did not look Jewish. However, her unconscious mind did not cooperate with her attempt to repress her Holocaust experience, and despite her attempts at suppression and or repression she was tormented with severe nightmares for decades. Eventually, Rina was able to work through her experiences in psychotherapy and this allowed her both to recall more of her experiences and to recognize that her mother's censure stemmed from an impulse to protect her. Both Rina and Helene described how they suppressed their traumatic memories and presented a "happy" face to the world that enabled them to fit into their post-Holocaust environments.

Compulsion to Repeat the Trauma

Dave: *I would rather die than be humiliated again.*

Freud (1920) and Van der Kolk (2007) explain the concept of compulsion to repeat the trauma, which is highlighted in the following testimony. They argue that repetition may reflect attempts to establish retrospective mastery over events in which the traumatized individual previously lacked control.

At the time of the interview, Dave reported that he would walk around his residential area, after dark, with a gun to protect himself. In addition, he would walk around areas that he perceived to be crime ridden during the day. It was clear that Dave was setting up the possibility of an attack so that he would have the opportunity to fight back. He said that he would choose to die or kill rather than face humiliation again. Dave said that the night that he and his family were told to leave their home made him decide that he would never be victimized again. He said that after the Holocaust he took up shooting as a hobby and competed on an international level:

> Dave: *If it hadn't been for the war, I don't think I would have developed this need for shooting. I had been a victim and did not want to be a victim anymore.*

> Tracey: *I am thinking that during the war years you were developing an identity as a young man. During this time, you were attacked and humiliated, and after the war, you chose to become a fighter, do you think that gave you a sense of mastery?*

> Dave: *Yes, I am not afraid anymore. I used to be afraid. I am not a sadist I just wanted to protect myself. I would rather die than be humiliated again!*

Dave's compulsion to repeat the trauma was so powerful that he ignored both his logic and his wife's pleas to behave in a less risky manner. He was desperate to reclaim his dignity and his potency, no matter what the consequence. In his attempt to deal with his fear of humiliation, Dave was willing to court danger in the behavior described above. He continued in this behavior over a period of many years, illustrating how powerful this compensatory drive was. The repetition compulsion is evident in the fact that even when he has apparently gained mastery in getting a gun and learning to shoot, this does not feel enough—he has to seek out and master conditions of threat again and again.

Further more subtle examples of compulsion to repeat the trauma are evident perhaps in the accounts of Anne and Lenna who both complained about their experiences of being abused in their interpersonal relationships—Lenna said she felt she was trampled on and Anne experienced difficulties in her first marriage where she felt abused. While such experiences clearly did not replicate those of the camps in severity it is possible that both women unconsciously engaged in relationships that replicated elements of dominance and submission (as observed is characteristic in CPTSD) with the hope of achieving different kinds of outcomes. The fact that Anne was no longer married to her first husband may have been indicative of her capacity to extract herself from this problematic kind of relational dynamic

Compartmentalization

Miriam: *I put my feelings aside and focused on my work and my hobbies.*

Dasberg (2001) describes one of the common ways in which survivors manage their unbearable feelings. He called it "splitting," which refers to a splitting off of feelings and memories, or perhaps what others might refer to as compartmentalization, rather than the traditional Kleinian idea of splitting, which refers to attempts to keep good and bad aspects of self and other separated out (although there may be overlaps between Klein and Dasberg's usages of the term "splitting"). Compartmentalization is defined as a subconscious defense mechanism that underpins attempts to cope with conflicting feelings or cognitive dissonance (Leary and Tangney 2012). Krell (2019), a psychiatrist, described his own experiences as a child survivor during the Holocaust. In explaining resilience, he describes Holocaust survivors as having "developed the ability to compartmentalize their personal tragedies from daily life." He added that sometimes these effort fails (Krell in Brenner 2019, 43).

In our analysis, the term is understood to refer to a form of separating out of life experiences in such a way that Holocaust experiences coexist alongside a more functional present-oriented self, but remain largely locked out of awareness. However, these facets of history can readily be reintroduced into consciousness under specific circumstances, such as in this instance in response to the invitation to describe and talk about Holocaust-related experiences.

Lenna described highly successful functioning and resilient behavior. However, she used compartmentalization to block off her Holocaust experience, as focusing on it left her feeling traumatized and miserable:

> Lenna: *I avoid talking about the Holocaust because it brings up feelings I would rather not think about. I try to push it back. I don't know if I can talk about the camps. I try blocking it. There are things that come to my mind very often, and I push them away or try to do something or go somewhere to distract me, and sometimes I succeed, and sometimes I don't.*

> Tracey: *When you don't succeed, what happens?*

Lenna: *It goes around and round inside me, and I get more and more hurt.*

Lenna functions well externally but at times battles to block her Holocaust experiences and feels consistently upset when she thinks about them. Nevertheless, she has managed to largely successfully lock these associations away for much of her life. This is consistent with what Dasberg (2001) described as an inside/outside split where survivors look resilient on the outside, but experience suffering in their internal world. As Lenna mentioned, she struggled with survivor guilt and experienced anhedonia, despite functioning adaptively in her everyday life. This is consistent with what Cohen et al. (1998) described, where although many survivors functioned very well, at the same time they lived with a traumatized internal world that could be relatively quickly accessed under certain circumstances. As she ages Lenna finds that her survivor guilt remains intense and contributes to her sense of despair.

Lenna added that she avoided conflict in her close family relationships and never discussed her feelings with anyone, consequently her communication skills within relationships were very limited. Lenna blocked and avoided all feelings and reported that she was unable to communicate feeling in her interpersonal relationships. However, she functioned at a high level and was a successful business woman. Externally, in terms of occupational success she coped well, however internally she experienced a level of suffering that was too difficult to articulate (Dasberg 2001).

Shlomo described compartmentalization in a similar way that highlighted a parallel process of outward apparently adaptive functioning together with inward suffering. Shlomo was resilient and very successful in his external world. When he was interviewed, he spoke about his ongoing sense of catastrophic grief about his parents, and his deep disappointment in God. It was clear that he was secretive about the suffering in his internal world. It emerged that he had never discussed the details of this with his wife and family, despite claiming that he was very close and attached to them. With compartmentalization it is evident that inhibition of memories and states associated with personal Holocaust history is employed as much in the service of the individual as it is to protect those around them from the magnitude of their experiences. The damaged Holocaust-infused part of the self exists alongside the socially functional part of the self, but is as far as possible kept boxed up or compartmentalized away in some manner.

Miriam, Dave, and Rina survived with their mothers. Clearly, their mothers were deeply traumatized and, in some sense, must have been emotionally unavailable. They were preoccupied with their own sense of loss and grief, as well as having traumatic symptoms. Miriam said; *When we came to South Africa nobody asked about our experiences, nobody wanted to know. I put it aside. My mother also didn't talk about it.* Dave also said that his mother never asked him what he went through after they were separated and he was sent to the men's concentration camp at Ravensbruck. He and his mother did not discuss the Holocaust. Rina said her mother never discussed the Holocaust with her at all. These mothers did what they could to protect their children during the Holocaust and were so badly traumatized that they were unable to discuss or help their children to process their traumatic experiences. The mothers' silence may have reinforced their children's need to split off the trauma and focus on functioning. In Danieli's (1985) terms, their parents were role models to the conspiracy of silence.

Where compartmentalization differs from repression or suppression is in the fact that Holocaust-related associations and recollections can rapidly be brought into the foreground of conscious awareness, suggesting that they remain psychically active. At the invitation to share such experiences the participants were able to revisit or access these dimensions of personal history in vivid and affectively loaded form in the present. This form of presentation seems to resonate with that described by Dasberg (2001) when he employs the term splitting.

Emotional Detachment and Dissociation of Affect

Dave: *To cope you harden yourself.*

Emotional detachment is described as an avoidant symptom of PTSD and Herman (1992) explains how emotional detachment and dissociation enables the trauma survivor to survive unbearable pain. Dissociation in response to trauma exposure, as described in the literature is the splitting of thought from the feeling self (Herman 1992; Wardi 1992), causing a rupture in the self that leads to a deadening of feeling.

Isaac said he was very detached from compassion and did not feel sorry for people. When he read something terrible in the paper, he would think *Ag, tough luck.* Also, he said that he did not get upset about discussing the Holocaust. This suggested that his capacity for empathy had become muted. The ease with which he discussed his trauma, pointed to his use of dissociation, where he distanced himself from experiencing emotion. Dave said that in looking back he was aware of the way in which he had cut off his feelings in order to cope. Dave said that he saw grown men cry from cold and torture and was surrounded by people dying of hunger and disease.

> Dave: *In order to cope you hardened yourself . . . In the morning, I collected the corpses.*

> Tracey: *How did that feel?*

> Dave: *I felt nothing it didn't mean a thing to me, you know corpses leak, it's not a pretty sight, never worried me. It was like picking up a sack of potatoes.*

Here Dave described the way in which he split off any feelings of revulsion or empathy. He relied on being self-sufficient and emotionless, a narcissistic defense (Kohut 1976) that helped him to survive and cope with the horror he was forced to endure. He did, however, acknowledge that he suffered from PTSD and depression. He explained that the nature of his depression was of being emotionally blunted, as described in the literature (Herman 1992; Kellermann 2001; Wardi 1992).

It is noted that Miriam suffered terrible losses and ongoing terror in the camps, despite being with her mother. In the following quote, she shows how she split off her vulnerability in the service of coping. Like Dave, she used this defense in the service of survival:

> Miriam: *After you have been through the Holocaust, nothing else is significant. I am not sensitive and don't cry easily.*

> Tracey: *Are you saying that after you have been through that level of pain, whatever else happens in your life you take with a pinch of salt?*

> Miriam: *Exactly. I am very stable and can tolerate a lot of things without making a drama. Depression is not my scene.*

The last comment was said in a very derisory tone as if Miriam considered depression a sign of weakness or attention seeking behavior. The manner in which Miriam split off her pain and vulnerability were extreme, and she acknowledged no emotional vulnerability at all. She seemed to see her stoicism and lack of sensitivity as positive qualities and that she idealized the coping capacities of both herself and her mother. This omnipotent grandiose defense may have been a manic defense (Melanie Klein 1935) against her helplessness and terror.

The deadening of the self or one's emotional responses to life is also understood as part of a basic rupture in the self (Herman 1992; Laub 1998). As Greif (2005) described in his interviews with the *Sonderkommando*, those who were forced to work with dead bodies in the camps appear to have shut down emotionally. This was described by participants in this study as well as just illustrated in the material from the interview with Dave. Dave elaborated on his responses towards dead bodies, saying he felt: *nothing, it was as if a dead body was a sack of potatoes . . . that's not true; I was starving! I would have shown more interest in a sack of potatoes!*

Menachem was responsible for collecting dead bodies, including dead babies in his town and delivering them to the cemetery, as he worked for the Jewish Council. He said: *You get used to it; I have seen hundreds of dead bodies.* It is possible that Dave and Menachem used dissociation, like those used by member of the *Sonderkommando* (Greif 2005). Being forced to handle dead bodies was a risk factor for developing PTSD in both these men. However, both demonstrated emotional detachment as a way of coping.

The permanent damage of prolonged employment of dissociation was observed in the participants' testimonies. Their narratives described how they shut down emotionally to cope with the horror of enduring ongoing trauma during the Holocaust. This trauma was experienced in childhood or adolescence and seemed to lay down the pattern of dissociation in their developing adolescent identities. Their defenses endured over several decades and were apparent in the aging survivors who participated in the present study. The defenses enabled them to cope, however it seemed that shutting down emotionally may have had consequences for their capacity to experience a full range of both positive and negative emotions. In addition, the limited range of emotion may have had consequences for their capacity to attach deeply and share their inner worlds. As noted, most reported that they did not share their Holocaust experiences with their spouses or children. These examples illustrate the way in which defense mechanisms served to block traumatic memories and horrific experiences from the ghettos and concentration camps, as discussed by Laub and Auerhahn (1989), who were both child Holocaust survivors.

The splitting of thought and feeling, as in dissociation, was described by Menachem, Dave, Miriam, Shlomo, Lenna, Rina, and Isaac. Their testimony indicated that dissociation was used as a means of coping with the horror of the concentration camps. This was clearly demonstrated by the way they discussed horrific experiences in an emotionally disconnected manner.

It would seem that dissociation is a paradoxical defense mechanism. It blocks the pain of trauma and kills the capacity to feel, protecting the individual from overwhelming pain. The paradox is that dissociation enables functioning at the price of a fully feeling, emotionally integrated self.

Summary

There were both differences and similarities in styles of coping and forms of processing trauma. In comparing and contrasting the defensive styles used by the participants, it was clear that, for example, while Helene suppressed her bereavement, Anne was overwhelmed by grief during the interview process. However, it was evident that all the survivors had in some way blocked their catastrophic grief as a way of coping as there was no time and space for grief during the Holocaust because survival was the priority. In addition, adjustment and building a new life in the post-Holocaust period became the focus. The defense mechanisms were instrumental in helping survivors to cope both during and after the Holocaust (Herman 1992; Laub and Auerhahn 1998; Wardi 1992), but came at some cost to psychological functioning. This will receive further attention in clarifying the impact of trauma on the developmental stage of "integrity versus despair" in old age.

Indicators of Despair and Indicators of Resilience in Child Holocaust Survivors

Tracey Farber

The discussion will now look at Erikson's (1982) stage of "integrity versus despair" and focus on the long-term impact of the Holocaust trauma on the aging survivor. Firstly, indicators of despair will be discussed such as catastrophic grief, depression, anger, and survivor guilt. Then the discussion will look at the indicators of resilience such as mastery, hope, and meaning.

Indicators of Despair

The long-term impact of complex traumatic stress and catastrophic grief led to elements of despair in aging survivors. There is indeed an overlap of mental health impacts and the existentially mediated aspect of despair in old age. When looking at the child Holocaust survivors who are entering their final stage of aging, a developmental lens aims to connect the impact of the developmental disruption and link it to their functioning as aging survivors. Dasberg (2001) cautioned that now that child survivors were entering the stage of "integrity versus despair," there would be complicated consequences. He cautioned that their use of defenses such as repression and splitting, to cope with their loss and trauma, would compromise their capacity for ego-integration. This study proposes that not only is depression an indicator of despair (as argued by Erikson 1982), but that in addition in the case of child survivors' catastrophic grief and its nuances of anger and survivor guilt appeared to be further indicators of despair in old age. This discussion will now elaborate on the links between catastrophic grief and despair in aging child survivors.

Catastrophic Grief as an Indicator of Despair in Aging Survivors

Shlomo: *Until the age of eighty it's still difficult for me to go to a cemetery. No gravestones for my parents, nothing.*

A ubiquitous finding in the present research was that all the participants experienced catastrophic bereavement. Examples were given of how survivors carry a sense of continuous, catastrophic grief, several decades after the Holocaust. Although this phenomenon in Holocaust survivor experience was described in the literature review (Barak 2013; Dasberg 2001; Durst 1995; Malkinson and Tur 2005; Witztum and Malkinson 2009) the depth and breadth of traumatic bereavement in the present study was striking. Both the resilient and vulnerable survivors reported the experience of catastrophic bereavement. It was evident that the intensive interview process that underpinned the research enabled a deeper and more elaborate exploration of the gravity of catastrophic grief in the participants. While many of the survivors in this study were resilient and functioned well and would in all probability have had a low score on a depression scale, their grief and enduring mourning experiences were still a significant feature in their lives. The nature of a qualitative research interview seemed to allow ostensibly resilient survivors to let down their guard and express their unremitting sense of loss that has followed them for decades and left them with a sense of a lack of closure despite the passing of time and other compensatory life experiences. They were also revisiting their losses at the life stage of "integrity versus despair" (Erikson 1982), as is anticipated to be part of one's life task at this time of life.

In attempting to understand the place of catastrophic grief in relation to integrity and despair the experiences of the "clinical group" were instructive. Anne, Menachem, Isaac, and Dave were able to express how catastrophic bereavement interacted with their depression and PTSD symptoms. All these survivors highlighted the way in which catastrophic loss was implicated in and underpinned their depression and ultimately their sense of despair. It is possible that catastrophic bereavement is a critical feature in all child Holocaust survivors. This is because they faced multiple traumatic losses, including parents, siblings and their childhoods (Dasberg 1987/2001; Durst 1995/2003). This is a central issue in genocide survivors, because of the scale of losses sustained and the fact that the task of processing loss cannot be managed or prioritized when survival is of paramount importance (Gerson 2009). It is also evident that with a few exceptions there was an absence of caretaking or containing persons to assist in processing the loss. Even when present, those caretaking persons could not function fully as emotional containers due to their own trauma. Researchers and writers have highlighted PTSD and depression and argued about the resilience versus vulnerability of child survivors, however it would seem from the present research that all child survivors share the emotional wound that never heals, that of catastrophic grief (Barak 2013; Dasberg 2001; Durst 2002) that contributes to despair in old age.

Researchers in the Holocaust field have argued that a central task of aging is a retrospective view of one's life, one's achievements and one's losses (Aarts and Op den Velde 2007). As Holocaust survivors enter the stage of "integrity versus despair," their catastrophic grief and PTSD impacts their capacity to integrate their identities and leaves them vulnerable to despair. This was perhaps why Dasberg (2001) cautioned that this life stage could potentially be a struggle for child survivors. In old age, the extent of catastrophic grief may plunge survivors into deep levels of despair, although this may be mediated to some extent by the use of defense mechanisms to repress or compartmentalize ongoing grief. Nevertheless, it appeared that there was something about interviewing people at this particular life stage that brought to the fore just how raw, present and palpable their sense of loss and associated grief was. At this life stage child survivors were more physically vulnerable and some were frail—there was an awareness of the imminence of an approaching death. There was an awareness that their grief and loss would never leave them. Some may have hoped that they would be reunited with lost family or at the very least gain some closure by finding some relevant facts about their loved ones. At this stage they were having to come to terms with the permanence of the loss and give up any fantasies of recovery of the dead or even of information about the circumstances of their deaths in some instances. In addition, their defenses were somewhat compromised because of the losses and frailties associated with this life stage. Indeed, some survivors may have hoped that they would feel better or find some meaning and as old age advances, they know they will never find closure.

It is proposed that the "trauma trilogy" of child survivors linked catastrophic grief to anger and survivor guilt. In this section it is suggested that both anger and survival guilt are additional markers of despair in old age. This is argued because the experience of catastrophic grief and its impact on despair was expressed in a complex manner across participants in this study. The different expressions of loss, anger and survival guilt were pervasive and affected the present life of the aging survivor and as a result their lives in old age were marred by different nuances of despair.

In the depressed group Anne and Menachem were overwhelmed with sadness, whereas Dave was obsessed with Auschwitz and the morbid deaths of his family there. Amongst these three their conscious daily life was marred by the experiences they carried, leading to an overwhelming experience of depression and despair in old age. Helene and Rina, although largely highly functional, both expressed an overwhelming grief that they had compartmentalized for decades. They reported that it was only at this late stage that they were able to face some of the grief about the devastating losses they endured. Their sense of despair for the catastrophic grief they endured was expressed in the interview, which they appeared to relate to as something of a life review process.

Many of the participants made special mention of the unrelenting grief they experienced for their siblings that died in the Holocaust. For example, Shlomo, Lenna, Menachem, and Anne expressed the continual pain of this loss as well as that relating to their parents. At this stage of their lives, they were again deprived of the camaraderie of their siblings who did not have the opportunity to reach old age. In addition, this overwhelming sense of loss and mourning left child survivors feeling terribly alone and isolated, further contributing to their sense of despair.

Depression as an Indicator of Despair in Aging Survivors

Dave: *I am numb. I feel nothing.*

The incidence of depression in survivors is widely mentioned in the literature (Barak 2013; Barak et al. 2005; Dasberg 1987/2001; Durst 1995; Joffe 2003; Krell 1985). Kellermann, (2001/2009) describes the prevalence of both PTSD and chronic depression in Holocaust survivors. Within the present study, five participants voluntarily disclosed that they were depressed and four were apparently not depressed. The following vignettes describe the way in which depression was experienced by participants in this study:

Dave said that part of the *emotional damage* of the Holocaust was that he struggled to relate to people and often felt angry and depressed. He described his depression as an *emotional flatness. I often feel nothing. I read about the Holocaust all the time.* He said that his psychiatrist diagnosed him with depression and post-traumatic stress disorder and that he had been on antidepressant medication for the past thirty years. Although he was depressed it is possible that medication was not helpful in the usual way due to the complex nature of the depression and its association with catastrophic grief. He spoke incessantly about the Holocaust and was fixated on Auschwitz and the death of his father and sixteen members of his family there. Menachem said that he had been depressed since the end of the Holocaust. Two years ago, medication was prescribed, however, he discontinued treatment. He said that he was unable to stop thinking about the loss of his family during the Holocaust, and was continually sad, six decades later. Both Dave and Menachem's comments reflect the way in which catastrophic grief led to depression that continued into their seventh decade and contributed to a sense of despair.

Anne said that she continued to mourn her mother and sister who died when she was five years old:

> Tracey: *Do you think it had something to do with your depression now?*
>
> Anne: *I am sure!*

Anne said that her depression started soon after she arrived in South Africa when she was fourteen years old. Anne was deeply depressed. Her type of depression appears to have been similar to that described by Garland (1998) as severe melancholia, where in some respects she had identified with her dead mother and had "died" herself. As such she was consumed by her grief and engulfed by her sadness.

At the time of the interview Isaac was clearly suffering from an agitated depression, which he expressed through his unremitting irritability and rage. He said that his wife and sons had complained about his behavior to the family doctor, who had suggested antidepressants. Isaac said that that made him angry as there was *nothing wrong with him!* However, his capacity to self-regulate his rage was problematic.

All these survivors show extreme dimensions of depression as a result of catastrophic grief and continued to experience depression into their old age as described was common in aging adult survivors (Barak 2013; Barel et al. 2010; Dasberg 1987/2001; Joffe et al. 2003; Kellermann 2001; Wardi 1992).

Loneliness as an Indicator of Despair in Aging Survivors

The link between depression and loneliness was highlighted by a recent study O'Rourke et al. (2018) who compared the depression scores of two hundred and ninety-five randomly selected aging child Holocaust survivors to aging control group in both Israel and Canada. The Centre for Epidemiological Studies Depression Scale (Radloff 1977) was administered. Findings confirm that the early life trauma of the Holocaust affects elevated depressive symptoms in child survivors. Their scores for depressive affect and the absence of wellbeing were raised when compared to the control group. However, they had good coping skills despite their chronic sadness. Most significantly child Holocaust survivors experienced depression differently when compared to the control group—they reported higher levels of "loneliness" on the depressive affect scales administered (O'Rourke et al. 2018, 666). This finding suggests that loneliness may be a hallmark of depression in child survivors (O'Rourke et al. 2018). Indeed, trauma survivors can feel alone even in the company of others and this has been described as the "trajectory of loneliness" (Solomon, Bensimon, Grenne, Horesh, and Ein Dor 2015, 1) or interpersonal disconnection (Dohary 2010). This echoes what Herman (1992) describes as the way in which trauma disconnects the survivor from others. Solomon et al. (2015) suggest that loneliness is related to PTSD and is connected to what Lifton (1967) describes as the "death imprint," which is an experience that involves witnessing death on a massive scale that leaves a permanent impression on the survivor's consciousness. The survivor experiences the world as place of "failed empathy" (Laub and Auerhahn 1989) as a result of experiencing ongoing trauma and this may lead to a sense of existential alienation that may also extend to a spiritual alienation.

O'Rourke et al.'s (2018) research analyzed depression offering quantitative data that supports the findings of the present qualitative research. Firstly, higher depression scores were found in survivors compared to controls. However, these survivors were also resilient and seemed to manage their ongoing sadness, suggesting that perhaps they use compartmentalization to help them to function in spite of their ongoing sadness.

Secondly, the researchers emphasize the early loss sustained by the child survivors and the long-term effects of raised depression and loneliness. It is possible that this sense of loneliness and existential alienation may be related to catastrophic grief and a sense of ongoing mourning and melancholia. This was seen in Rina, Anne, and Lenna who remained attached to their dead parents and struggled to attach to their own children, and Miriam who said that she felt that no one who hadn't "been there" could understand her Holocaust experience.

Finally, raised depression levels and specifically loneliness can be understood as contributing to the experience of despair in both resilient and depressed survivors. Although they had compartmentalized their emotional pain, they made it clear that their present families and success did not compensate for their inner turmoil and mourning related to their losses in the Holocaust. Their emotional loneliness and interpersonal disconnection were demonstrated by the way in which they all struggled to share their early loss and trauma with their present families. Although none of them were alone, they were alone in their despair at carrying their trauma and grief, feeling disconnected from others. For some survivors, for example, Shlomo, Menachem, and Dave, this sense of existential loneliness also led to a sense of spiritual alienation where they also felt disconnected from God. This existential loneliness seemed to be an important theme in aging child survivors related to the trauma and catastrophic grief they experienced as a result of the Holocaust.

Anger as an Indicator of Despair in Aging Survivors

Anger was experienced as a result of catastrophic grief; however, the child survivors in this study varied in the way they expressed their anger and whom they blamed for the loss of family members. Most were angry with the Germans and some were angry with their religious leaders or God. Isaac carried a rage for the Germans, which pervaded his present experience, and he unleashed his anger at his family, whereas Miriam was angry at religious leaders for not acknowledging her losses and her anger was expressed more passive-aggressively. Shlomo was angry directly with God, which contributed to his overarching difficulty in finding spiritual comfort. It is possible that all these participants were using anger as a defense against their loss, grief, and helplessness. However, the pervasive experience of anger left an embittered perspective in their present life experience, namely, aging.

Survivor Guilt as an Indicator of Despair in Aging Survivors

The experience of survivor guilt can have an all-consuming impact in the present. Child survivors may remain preoccupied with guilt that leaves them with a sense of anhedonia, and as a result they may well struggle to fully enjoy aspects of current experience. For example, this was expressed by Lenna who said that she struggled to enjoy what she had achieved because she felt survivor guilt in relation to her brother who died in the Holocaust. Menachem was overwhelmed by survivor guilt in relation to his siblings, and this intensified his depression. In both cases the impact of survivor guilt held a sense of torment and blocked full life enjoyment as they felt they did not deserve pleasure that was felt in some manner to be at the expense of another. Their acknowledgment of the arbitrary nature of their own survival and the deaths of others served as a kind of ongoing memorial for the latter. Dave and Rina were both plagued with a sense of guilt regarding their fathers, which complicated their grieving experiences. In all these examples, guilt, especially survival guilt, left participants feeling a sense of obligation to the dead, resulting in a complicated sense of despair. In a sense, perhaps, reparation could never be completed.

Catastrophic grief that resulted in depression, anger, and survivor guilt colored the different aspects of despair described by child survivors in this study. Although some were depressed and others were largely resilient, the experience of catastrophic grief took all of them at times to deep levels of despair in old age. The "trauma trilogy" identified in child survivors—that of catastrophic grief, anger, and survivor guilt—was also recognized as indicators of despair in old age. The difference between those who were overwhelmed by despair and those who were not lay primarily in their differing capacity to compartmentalize.

This discussion will now focus on how the experience of catastrophic grief led to the rupture of the self and its impact on the experience of despair in old age.

Catastrophic Grief and the Rupture of the Self

Theorists and researchers (Benyakar et al. 1989; Cook et al. 2017; Herman 1992; Klein 2012; Laub and Auerhahn 1993; Van der Kolk 2007) explain that trauma ruptures the self with regard to a sense of cohesive identity, autonomy, mastery/agency, and the capacity to self-regulate. This applies to participants in this study in terms of the developmental disruption they endured and the manner in which this left its mark on their identities and personalities in old age.

Lack of a Cohesive Identity

The lack of a cohesive identity in child survivors appeared to stem from the traumatic disruption of their developmental identity during the Holocaust and the damage of a dehumanized identity that they internalized. The lack of self-cohesion was seen in the dual identity that they used to survive, an exterior functioning presentation that hid or belied their experience of internal trauma and grief, which they were reluctant to share and which set them apart from others. This was described by Dasberg (2001) as "splitting" and by Kellermann (2001/2009) as paradoxical integration in their sense of self, signaling that in fact the self was not well integrated in this respect. The present research confirms the way that many Holocaust survivors appear to have compartmentalized their trauma and maintained a level of adaptive or apparently non-damaged functioning throughout their lives.

The Survivor Identity

Participants in the present study expressed their identities as Holocaust survivors in different ways that reflected how their identities had been shaped by this aspect of their life history. For example, Dave and Miriam spent a large portion of their time speaking publicly about their Holocaust experiences. They both said that this was sometimes traumatic, and Dave said that sometimes his distress was triggered and he would cry. The constant engagement with Holocaust trauma and the identification with the Holocaust may have been their way of trying to gain some sort of mastery over the trauma. However, most of the other survivors said that they did not like to speak about their Holocaust experiences. Rina, Helene, and Anne said that they refused to speak publicly and preferred not to discuss it socially or with their families. At the opposite extreme of Dave and Miriam, Isaac and Menachem never spoke about their complicity with the Germans as they feared the consequences of such disclosure, and Lenna did not speak about the Holocaust at all. The participants in this study to a large extent did not like speaking about their Holocaust experiences and kept their loss and trauma compartmentalized, thereby holding a split identity or presenting paradoxical integration (Kellermann 2009). This incapacity to fully integrate their traumatic history compromised their ability to form a cohesive sense of self.

Autonomy

Many Holocaust survivors give the appearance of being autonomous; however, this may have been a defensive attempt to survive by being self-sufficient and self-reliant. Aging is fraught with a loss of autonomy and a sense of frailty. At the time of the interviews, most of the survivors were in reasonable health, with the exception of Anne, Menachem, and Isaac. They expressed their sense of struggle with being physically disabled as a result of aging. Dave expressed his fear of becoming dependent. Indeed, survivors survived because of their self-sufficiency and the loss of autonomy is a particularly difficult struggle for those who have had to place such importance on stoicism, stamina, and self-reliance in earlier life. In the case of Anne, Isaac, and Menachem, their experience of physical frailty contributed to their depression.

Autonomy was seen in the manner in which many survivors had attempted to cope alone and remain self-sufficient even within later intimate relationships. Both Rina and Helene said that they felt different in their post-Holocaust lives, so they did their best to fit in and tried not to attract attention to their difference, keeping aspects of their "true selves" hidden. Although they formed attachment in their post-Holocaust lives, they kept their traumas to themselves. Dave expressed this clearly in the following way:

> Dave: *When I went to the men's camp, I was fourteen and had to depend on myself, and I had to break the dependence of a child from his mother. From that time onwards I only depended on myself . . . and never depended on people.*

> Tracey: *So, you had to fend for yourself and detached yourself from people?*

> Dave: *Yes. There are still survivors who keep in touch, cling to each other for comfort. I walk alone I don't need anybody. I was alone in those men's camps. So, I had to look after myself in every possible way and could not depend on anybody, emotionally or otherwise, and have remained that way to this day. I don't have attachments besides my wife, and I was very attached to our small dog that was like our child. The only time I ever cried was in the presence of my dog.*

This quote indicates that Dave only felt he could trust his dog with his vulnerability. Even though he claimed to have a good marital relationship, he was unable to let down his guard with his wife.

It seems that, although many of the participants had successful long-term relationships, their capacity for emotional intimacy was limited. For example, Lenna, Rina, Dave, and Shlomo had "good marriages" in the context of which they still did not share with their spouses the severe trauma and loss they had experienced. They all expressed that their lack of trust in others and in God isolated them on a relational level. Internally, they compartmentalized their emotional trauma and appeared to need others to a lesser degree. Most of them were extremely autonomous and self-sufficient. It is possible that after such intense catastrophic loss they were no longer able to depend on others or fully invest in later relationships, including those with God or a spiritual being. The emphasis on a fairly rigid form of autonomy distorted their capacity to rely on others, which manifested in an exaggerated self-reliance. The sense of mistrust towards others and the need for self-reliance formed part of the survivor identity. This defensive style enabled survival but contributed to a sense of isolation and aloneness and compromised their ability to form close attachments to some extent.

Self-Regulation

In general, most of the survivors were emotionally constricted and used compartmentalization or suppression to cope with their overwhelming feelings. It is argued that this form of suppression was related to their attempt to regulate difficult and painful emotion. It was clear that Isaac struggled to regulate his rage, which he used as a defense against his vulnerability and shame. Anne and Menachem struggled to regulate their unremitting melancholia and were overwhelmed by constant sadness. In addition, PTSD symptoms broke through their attempts at self-regulation and overwhelmed their sense of coping and their ability to focus on the present. Flashbacks or triggers interfered with emotional regulation. In addition, a sense of despair caused by ongoing trauma and grief further compromised their capacity for emotional regulation, as many actively felt a deep sense of sadness, anger, and survivor guilt in their lives, continuing into their aging years.

Summary

A compromised ability to form a healthy sense of a cohesive identity, sense of autonomy, agency/mastery, and a capacity to self-regulate in old age impacted the task of "integrity versus despair." The present study to a large extent bears out Dasberg's (2001) concern that aging survivors would struggle to integrate their experiences in old age because of the way that they had "split" or compartmentalized their trauma. High levels of despair were found in both the resilient and the clinical group—the despair was related primarily to their ongoing catastrophic grief, which was also in some instances associated with unfulfilled fantasies of revenge and an inability to reconcile with survivor guilt.

This discussion will now focus on the impact of trauma on aging survivors at Erikson's stage of "integrity versus despair," regarding relationships with others and their relationship with God.

The Impact of Holocaust Trauma on Relationships with Others

Helene: *I was scared I would not be a good mother.*

The rupture of the self as a consequence of trauma will impact the survivor's ability to trust and attach (Herman 1992). The question of how their Holocaust trauma affected the survivors' attachments in old age will be addressed in this section.

Helene explained that the first time she got depressed after the Holocaust was in the hospital after the birth of her daughter, when she was nineteen years old: *When I looked at my baby, I could empathize with the pain my mother felt when she gave me to the authorities to save me. I was alone I didn't have my mother; I was scared of how I would bring her up, I was scared I wouldn't be a good mother. I had no support system; my aunt and uncle were far away. The nurses saw me cry for a few days. When I got home, I did not go into a heavy depression; I never cried in front of my husband. This child bore the brunt of my Holocaust experiences.* The sense of utter aloneness is described by this child survivor, who became a mother at nineteen years old. She had repressed her own catastrophic grief and she was faced with adult responsibilities without support. It seems that her confrontation with her own baby changed her repression of the grief she carried for her parents. She described how she was afraid to attach to and bond with her first child, for fear of further loss, although this experience seems to have given her access to the repressed grief she felt regarding her own deceased parents. She claimed not to be suffering from depression at the time of the interview; however, it was clear that she had suffered with depression in the past. She said that at the time of the interview she continued to struggle in her relationship with this daughter.

Shlomo was very attached to his family, however, it emerged that he had not shared his Holocaust trauma and grief with them. Dave had a good relationship with his wife, but he reported that he was very much a loner and had struggled to integrate socially after the Holocaust. Miriam did not acknowledge any difficulties in the area of relationships, which was in keeping with her dissociation and defense against vulnerability. Anne acknowledged that she never fitted in socially after the Holocaust and said she had a problematic relationship with her first husband. She also struggled with mothering to some extent, particularly with her daughter. Helene said she always questioned her lovability after being separated from her parents, and was always insecure in her relationship with her husband. She said that after her massive losses she struggled to allow herself to attach. This affected her bonding with her children and in particular with her eldest daughter. Lenna said she often felt used by her family members and struggled to articulate herself. She said that her children knew she was *mad*. Isaac struggled to trust his wife and said he could not control the way he screamed and shouted at his wife and sons. Rina said she struggled to get on with her only daughter and was an anxious and overprotective mother to her children.

The impact of the Holocaust on the second generation is widely acknowledged (Kellermann 2001; Klein 2012; Wardi 1992). Although not the topic of the present research, most of the survivors in this study were able to recognize and acknowledge the impact of their Holocaust experiences on their close attachment relationships. Their relationship with their children was complicated, with several survivors admitting that they struggled to form secure attachments. Perhaps they were avoiding the pain of potential loss and separation in the future. In addition, most survivors said they did not tell their children about their Holocaust experiences as they feared potentially contaminating their children with their traumatic experiences.

There is the sense that in most instances they formed relationships but kept some part of themselves secret or hidden and perhaps could never be fully vulnerable. It is possible that the extensive defense mechanisms they used also made it difficult for them to fully process their trauma and grief and therefore they were unable to share their Holocaust trauma within their intimate relationships. Many seem to have made one very significant exclusive attachment to a partner with a particular dependence or intensity—a sense of loyalty in acknowledgment that this person was able to live with them despite their damage. However, in spite of this apparent closeness, they were not generally able to fully share their Holocaust experience. Perhaps, it was easier for them to confide in a researcher as I was outside their family and a neutral person.

The Impact of Holocaust Trauma on the Relationship to God

Menachem: *Babies being thrown from the third floor of a building! So how could I believe in God at all?*

Several researchers have indicated that trauma disrupts the survivor's relationship with God (Greif 2005; Herman 1992; Juni 2015; Klein 2012; Lassley 2015; Lifton 1973; Wiesel 1974). In the present research, the following responses indicated how participants were dealing with their religious beliefs and their relationship to God. There was a continuum of responses. Some believed they were saved by a miracle while others believed that God had abandoned them and in the worst extreme some claimed that they became atheists as a result of their Holocaust experiences. It seemed that all participants had to grapple with reconciling a sense of a benign or compassionate God with the trauma that they endured. Their trauma in the Holocaust seemed to raise profound existential questions that became more prominent as they developed more advanced cognitive capacities as adults, which are likely to be very salient at the end-of-life stage.

> Shlomo (saying that he attended synagogue): *I don't really believe in God, because if he didn't prove himself at Auschwitz then how can I believe in him?*

> Tracey: *Do you feel God doesn't exist or that He let the Jews down?*

> Shlomo: *It's difficult to say, more that He let them down, but it isn't the only time He let them down; He let them down during the Crusades, the Russian pogroms, and the Spanish Inquisition.*

Shlomo said that he grew up in a religious home and was tormented by the question of why God performed miracles to save the Jewish people in Egypt, by the miracle of opening the Red Sea, yet did not save the Jews from the Holocaust. He said that he had tried to discuss it with rabbis; however, he found that they *ran away* from him and could not provide an answer. He said he did not challenge them, even though he had a lot of questions. In keeping with Juni's (2015) observations, Shlomo describes his deep disappointment in God. His religious upbringing may have exacerbated his sense of abandonment and betrayal. His expectation was that, if God could save the Jews in Egypt, He could save the Jews in the Holocaust. *I am sadder about God; it gets harder as I get older.* This quote shows that as survivors get older it becomes more apparent that there is no good explanation for the Holocaust—it was an experience of meaningless loss and suffering.

Helene said: *I am proud to be Jewish and being part of a people. I think I am ambivalent about God. I don't think God should be something you fear, rather something you love, but it's difficult for me to love. It's not easy . . . I loved my husband and children but I don't think there is anything in the world that is close to me.* Helene acknowledged that it was difficult for her to love God in the same way that it was difficult for her to make close attachments. This illustrates Juni's (2015) point about theistic object relations, wherein one's attachment to others is mirrored by one's attachment to God. Most significantly, Helene's capacity to attach was compromised by her experiences of catastrophic loss. Just as she felt unable to be close to her family members, she felt a distance and remoteness from God.

Dave said that the night before the war ended he prayed with *all his might.* After the Holocaust, he ceased to believe in God. He does not believe in the existence of God.

> Dave: *If there was a God why did the Holocaust happen in the first place? No, I don't believe. It's as simple as that.*
>
> Tracey: *But you said that you prayed on the last night of the war?*
>
> Dave: *After the war, I started to think and question how could there be a God and a Holocaust? The night before the war ended, I couldn't afford to think and question I needed that "man upstairs." Looking back now I ask what did I have for being a Jew? Two and a half years of concentration camps.*

Dave described the way in which he felt so angry, disappointed, and betrayed by God. He reacted by denying the existence of God. As mentioned in the literature review, the experience of a "failed empathy" (Benyakar et al. 1989, Garland 1998; Gerson 2009) in the case of Holocaust trauma has led to a rupture between the self and the other. In this case the "other" included God.

This extends to personal and spiritual relationships (Eagle 2013; Herman 1992; Laub and Auerhahn 1989). God was understood to have no empathy in allowing this suffering. At times Dave appeared to be angry with God and his claim of being an atheist appeared to be an act of defiance and revenge.

Despite his insistence on being an atheist, Dave told me about the song of the concentration camps, known as *Ani Ma'amin* ("I believe"), a song that Jews sang on the way to their deaths in the gas chambers of Auschwitz. It was introduced by a Hassidic Jew in Auschwitz, and soon it became known as the "hymn of the concentration camps." Dave sang the song beautifully during one of his interviews and subsequently wrote out the English translation for me, which reads: "I believe with perfect faith in the coming of the Messiah. And even if his arrival is delayed, I still believe." I wondered whether he was truly an atheist or a man disappointed and angry at God because He had allowed the Holocaust to happen. The song and the story express deep tragedy and heartbreak about Jews who hold onto their faith and hope in God in the face of death. Dave's comments appeared somewhat ironic and paradoxical in that he vehemently claimed to be an atheist and then gave a moving rendition of this song that is considered very holy as it professes one of the thirteen principles of the Jewish faith. I wondered about the loss of a theistic object, when a traumatized believer, such as Dave, moved from praying to being an atheist. Dave's comments mirrored what was said by Juni (2015) where he felt abandoned and betrayed by God. He was clearly ambivalent and continued to participate in Jewish rituals and had a good relationship with his rabbi despite his claim to be atheist.

Miriam said, *I believe I survived because my Catholic nanny prayed for me. I don't pray as such, and I don't know if I can relate to God. I never analyze it, never think of it. Must I condemn God or thank God? So, I never think about it ... I once told a rabbi that the Holocaust is not honored enough. He said it was the "kapora" (sacrifice) of the Jewish people. That really made me angry ... that my father died as a "kapora"! I feel the rabbis push the Holocaust aside. They should have a special day of mourning or a "Haggadah" about the Holocaust* (on Passover Jews read a *Haggadah* to commemorate the exodus from Egypt). *They think the destruction of the Temple is more important than this.* While Miriam expressed her ambivalence in relation to God, her comment reflects her rage at the lack of recognition of her own and her family's suffering. Her comments about the rabbis reflected her rage about the futility of her father's death and her feeling that the Holocaust does not receive enough special attention in the religious Jewish world. It was her catastrophe, and she felt that the Holocaust had been minimized and dismissed by religious Jews. It seemed that Miriam was angry with the religious community for not properly acknowledging the Holocaust trauma and for trying to positively reframe it in some way. It seemed that she felt more alienated by religious persons than by God per se. Miriam's theistic object relations reflected her sense of detachment from God. She appeared to acknowledge the existence of God but was disinclined to have a relationship with her God. This ambivalence appears to reflect her anger and disappointment. She was more able to engage her anger with the rabbis who she felt did not prioritize the Holocaust and its victims.

By contrast, Rina said: *I have no gripes with God at all and would never say, "Why did He allow this to happen?" God gave humanity a choice and humanity is responsible for what happened during the Holocaust. "Where was man?" is a very good answer! Although I believe in God, I am not religious. My mother used to say Psalm 23 every night, even in the camp, and I say it every night. I pray for my children and my health.*

It is possible that Rina recited Psalm 23 as a ritual to remember her now deceased mother and retain some connection with her. It appeared that Rina's view of God excluded any direct accountability and she placed the moral debt of the Holocaust at the door of the men and women who exercised choice. By placing the moral debt for the Holocaust at the door of humankind, Rina avoided feelings of ambivalence towards her God. She believed God gave humankind a sense of agency and they used this agency to do evil. The omnipotence of God did not feature in her understanding of why the Holocaust occurred.

Menachem was deeply troubled by spiritual issues regarding God. He said that he was not sure of the existence of God.

> Menachem: *In the beginning, I couldn't believe it! Never in my life have I seen such a thing! Babies being thrown from the third floor of a building! So how could I believe in God at all?*
>
> Tracey: *So, what did you believe?*
>
> Menachem: *I believe in God because I read the Bible a lot but I don't know if God really exists.*

Menachem struggled with a belief in a God and his knowledge that such a God could permit the suffering of babies. His comments demonstrate how catastrophic trauma shatters a sense of God's justice (Janoff-Bulman 1992) and ruptures the connection between the Holocaust survivor and his/her spiritual beliefs. As described by Juni (2015), this rupture exacerbated Menachem's sense of abandonment and confusion. He was left believing in a God but could not accept that this God could permit the Holocaust.

Anne, although significantly depressed, explained that she had a good relationship with God as he had saved her by a miracle. However, she said her brother became an atheist as a result of the trauma they went through. Anne said that she believed in God and sometimes prayed. She said that when they were in hiding her father said *Kaddish* (the Jewish prayer of mourning) for her mother and her sister. She said that, although she converted to Catholicism when she was eleven years old, *I remained Jewish in my heart.* It appears that Anne retained a belief in God and a sense of Jewish identity. However, she avoided the ambivalence associated with a belief in a God that allowed cruelty and suffering.

Isaac said he believed in God and that *the Holocaust was a punishment for the Jewish people, otherwise, how could something like that happen? Maybe they didn't keep the laws; there is a reason for everything.* He said he came from a religious home, accepted God's will, and never felt angry with God. *I believe God saved me in the Holocaust; he saved all of us.* At the time of the interview, he continued to be an active member of his synagogue and felt very connected to his rabbi. In Juni's (2015) terms, Isaac was rationalizing the Holocaust and justifying God's omnipotence. Isaac's religious beliefs precluded him from questioning his God's authority. Nevertheless, Isaac did demonstrate Juni's (2015) splitting in theistic beliefs when he claimed that his God saved him from the Holocaust but avoided the reality that his God did not save others.

The findings of this study largely confirm Juni's (2015) description of God as a paternal figure who had failed almost all the participants who believed in God prior to the Holocaust. The majority of the participants felt abandoned and at times betrayed by an omnipotent figure who did not intercede to save their beloved families. Each dealt with this perceived act of abandonment differently, some through a rejection of God, others through rage and disappointment, while yet others detached themselves from God. Most held contradictory or ambivalent positions in their view of God. Some became atheists and some retained faith by different means, for example by splitting human intention and agency from God. Others practiced religious rituals in a way that created a partial commitment, for example, by retaining some parts of their belief and rejecting others.

Indicators of Resilience and Integration

Although examples of integrity were given under the case history section, a number of common themes will be highlighted in the following section. The themes will cover generativity, resilience and meaning making as indicators of ego integrity.

Generativity as an Indicator of meaning

The following examples will describe how child survivors were able to attain a deep sense of satisfaction from being parents and grandparents. Rina said that having her four children was *the best thing I ever did*. This was the source of mastery and self-healing for her where she was able to give her children the secure kind of childhood that she missed. Having experienced a loving attachment to her parents, she felt she was able to attach to her children, albeit that she was overprotective towards them. She said she found it very rewarding to be a mother and appeared to have been able to make reparations to her own internal damaged child introject by offering her children a different experience to what she had. She felt her life was meaningful. Significantly, she compartmentalized her own Holocaust experience and did not share it with her children at all. As her mother protected her in the camps by covering her eyes, so it seemed that she protected her children from her Holocaust experience by "covering their ears" and keeping her trauma a secret.

Miriam, Rina, Anne, and Shlomo spoke at length about their pride regarding their children's academic achievements. Shlomo said that he was especially proud of his son who was well educated and financially successful. He told me that he had a secure marriage and loved his children and grandchildren. It is interesting that although his family had a vague idea about his story, he never shared his traumatic loss of his mother and other Holocaust traumas with them. Perhaps, like Rina and others, he was protecting them for fear of contaminating them with his trauma. Also, he tended to compartmentalize his trauma as to expose it would be too traumatic for him. It seemed that he had a sense of having been successful at achieving mastery over his trauma as well as having established meaningful relationships with his wife and children despite his Holocaust experience.

Miriam also mentioned her children and spoke at great length about them. She said that being a mother and knowing that she had produced four kind and responsible children was extremely gratifying for her. She said that two of her children refused to listen to her Holocaust experiences, while the other two were sympathetic towards her. Lenna, Anne, and Helene also mentioned their grandchildren with whom they shared close relationships. Isaac and Menachem were overwhelmed with despair, although both mentioned a glimmer of hope in their ongoing appreciation of their grandchildren. This indicated that their sense of generativity had been well established and provided a sense of meaning for them despite their apparent despair. Having lost their own families, they attached a special meaning to their children and grandchildren.

Generativity within the work sphere was mentioned by Shlomo and Lenna who had both built very successful businesses. Miriam and Anne both volunteered to show me the jewellery they had made during their working years before they retired. Dave and Miriam were deeply involved in Holocaust education and hoped to make the world a better place through this. Dasberg (2001) says that these memoirs serve as a memorial for their families and pre-war lives, as well as a heritage for their children. It was evident that the majority of the group felt they had been able to put into the world something of value that they could treasure or feel some sense of accomplishment in having produced it. This contributed to a sense of integrity as they looked back over their lives.

Mastery as an Indicator of Resilience

Resilience can be understood as part of ego integrity, as it refers to the capacity to adapt in a resourceful way. In accordance with the research literature, the roots of resilience in childhood are established to a large extent within emotional attachments (Cook et al. 2017; Durst 2003; Isserman 2013; Klein 2012; McFarlane and Van der Kolk 2007; Rutter 1985). This dovetails with what Erikson (1965) emphasizes as contributing to the establishment of trust and hope in infancy. As a result, resilience in old age can be understood to be the resourceful hopeful part of the child survivor. Within the present research, resilience endured across a lifetime and expressed itself as a sense of appreciation of survival in old age that parallels with what Erikson (1965) describes as ego integrity. Barel et al. (2010) describe resilient survivors as having a combination of good ability to adapt and effective defense mechanisms that moderated their PTSD symptoms, a pattern that seemed evident in the resilient group of participants.

In describing the way that survivors hid their vulnerability and presented a resourceful and dignified face to the world, H. Gordon (personal communication, February 1989) described Holocaust survivors as wearing "silk bandages." This referred to a physical presentation in such features as wearing of quality clothing and cultivating excellent grooming to achieve the appearance of dignity and respect and to cover their wounds. Indeed, survivors appeared to have largely hidden their vulnerability and did their best to build successful lives to compensate for the devastating trauma, loss, and indignity they suffered. The physical attributes of the participants in this study were not mentioned owing to confidentiality and anonymity. However, it was remarkable that most of the survivors took pride in their self-presentation, where great care and attention to detail was evident in their physical appearance. This seemed to echo the idea that survivors could be viewed as displaying a physical expression of the "silk bandages."

Resilience is another expression of the capacity to triumph over trauma and achieve a sense of mastery. The following discussion of participant material will demonstrate the expression of resilience by participants in this study.

Tracey: *Helene, what helped you survive?*

Helene: *Being loved by my parents I think it gave me strength to face life and not focus on the negatives.*

Tracey: *And you have not focused on negatives?*

Helene: *No, I just don't think it's helpful feeling sorry for oneself. I have never asked why it happened to me.*

Here Helene, who had never received therapy, had personal insight and credits her early attachments as the basis for building her resilience. This is substantiated by previous research (Cook et al. 2017; Isserman 2013; Paris 2000). Helene reported that she had never suffered from depression. She adjusted well in her post-Holocaust years and expressed an appreciation for her life despite the difficulties. In Erikson's (1982) terms, she seemed to have achieved a reasonable level of ego integration. Helene demonstrated a capacity to adapt in resourceful ways as she was functional, reared her children, had a job, made a home, and was a wife. Rina and Miriam also described how they survived the Holocaust because their mothers loved and protected them at all times. Both claimed that this was a major factor in building their resilience. Rina described herself as strong because she had survived cancer twice as an adult as well as two vehicle hijackings. She describes her coping skills in the following way: *I don't dwell on the past, I move forward. Whenever something unpleasant happens, I always think to myself: I have been through worse.*

In terms of the importance of early attachments in building personal resilience against life stressors, most of the participants in the study had at least one if not two positive attachment figures, as seen in the case histories. Shlomo, Helene, Rina, Dave, and Anne reported that they were very attached to their mothers, while Menachem was close to his father. Isaac and Lenna both lost a parent before the war, rendering them possibly somewhat less resilient. In the main, however, it was evident from the description of their marriages that most of the participants made good object choices in picking a spouse, except for Isaac and Anne who had both had difficult marriages. Klein (2012) emphasizes the "good enough" experience with an attachment figure before the war as a hallmark of resilience, critical in the survivor's ability to preserve a sense of self and a sense of renewal after the Holocaust. Barel et al. (2010) and Paris (2000) suggest that, although child survivors were very traumatized, the perpetrators were strangers, not their parents or people known to them. This allowed them to hold onto internalized good objects, thus preserving a sense of self (Klein 2012).

Interestingly, all the participants in this study for whom this was salient spoke extensively about the righteous gentiles who contributed to saving their lives during the Holocaust. Non-Jews who saved Jews put their lives at risk: they could be murdered with their families if they were caught. These gentiles offered islands of hope in humanity and served as an empathic other in the psychotic world of the Holocaust survivor (Davidson 1979; Klein 2012). For example, Miriam's creative work and hobbies seemed to have helped her to cope with her loss and trauma and, as was suggested previously, these activities may have been a way for her to connect with her nanny who was an internal object that could soothe her. It is possible that the righteous gentiles offered a sense of hope for child survivors that reinforced their resilience.

Both Rina and Dave attended psychotherapy and said that this experience helped them to cope with their Holocaust experiences and built their resilience. Rina went twice a week for psychotherapy for a period of six months, to deal with her Holocaust trauma and consequent nightmares, when she was in her thirties. She reported that, after telling her psychiatrist about her Holocaust experiences during the session, sometimes she would just sit and cry as he instructed her to go home and write down everything she had said. Rina reported that during the following session he would ask her to read what she had written. She reported that this process was helpful and the nightmares stopped. However, her nightmares returned when her grandchildren were born. She went back to her therapist who told her to start reading books about the Holocaust, as she had previously avoided anything to do with the Holocaust. She indicated that the content of the books upset her; however, her nightmares stopped. She continued: *My therapist said, "It's normal to wish that it didn't happen, you can't change what happened, you are who you are because of your experiences. You need to read books about the Holocaust when you are ready, so you know what happened and you know it didn't only happen to you."* Rina shared how her therapy experience helped her to work through her trauma. Dave said that his therapist helped him to understand that he was deeply traumatized by his experiences in the concentration camps and how this impacted his long-term experience of PTSD and depression. He said that his therapist helped him to process the horrors of what he experienced.

Shlomo gained a sense of mastery in the camps and he was able to use this experience after the Holocaust. As indicated previously, during his internment he was sent to assist a German engineer who taught him how to weld steel. He proudly told the me that he used this skill to build machine guns in the Israeli Army after the Holocaust, and he built machinery in his work in South Africa. Shlomo was very proud of the fact that he had succeeded financially after being a fifteen-year-old penniless survivor after the war. He told me that he did not receive financial repatriation from the Germans due to late registration. He said: *I tell you what! I managed without the Germans!* This comment clearly states his sense of mastery over his persecutors and his trauma. This resilient response underscores what Cyrulnik (2009) says regarding the protest aspect of resilience.

It seemed that resilience and attaining a sense of mastery was reinforcing for these survivors as they had a sense of accomplishment in spite of their suffering, which may have contributed to restoring a sense of self. This may have added to their sense of ego integration as they were able to view themselves as capable and their lives as meaningful despite great loss and suffering.

Finally, the capacity to play and be creative served as a hallmark of hope, as demonstrated by Rina. She said that in the camp at the age of seven and eight years she and the other children would play while their mothers went to work: *We used to imagine we were living in a castle, we drew in the mud with a stick, and we used to imagine things. My biggest dream was to imagine growing wings, and I would fly over the camp wall* (with tears in her eyes). It is possible that this ability to play creatively, despite being in a camp, provided evidence of hope and resilience that evolved over the course of people's life trajectories. I felt deeply moved by Rina's account as it emphasized how intrinsically deprived and traumatized children in the concentration camps were and yet that their capacity to play and dream was not destroyed. This was seen in all the survivors in the way in which they were able to invest in life despite their damaged histories and to have carried some sense of having overcome or transcended adversity. With the kind of hindsight and review that aging brings, participants were able to more deeply own the fact that they were indeed survivors.

Making Meaning of Suffering

The trauma literature as well as the literature on aging emphasize the importance of making meaning in order to be able to integrate and transcend life-changing experiences (Aarts and Op den Velde 2007; Frankl 1962; Herman 1992; Klein

2012). The following testimony described the manner in which participants found a sense of meaning in their trauma.

Lenna expressed her ongoing spiritual connection with her family:

> Lenna: *When I visit Auschwitz, I feel my family around me.*

> Tracey: *So, you believe that souls exist after death?*

> Lenna: *I do believe the soul continues living after death. I think people who went through the camps, we got to believe that, otherwise we would all go nuts. To imagine you lost everything that was dear to you, close to you, and there is nothing left of them.*

This comment shows that the hope of reunion with the deceased in the afterlife persists alongside the catastrophic loss endured across the lifespan.

Dave had devoted considerable effort to meaning making, despite having been diagnosed with both depression and PTSD. Dave said: *not all Germans were bad, some saved Jews. A German SS woman saved me . . . This same woman was responsible for the deaths of many women that she had beaten to death. In all of us, there is a devil and an angel, a good part and a bad part I know this because I saw it in myself. I was capable of looking after my younger friend in the camps and shared food with him and looked after him and was also responsible for cruelly beating up a Jewish boy who betrayed us to the guard. In certain conditions, I could become very hard and cruel, and in other conditions, I could just about save people's lives.* Here Dave attempts to reconcile the cruelty and kindness of the German guard who saved his life, in part by recognizing his own propensities towards aggression.

Dave appeared to have a deep level of wisdom from surviving this experience, as evidenced in his observation: *There is good and bad in every person, and certain circumstances will bring out one aspect or another. Everybody has a devil and an angel in them.* He felt it was a priority that he told his story, and he hoped that children would learn tolerance from his experience and make the world a better place. *My mission is to tell the story on behalf of six million.* I was struck by Dave's expression of appreciation of the kind of internal splits in personality. As observed by Melanie Klein, one can be both a *devil and an angel.* Dave's intuitive understanding of the split in himself and in others was both honest and deeply insightful. This acknowledgement of both good and evil is consistent with a depressive position stance.

Dave also struggled to grasp the reasons for the Holocaust: *It happened because of hatred. And because people were induced to hate, I don't believe that there* is a race, which is supremely bad. Which is what everybody after the war believed. "German monsters," they regarded us Jews as monsters, subhumans; which I knew was not the case. I also knew if there were such things as subhumans, the only ones who had conclusively proved that there were subhumans were the Germans because what they did was subhuman.

Shlomo said: For eighty percent of Germans, Hitler was God, and I hate them. But not all Germans were bad. There is good and bad in every nation; there were good Germans and bad Jews. He said that he gleaned no wisdom from the Holocaust. I just had to grow up and do what I needed to do. Here, Shlomo expresses his sense of meaningless in the catastrophe associated with the Holocaust. Given that he was one of the more resilient participants in the present study, it is interesting that he found no meaning in his suffering. Another interpretation would be that he thought finding meaning was futile. He focused on building and creating and this distracted him from his pain. His sense of meaning was to focus on mastery and build his business.

We see that both Dave and Shlomo were struggling to integrate contradictory aspects of human motivation and actions. They were in a position where they had seen the best and the worst of human behavior and they were able to entertain a non-categorial and somewhat ambivalent perspective towards the perpetrators.

Miriam expressed her sense of meaning in the following way:

> Miriam: The minute you hate; you want to harm another person. Hate caused the Holocaust! Hitler hated the Jews! My philosophy is that if you hate, it makes a misery of your life. If you hate it kills you, you can't live a normal life. The more that people know about the Holocaust, the better for the next generation.
>
> Tracey: What do you want the next generation to know?
>
> Miriam: Be cautious about man's evil.

Here, Miriam was describing that, for her, the Holocaust destroyed her sense of trust in the world, and she carried this wariness about the existence of evil in humankind into her old age. Her sense of meaning was to be prepared for the potential evil in the other and to attempt to quell hateful sentiments in the self. She recognized the destructive impact of human hatred and how it damaged both the individual and his/her projected enemy.

Anne says that the wisdom learned from her experiences is self-restraint with regards to aggression. This was an interesting response as Anne was involved in a difficult marriage for years and it is possible that her trauma ruptured her sense of identity, leaving her with a sense of herself as a victim. Perhaps she was unconsciously afraid of the rage she could unleash in response to her catastrophic loss of her mother and sister. It is possible that she repressed her rage as a result.

Miriam, Rina, Anne, and Shlomo spoke at length about their pride regarding their children's academic achievements. For all of them, this was a source not only of generativity but also of meaning. Lenna, Isaac, and Menachem also mentioned their children with pride. Dave and Miriam were deeply involved in Holocaust education and hoped to make the world a better place through this. Participating in such educational endeavors appeared to allow them to generate new meanings as they spoke and also to see that others could draw useful and important life lessons from their past suffering. This created a different layer of meaning for them.

Both Isaac and Menachem were unable to articulate any sense of meaning at all. Perhaps it is because the trauma of the Holocaust had caused such severe ruptures in their identities (Benyakar et al. 1989; Herman 1992). They were overwhelmed with despair; however, both mentioned a glimmer of hope in their ongoing appreciation of their grandchildren.

As an additional element of meaning-making survivors in this study were asked how they felt about having living under the Apartheid regime, given that this dispensation also contributed to enormous human suffering and was based on relations of oppression, dehumanization, and stripping of rights. All participants said that they empathized with the oppression of Black people. For example, Miriam said she felt very critical of how unfairly Black people were treated in South Africa. When she voiced her criticism to her matric teacher, she recalled that he had warned her: *If you talk like this and someone hears you, you will be arrested.*

> Miriam: *If you take it globally, there was a parallel between Apartheid and Nazi Germany but compared to what we went through there was no parallel.*

> Tracey: *Are you saying that the discrimination was a parallel, but when you look at the mass murder there was no parallel?*

> Miriam: *Of course. In South Africa, there were no gas chambers or crematoria. Mandela knew why he was going to prison. He risked*

his life for his people. The Jews did nothing against the German government.

It was evident that Miriam had been able to identify with apartheid victims but also felt that there were clear differences both in the nature of oppression suffered and the form of resistance to this. There is some recognition here of the universality of human suffering but also of historical and contextual distinctions. Since reflections on living under Apartheid did not emerge as a strong feature of participants' testimonies across the group, it is difficult to make any further general observations about the perceived relationship between Holocaust- and Apartheid-related abuses and consequences.

From the interviews it was evident that the survivors in this study were able to experience some sense of meaning-making. In the literature review, it was argued that survivors struggle/d to make meaning, owing to the catastrophic characteristics of the Holocaust and the fact that the cruelty and inhumanity of the events in the camps and beyond defied comprehension (Aarts and Op den Velde 2007). It is clear from the present study that most survivors were able to find and express some sense of meaning, as expressed by both Frankl (1962) and Klein (2012). It would appear that having a clinical diagnosis of depression and PTSD does not preclude survivors from making meaning. Klein (2012) said that some survivors were able to salvage a sense of self that was not destroyed by Holocaust trauma and perhaps the capacity to make meaning is some evidence of this. It is possible that some survivors (such as Menachem and Isaac) are totally shattered by their trauma, as described by Barak (2010) to the extent that they are unable to salvage any meaning at all, while others have some degree of resilience and are able to attempt to think about or reflect upon their Holocaust experiences in a way that produces some meaning, as mentioned by Valent (1998) and Hass (1995). Nevertheless, there was a wish in some to retain fidelity to experience and to preserve and convey memories rather than to distance from such. Several saw the legacy of their stories as a testimony for others in the hope that it would potentially prevent further suffering.

Resilience versus Vulnerability in Child Survivors

The loss of health and functioning in aging needs to be considered as an important factor when assessing the functioning of survivors, as suggested by Aarts and Op den Velde (2007).

Frailty plays a large role in aging. Anne and Menachem had serious difficulties with their health and mobility. This needs to be taken into account when looking at their general coping. Physical frailty is a risk factor for depression and PTSD in the aged (Aarts and Op den Velde 2007). This also has significance for survivors who have depended on their bodies to survive. For them, weakness, dependence, and vulnerability associated with old age are a severe threat to their identities as survivors. The loss of health and autonomy could be linked to the severe despair seen in Isaac, Menachem, and Anne. The other participants were in good physical health.

Despite being a community-selected sample, half of the group interviewed had received psychiatric intervention and were on medication. Dave and Menachem received antidepressant medication for depression and PTSD. Isaac said that his doctor had suggested antidepressants, but he refused to take them as he *didn't believe in it*. Anne had been prescribed antidepressants but was resistant to taking them. Rina had received psychotherapy for her ongoing nightmares. The relevance of this is that half the group were clinically representative of what Kellermann (2001) describes as suffering from both PTSD and depression. The other half were a generally high-functioning resilient group, as described by Valent (1998). The criticism of previous studies on survivors is that they focused on only clinical populations who presented for help, and the more resilient survivors were generally overlooked (Fishman 2014).

The self-selected volunteer community sample of this study seemed to represent both resilient survivors and those from a clinical population. Even though this was a small group of survivors, each one represented a type described in the literature. For example, Shlomo and Lenna could be described as very successful and resilient survivors, as described by Valent (1998). However, Lenna was so traumatized that she was unable to share her story, whereas Shlomo spoke of deep levels of despair despite his resilient functioning. Miriam, Helene, and Rina also fall into the resilient category as they lived lives where they coped and functioned well. As per Dasberg (2001), these survivors lived parallel lives where they appeared highly functional on the outside but, internally, they expressed intense suffering related to their Holocaust experiences, demonstrating an inside/outside split where they compartmentalized their trauma. Research showed that these kinds of survivors could appear and in fact operate in a highly functional manner at the same time as suffering from high levels of PTSD symptoms (Cohen et al. 2001). In contrast, Dave, Anne, Menachem, and Isaac represent the clinical group who suffered from diagnosable PTSD and depression, as also described was common amongst this population in the literature review (Elran-Barak, Barak, Lomranz, and Benyamini 2016; Kellermann 2001). Findings in the present research suggest that, although three survivors had diagnosed PTSD (Dave, Menachem, and Isaac), all survivors suffered from PTSD and complex traumatic symptoms. However, some were deeply depressed in such a way as to compromise daily functioning, while others were highly functional and resilient. Of those in the resilient group it appeared that they all carried deep levels of despair regarding the unresolved catastrophic grief that they had successfully compartmentalized. Indeed, it appeared that the capacity to successfully compartmentalize was the distinguishing feature when comparing vulnerable versus resilient survivors. Yehuda (2014) says that many resilient individuals have a capacity to "fight back against adversity" (5). She states that resilient people struggle every day with PTSD symptoms but don't give in to its negative consequences. It involves the decision to "keep moving forward" (Yehuda in Southwick et al. 2014, 3).

Integration versus Despair on a Continuum

When trying to conceptualize the variance of survivor resilience versus vulnerability in old age, it would seem that their negotiation of Erikson's (1982) stage of "integrity versus despair" falls on a continuum. The survivors who had some level of ego integrity also demonstrate areas in which despair was prominent. For example, both Helene and Rina were resilient and appreciative of their lives; however, both had pockets of deep despair and catastrophic grief regarding the loss of their parents and siblings. Shlomo, although very successful on the outside, was deeply despairing about the loss of his family and his disappointment in God. On the other hand, Dave, although diagnosed with depression and PTSD, was able to express some appreciation and meaning in his life. Despite the fact that there was significant despair in his world, there were also pockets of meaning and wisdom. Both Anne and Menachem were deeply depressed and despairing. However, Anne was able to express her gratitude about her happy second marriage, and Menachem was also able to acknowledge that his wife was a huge support in his life. Lenna, although very successful, expressed much inner despair. Yet, her pockets of hope were expressed in her wish to live in Israel. Isaac was raging, and deeply despairing about his life, but retained a small amount of hope in expressing his joy about his grandchild. From this perspective, pockets of hope were indicators of some ego integrity, as described by Erikson (1982).

From the understanding gleaned in this study, it would seem that Dasberg (2001) was correct in saying that survivors are faced with their defenses and struggle to face the pain of their past in the process of integrating their experiences of loss and trauma in old age. Two of the survivors in the study, Anne and Menachem, were deeply depressed and despairing. They had few defenses against their pain and were overwhelmed by it. Isaac coped with his overwhelming pain by being in a state of paranoia or rage; it seems that rage was his defense against his pain. The other survivors suppressed or compartmentalized their pain about the Holocaust. Dissociation, compartmentalization, and repression were identified as the defenses most often used. However, as just indicated, there were markers of wisdom and resilience, even in the most depressed survivors. Conversely, there were pockets of despair in the most functional and resilient survivors. "Integrity versus despair" is understood as a continuum, whereby there is an extreme at each polarity. It is potentially helpful to understand the position of child holocaust survivors as falling at different places on this continuum.

All the survivors in this study had some difficulty with the aging process as it brought into focus their catastrophic grief stemming from losses sustained during the Holocaust. This was in addition to the other affective impacts they carried discussed in previous sections of the discussion, as well as the complex traumatic stress symptoms that many of them had experienced for decades. Aging comes with the loss of youth, mobility, and health. Financial security and health are certainly protective factors against despair, as are psychological factors of resilience in relation to early attachment. Survivors have a sense of mastery that is lodged in their identities in which they needed to rely on their wits, physical stamina, and social supports to survive. It was difficult for survivors to lose the capacities that had previously contributed to their sense of mastery and survival. This was observed regarding Isaac's rage at his failing health, Anne's despair at her difficulty walking, and Menachem's despair at his worsening financial position. In Garland's (1989) terms, present losses and traumas echo early traumas, and the loss of mastery may feel unconsciously tantamount to the loss of survival for these child survivors.

Hope is a central affect in revival (Klein 2012) and aging (Erikson 1982). Each of the survivors in the study expressed some hope. For example, Lenna hoped to emigrate to Israel, Helene and Rina hoped to spend time with grandchildren, Dave hoped to educate more children about the Holocaust, and Isaac spoke of his hope of seeing his grandchild who lived overseas. Even in the most despairing survivors, the hope of attachment featured. Thus, reading off this population, Klein (2012) was correct in his emphasis that hope, agency, and attachment are central to survival. Erikson (1982) made the link between hope at different periods over a person's lifetime, beginning in establishing trust in infancy, to holding onto hope and wisdom in the closure of old age. It would seem that within the paradigm of "integrity versus despair," hope and hopelessness are on a continuum. This is especially apparent in the case of child survivors. All the survivors in this research expressed deep despair and hopelessness regarding their losses, no matter how well they functioned. However, for some this pain was more actively present and more pervasive than for others. As indicated earlier, it seemed that the capacity to compartmentalize unresolved or unresolvable grief was a mediating factor in how well they functioned.

McFarlane and Van der Kolk (2007) mention that trauma survivors feel betrayed by humankind and abandoned by God. Aarts and Op den Velde (2007) questioned whether Holocaust survivors were able to make meaning in view of their catastrophic grief and levels of severe traumatization. It was clear that resilience and the capacity to make meaning are not necessarily linked. As previously discussed, the capacity to be resilient is based on strong defense mechanisms that often block the capacity to feel. The capacity to make meaning varied in this study. Some of the most resilient participants said they were unable to make meaning of their suffering, yet their mastery was evident in their high level of functioning. Conversely, some of the depressed participants in the study were able to articulate a personal capacity to make meaning despite struggling to function or being impaired because of PTSD and related depression. In this respect it seemed that resilience was not necessarily a prerequisite for the capacity to make meaning. Rather, enduring suffering and wisdom gleaned from life itself was perhaps necessary to establish and create a sense of meaning.

5

Reflexivity and Countertransference

Tracey Farber

Reflexivity can be understood to constitute an exploration of the intersubjective space between the researcher and participants in particular kinds of research. From this perspective, the personal values and history of the researcher have an impact on the research (Berger 2015) that may be important to examine in reviewing the form that a research study takes. I shared a religious and cultural background with the survivors as I am both Jewish and Ashkenazi in lineage. In addition, I had two grandfathers who had lost close family in the Holocaust so I understood something of the impact of unresolved mourning and lack of closure. My immersion in the community and personal family loss in the Holocaust contributed towards insight into and empathy for the world and culture of the survivors. It is also likely that I was affected by the level of traumatic countertransference I experienced in conducting the study as I could in some way identify with the survivors.

In psychoanalytic thinking, countertransference may be employed as the related term used to describe the researcher's interpretation and analysis of the data, as well as his or her emotional reaction to the research participants, although it is recognized that the term "countertransference" is generally employed largely within the clinical consulting room (Parker 2005). In Long and Eagle's (2009) opinion, the clinically trained researcher needs to be aware of the transference and countertransference issues that may emerge in the process of data collection and analysis, as well as the possibility of projective identification, as part of the reflexivity process.

Laub (1992) worked both as a psychoanalyst of Holocaust survivors and also as the interviewer of Holocaust survivors for the Testimony Project at Yale. In his understanding, the role of analyst and the role of interviewer, while they have essential differences, are also very similar in impact and dynamics. In Laub's (1992) understanding there is a big emotional investment in the interview as there is harsh destructiveness, death, loss, and hopelessness that is revealed, that "there has to be an abundance of emotional holding and of emotional investment in the encounter, to keep alive the witnessing narration" (71). As part of the process, the listener is impacted by the trauma and faced with the existential questions raised by the Holocaust. Issues around death and the meaning of life are raised as well as around love, loss, helplessness, and our ultimate aloneness as human beings.

While conducting the study, not only during the interview process, but also particularly when transcribing the material, I became powerfully affected by the testimony such that I experienced what I understood to be vicarious traumatization (McCann and Perlman 1990). I had nightmares related to the content of peoples' stories and found myself disturbingly preoccupied with accounts and images. I experienced anxiety and sad mood at points, finding my own beliefs about humanity's capacity for destructiveness and care challenged. One of the concrete consequences of this vicarious traumatization is that the study project stalled for a period and it required considerable determination and working through the impact of the research process on my psyche for me to continue. While I had anticipated at the outset that conducting the study would prove emotionally taxing, I had no comprehension of quite how challenging the process would prove to be.

I am aware that I still carry projections of massive horror and that, albeit indirectly, I became a witness to man's inhumanity and capacity for evil. Hearing Menachem's account of the dead babies, Lenna's description of the screaming in Auschwitz, Shlomo's description of Jews chocking to death on the mud in a stampede in Blechammer concentration camp, and Miriam's description of the liquidation of the Dvinsk Ghetto was horrifying, and the imagery associated with these events is haunting. However, when I was with the participants, my professional identity and my defenses were in focus. I found the interviews deeply meaningful and was most grateful to the participants for their testimony. The struggle was in the writing up of the study. In keeping with Laub's (1992) description of the overwhelming nature of Holocaust material, I became paralyzed in the face of writing about overwhelming suffering. Indeed, the writing up of the testimony was more painful in some way than the interview process as I was silently alone with the testimony. The gravity of the loss and trauma was clear and palpable. Also, I did not have the distraction of needing to remain empathic and attentive to the participants and my defenses were lowered. Sometimes I would "forget" the horrors of the testimony and was reminded on my return to reading the material. The projections that I received in the interviewing process were reactivated in the process of transcribing and writing up the research. However, I was aware that I bore some responsibility to the participants to justify their participation in the project and this was one of the factors that assisted me in remaining motivated to complete the thesis.

As part of the ethical guidelines for conducting the project I was assisted with frequent supervision and trauma debriefing in the course of the present research, inputs that proved invaluable in helping me to continue to do this difficult, yet meaningful work. Thus, in many instances research supervision sessions with Cora Smith took the form of containment and debriefing rather than academic reflection and task orientation. This underscores the importance of trauma debriefing in the process of trauma research as countertransference experiences can be extremely difficult (Eagle 2013; Herman 1992; Laub 1992). I understood that I needed to receive many of the traumatic projections of both horror and catastrophic grief and to serve as a witness to the unbearable experiences of the survivors. Gerson (2009) emphasizes the importance of being a witness to the hopelessness of the Holocaust survivors, and that this interaction lessens the load of their aloneness in their suffering. In this regard I aimed as far as possible to retain the stance of being an empathic witness. The parallel process of having my own experiences witnessed by my supervisor was essential to give me an opportunity to process the trauma that I experienced from being a witness to the survivors.

Over time I came to more fully appreciate that, in the intersubjective space that the extended interviewing created, transference and countertransferential dynamics were colored with the experiences of Holocaust trauma. Most of the survivors developed a positive or in some instances even idealized transference in relation to me. This may have been related to their attempts to reintroject a good enough container into their internal worlds (Eagle 2013). In speaking about their life trajectory before, during, and after the Holocaust, the participants were offered the space to integrate and evaluate their pre-Holocaust, Holocaust, and post-liberation experiences. The extended interviews offered participants the opportunity to express their trauma and grief, an opportunity for catharsis, and in that way the interviewing process may have had an unintended therapeutic function. The research process appeared to have a containing and interpretive function (Eagle and Long 2009). This may have enabled the survivors to integrate some of their traumatic experiences. Long and Eagle (2009) observe that at times, participants may consciously or unconsciously use research interviews as therapeutic opportunities. In the present study, for example, Menachem spoke of the horrors he saw, and Isaac confessed to being forced to hang other Jews in the ghettos—in this way they were able to share with me the shameful secrets that they had carried alone for decades. The anonymity of the research and the neutrality of the researcher as a significant person in their lives facilitated this process. In addition, both Helene and Rina cried about the loss of their parents in a manner that seemed intense and to some extent cathartic for them, again appearing to use the presence and containment of the research process in a therapeutic manner.

Most of the participants expressed their gratitude to me for having the opportunity to unburden themselves during the research process. It is possible that survivors in the present study felt contained because their testimony was heard by an empathic witness and also because I asked detailed questions about their lives in a more comprehensive manner, trying to build up a picture of them as people who had histories prior to and after their time in the camps. As part of the interview process, I asked participants about their early attachments and attachment figures before the Holocaust. This description led to reminiscing, which may have put them in touch with early good objects and may have added to their gratitude and their sense that they benefited from the interviews. This substantiates what Auerhahn and Laub (2018) describe as a critical process whereby Holocaust survivors are able to think about pre-Holocaust love objects so that they can remember and reexperience themselves as "someone who can be loved" (61). This view was also echoed by Durst (2005) who said that when working therapeutically with survivors it is important to get them to remember the love that they received from significant others before the Holocaust, allowing for some integration of good and bad experiences (in conversation, May 2010).

Although the transference-related dynamics that appeared evident during the interview process were dominantly positive there were also some exceptions to this. Some negative transference appeared with Miriam, who told me in an aggressive tone that I would *never understand what it feels like to be a Holocaust survivor.* My response was to say, *You are correct I can never understand.* In this way I sought to acknowledge her anger and her sense of isolation in carrying the enormity of her trauma. Miriam was enraged and indignant that her trauma had separated her from others. I used my clinical skills in the service of containing the projections and projective identifications of the participants (Long and Eagle 2009) where necessary or apparently helpful, as in this instance with Miriam.

However, I was as mindful as possible not to overstep the boundaries between researcher and therapist, even when pulled to do so on occasion. For example, Shlomo phoned me on three occasions imploring me to write a book about him and his experiences. He was aware that he would soon die and feared he would be forgotten and his life be rendered meaningless. It was very difficult to resist this kind of pressure and to be reassuring but not to respond to his heartfelt request. Again, research supervision was helpful in this regard and it was immensely helpful when we thought collectively about some of these unanticipated ethical dimensions of the study and the level of personal relationship that many participants experienced and sought to continue in some way. My training as a psychodynamic therapist helped me to keep the boundaries and helped me to address my countertransference experience. Finally, years after his death we are able to grant Shlomo his wish and include his story in our book.

Laub (1992) states that at their core survivors are deeply wounded: "a fragility, a woundedness that defies all healing" (Laub 1992, 73). For Feldman and Laub (1992) the act of giving testimony is a process of facing loss and mourning. "It is the realisation that lost ones are not coming back" (92) and in listening to testimony the listener becomes a witness to the grief of the survivor (Feldman and Laub 1992). This happened for me with the research participants. For example, when listening to Helene sob inconsolably for hours, I became a witness to raw grief. This also happened to a lesser extent with Rina, who briefly cried when she spoke about her father. There was a sense of maternal reverie as mentioned by Eagle (2013) is sometimes important in trauma work, where I felt that I was listening to the cries of the children within the aging survivors. This crying was an acknowledgement that the grief had endured for decades and that parental loss had always remained a significant aspect of life experience. Although Shlomo did not cry, his sadness about his parents was palpable, and he eloquently expressed his longing for his *Yiddisher Mamma*. I felt his deep sadness. There were many other examples of being witness to intense grief, horror and torment across the interviews of having to bear the feeling states that were evidenced by participants as a form of respect for what they had endured and what they were willing to share with me. In addition to tolerating the affective impact of the interview process and subsequent data transcription, I was also aware of my own meaning systems becoming challenged through the process.

Laub (1992) states that working with survivors raises issues about life, death, and meaning. I was distressed by the existential sadness associated with the spiritual disconnection and disappointment in God, as expressed by Menachem, Shlomo, and Isaac. The spiritual rupture that can be caused by trauma was mentioned by Herman (1992); frequently this kind of experience is also accompanied by a great sense of loss of faith in a benevolent God (Juni 2005). This dynamic worsened the sense of loss and loneliness expressed by the survivors and was deeply sad to witness. The necessity of supervision is underscored for researchers who bear witness to traumatic testimonies as it becomes difficult to navigate the existential questions related to profound human cruelty and suffering, especially in cases of intentional human-inflicted trauma.

When confronted by man's capacity for evil, I became aware of the importance of the death instinct, as described by Freud (1920) and echoed by Laub (1992). For Laub (1992), Freud's understanding of Thanatos is well documented. When I allowed myself to comprehend the horror and death in genocides, and the fact that these continue to occur, I have become more open to the idea that humankind holds destructive, aggressive and breaking down potentialities as linked to the death instinct. Despite this, I also have a renewed appreciation for the role of hope and the capacity for growth and meaning and the importance of human connection (Frankl 1962; Klein 2012). I felt a deep gratitude to have witnessed the paradox of both despair and hope in hearing survivors' accounts of their own existential struggles.

My research trajectory and the final writing of this document was both enormously demanding and enormously meaningful. Despite the difficulty, I felt very privileged to have interviewed the child survivors and very grateful for the way in which they confided in me. My meaning structure gave me a new hope in the concept of attachment and its importance in resilience. Finally, I realized what Eagle (2013) meant when she said that the trauma therapist has to hold onto their own good objects for dear life in the face of the horror and trauma. I found that I had a renewed appreciation for my own good objects and a revival of understanding of hope and attachment. I had a definite sense of the importance of being an empathic listener and its critical aim of offering trauma survivors an experience of being heard, as described by Laub (1992/2005). Empathy and feeling heard may on some level lessen survivors' hopelessness and despair. My experience in this research is that pain and grief, no matter how catastrophic, needs to be witnessed as this is therapeutic in some manner. The process of completing this research honed my skills as a therapist as I became more adept at hearing themes presented in the narrative of my clients. In addition, I had a renewed understanding and appreciation of the therapist's role as a witness. Krell (2013) explains from his perspective as both a child survivor and a psychiatrist: "No survivor truly expects to be understood. Our need is to be heard" (7). He continues that after all the development and sophistication of psychotherapy—"it all still comes down to the wounded teller and the healing listener" (Krell 2013, 7). Gerson (2009) quotes a patient who said, "I would be entirely hopeless, if I couldn't be truly hopeless with you" (1354). In other words, the empathic listener offers some capacity for reparation, in the world of the trauma survivor, whose trust in the world has been ruptured leading to a sense of existential loneliness and despair.

Looking back retrospectively, the research had taught me the power of being a witness. In the therapeutic process basic empathy builds a bridge between therapist and client and lessens the existential isolation of the trauma survivor and the same process may be to some extent replicated in conducting in-depth research interviews over many hours. Being equipped with knowledge as a result of having completed my doctoral research made me want to share these important experiences so that therapists are reminded of the important roles that they play in offering empathy and hope to survivors of trauma. In my role as a supervisor of mental health workers I was able to encourage supervisees and underscore the importance of what they offered their clients in the process of presence, attunement, and empathy. So often we feel helpless in the face of great suffering, and being reminded of the power of empathy and witnessing in the process of therapy is an empowering core issue as was outlined by Laub (1984).

6

Interventions

Tracey Farber

It was interesting that after I completed the research, only Miriam, Dave and Isaac reached out specifically to me, whereas the other participants were able to terminate contact with me or to bond to therapists who were assigned to them. I thought that perhaps the extended research interviews performed an integrating function for the participants. Laufer (1988) explained that trauma causes a split between the pre-traumatic, traumatic, and post-traumatic self. Perhaps the in-depth, extended interviews offered some level of containment and integration of the trauma for the participants. Possibly, after exposing their vulnerability, Miriam, Dave, and Isaac needed to keep ongoing contact, as they felt some level of containment and understanding was offered to them. In December 2017 on completing the data collection and analysis dimensions of the research I approached Johannesburg Jewish Community Services with the support of my two supervisors (Cora Smith and Gillian Eagle). I appealed to them to offer a psychosocial program to address the needs of Holocaust survivors based on the findings of this research. They conducted a needs assessment and agreed to set up a special psychosocial service for Holocaust survivors. This service has been operating for the past four years and caseworkers have reached out to all the known thirty survivors in Johannesburg. I met with a leader in the Jewish community who offered to make a donation to assist in supporting these services for Holocaust survivors in Johannesburg.

The Johannesburg Jewish Community Services have now formalized a service for Holocaust survivors, which includes financial, medical, and dental assistance, psychiatric consultations and free psychiatric medication for those suffering from PTSD and depression, visits from a caseworker, nursing care, physiotherapy, financial assistance, and lifts from a driver. This service is aimed to help survivors live independently with dignity in their advanced years. In addition, the caseworkers offer to hear testimony from the survivors who wish to speak about their Holocaust experiences. The research served as catalyst for initiating psychosocial services for aging Holocaust survivors and highlighted their special needs in their final developmental stage. At present I am supervising and debriefing the two caseworkers who are hearing testimony as part of the psychosocial support they are offering to survivors and I have been able to draw upon my own experiences of conducting this research in order to support them through this difficult process.

At the beginning of 2020 during COVID-19 lockdown in Johannesburg I was given a license by Jewish Community services to visit child survivors in isolation. These were survivors who were identified as being "at risk" for various reasons. Thus, I saw four child survivors for supportive psychotherapy, some in their homes and some on the internet, on a weekly basis over a six-month period. As I witnessed some of the survivors being triggered by isolation and fear, I also saw their resilience being activated. Themes that I had written about in my research emerged as core issues: helplessness, fear, dread of suffering, ongoing grief, existential loneliness, spiritual crisis, and yet simultaneously there was evidence of the capacity for hope and resilience. Each of the survivors had a different story; however, they were able to use the therapy as an opportunity to process and organize their trauma.

One survivor died of COVID during the therapy process. Another one, who was isolated in her flat, said to me, *When I was in the Holocaust it was "gehaynem"* (Yiddish word for hell)—*now I feel I am in "gehaynem" again!* From this experience I learned that therapeutic contact has a benefit for trauma survivors even in their final years.

As I navigate being an immigrant to Israel myself at this present time, I often think of how hard it must have been for these child survivors to have arrived in a strange land, unable to speak the language, having lost one or both parents and bearing grief and horror. I think about how each survivor showed me something personal about themselves at the end of the interviews: Helene a poem about individuation, Anne and Miriam pictures of the jewellery they made, Lenna her art, Rina her gift of perfume, Shlomo the gates he built, Isaac showing me his pictures, and Dave singing his song *Ani Ma'amin.* It is only years later that I think they were showing me that, despite all the heartbreak and brokenness that they endured, they were able to build and create. It was my privilege to know the child Holocaust survivors as a researcher and then as a therapist. They shared their experiences and their wisdom so generously. Their stories of trauma, grief, resilience, and hope remain with me.

In my final meeting with Dave before I came to Israel he said: *You know, I am starting to think that maybe there is a God. I was reading a book, about the Jewish people and there are so many miracles that there must be a God. I will never understand how he allowed the Holocaust—how can I?—but I can't deny His existence anymore.* In the process of the research, I had seen Dave claim that he was an atheist and then wrestle with his ambivalence about his spiritual beliefs. It was a difficult process to witness and also a privilege.

In the following chapter Cora Smith with look at how child survivors view their traumas as they age.

7

Temporality and the Reevaluation of Memories in Aging Child Holocaust Survivors: A Developmental Trajectory

Cora Smith

The future is always the same, it's the past that keeps changing.

—*Russian proverb (in Prince 2016, 205)*

Child Holocaust survivors constitute a unique category of survivors as their period of post-Holocaust survival is both long and refracted through most adult developmental stages. The current research recounts the narratives of child Holocaust survivors some seventy years after the Holocaust, resulting in testimony from survivors currently in their late seventies and eighties. Temporality becomes a major component of the aging survivors' narratives as they reevaluate their traumatic life experiences from ever advancing developmental positions. Survivors differ in their focus on Holocaust events as they age and their developmental perspectives often change their views and sometimes even their emotional responses. This chapter will focus on the impact that the passage of time has on the reappraisal of traumatic events experienced by child survivors. It further explores how these experiences contribute to a restorying of their life narratives and promote a sense of survival and mastery in some, and a sense of despair and helplessness in others, as each navigates the developmental stage of old age.

The child survivor Dave, aged seventy-five at the time he was interviewed for the study, related the following incident. Dave celebrated his *bar mitzvah* in Westerbork concentration camp in the Netherlands, where his father gave him his watch as a present. This was the only valuable possession that the father had to commemorate his son's *bar mitzvah*. Later, when Dave was told that his father was to be transferred to Buchenwald concentration camp in Germany, he slipped the watch into his father's back pocket as a gesture of goodwill. At the time Dave had wanted his father to understand that it was a *gift of love*. Years later, Dave felt tormented by the idea that his father may have been upset or angry when he found it. He felt tremendous guilt at the thought that his father might have thought that he had rejected his precious gift. Dave reported that he continued to feel guilty and sad about this action he took as a thirteen-year-old boy and that even at the age of seventy-five he had *no closure* on this issue. With the advance of age, maturity, and experience, Dave had realized retrospectively that, in his good intention to please his father, he had deprived his father of the opportunity to give his son a gift of a watch as a symbol of his legacy. It is possible that the father was aware that he may not survive the move to Buchenwald concentration camp (he did perish there), and while this information was not known, the idea tormented Dave throughout his adult life. It is clear that as a young boy he could not have foreseen that his actions could potentially distress his father and yet as an adult he felt guilty and traumatized by his lack of foresight at the time. This realization achieved retrospectively with the passage of time and the acquisition of life experience only served to retraumatize Dave. It is also clear that this retraumatization was not a single episode but instead a continuous retraumatizing experience each time he recalled the incident.

In commenting on this example, it is apparent that several issues arise as part of our potential understanding of concepts such as trauma, memory, aging, and subjective reappraisal of past events. In the current example, is it clear that the Holocaust was not a single episode of trauma but rather a continuous complex trauma that was catastrophic in the scope of the pain, suffering, and losses that were experienced (Farber et al. 2018). Much has been written of the role of memory with regard to Holocaust experiences, including the notion of repressed and delayed memories that surfaced later after being triggered by current events or unearthed during personal psychotherapies. Perhaps the most obvious concept to consider is that of Freud's concept of *Nachträglichkeit* (Freud 1897). The term was never actually defined by Freud but he used it to describe a repressed memory that later becomes a trauma by deferred action. Similar ideas related to the concept of *Nachträglichkeit* or "deferred action: are those of Laplanche's (1999) concept of *après-coup* or "afterwardness" as well as concepts such as "retroactive temporality" and "retrospective attribution" (Eikohoff 2006). The concept of *après-coup* lies in the relationship between the original traumatic event and the renewed meaning it later acquires (Fohn and Heenen-Wolff 2011).

However, the concept of delayed trauma in each of these understandings implies some form of dissociation or unconscious process whereby an extreme trauma overwhelms the individual's coping resources and cannot be cognitively assimilated at the time, so that it manifests belatedly. In the current example, there is no unconscious defensive process that has been dissociated or repressed but rather a perfectly well-remembered event that is reappraised with the passage of time and with renewed insight. Nevertheless, several writers have described this phenomenon of afterwardness as also encompassing the reappraisal of meaning as determined by changing contexts over time (Eickhoff 2006; Pedersen 2019; Prince 2016). They also address the constructive quality of memory as it may be reconstituted through subjective experience. In addition, it is suggested that memory is not static and that changes occur over time not through a concrete misremembering of details or presence of inaccuracies but through the individual subjectivities encased within ongoing human experience (Bistoen et al. 2014). The idea that traumas not understood in the past return as anticipated horrors at some point in the future has been widely accepted through the writings of Winnicott (1974) on the fear of breakdown remembered.

A contentious debate concerns the issue of consistency versus change in the study of Holocaust narratives over the passage of time. However, Schiff (2005) notes that despite the passage of time there remains enormous consistency in the structure and content of the narratives of aging Holocaust survivors. While the survivors may understand their past in a different or new way due to the passage of time and changing contexts in their lives, the core of their narratives remained consistent. Schiff (2005) is at pains to point out that the narrative approach to understanding that any change in past comprehensions of Holocaust memories due to contextual shift should not be misunderstood as a reflection on the effect of age on the accuracy or quality of memories. He recognizes that as survivors age their perceptions of events may change due to different life experiences and insights. The strength of the narrative approach is not just a focus on retelling the past but on the meaning and understanding attributed to past events and memories (De Vries and Suedfeld 2005).

In the example given by Dave it is clear that the there are no issues regarding a reconstructed memory of a particular event but rather a belated understanding of the original context, which became retraumatizing. It was not only the understanding that as an adult he realized that he had deprived his father of giving him some form of legacy on his *bar mitzvah* but also the realization that his father had tried to acknowledge and recognize his son's rite of passage in circumstances of extreme deprivation in which his fathering role was severely limited. Part of the trauma suffered by Dave was his recognition that his father had little to give and the little he had to give had been returned to his father by a young well-meaning boy anxious for his father's approval. The memory is both poignant and tragic as one observes the love of father and son struggling to meet one other. Although, as a mature adult, Dave can consider that his father may well have realized that his son was well-meaning, it distressed him that his father may have been angry or upset given that the circumstances in which the event took place were extreme and that shortly after this event the father perished in a concentration camp. As it was likely that his father knew he was being sent to his death and this was the last gift of love he could bestow upon on his son, his disappointment at being unable to do so, may have been devastating. It is this realization that plagued Dave as he revisited this memory. As Dave recounted this memory, he said that over the years there was *no closure* and he was unable to find peace.

What becomes clear is that, embedded within the overall trauma of the Holocaust experience, there are specific memories that continue to plague the survivors. It is also more likely that it would be the child survivors most suffering from this kind of retrospective reappraisal of events as they all experienced the Holocaust during a period of cognitive immaturity and limited life experience. As their cognitive abilities matured, so too would their insights into the events that took place change with the passage of time.

A second example is that reported by Anne, aged seventy-four at the time of interview. Anne remembered an instance at the beginning of the war when she was six years old, when German soldiers came to her house for supper. During the meal, one of the soldiers took her mother to the bedroom. During this time her father remained seated at the table with his four children. After a period of time, the mother and the soldier returned. Anne recalled feeling confused about her mother going to the bedroom with this soldier and sensing that something was wrong. She also remembered feeling that something *bad* had happened. Years later, as an adult, she realized that her mother had been raped by this soldier and that her father had been helpless and unable to protect his wife. She reported feeling a deep sense of *disgust* at what took place. She was extremely distressed because of her mother's trauma and her father's helplessness as well as their joint humiliation at the hands of these soldiers. Anne suffered multiple losses during the Holocaust, including the death of her mother and sister. Her trauma has resulted in a lifelong experience of depression, sadness, and unresolved mourning. In addition to her losses, she continued to be retraumatized by her adult understanding of past events that occurred when she was a young child. This particular event continued to distress Anne as she recognized the helplessness and humiliation that her parents suffered at the time.

A further example is that given by the child survivor Helene, aged seventy-two, at the time of interview. At the age of seven, Helene was placed in Rivesaltes camp in France together with her parents. In an attempt to save her life, her parents sent her away with French and Jewish authorities who had agreed to place a group of Jewish refugee children in two children's homes. Helene was not aware that she was in grave danger or that her parents were likely to be murdered when she was sent to the children's home. She recalls her father telling her to *always pray and everything will be okay.* Her mother gave her a purse that she had made for her but she did not say a word. This distressed Helene for years and she felt that her she was in some way unworthy or a disappointment to her mother. It was only later she realized that: *as an adult now, I think she was incapable of speaking because it was so hard for her to say good bye. What can a mother say if she knows that there is a good chance she will not see her child again? My grandmother told my aunt that it took a lot of persuasion from everybody for my mother to give permission for me to go. I remember my father waving his handkerchief as far as he could see me. I didn't cry. I didn't know I would never see them again.*

In this example Helene reinterprets a tragic significant moment in her childhood and realizes that her mother's silent behavior was an expression of her helpless trauma when she as a mother struggled to say good bye to her daughter. With the passage of time Helene was able to place herself in her mother's position and empathize with the sorrow and pain that she must have experienced at that time. It became clear from the information Helene received from her surviving relatives that her mother did not wish to separate from her daughter and that this was an extremely painful decision for her to undertake. In this sense, the retrospective adult reinterpretation of a past event gave some comfort to Helene as she realized that her mother's silence was a sign of love and hence a symbol of Helene's value to her mother. However, it is also the case that, as Helene retrospectively reinterpreted her mother's silent response to sending her daughter away, she also became acutely aware of the pain her mother must have endured in making this choice. At the time there would have been tremendous anxiety and uncertainty as her mother would have had no guarantee that her choice to send her daughter away would result in her survival. This aspect of Helene's memory only served to retraumatize her as she realized the untenable choices her parents had to make.

Survivor guilt is described as ubiquitous among Holocaust survivors. This construct may not necessarily be accompanied by any justifiable culpability on the part of the survivor. However, the moral dilemmas faced by many survivors in their efforts to survive the concentration camps are well described by Primo Levi (1979/1986/1989/1993) who argues that any judgment of the actions of these individuals ought to be suspended given their extreme suffering and the very real threat to survival they faced. One of the crucial aspects of Nazi practice was to turn victims into accomplices. Levi (1979/1993) goes to great lengths to describe the long-term destructive dehumanizing impact this Nazi practice had on survivors. This led to Levi (1986/1989) pointing out that the notion that a simple binary separation of victims and persecutors in the context of the Holocaust completely ignores the complexity of the situation. Levi (1986/1989) coins the term "the grey zone" to describe the position of Holocaust victims who collaborated with their oppressors through compromised actions with variable degrees of freedom of choice in exchange for preferential treatment.

Many of the debates surrounding the ethical judgment of such actions undertaken by some survivors during the Holocaust are centered on the argument of context. The argument that context plays a role in the culpability of any crime underpins most systems of law globally. The central idea is that the particular context of a given action serves to explain and mitigate culpability, guilt, and responsibility for the action that may transgress universal notions of moral conduct. While this position is logical and fair in the context of ordinary living, it does not export comfortably to the context of the Holocaust or other genocides. Hence the emphasis of context in so many ethical debates about the Holocaust and other genocides.

This view of considering the ethics of behavior according to context in the case of the Holocaust and other genocides is sound but not without limitations. The argument put forward by Langer (1980) in many ways may be considered more convincing and possibly more ethical. He does not view the morality of choices according to the context of the survivors but rather disputes the fact that they were choices at all. Langer (1980) writes eloquently on the false moral dilemma of choices in the death camps and cogently argues the case for "choiceless choices" (Langer 1980, 224) that were faced by concentration camp inmates. The view being taken here is that choices facing many victims of the Holocaust were not meaningful choices. As a consequence, behavior in the camps cannot be judged by the same standards as similar behaviors in ordinary circumstances as the choices available for human decision making were not permitted in the concentration camps. Victims of the Holocaust were faced with *choiceless choices* where critical decisions did not reflect options between life and death but between one form of abnormal response and another). Langer (1980) further argues that many camp inmates who tried to cling to any form of principled behavior despite the dehumanizing conditions in concentration camps found that attempts to salvage such moral baggage suffered fatal consequences. For example, there were inmates who on principle would not eat non-kosher food. They perished fairly quickly in the camps. Langbein (2003) describes a group of camp inmates being escorted to the gas chamber where an old man barely able to walk tries to sit down along the way. He is accosted by a guard who threatens to beat him to death. The old man hurries back into line pleading not to be beaten to death. The point made by Langer (1980) is that this is a choiceless choice. It is not a choice between life and death, it is only a choice between two forms of humiliation as in this case either choice would lead to death. In a similar vein, Mintz (2001) refers to the untenable choices faced by many during the Holocaust as *bête noire*, meaning black beast, a French idiom referring to something that is anathema or strongly detested and to be avoided.

While the moral dilemmas faced by Holocaust survivors have been thoroughly discussed in the research literature, very little has been written of child survivors who were faced with these untenable choices at a time when they were vulnerable minors, traumatized, without their parents but nevertheless left to face the emotional consequences as adults later in life.

This brings us to the case of Menachem who was eighty-one years old at the time of interview. Menachem was thirteen years old when the Holocaust started and the Nazis took over his town in Poland. He was later interned at a labor camp, Pustkow, for six months and then transferred to Blechammer, a subcamp of Auschwitz, until the end of the war.

As a young adolescent, Menachem got a job working for the Judenrat. His job entailed going to Jewish homes and warning them that, if they did not obey Nazi orders, they would be shot. As a member of the Judenrat he had some authority over fellow Jews and some protection from being persecuted and sent to a concentration camp. Menachem reported that many of the Jews from the town were taken to the cemetery, forced to dig their own graves, and then undress. Once their valuables were seized, they were shot. Menachem was forced to work with a Polish policeman who made him remove the victims' wallets and hand the money over to him.

Menachem continued to be plagued by this experience throughout his life. He continued to have flashbacks about all his Holocaust experiences and felt a deep sense of rage, helplessness, and guilt. He was particularly preoccupied with a need for revenge. He reported that after the war he purchased a gun with the intention of tracking down this Polish policeman and killing him. He said he was never able to trace him.

As an adult, later in life, Menachem recognized that he would have been killed himself had he not complied with the requirements of the Judenrat or with the instructions of the Polish policeman. Nevertheless, he felt a strong sense of helplessness because of his predicament and relentless hatred for this policeman. Menachem remained enraged and spoke of a perpetual preoccupation with revenge to compensate for his sense of helplessness and self-loathing. He also felt a profound loss of faith and belief in God. Menachem lost his entire family, both his parents and all three of his siblings, in the Holocaust. He vacillated between believing that God did not exist and that God had abandoned him. This loss of faith left him feeling bereft, alienated, and despairing about meaning of his life.

Menachem was not able to forgive his young adolescent self, who, faced with meaningless choices, worked for the Judenrat and the Polish police for his own survival. As time passed and he grew older, his feelings of helplessness and hatred at the hands of the Nazis worsened and his rage became more intense. He remained perpetually traumatized by these actions, and the passage of time served only to enhance his sense of adult accountability without access to his youth, immaturity, and powerlessness at the time. The adult sense of accountability only increased his sense of humiliation and helplessness in the face of the Polish policeman's sadism and thereby enhanced his obsession with vengeance.

Isaac was eighty-one years old at the time of interview. Soon after the war began, his father was sent to a labor camp where he was shot en route. His sister, stepmother, and half-brother were sent to Auschwitz where they perished. As a young adolescent he was forced by the Nazis to hang other Jews. These victims were hanged for invented false crimes such as stealing bread. Isaac reported that he was forced to be involved in these public hangings six or seven times. As an adult, later in life, Isaac recognized that he would have been killed himself had he not complied with this injunction. Nevertheless, he felt a strong sense of self-loathing, guilt, and a relentless hatred toward the Nazis who forced him to kill. He remained enraged and spoke of a perpetual preoccupation with revenge to compensate for his sense of shame and self-loathing at these forced killings. This survivor was not able to forgive his young adolescent self, who, faced with meaningless choices, hanged fellow Jews for his own survival. As time passed and he grew older, his feelings of helplessness and humiliation at the hands of the Nazis worsened and his rage became more intense. He remained continually traumatized by these actions and the passage of time served only to enhance his sense of adult accountability, losing touch with his youth, immaturity, and powerlessness at the time. The adult sense of accountability only increased his sense of helplessness, humiliation, and rage in the face of Nazi sadism and thereby deepened his shame and self-loathing. Isaac reported that he had never spoken about these incidents for fear of being judged and attacked. The secrecy that surrounded these events enhanced his shame and self-loathing. He tormented himself with this secret over many years, and at the end of his life, when he was ill with cancer, he was afraid that God was punishing him for what he had done.

As child survivors age, their newly attained developmental stages in adulthood provides them with a new lens with which to reflect on their perceptions of their parents and their own views of their relationship with their parents. The resulting consequences of such a reappraisal of earlier events that occurred during the Holocaust has had both positive and negative outcomes. The reevaluation of specific traumatic events not only elucidates insights facilitated by age and experience of the now adult survivor but also allows some of the survivors to reflect on the possible subjective experiences their parents may have had when responding to the needs of their children whom they felt inadequate to protect. Such retrospective reappraisal of past traumatic experiences as the aging child survivors reflect on their lives translates into a reevaluate of the choices of their parents and contributes to a renewed reflection on their own changing responses.

Rina was seventy-one years old at the time of interview. When she was five and a half years old, she, her brother, and her mother were placed in Ravensbruck women's concentration camp in Germany. As an adult, Rina reported being tormented by her mother's shame and humiliation at being forced to parade naked in front of the Germans. Her recognition of her mother's helplessness and loss of dignity plagued her. Rina also commented in anguish that *it must have been terrible for my mother to see her children hungry and worry about us all the time.* As an adult Rina recognized the suffering her mother must have endured in her helplessness to protect her children and, indeed, her helplessness to protect herself. Rina was also tormented by the information she had about her father's death. She had heard that he died a *Muselmann* (a term used for camp inmates who were on the verge of death from starvation, exhaustion, and despair). She said that he became like the *walking dead. He died in the mud and collapsed and that was that.* Rina said that she had never been able to come to terms with her father's suffering and death. His loss of dignity, his impotence, and inability to protect himself continued to torment her.

The child survivor Helene sobbed when she described how her thoughts of her parents' suffering and death plagued her. She reported: *They must have been hungry and cold, living in that hellhole. I cannot bear to think of them as walking skeletons or fighting for their last breadth in the gas chambers . . . I cannot come to terms with their suffering they must have felt. I feel so sad and angry that they died in Auschwitz.* As an adult, Helene has been able to consider the realities of her parents' plight and the likely details of their suffering in the gas chambers left her distraught and inconsolable.

The survivor Dave reported that his realization of his parents' suffering tormented him throughout his life. He said: *I was told my father was so thin that he had little flesh on his body, and he was so weak that the Germans did not bother to take him to work anymore.* Dave reported that, looking back retrospectively, he felt angry that his father was stripped of his dignity in this way. He also reported a deep sense of empathy for his father's pain and helplessness in not being able to protect his children. Dave also could not bear to think of his mother's pain who had to watch helplessly as her children starved and suffered cold. The realization of the anguish his parents must have endured, as they were prevented from fulfilling their parental roles as protectors and providers for their families, came later in life with the maturity of adult understanding.

The survivor Anne was tormented by the humiliation and helplessness her parents endured when her mother was raped in the family home and her father made to sit at the dinner table and provide a meal to his tormentors, knowing he was helpless to protect his wife. It was only with hindsight and adult understanding that Anne recognized the trauma her parents suffered at the time.

Much has been written about the aging Holocaust survivors (Ayalon et al. 2007; Elran-Barak et al. 2018) although less about the aging child Holocaust survivor. The aging child survivors, by virtue of their cognitive immaturity at the time of their Holocaust experiences, have had to reevaluate some of their past experiences and memories with the passage of time. This process has in many instances served to retraumatize survivors as they realize with adult reflection the pain and suffering implicit in many of the events they were unable to comprehend at the time. Despite an intellectual understanding of their own cognitive limitations due to youth and inexperience at the time, many of the survivors were unable to forgive themselves for their lack of insight and foresight.

The child survivors in the present study certainly demonstrated considerable resilience as they rebuilt their lives after the Holocaust. However, what is clear is that the catastrophic grief experienced by all these child survivors cannot be attributed solely to the Holocaust events experienced in the past or to the difficulties in post-war adaptation alone. What is clear is that there has been ongoing and continuous traumatization of these child survivors as they revisit childhood memories and reevaluate their past experiences with the maturity of adult insight. It is possible that the "trauma trilogy" of catastrophic grief, anger, and survivor guilt is triggered at different points in the developmental trajectory as child survivors age and understand their parents' suffering through a retrospective lens. The role of temporality and retrospective reinterpretation of the perception of past traumatic experiences needs to be considered when evaluating the impact of trauma on child Holocaust survivors.

In the following chapter, Gillian Eagle will explore complex traumatic stress in child Holocaust survivors.

8

A Particular Form of Complex Traumatization

Gillian Eagle

Introduction

In exploring the experiences of the nine child Holocaust survivors who generously offered accounts of their past and present lives, one of the interesting findings that emerged concerned the nature of their traumatic stress-related responses. The discussion in this chapter focuses on how the experiences of the survivors in this regard allow us not only to better appreciate the impact of Holocaust and internment trauma that they suffered, but also to contribute to some of the active debates regarding formulations of complex traumatic stress conditions.

As discussed previously, Judith Herman (1992) has made a highly influential contribution to the trauma literature in arguing that exposure to "prolonged and repeated" trauma produce different outcomes for individuals as compared to once-off events. Herman's observations resonate with those of Lenore Terr (1995), who in a parallel formulation argues that children exposed to what she termed Type II traumas (such as chronic physical or sexual abuse) will present with a different symptom picture from those exposed to single-incident Type I traumas. Both Herman and Terr observe that survivors who have been compelled to adapt to chronically harmful environments develop what might be understood as personality changes, "practiced" ways of being that endure beyond situations of captivity and abuse. Writing on complex traumatic stress continues to emphasize the fact that pathology arising from exposure to such environments needs to be recognized as previously protective for the individual. This perspective resonates with some of the earlier discussion about the contestation in writing about mental health among Holocaust survivors and whether resilience should be emphasized over vulnerability.

As has been evident in the testimonies, all nine interviewed survivors reported compromised psychological wellbeing and several of them (Dave, Isaac, Menachem, Anne) had received formal psychiatric diagnoses. However, in keeping with the emphasis in the literature on situational causation, survivors viewed mental health difficulties to stem from their Holocaust-related experiences, as opposed, for example, to thinking of themselves as having some kind of intrinsic or inherited psychic vulnerability. Although in many instances they suffered severely from difficulties such as sleeping problems, low mood, and anxiety, there tended to be anger and distress around these burdens rather than the shame that often accompanies psychiatric illnesses. For example, Dave angrily stated: *I have been on psychiatric medication for decades because of what I went through as a child in the Holocaust*; and Anne indicated: *My depression is from how my mother died in the Holocaust—because she died coming to save me.* Psychological scars provided evidence of the severity of the trauma survivors had suffered and added veracity to their recollections. In a sense they wore their symptoms like battle scars in the same way that combatants might present with physical injuries.

Conceptualization of Complex Traumatic Stress, Diagnosis, and Presentation

In writing about the kinds of circumstances that might give rise to complex post-traumatic stress (CPTS) and complex post-traumatic stress disorder (CPTSD) Herman suggested the survivors had generally been trapped in inescapable conditions of captivity or material and psychophysiological dependence, within which they were exposed to multiple traumatic impingements (polyvictimization) on an ongoing basis. Complex traumatization can take place on an individual and collective level, and within both intimate, familial and larger repressive, social formations (McDonnell, Robjant, and Katona 2013). It is apparent that Herman understood concentration camp confinement, and by implication the circumstances of the child Holocaust survivors such as those whose interviews are presented in this book, to be an emblematic form of trauma exposure leading to CPTS. As is evident from all the testimonies, the interviewees were acutely aware of their imprisonment, subjugation, and limited agency and were subjected to multiple traumatic events such as being beaten, degraded, and witnessing the injury and death of others.

For example, in the arbitrariness of decisions made in Shlomo's case about who within his family would remain and who would be transported to other camps (his mother was sent away to Auschwitz) it was evident that absolute power lay in the hands of Nazi captors. In Shlomo's description of witnessing fellow prisoners falling and dying in the mud under instruction to move, it is evident that as a young adolescent he appreciated the helplessness of himself and other prisoners in the face of ruthless exercise of power. The survivors' testimonies are saturated with accounts of exposure to traumatizing events, from having one's pubic area inspected for lice, to hearing an account of one's mother's finger having been cut off, to witnessing infants being thrown to their deaths. In each person's narrative there is evidence of exposure to multiple traumatic stimuli and there is evidence of the inescapability of their conditions. They were all exposed to such conditions over months or years, indicating the requirement to have adapted to these circumstances to the best of their capacities over an extended period of time.

In response to surviving under such conditions theorists have postulated a descriptive picture of likely outcomes, whether considered as disorders, commonly referred to as complex traumatic stress disorders (CTSD), or as possible personality or response tendencies. As elaborated at some length previously, Herman provided a comprehensive picture of CPTSD that may be summarized as follows:

> Clinical observations identify three broad areas of disturbance which transcend simple PTSD. The first is symptomatic: the symptom picture in survivors of prolonged trauma often appears more complex, diffuse and tenacious than in simple PTSD. The second is characterological: survivors of prolonged abuse develop characteristic personality changes, including deformations of relatedness and identity. The third area involves the survivor's vulnerability to repeated harm, both self-inflicted and at the hands of others. (Herman 1992, 378)

Herman and others (Ford 2020) have noted that many of these features of CPTSD overlap with the diagnostic presentation of people with borderline personality disorder (BPD), although research indicates that the two conditions are distinct. It is noteworthy that BPD diagnoses have not generally been associated with assessment of psychopathology in Holocaust survivors.

During the refinement and construction of the most recent version of the Diagnostic and Statistical Manual of Mental Disorders, DSM-5 (American Psychiatric Association 2013), there was considerable contestation around whether complex post-traumatic stress disorder (CPTSD) should be included as a separate disorder in addition to PTSD, with strong lobbying for inclusion from certain quarters. Ultimately, it was decided that CPTSD did not warrant recognition as a standalone diagnostic condition, but a particular dissociative form of PTSD was added into the category (Resick et al. 2012). However, complex post-traumatic stress disorder (CPTSD) was included in the most recent version of the International Classification of Diseases (ICD), ICD-11 version (World Health Organization 2018). Based on symptom presentation, individuals can be classified as having either PTSD or CPTSD but cannot have both (as in some other conceptualizations). "CPTSD includes the three core elements of PTSD as well as three additional elements called disturbances in self-organisation that are pervasive and occur across various contexts: emotion regulation difficulties (for example problems calming down), negative self-concept (for example beliefs about self as worthless or a failure) and relationship difficulties (for example avoidance of relationships)" (Cloitre 2020, 130).

Although the interviews on which the book is based were not designed to assess mental health and psychiatric conditions in a systematic manner, there was nevertheless a great deal of information gathered about psychological functioning. The extended interviews allowed us to gauge reasonably well how survivors had observed their psychological states and strengths and difficulties through their life course development and in the present. From these observations what appeared somewhat surprising is just how functional in the world the elderly survivors appeared to have been in their lives subsequent to the Holocaust, despite their extended, majorly traumatic experiences as children. Using some of the kinds of markers that would indicate psychological health and/or vulnerability to CPTSD, a number of observations are relevant.

While several of the survivors spoke about trying not to think about or recollect traumatic Holocaust-related material, and appeared to dissociate, or, as we have argued, "compartmentalize," these experiences away in their minds, there were no reports of self-harming behavior or any impulse towards this, nor were there any indications of substance addiction. While all of the nine suffered from depression of differing severity and chronicity, this seemed to be tied to loss and chronic grief rather than purely to their own direct trauma exposure. There was indication of emotional constriction in a number of survivors, as in Helene's discussion of the fact that up until the interviews she had never wept openly about the loss of her parents, but less evidence of suffering from extreme emotional displays, except for Isaac's descriptions of intense feelings and displays of anger. It was not generally evident that the survivors carried general feelings of low self-worth. Many of them made very successful careers and held positions of high standing or responsibility in their communities. For example, Lenna, Shlomo, Miriam, and Helene ran successful businesses. These "external" markers suggested a capacity to be generative out of a confidence in their capacities or abilities and some expectation of being well-received by others. Although we know that internal states may not map directly onto external performance, these achievements reflect a degree of agency and social recognition.

In terms of relationships, all nine interviewees had married, and even though some discussed having experienced marital difficulties, only Anne had divorced. Recognizing there may have been cultural pressures and supports that helped to sustain these marriages, in the main there was a considerable degree of stability in their long-term partner relationships. All but one of the survivors had children and grandchildren to whom they were clearly attached. However, Helene acknowledged some alienation from her daughter that she attributed to her own emotional constriction, and Isaac was inclined to have altercations with his sons. In keeping with literature on problems in second-generation Holocaust survivors, it is possible that relationship difficulties were most evident for survivors in relation to their offspring, although these kinds of problems were reported in a minority of cases. What was not generally evident was the repeating of pathological victim-perpetrator dynamics in later life relationships. None of the interviewees reported fears of having become abusive towards others themselves, or of having become involved in abusive relationships.

Having discussed our observations about the presentation of the nine child survivors it is rather striking that although many features of CPTSD were evident (as elucidated in the case study material), many of the more borderline crossover type features were not generally present. In the last section of the chapter, we present some suggestions as to why this might be the case and highlight how this deepens our understanding of child Holocaust and other complex trauma survivors.

Salient Features of Child Holocaust Survivor Histories in Relation to Complex Traumatic Stress

In keeping with some of the ongoing debates in the complex trauma literature (Sar 2011), the key argument that we advance, based on observations from this case-study based research, is that there may be significantly different outcomes for populations of people who have been traumatized in "intimate" or family-type environments than for those who have been traumatized by "strangers" or in more anonymized environments.

In listening to the testimonies of the survivors it was apparent that while they had been acutely aware of humiliation, risk of harm, and life threat, they had suffered as part of a collective of people and had also been abused by a collective of people, "the Nazis." Within their accounts there are few references to individual agents of terror, (although these are present in some testimonies). Perpetrators tend to be described as "the soldiers," "the guards," "they," "the Nazis," suggesting a lack of individualization of relationship to perpetrators. In Herman's original work and much of the subsequent literature what is viewed as contributing to the most problematic intrapsychic constellation for CPTS sufferers is the necessity of having to attach to the very person/object who is causing you harm. The emphasis is upon what in some literature has been referred to as "traumatic bonding" or "betrayal trauma" (Gobin and Freyd 2014). Although this kind of relationship is most common in situations of chronic child abuse by a caretaker or caretakers, it has also been demonstrated that even adults who are kept in hostage situations over prolonged periods may develop complex attachments to perpetrators, as captured in the popularized notion of Stockholm syndrome (Sar 2011). In situations in which survival is dependent upon compliance with the perpetrator, who holds the power of daily sustenance and life and death over the victim, a very primitive sense of dependence develops, that may translate into gratefulness for any lenience. Captors often seek to exploit precisely this form of dependence, abjection, and lack of agency. For young children growing up in abusive environments it is apparent how this perverse kind of internalized object-relational constellation becomes the prototype for subsequent relationships. Even for adults subjected to these kinds of conditions, the intensity of the experience produces a level of regression that may mean that internalized victim-perpetrator object-relational constellations come to shape and be enacted in subsequent relationships.

In the case of the interviewees there was an absence of evidence of traumatic bonding with Nazi perpetrators and an absence of indications of patterns of relationships in adult life in which victim and perpetrator dynamics were replayed. They did not appear to have internalized an object-relational template that mapped this kind of dynamic onto subsequent relationships. However, some aspects of their subjugation, albeit as a member of a group as opposed to an individual, did appear to have affected their sense of identity. In individual situations victims are often held accountable for their own suffering by the perpetrator who arbitrarily indicates their actions as deserving of punishment (as in child abuse, domestic violence, and torture situations). Within the camps, internees were generally subject to degradation, violence, and annihilation based on a doctrine that justified their infra-humanization—a doctrine that was communicated constantly to them. Although survivors may not have internalized the individualized, defective self-representations that accompany more intimate situations of abuse, it was very difficult to resist the sense of being identified as part of a degraded and helpless group. In this respect it seemed that survivors had worked hard to regain a sense of agency, legitimacy, and value in post-camp environments and that collective and cultural resistance to negative framing of their Jewish identity had been important. For several of the participants, their willingness to provide their testimonies for the research study represented their wish not only to have someone witness their trauma but also to be people who had something to contribute to others by virtue of sharing these experiences. Dave said: *I speak for the 1,5 million children who died.*

In addition to the less personalized nature of survivors' abuse experiences, a second major feature of their testimonies that appeared to play a role in how they were vulnerable to CPTSD was the quality of prior attachments and the role played by some caretakers in attempting to ameliorate or protect against traumatizing experiences. As discussed earlier, most of the nine participants described stable, content, and loving relationships with parents, siblings, caretakers, or extended family members in their pre-Holocaust lives. These positive attachment relationships seem to have provided them not only with a reasonably healthy sense of self and ongoing being, but also with a propensity for trust in others and the world. Although their attachments rendered the survivors highly vulnerable to grief with the loss of many, if not most, of these loving figures, the survivors had retained their positive representations of significant others throughout their lives, as indicated in the interviews. These loving (good) object introjects sustained survivors in certain respects both during their internment and subsequently. In addition, for those of the nine who were interned with a significant caretaker (Dave, Rina, Miriam, Helene, and Anne), it was apparent that their efforts to protect them from or minimize harm had stayed with them. Participants described the devotion with which their parents looked after them in the worst of conditions: *My mother did everything she could, she would rub my sores and comfort me* (Miriam); *My mother would say to me when we were in the camp, "Stone walls do not a prison make," meaning that in my mind I was still free. She told us stories and I was devastated when they separated me from her and sent me to Ravensbruck men's camp* (Dave); *My father looked after me, my brother, and sister in the hay barn, he was a wonderful man* (Anne). The fact that Dave's father gave him his watch, even though this became complicated with its secret return, similarly conveyed to Dave that his father had wanted to provide some kind of transitional object to allow him to be symbolically present to his son when he could not be physically present.

Throughout the testimonies there is appreciation of gestures of support, sacrifice, and care that were shown between family members and caretakers, indicating that internalized bonds with good objects remained intact. Although these relational connections could not be elaborated in reality over subsequent years with living parents or siblings, in all but one case (that of Isaac, discussed previously) they appear to have provided some protection against coming to view all relationships as potentially untrustworthy or harmful. As noted previously, the manner in which traumatic experiences in childhood are mediated by significant adults is as significant to outcomes as is the nature and severity of the trauma itself. The fact that parents (or other adults) demonstrated efforts to protect their children is significant for the survivors.

While efforts at protection were important, especially in that they conveyed to survivors that they were worthy of care by adults, the failures of caretakers (good objects) to protect themselves and their children from harm contributed to a different aspect of complex traumatization. Psychoanalytic writing on trauma impact indicates that how external events are processed is filtered through pre-existing object-relational constellations (Garland 2018). Being subject to violation and terror indicates a failure of good objects to operate as potently and protectively as desired in terms of core introjects. For children in early stages of development it is important to have a sense of caretakers as sufficiently powerful and attuned to provide a sense of safety and containment. Adequate provision and care in early life is understood to underpin basic trust (Erikson 1965) and the fundamental assumption that the world is benign (Janoff-Bulman 2010). It is evident that, rather than being able to internalize caretakers as potent, protective, loving objects, survivors were compelled to engage with experiences of caretakers who were unable to intervene to assist children in many instances and who were themselves subjugated, violated, and literally destroyed. Images of distressed, damaged, and dead parents haunted several of the participants throughout their lives (with shifting engagement with this knowledge over time as discussed in the previous chapter). It was evident that some of the most intense affect during the interviews emerged in association with the bringing to mind of images of parent destruction, such as that of Anne's mother's shooting and disfigurement in having her finger cut off and Rina's knowledge that her father had died too weak to continue to walk. In addition, Dave, Miriam, Helene, Lenna, and Shlomo were told that their parents died in concentration camp circumstances in which they were helpless to defend themselves. What was very evident in survivors' attempts to fully comprehend the impact of destruction of caretakers, and by implication damage to good internal objects, was considerable bitterness and disillusionment and felt ambivalence about the place of religion and relationship to spiritual forces (the "cultural good"). As indicated in the discussion of integrity and despair, it was difficult to find existential meaning in the face of early exposure to the power of evil. In some formulations of CTSD it has been noted that negative alterations to belief systems may be a long-term feature of prolonged human-inflicted trauma exposure.

Conclusion

In concluding the discussion of CTS in relation to the nine interviewed child Holocaust survivors it is important to reemphasize that framing of the impact of their trauma exposure in terms of complex traumatic stress is useful and apt. However, in examining their narratives in considerable depth it appears that they present with a form of complex traumatic stress that meets certain aspects of the described condition and not others. It appears that although this group of participants presented with several PTSD and CPTS symptoms, in the main they did not display what might be referred to as the more borderline-type or disorders-of-self-related (DoS-related) symptoms of CPTSD (Cloitre et al. 2009), such as externalized enactments of affective distress or repetitive enactments of abusive dynamics in relationships. It is hypothesized that particular kinds of risk and protective factors seem to have contributed to this picture.

Within the complex traumatic stress literature there has been some discussion as to whether there may be different subtypes of CPTSD, associated with different kinds of complex trauma exposure and related symptom patterns (Ford 2020; Karatzias and Levendosky 2019; Landy, Wagner, Brown-Bowers, and Monson 2015). The picture that emerged from Farber's (2019) research would seem to confirm that there may well be subtypes of CPTSD, and that one important differentiating feature may be the degree to which abuse or damage is inflicted by an "intimate" other (be this family member or abductor, for example) in a situation that generates some kind of traumatic bonding. In this instance, even though exposure to prolonged and inescapable trauma took place during childhood or adolescent years, the fact that it was not personalized may have protected survivors from forming the perverse kinds of internal object-relational constellations that one finds when care and harm are meted out by the same person/object. However, Holocaust survivors were extra-vulnerable in relation to witnessing the powerlessness of good caretaker objects.

In concluding, we believe it is important to reiterate that differences in emphasis rather than absolute differences in complex trauma presentation are being proposed. Given the case study-based approach and that the original study was not designed to focus systematically on mental health or complex traumatic stress the arguments put forward here are necessarily tentative and only partially substantiated. It is hoped that the reader has been invited to think together with us about the complexity of formulating the form of traumatization that child Holocaust survivors suffered and its impact. Doing so may help us to understand what kinds of support they require and may hopefully contribute to theorization of nuances and distinctions in relation to mechanisms of traumatization in related populations.

As a final note, it is also worth observing that alongside personal traumatization (in the sense of experiencing, witnessing, and hearing about damaging and life-threatening events), these survivors had also suffered catastrophic loss and it was difficult to distinguish between features of complicated grief and complex trauma. It is also likely that partners and close family members may have described relational difficulties with these survivors in a different manner to their self-accounts, and that second-generation survivors may have carried complex trauma residues on behalf of their parents that were not immediately evident from interview data with the survivors themselves.

9

What Can Be Learned from Child Concentration Camp Survivors about the Impact of Severe Trauma and Its Long-Term Impact on Aging

Tracey Farber, Gillian Eagle, Cora Smith

This book aimed to describe and explore the long-term impact of the Holocaust on child survivors as they reached old age. More specifically the focus was to explore the impact of Holocaust trauma on the developmental trajectory of child survivors and its long-term effects across the life cycle. At the time of the research interviews all of the child survivors interviewed for the purposes of the study were in Erikson's (1965) eighth stage of "integrity versus despair," and the impact of Holocaust trauma was understood within this context.

Common themes indicated that all the participants in the study experienced some form of developmental disruption and suffered from child survivor syndrome as described by Dasberg (2001). They were all deprived of aspects of "normal" childhood and exposed to ongoing deprivation, horror, and loss. Significantly, in many instances they lost parental figures at early stages of life. In addition, those that survived with a parental figure observed damage done to their caretakers, leaving child survivors with anxiety about the capacity of parental figures to protect them from harm. They were compelled to engage with and take in a highly persecutory environment and developed various kinds of defenses to do so, some of which proved long-lasting and to some extent counterproductive in later life. However, the present study confirms previous research (Klein 2012) that showed that strong early attachment prior to the

Holocaust built resilience in child survivors. Keilson's (1979) research was also confirmed, in that it appeared that child survivors who had a supportive post-Holocaust environment were also more likely to be resilient.

Participants within this community-based sample were both "vulnerable" survivors who formed a clinical subgroup (many of whom had formal psychiatric diagnoses) and "resilient" survivors who functioned well in terms of general life adaptation. All child survivors in the present study, both "resilient" and "vulnerable," described PTSD symptoms that they endured for many years after the Holocaust. The PTSD symptoms can perhaps be likened to the metaphor of "shrapnel" from a bullet that remains lodged in the body and is impossible to remove, serving as a reminder of the trauma even if not necessarily compromising daily functioning or overall health. The findings of the study dovetail with those of previous researchers who also established the presence of enduring PTSD symptoms in both "resilient" and "vulnerable" survivors (Barak 2010; Brom 2001; Durst 2002; Cohen et al. 2001; Joffe 2003). Although all survivors had symptoms of PTSD, they differed in intensity. Most participants had full-blown PTSD, although some had limited or single symptoms and did not qualify for the full diagnosis. However, the "vulnerable" survivors who were part of the clinical subgroup in this study had more severe PTSD and also had a dual diagnosis of PTSD and chronic depression, in keeping with what was observed by Kellermann (2001). Herman's (1992) construct of complex traumatic stress was useful with reference to child survivors. This diagnostic construct underscored the long-term impact of trauma on the personality makeup and defensive styles of child survivors. For example, there was evidence of restricted affect, emotional dysregulation, and self-esteem impairment in some participants. However, as discussed in the previous chapter, it is argued that this group of survivors did not fit the typical picture of CPTSD and it is likely that there is a subtype of CPTSD that may be specific for child Holocaust survivors. In addition, the catastrophic loss experienced by all survivors, especially child survivors, only served to conflate their presentation of trauma. Although there may be some similarities between the mental health presentation of child abuse survivors and child survivors of the Holocaust, there are also notable differences. Child Holocaust survivors mostly had secure attachments to their parents and were tormented by strangers, enabling them to hold onto a more stable and secure sense of self (and caretaker figures) that built resilience, as opposed to having to struggle with the difficulty of integrating contradictory experiences of abuser-caretakers.

A ubiquitous finding of the present research was that all child survivors described the massive losses they endured as children and their ongoing grief and lack of closure regarding such losses in their old age. Witztum and Malkinson (2009) suggested that Holocaust survivors be understood through the lens of traumatic bereavement. As highlighted previously, the magnitude of losses and the violent or dehumanizing circumstances of the dying of attachment figures created particular difficulties, as did the lack of preparation for leave-taking. It is proposed that the term "catastrophic grief" be used to describe the experiences of child survivors as they suffered from multiple traumatic bereavements, associated with a range of complex emotions and memories. The term "catastrophic grief" appears to capture something of the extent and intensity of the loss in the context of a catastrophe such as the Holocaust. It is suggested that catastrophic grief differs from complex PTSD, complex bereavement, and/ or complicated grief in that this term captures the experiential intensity of the magnitude and pervasiveness of the loss and trauma suffered by child Holocaust survivors as well as the permanent ruptures suffered in self-formation and distress that is beyond consolation. Unlike PTSD, depression was not experienced by all the survivors in the study, yet they all suffered from ongoing bereavement. In addition, most of these survivors remained functional in their lives in contrast to sufferers of complex bereavement or complicated grief (Farber et al. 2021).

All the survivors in this study described the presence of catastrophic bereavement in their old age as was evident in the intensity of their affective expression, preoccupation with the manner of peoples' leave-taking and dying, and the guilt they carried in many instances for having survived. Child survivors continued to mourn their parents and siblings into their old age. It is proposed that survivors appeared to present with a "trauma trilogy" of catastrophic grief, anger, and survival guilt, which appeared to have endured across the life trajectory (Amir and Lev Wiesel 2003; Durst 1995, Farber et al. 2021). The "trauma trilogy" is important because some survivors presented with strong affects of anger and survivor guilt, however, when these emotions were deconstructed during the interviews, what lay beneath was an anger and/ or survivor guilt that related to the catastrophic grief they had experienced. It was evident that they carried the burden of the "trauma trilogy" across decades of their life, resulting in despair and existential loneliness (Farber et al. 2021).

This research demonstrated that in the stage of "integrity versus despair" indicators of despair were continuing grief and vulnerability to depression, as well as compromised spiritual beliefs and complex relationships to religion and God. It must be emphasized that the extent of the catastrophic grief intensified the survivors' sense of despair in old age, and the sense of disconnection from others and God left them with a sense of existential loneliness. This sense of despair and loneliness was found in both resilient and depressed survivors. This research substantiates previous research that demonstrated that child survivors have high levels of loneliness (O'Rourke et al. 2018). However, it was also noteworthy that all survivors mentioned that they were able to glean a sense of meaning and satisfaction from their children and/or grandchildren, indicating that later-life human attachments could yield a sense of renewal and hope.

Some of the debates regarding the apparent resilience of Holocaust survivors were outlined in the literature review (Barel et al. 2010; Hass 1995; Vallent 1989). As predicted by Dasberg (2001), child survivors in this study grappled with issues of aging. This appeared to be related to the suppression of their grief, as well as the loosening of the split between their outer adaptation and inner turmoil. The present study confirmed Dasberg's (2001) explanation of a vertical split where survivors carried significant internal or hidden distress and yet externally displayed adaptive functioning. The participants described vivid recollections that were visceral and had a strong sensory immediacy. This suggested that their trauma-related memories were still very much "alive," and it appeared that the trauma was compartmentalized and walled off in the psyche. This was also evident in the way that the catastrophic grief and traumatic memories were encapsulated in a survival shield that endured across decades and served as a defense mechanism. This study confirmed and reinterpreted the split as described by Dasberg (2001), reframing this defensive style as the compartmentalization of the trauma as this term seemed to best fit the presentation of the participants. The integration of their mourning and Holocaust trauma was a complicated process in the final stage of aging particularly because it had been kept shut out of conscious view for so long. This group seemed to function in line with the paradoxical integration described by Kellermann (2009). In normal circumstances, the use of the kinds of defenses associated with splitting, dissociation, repression, suppression, and compartmentalization may be viewed as "unhealthy" as they block access to emotional experience that then remains unprocessed. In the case of child Holocaust survivors, however, these defenses appeared to have been functional in blocking out unbearable trauma and catastrophic grief not only at the time of the original events but also in subsequent life, enabling outwardly adaptive adjustment and functioning. Suppression was aided by post-war environments where there was an injunction not to speak about Holocaust experiences. The survivors' resilience and adaptation in their present life was generally remarkable given their historical experiences. However, they retained Holocaust-related damage and both the experience of complex traumatic stress and of catastrophic grief contributed to the experience of despair in old age. As children, the tragic losses they sustained destroyed their overall sense of trust in a benign and lawful world.

This caused them deep and persistent sadness. The metaphor of "silk bandages" (H. Gordon, personal communication, February 1989) is used to describe the way in which they hid their wounds and went to great lengths to preserve their sense of dignity in the outside world. What lay beneath the "silk bandages" was the encapsulation of profound suffering and loss, some of which became more prominent as they moved into end-of-life stage.

Herman (1992) describes the way in which horrific trauma is unspeakable and there is a sense that repression operates at a group level as the group or community is unable to process and metabolize the trauma. This climate of group and personal repression helped the child survivors to focus on functioning while their trauma and grief remained unprocessed. Historically, psychology had not reached popular culture immediately after the war, and there were few mental health services available to help survivors to deal with trauma. In addition, Danieli (1984) describes how in the decades after the Holocaust mental health workers did not unpack Holocaust trauma and unintentionally supported the "conspiracy of silence."

The present study opens an inquiry into the role of research in exposing what has been compartmentalized or split off. The nature of the research interviews facilitated an unpacking of the suppressed trauma and grief in some survivors who had compartmentalized their trauma for decades. Perhaps their knowing that they were talking to a clinician helped them to acquire a sense of safety and because it was "research" they did not feel stigmatized about speaking to a professional. Those who spoke expressed their gratitude as it allowed them to unburden themselves of the trauma and grief that they had repressed and/or suppressed for decades. As reported in the follow-up with participants in this study, none were negatively affected in the sense that they reported research-related traumatization. The participant who refused to tell her story was not pressurized and her silence was respected. It is possible that participants volunteered for this study as it was a final opportunity at this late stage of life to tell the truth of their life story, as there was a parallel process occurring as a developmental task of old age where they were in any case reflecting on their personal history. This process of reflection is part of "integrity versus despair" and it is possible that the research offered the child survivors a structure and a platform to integrate their experiences of both the traumatic and positive aspects of their lives. Their recorded research interviews offered them an opportunity to leave a legacy in contributing towards the understanding of child survivors in the Holocaust. The confidentiality offered some of them an opportunity to tell, for the first time, the truth about events that they had experienced but found difficult to acknowledge. The research interviews offered an opportunity of "final confession" for some survivors and the opportunity to speak openly and have an empathic but non-personally related listener to "bear witness" to their story. As such, one of the findings of the research was that survivors reported that they benefited from the interview process, which substantiates what Auerhahn and Laub (2018) emphasize in the value of giving testimony.

Kellermann (2009) points out that exploring Holocaust trauma presents a paradox in that survivors represent a community who have been deeply traumatized and at the same time offer an example of resilience and hope. The capacity of survivors to have a sense of hope, meaning, and wisdom in old age may be linked to a sense of early trust established in relation to attachment figures (Klein 2012). This helped participants to survive and revive and hold onto a sense of hope and gratitude, despite their catastrophic loss. As Erikson (1982) says, basic trust lays down a sense of hope in needs being met. The task of old age is to glean a sense of wisdom and hold onto appreciation for a life well-lived. The horrors of the Holocaust were inflicted by strangers, not attachment figures. The glimmers of hope and appreciation indicate that in some survivors there was a remnant of self that survived the trauma, owing to early attachment (Klein 2012). However, it is also because of the influence of early attachment that catastrophic grief continued over decades. The ability to compartmentalize was the mediating factor that enabled some to be more resilient than others. Nevertheless, the experience of despair compromised their capacity to achieve full ego integration—as predicted by Dasberg (2001).

The findings of this study underscore the importance of attachment on multiple levels. First, aging survivors who had a good sense of early attachment tended to demonstrate a capacity for resilience, hope, and creativity in building their lives after the Holocaust. However, secondly, it was also apparent that the rupture in attachments, caused by the loss of parents and siblings in the context of the Holocaust, led to an experience of catastrophic grief that impaired subsequent life quality. The ongoing sense of loss, trauma, loneliness, and feeling like a refugee in a strange land, resonating with the words of the nine participants of this study, are eloquently expressed by Auerhahn and Laub (2018):

> The dead continue to be acutely and painfully absent. Homelessness and utter aloneness continue to haunt the survivor, even if he or she was able to build a family, a community, and a home. The traumatic experience remains unfinished between the survivor and the perpetrator. (Laub and Auerhahn 2018, 59)

It is the core of love that the survivors experienced in their early attachment that built their resilience. We were deeply moved at how clearly all the survivors remembered their parents with much detail and how they held onto the memory of being treasured and loved by the parents that they had lost. It is this resilience that enables survival and so this is a book both about deep despair and the power of love and hope in the service of survival.

10

Responding to the Needs of Aging Child Holocaust Survivors and Other Survivors of Severe Early Trauma

Tracey Farber, Gillian Eagle, Cora Smith

It has been over four years since a social service was established by Jewish Community Services in Johannesburg as a result of the findings of this research. We are aware that there are still many aging child Holocaust survivors worldwide. Child survivors range in ages from 76 to 100. The numbers are deceptive as not all child survivors were registered after the Holocaust; however, a rough estimate is 180,000 in Israel (Surkes 2021). They are a "lost" generation as many were never formally recorded as being Holocaust survivors (Dr. Jenni Frummer, in conversation, August 20, 2021). There are also large numbers of child survivors in the United States, Canada, Europe, and Russia and the worldwide estimate is that there are currently 24,000 Holocaust survivors worldwide (Rising 2020). Aging child survivors are in their twilight years, and they have differing financial and psychosocial needs. In many communities worldwide, aging child survivors live in poverty. Governments and communities can make a significant difference by making sure that they address the financial, medical, and psychosocial needs of aging child Holocaust survivors. Special psychosocial services are needed for aging survivors to help them to process their loss and trauma in their final life stage. In addition, psychiatric services should screen them for depression and PTSD and offer medication if it can be helpful. Casework services should check in on survivors who live independently and offer financial assistance/practical services and emotional support, with the acknowledgement that they are a group who carry deep levels of despair despite their apparent resilience.

Appreciation of the burden of the "trauma trilogy" underscores the continued importance of offering supportive psychological services for child Holocaust survivors if they chose to access such services. From the cases reported on here it seems that aging survivors may be more inclined to speak about their experiences or to use therapeutic and support services as they become more vulnerable in their declining years. It is hoped that the concept of the "trauma trilogy" may be clinically helpful to those who may intervene, where grief, anger and survivor guilt are understood to form a psychic constellation that shapes the experiences of clients who struggle to come to terms with massive traumatic bereavement and therefore form an important nexus for any intervention that aims to deepen empathy and alleviate suffering (Farber et al. 2021). The important benefit of giving testimony was a finding of the present research. It is suggested that Holocaust and genocide survivors be afforded the opportunity to give testimony to an empathic witness should they so choose. The struggle to incorporate the impact of the Holocaust on their life trajectories and the lived experience of carrying the burden of the "trauma trilogy" inevitably contributes to some weight of despair in this final developmental period of their lives. At the time of writing this book, aging child Holocaust survivors are facing additional isolation as a result of COVID-19, where their previous traumas and losses may be retriggered (Farber et al. 2021). Recent research (Fortmeiester et al. 2020) has demonstrated that aging child survivors can benefit from life review therapy. This would give them the chance to articulate their losses and describe their traumas and find a sense of meaning in the process of telling their stories in a therapeutic context.

Healthcare providers who work with survivors should be educated about their sensitivities and special needs. Community leaders and religious leaders could benefit from understanding the impact of Holocaust or genocidal trauma on the spiritual world of the survivor, and to offer to help them voice their distress and spiritual dilemmas.

This research highlighted the vulnerability of child survivors of the Holocaust. This knowledge can be extrapolated to all child genocide survivors who experience complex traumatic stress and catastrophic grief. There are notable cases of child survivors traumatized in the Khmer Rouge genocide of Cambodia (Kierman 2003), the genocide of Rwanda (Meierhenrich 2020), the genocide of Turkish Armenians, Guatemala, and Bosnia/Srebrenica (Benjamin 2004), or the current ethnic cleansing of the Nuer in South Sudan, the Rohingya in Myanmar, or the Christians and Yazidis in Iraq and Syria, to name a few. These genocidal events produce a multitude of traumatized survivors, both adult and child. Protective factors in such circumstances include a supportive environment after the trauma, as described in the research literature (Herman 1992; Keilson 1979). Results show that there is a high risk for depression and PTSD and services should focus on providing support and psychotherapeutic help for child genocide survivors who are in need. In addition, they are at risk over the course of the life cycle and need ongoing monitoring.

It is suggested that more qualitative research is conducted on child survivors as well as second- and third-generation survivors. This is because checklists are unlikely to capture the depth of the impact of intergenerational trauma. Qualitative research is likely to highlight issues such as the impact of living with those suffering from complex traumatic stress, catastrophic bereavement and the "trauma trilogy." In addition, the interview process can facilitate a climate where survivors are encouraged to offer testimony as the researcher is there to "bear witness" to their story.

The needs of second-generation survivors should receive attention. Being the child of a child survivor leaves the second-generation survivor potentially vulnerable to multiple distress through intergenerational transmission. Special therapeutic services should address these issues and additional research into the experiences of the children of child survivors is to be encouraged.

Psycho-education around trauma and resilience in communities affected by mass trauma is important. Cultivating and promoting resilience—the capacity to adapt to a trauma and "bounce back"—is a universal challenge. This is particularly relevant in recent times, when we have been challenged as a human community with the COVID-19 pandemic. The concept of building resilience is widely applicable and child concentration camp survivors offer a base of experiential knowledge that we can learn from. This includes the importance of early attachment in building resilience, finding agency, and emotional regulation, as well as the capacity to hold onto hope.

Bibliography

Aarts, P. G. H., and W. Op den Velde. 2007. "Prior Traumatization and the Process of Aging: Theory and Clinical Implications." In *Traumatic Stress: The Effects of Overwhelming Experience on Mind, Body, and Society*, edited by B. A. Van der Kolk, A. C. McFarlane, and L. Elisabeth, 359–377. New York, NY: The Guilford Press.

Abramowitch, M. 2002. *To Forgive . . . but Not Forget. Maja's Story.* Ilford: Vallentine Mitchell.

Amcha—The National Israel Centre for Psychosocial Support of Survivors of the Holocaust and Second Generation, founded in 1987. www.amcha.org.

American Psychiatric Association. 2000. *Diagnostic and Statistical Manual of Mental Disorder* (4th ed., text revision). Washington, DC: American Psychiatric Association.

———. 2013. *Diagnostic and statistical manual of mental disorders* (5th ed.). Washington, DC: American Psychiatric Association.

Amir, M., and R. Lev-Wiesel. 2003. "Time does Not Heal All Wounds: Quality of Life and Psychological Distress of People who Survived the Holocaust as Children 55 Years Later." *Journal of Traumatic Stress: Official Publication of The International Society for Traumatic Stress Studies* 16, no. 3: 295–299.

Andrews, B., C. R. Brewin, S. Rose, and M. Kirk. 2000. "Predicting PTSD Symptoms in Victims of Violent Crime: The Role of Shame, Anger and Childhood Abuse." *Journal of Abnormal Psychology* 109: 69–73.

Aron, L., and K. Starr. 2013. *A Psychotherapy for the People.* New York, NY: Routledge.

Assael, M., and M. Givon. 1982. "Aging of Holocaust Survivors in Israel." *Gerontologia* 21: 55–64.

———. 1984. "The Aging Process in Holocaust Survivors." *American Journal of Social Psychiatry* 4: 32–36.

Auerhahn, N. C., and D. Laub. 1984. "Annihilation and Restoration: Post Traumatic Memory as Pathway and Obstacle to Recovery." *International Review of Psychoanalysis* 11: 327–344.

———. 1998. "The Primal Scene of Atrocity: The Dynamic Interplay between Knowledge and Fantasy of the Holocaust in Children of Survivors." *Psychoanalytic Psychology* 15, no. 3: 360.

———. 2018. "Against Forgiving: The Encounter that Cannot Happen between Holocaust Survivors and Perpetrators." *The Psychoanalytic Quarterly* 87, no. 1: 39–72.

Auerhahn, N. C., D. Laub, and H. Peskin. 1993. "Psychotherapy with Holocaust Survivors." *Psychotherapy: Theory Research, Practice, Training* 30, no. 3: 434–442.

Ayalon, L. 2005. "Challenges Associated with the Study of Resilience to Trauma in Holocaust Survivors." *Journal of Loss and Trauma* 10, no. 4: 347–358.

Ayalon, L., C. Perry, P. A. Arean, and M. J. Horowitz. 2007. "Making Sense of the Past—Perspectives on Resilience among Holocaust Survivors." *Journal of Loss and Trauma* 12, no. 3: 281–293.

Bachner, Y. G., S. Carmel, and N. O'Rourke. 2018. "The Paradox of Well-Being and Holocaust Survivors." *Journal of the American Psychiatric Nurses Association* 24, no. 1: 45–52.

Bakermans-Kranenburg, M. J., M. H. Van Ijzendoorn, and F. Juffer. 2003. "Less is More: Meta-Analyses of Sensitivity and Attachment Interventions in Early Childhood." *Psychological Bulletin* 129, no. 2: 195.

Barak, Y. 2013. "Aging of Child Holocaust Survivors." *Kavod* 3: 1–11.

Barak, Y., D. Aizenberg, H. Szor, M. Swartz, R. Maor, and H. Y. Knobler. 2005. "Increased Risk of Attempted Suicide among Aging Holocaust Survivors." *The American Journal of Geriatric Psychiatry* 13, no. 8: 701–704.

Barel, E., M. H. Van Ijzendoorn, A. Sagi-Schwartz, and M. J. Bakermans-Kranenburg. 2010. "Surviving the Holocaust: A Meta-Analysis of the Long-Term Sequelae of a Genocide." *Psychological Bulletin* 136, no. 5: 677–698.

Bar-Tur, L., and R. Levy-Shiff. 2000. "Coping with Losses and Past Trauma in Old Age: The Separation Individuation Perspective." *Journal of Personal & Interpersonal Loss* 5: 263–281.

Benjamin, V. A. 2005. *Final Solutions: Mass Killing and Genocide in the 20th Century.* Ithaca, NY: Cornell University Press.

Benyakar, M., I. Kutz, H. Dasberg, and M. J. Stern. 1989. "The Collapse of a Structure: A Structural Approach to Trauma." *Journal of Traumatic Stress* 2, no. 4: 431–449.

Berger, R. 2015. "Now I See It, Now I Don't: Researcher's Position and Reflexivity in Qualitative Research." *Qualitative Research* 15, no. 2: 219–234.

Besdin, A. R. 1993. *Reflections of the Rav: Lessons in Jewish Thought Adapted from the Lectures of Rabbi Joseph B. Soloveitchik.* Vol. 1. Jerusalem: Torah Education.

Bialystok, F. 2000. *Delayed Impact: The Holocaust and the Canadian Jewish Community.* Canada: McGill-Queen's University Press.

Bistoen, G., S. Vanheule, and S. Craps. 2014. "Nachträglichkeit: A Freudian Perspective on Delayed Traumatic Reactions." *Theory and Psychology* 24, no. 5: 668–687.

Bion, W. R. 1985. "Container and Contained." *Group Relations Reader* 2, no. 8: 127–133.

Boag, S. 2010. "Repression, Suppression, and Conscious Awareness." *Psychoanalytic Psychology* 27, no. 2: 164–181.

Bolton, E. 2015. *PTSD in Refugees.* National Centre for PTSD Research. http://www.ptsd.va.gov/proessional/trauma/other/ptsd-refugees.asp.

Bowlby, J. 1973. *Attachment and Loss,* vol. 2: *Separation.* New York, NY: Basic Books.

Braun, V., and V. Clarke. 2008. "Using Thematic Analysis in Psychology." *Qualitative Research in Psychology* 3, no. 2: 77–101.

Brenner, I. 1988. "Multisensory Bridges in Response to Object Loss during the Holocaust." *Psychoanalytic Review* 75: 573–587.

———, ed. 2019. *The Handbook of Psychoanalytic Holocaust Studies: International Perspectives.* N.p.: Routledge.

Brice, J. S. 2005. "Holocaust Literature: Trends and Tendencies." PhD diss., University of Constanz, Constanz, Germany.

Brom, D. 2001. "The Consequences of the Holocaust on Child Survivors and Children of Survivors." *Israel Journal of Psychiatry and Related Sciences* 38: 1–2.

Brom, D., N. Durst, and G. Aghassy. 2002. "The Phenomenology of Posttraumatic Distress in Older Adult Holocaust Survivors." *Journal of Clinical Geropsychology* 8, no. 3: 189–201.

Brom, D., and R. Kleber. 2000. "On Coping with Trauma and Coping with Grief: Similarities and Differences." In *Traumatic and Nontraumatic Loss and Bereavement: Clinical Theory and Practice*, edited by R. Malkinson, S. Rubin, and E. Witztum, 41–66. Madison, CT: Psychosocial Press.

Butler, R. N. 1964. "The life Review: An Interpretation of Reminiscence in the Aged." In *New Thoughts on Old Age*, edited by R. Kastenbaum, 265–280. New York: Springer Science and Business Media.

Calhoun, L. G., and R. G. Tedeschi. 1999. *Facilitating Posttraumatic Growth: A Clinician's Guide*. London: Routledge.

Carmil, D., and S. Breznitz. 1991. "Personal Trauma and World View: Are Extremely Stressful Experiences Related to Political Attitudes, Religious Beliefs, and Future Orientation?" *Journal of Traumatic Stress* 4, no. 3: 393–405.

Carmil, D., and R. S. Carel. 1986. "Emotional Distress and Satisfaction in Life among Holocaust Survivors: A Community Study of Survivors and Controls." *Psychological Medicine* 16: 141–149.

Chalmers, B. 2015. *Birth, Sex and Abuse: Women's Voices under Nazi Rule*. Surrey: Grosvenor House.

Cheng, S. T. 2009. "Generativity in Later Life: Perceived Respect from Younger Generations as a Determinant of Goal Disengagement and Psychological Well-Being." *Journal of Gerontology. Series B: Psychological Sciences and Social Sciences* 64, no. 1: 45–54.

Cicchetti, D., and D. Tucker. 1994. "Development and Self-Regulatory Structures of the Mind." *Development and Psychopathology* 6, no. 4: 533–549.

Cloitre, M. 2020. "ICD-11 Complex Post-Traumatic Stress Disorder: Simplifying Diagnosis in Trauma Populations." *The British Journal of Psychiatry* 216, no. 3: 129–131.

Cloitre, M., B. C. Stolbach, J. L. Herman, B. V. D. Kolk, R. Pynoos, J. Wang, and E. Petkova. 2009. "A Developmental Approach to Complex PTSD: Childhood and Adult Cumulative Trauma as Predictors of Symptom Complexity." *Journal of Traumatic Stress* 22, no. 5: 399–408.

Cohen, E., R. Dekel, Z. Solomon, and T. Lavie. 2003. "Posttraumatic Stress Symptoms and Fear of Intimacy among Treated and Non-Treated Survivors who Were Children During the Holocaust." *Social Psychiatry and Psychiatric Epidemiology* 38, no. 11: 611–617.

Cohen, J. 1977. "The Impact of Death and Dying on Concentration Camp Survivors." In *Advances in Thanatology*, 4, no. 1, edited by L. G. Kutscher, 27–36.

Cohen, J. A., and A. P. Mannarino. 2004. "Treatment of Childhood Traumatic Grief." *Journal of Clinical Child and Adolescent Psychology* 33, no. 4: 819–831.

Cohen, M., D. Brom, and H. Dasberg. 2001. "Child Survivors of the Holocaust: Symptoms and Coping after Fifty Years." *The Israel Journal of Psychiatry and Related Sciences* 38, no. 1: 3–12.

Cook, A., J. Spinazzola, J. Ford, C. Lanktree, M. Blaustein, M. Cloitre, and B. Van der Kolk. 2017. "Complex Trauma in Children and Adolescents." *Psychiatric Annals* 35, no. 5: 390–398.

Corley, C. 2010. "Creative Expression and Resilience among Holocaust Survivors." *Journal of Human Behaviour in the Social Environment* 20, no. 4: 542–552.

Cyrulnik, B. 2009. *Resilience: How Your Inner Strength Can Set You Free from the Past*. Penguin Books: London.

Danieli, Y. 1981. "Discussion: On the Achievement of Integration in Aging Survivors of the Nazi Holocaust." *Journal of Geriatric Psychiatry* 14, no. 2: 191–210.

———. 1984. "Psychotherapists' Participation in the Conspiracy of Silence about the Holocaust." *Psychoanalytic Psychology* 1, no. 1: 23–42.

———. 1985. "The Treatment and Prevention of Long-Term Effects and Intergenerational Transmission of Victimization: A Lesson from Holocaust Survivors and their Children." In *Trauma and Its Wake*, edited by C. R. Figley, 295–313. Bristol: Brunner Mazel.

———. 1988. "Confronting the Unimaginable." In *Human Adaptation to Extreme Stress: From the Holocaust to Vietnam*, edited by J. P. Wilson., Z. Harel., and B. Kahana, 219–238. Boston, MA: Springer.

———. 1997. "As survivors Age: An Overview." *Journal of Geriatric Psychiatry* 30, no. 1: 9–26.

Dasberg, H. 1987. "Psychological Distress of Holocaust Survivors and Offspring in Israel, Forty Years Later: Review." *Israel Journal of Psychiatry and Related Sciences* 24: 243–256.

——. 1992. "Child Survivors of the Holocaust Reach Middle Age: Psychotherapy of Late Grief Reactions." *Journal of Social Work and Policy in Israel* 5, no. 6: 71–83.

——. 2001. "Adult Child Survivor Syndrome: On Deprived Childhoods of Aging Holocaust Survivors." *The Israel Journal of Psychiatry and Related Sciences* 38, no. 1: 13–26.

David, P. 1988. "Meeting the Needs of the Aging Holocaust Survivor." *Mature Medicine* 1, no. 6.

——. 2002. "Aging Survivors of the Holocaust: Unique Needs, Responses and Long-Term Group Work Approaches." *Journal of Social Work in Long-Term Care* 1, no. 3: 73–89.

——. 2011. "Aging Holocaust Survivors: An Evolution of Understanding." *Kavod* 1: 1–6.

Davidson, J. R. T., D. Hughes, D. G. Blazer, and L. K. George. 1991. "Post-Traumatic Stress Disorder in the Community: An Epidemiological Study." *Psychological Medicine* 21: 713–721.

Davidson, S. 1980. "Human Reciprocity among the Jewish Prisoners in the Nazi Concentration Camps." In *The Nazi Concentration Camps*, 555–572. Jerusalem: Yad Vashem.

——. 1987. "Trauma in the Life Cycle of the Individual and the Collective Consciousness in Relation to War and Persecution." In *Society and Trauma of War*, edited by H. Dasberg, S. Davidson, G. L. Durlacher, B. C. Filet, and E. de Wind, 14–32. Sinai Series 4. Assen, the Netherlands: Van Gorcum.

Des Pres, T. 1976. *The Survivor: An Anatomy of Life in the Death Camps.* New York, NY: Oxford University Press.

Desbois, F. P. 2008. *The Holocaust by Bullets: A Priest's Journey to Uncover the Truth behind the Murder of 1.5 Million Jews.* New York, NY: Palgrave-Macmillan.

Dohary, M. J. 2010. "The Impact of Dissociation, Shame and Guilt on Interpersonal Relationships in Chronically Traumatized Individuals: A Pilot Study." *Journal of Trauma Stress* 23: 653–656.

Durst, N. 1995. "Child Survivors: A Child Survives . . . and Then What?" In *A Global Perspective on Working with Holocaust Survivors and the Second Generation*, edited by J. Lemberger, 291–303. Jerusalem: JDS-Brookdale/AMCHA.

——. 2002. "Emotional Wounds that Never Heal." *Jewish Political Studies Review* 14: 3–11.

——. 2003. "Child-survivors of the Holocaust: Age-Specific Traumatization and the Consequences for Therapy." *American Journal of Psychotherapy* 57, no. 4: 499–518.

Eagle, G. T. 1998. "An Integrative Model for Brief Term Intervention in the Treatment of Psychological Trauma." *International Journal of Psychotherapy* 3: 1–11.

——. 2000. "The Shattering of the Stimulus Barrier: The Case for an Integrative Approach in Short-Term Treatment of Psychological Trauma." *Journal of Psychotherapy Integration* 10, no. 3: 301–323.

——. 2013. "Traumatic Stress, Internal and External: What do Psychodynamic Perspectives have to Contribute?" In *Psychodynamic Psychotherapy in Contemporary South Africa*, edited by C. Smith, G. Lobban, and M. O'Laughlin, 109–137. Johannesburg: Wits University Press.

——. 2014. "Male Crime Victims: The Social and Personal Construction of Meaning in Response to Traumatogenic Events." PhD diss., University of Johannesburg, Johannesburg, South Africa.

Eickhoff, F.-W. 2006. "On *Nachträglichkeit*: The Modernity of an Old Concept." *International Journal of Psychoanalysis* 87: 1453–1469.

Elran-Barak, R., A. Barak, J. Lomranz, and Y. Benyamini. 2018. "Proactive Aging among Holocaust Survivors: Striving for the Best Possible Life." *Journal of Gerontology. Series B: Psychological Sciences and Social Sciences* 73, no. 8: 1446–1456.

Erdelyi, M. H. 2006. "The Unified Theory of Repression." *Behaviour & Brain Sciences* 29: 449–551.

Erikson, E. H. 1950. *Childhood and Society*. New York, NY: W. W. Norton & Company.

——. 1959. "Identity and the Life Cycle." *Psychological Issues* 1: 18–164.

——. 1964. *Insight and Responsibility*. New York, NY: W. W. Norton & Company.

——. 1965. *Identity and the Life Cycle*. New York, NY: International Universities Press.

——. 1968. *Identity Youth and Crisis*. New York, NY: W. W. Norton & Company.

——. 1977. *Childhood and Society*. St. Albans, VT: Paladin.

——. 1982. *The Life Cycle Completed*. New York, NY: W. W. Norton & Company.

——. 1994. *Identity: Youth and Crisis*. New York, NY: W. W. Norton & Company.

Fairbairn, W. R. 1952. *Psychological Studies of the Personality*. London: Routledge & Kegan Paul.

——. 1958. "On the Nature and Aims of Psycho-Analytical Treatment." *The International Journal of Psycho-Analysis* 39, no. 5: 374–385.

Farber, T. R. 2019. "Integrity versus Despair: The Experience of Traumatised Child Holocaust Survivors." PhD diss., University of the Witwatersrand, Johannesburg, South Africa.

Farber, T., G. Eagle, and C. Smith. 2018. "Catastrophic Grief and Associated Defences in Elderly Child Holocaust Survivors." *Psycho-Analytic Psychotherapy in South Africa* 26, no. 2: 49–83.

Farber, T., C. Smith, and G. Eagle. 2021. "The Trauma Trilogy of Catastrophic Grief, Survivor Guilt and Anger in Aging Child Holocaust Survivors." *Journal of Loss and Trauma* 27, no. 2: 99–119.

Felman, S., and D. Laub. 1992. *Testimony Crises of Listening in Literature, Psychoanalysis, and History*. New York, NY: Routledge.

Felsen, I. 2016. "Encounters with Chronic Psychiatric Holocaust Survivors: Trauma, Psychosis and Functionality." *Kavod* 6: 1–25.

——. 2017. "Adult-Onset Trauma and Intergenerational Transmission: Integrating Empirical Data and Psychoanalytic Theory." *Psychoanalysis Self and Context* 12: 60–77.

Felson, I., and D. Brom. 2019. "Adaptation to Trauma, Silence and Social Support." In *Starting Anew: The Rehabilitation of Child Survivors of the Holocaust in the Early Post-War Years*, edited by Sharon Kangisser and Dalia Ofer, 315–350. Jerusalem: Yad Vashem.

Fillit, H., and R. N. Butler. 2009. "The Frailty Identity Crisis." *Journal of the American Geriatrics Society* 57, no. 2: 348–352.

Fishman, Y. 2014. "Exploring Holocaust Survivors' Successful Coping and Adaption." *Kavod* 4: 1–18.

Fohn, A., and S. Heenen-Wolff. 2011. "The Destiny of an Unacknowledged Trauma: The Deferred Retroactive Effect of *après-coup* in the Hidden Jewish Children of Wartime Belgium." *International Journal of Psychoanalysis* 92: 5–20.

Ford, Julian D. 2020. "New Findings Questioning the Construct Validity of Complex Posttraumatic Stress Disorder (cPTSD): Let's Take a Closer Look." *European Journal of Psychotraumatology* 11, no. 1: article 1708145.

Forstmeier, S., E. van der Hal, M. Auerbach, A. Maercker, and D. Brom. 2020. "Life Review Therapy for Holocaust Survivors (LRT-HS): Study Protocol for a Randomised Controlled Trial." *BMC psychiatry* 20, no. 1: 1–13.

Fraiberg, S. H. 1959. *The Magic Years: Understanding and Handling the Problems of Early Childhood*. New York, NY: Charles Scribner's Sons.

Frankl, V. E. 1962. *Man's Search for Meaning: An Introduction to Logotherapy: A Newly Revised and Enlarged Edition of "From Death-Camp to Existentialism."* Boston, MA: Beacon Press.

Freud, S. 1897. *Die Infantile Cerebrallähmung*. Vol. 3. N.p.: A. Hölder.

———. 1910. "The Origin and Development of Psychoanalysis." *The American Journal of Psychology* 21, no. 2: 181–218.

———. 1917. "Mourning and Melancholia." In *The Standard Edition of the Complete Psychological Works of Sigmund Freud*, vol. 14: *On the History of the Psycho-Analytic Movement (1914–1916)*, 237–258. London: Hogarth Press.

———. 1920. *Beyond the Pleasure Principle*. London: Hogarth Press.

———. 1924. Mourning and Melancholia. *The Psychoanalytic Review (1913–1957)*, 11, 77.

———. 1926. *Inhibitions, Symptoms and Anxiety*. In *The Standard Edition of the Complete Psychological Works of Sigmund Freud*, vol. 20: *An Autobiographical Study, Inhibitions, Symptoms and Anxiety, Lay Analysis and Other Works (1925–1926)*. London: Hogarth Press.

———. 1948. *Collected Papers*. London: International Psycho-Analytical Press.

———. 1957. "The Future Prospects of Psycho-Analytic Therapy." In *the Standard Edition of the Complete Psychological Works of Sigmund Freud*, vol. 11: *Five Lectures on Psycho-Analysis, Leonardo da Vinci and Other Works (1910)*, 139–152. London: Hogarth Press.

Fridman, A., M. J. Bakermans-Kranenburg, A. Sagi-Schwartz, and M. H. Van Ijzendoorn. 2011. "Coping in Old Age with Extreme Childhood Trauma: Aging Holocaust Survivors and Their Offspring Facing New Challenges." *Aging & Mental Health* 15, no. 2: 232–242.

Gampel, Y. 1988. "Facing War, Murder, Torture and Death in Latency." *Psychoanalytic Review* 75: 449–509.

Garland, C. 1998. "Issues in Treatment: A Case of Rape." In *Understanding Trauma: A Psychoanalytical Approach*, edited by C. Garland, 108–122. London: Duckworth.

———. 2018. *Understanding Trauma: A Psychoanalytical Approach*. New York, NY: Routledge.

Gay, P., ed. 1995. *The Freud Reader*. London: Vintage.

Gerson, S. 2009. "When the Third is Dead: Memory, Mourning, and Witnessing in the Aftermath of the Holocaust." *The International Journal of Psychoanalysis* 90, 6: 1341–1357.

Goenjian, A. 1993. "A Mental Health Relief Program in Armenia after the Earthquake: Implementation and Clinical Observations." *British Journal of Psychiatry* 163: 230–239.

Goenjian, A., R. S. Pynoos, A. M. Steinberg, L. M. Najarian, J. R. Asarnow, I. Karayan, M. Ghurabi, and L. A. Fairbanks. 1995. "Psychiatric Co-Morbidity in Children after the 1988 Earthquake in Armenia." *Journal of the American Academy of Child and Adolescent Psychiatry* 34: 1174–1184.

Goldstein, E. 1995. "Ego Psychology and Social Work Practice." In *Treatment Approaches in the Human Services*, edited by F. J. Turner, 80–101. New York, NY: Free Press.

Goldstein, G., W. Van Kammen, C. Shelly, D. J. Miller, and D. P. Van Kammen. 1987. "Survivors of Imprisonment in the Pacific Theatre during World War II." *The American Journal of Psychiatry* 144: 1210–1213.

Green, A. 1986. *On Private Madness*. London: The Hogarth Press.

Green, A. H. 1983. "Dimension of Psychological Trauma in Abused Children." *Journal of the American Association of Child Psychiatry* 22: 231–237.

Green, B. L., M. C. Grace, and J. D. Lindy. 1990. "Risk Factors for PTSD and Other Diagnoses in a General Sample of Vietnam Veterans." *American Journal of Psychiatry* 174: 729–733.

Green, B. L., J. D. Lindy, M. C. Grace, and A. C. Leonard. 1992. "Chronic Stress Disorder and Diagnostic Comorbidity in a Disaster Sample." *Journal of Nervous and Mental Disease* 180: 70–76.

Greene, R. R. 2002. "Holocaust Survivors: A Study in Resilience." *Journal of Gerontological Social Work* 37, no. 1: 3–18.

Greif, G. 2005. *We Wept without Tears: Testimonies of the Jewish Sonderkommando from Auschwitz*. New Haven, CT: Yale University Press.

Gutterman, B., and A. Shalev, eds. 2008. *To Bear Witness: Holocaust Remembrance at Yad Vashem*. Jerusalem: Yad Vashem.

Harel, Z. 1995. "Serving Holocaust Survivors and Survivor Families." *Marriage Family Review* 21: 29–49.

Harel, Z., B. Kahana, and E. Kahana. 1988. "Psychological Well-Being among Holocaust Survivors and Immigrants in Israel." *Journal of Traumatic Stress* 1, no. 4: 413–429.

———. 1993. "Social Resources and the Mental Health of Aging Nazi Holocaust Survivors and Immigrants." In *International Handbook of Traumatic Stress Syndromes*, edited by J. P. Wilson and B. Raphael, 241–252. Boston, MA: Springer Science and Business Media.

Hass, A. 1995. "Survivor Guilt in Holocaust Survivors and Their Children." *A Global Perspective on Working with Holocaust Survivors and the Second Generation* 35: 163–183.

Hassan, J. 2013. "End of Life Issues for Holocaust Survivors." *Kavod* 3: 1–6.

Hemmendinger, J., and R. Krell. 2002. *The Children of Buchenwald: Child Survivors of the Holocaust and Their Adult Lives*. Jerusalem: Gefen.

Herman, J. L. 1992. "Complex PTSD: A Syndrome in Survivors of Prolonged and Repeated Trauma." *Journal of Traumatic Stress* 5, no. 3: 377–391.

———. 1992. *Trauma and Recovery: From Domestic Abuse to Political Terror*. London: Pandora Publishers.

Hollander-Goldfein, B., N. Isserman, and J. E. Goldenberg. 2012. *Transcending Trauma: Survival, Resilience and Clinical Implications in Survivor Families*. New York, NY: Routledge.

Isserman, N., B. Hollander-Goldfein, and S. N. Horwitz. 2013. "Wartime Experiences and Late Life Coping Styles." *Kavod* 3: 1–17.

———. 2017. "Challenges for Aging Holocaust Survivors and Their Children: The Impact of Early Trauma on Aging." *Journal of Religion, Spirituality & Aging* 29, no. 2–3: 105–129.

Janoff-Bulman, R. 1985. "Criminal vs Non-Criminal Victimization: Victims' Reactions." *Victimology: An International Journal* 10: 180–192.

———. 1992. *Shattered Assumptions: Toward a New Psychology of Trauma*. New York, NY: The Free Press.

Joffe, C., H. Brodaty, G. Luscombe, and F. Ehrlich. 2003. "The Sydney Holocaust Study: Posttraumatic Stress Disorder and Other Psychosocial Morbidity in an Aged Community Sample." *Journal of Traumatic Stress: Official Publication of The International Society for Traumatic Stress Studies* 16, no. 1: 39–47.

Juni, S. 2015. "Negative Emotionality and Relationships with God among Religious Jewish Holocaust Survivors." *Mental Health, Religion & Culture* 18, no. 3: 165–174.

Kahana, B., Z. Harel, and E. Kahana. 1913. "Predictors of Psychological Well-Being among Survivors of the Holocaust." In *Human Adaptation to Extreme Stress: From the Holocaust to Vietnam*, edited by J. P. Wilson, Z. Harel, and B. Kahana, 171–192. Boston, MA: Springer Science & Business Media.

Karatzias, T., and A. A. Levendosky. 2019. "Introduction to the Special Section on Complex Posttraumatic Stress Disorder. CPTSD): The Evolution of a Disorder." *Journal of Traumatic Stress* 32, no. 6: 817–821.

Karniel-Lauer, E. 2003. "Post-Traumatic Stress Disorder and Grief Response: Their Interrelationship, and the Contribution of Damage to 'World Assumption' and 'Self-Perception.'" PhD diss., Tel Aviv University, Tel Aviv, Israel.

Keilson, H. 1979. *Sequential Traumatization in Children.* Jerusalem: Magnes Press.

Kellermann, N. P. 2001. "The Long-Term Psychological Effects and Treatment of Holocaust Trauma." *Journal of Loss &Trauma* 6, no. 3: 197–218.

———. 2009. *Holocaust Trauma: Psychological Effects and Treatment.* New York, NY: IUniverse.

Kenyon, G. 2005. "Holocaust Stories and Narrative." *International Journal of Aging and Human Development* 60, no. 3: 183–187.

Kessler, R. C., A. Sonnega, E. Bromet, M. Hughes, and C. B. Nelson. 1995. "Posttraumatic Stress Disorder in the National Comorbidity Survey." *Archives of General Psychiatry* 52, no. 12: 1048–1060.

Kestenberg, J. K. 1972. "Psychoanalytic Contributions to the Problem of Children of Survivors from Nazi Persecution." *Israel Annals of Psychiatry* 10: 311–325.

Kestenberg, J. S. 1982. "A Meta Psychological Assessment Based on an Analysis of a Survivor's Child." In *Generations of the Holocaust,* edited by M. S. Bergmann and M. E. Jucovy, 137–158. New York, NY: Columbia University Press.

———. 1984. "The Response of the Child to the Rescuer." Paper presented at the panel on Psychological Research on Rescuing Behaviour at the conference "Faith in Humankind: Rescuers of Jews during the Holocaust," September 17, United States Holocaust Memorial Council, Washington, D.C.

———. 1987. "Imagining and Remembering." *Israel Journal of Psychiatry and Related Sciences* 24, no. 4: 229–241.

Kestenberg, J. S., and I. Brenner. 1986. "Children who Survived the Holocaust: The Role of Rules and Routines in the Development of the Superego." *International Journal of Psychoanalysis* 67: 309–316.

Kestenberg, J. S., and M. Kestenberg. 1988. "The Sense of Belonging and Altruism in Children who Survived the Holocaust." *Psychoanalytic Review* 75: 533–560.

Kiernan, Ben. 2003. "The Demography of Genocide in Southeast Asia: The Death Tolls in Cambodia, 1975–79, and East Timor, 1975–80." *Critical Asian Studies* 35, no. 4: 585–597.

Klein, H. 1973. "Children of the Holocaust: Mourning and Bereavement." In *The Child in His Family: The Impact of Death and Disease*, edited by E. J. Anthony and C. Koupernik, 393–409. New York, NY: John Wiley & Sons.

———. 1974. "Child Victims of the Holocaust." *Journal of Clinical Child Psychology* 3, no. 2: 44–47.

———. 1974. "Delayed Affects and After-Effects of Severe Traumatisation." *Israel Annals of Psychiatry* 12: 293–303.

———. 1983. "The Meaning of the Holocaust." *Israel Journal of Psychiatry and Related Sciences* 20: 119–128.

———. 1992. "Von Schuld zu Verantwortung" [From guilt to responsibility]. *Psyche* 46: 1117–1186. Transcript of the lecture given largely without notes at the Fall conference of the German Psychoanalytical Association in Wiesbaden in 1983 (from tape recordings prepared by Christoph Bierman).

———. 2012. *Survival and Trials of Revival: Psychodynamic Studies of Holocaust Survivors and Their Families in Israel and the Diaspora*. Boston, MA: Academic Studies Press.

———. 1935. "A Contribution to the Psychogenesis of Manic-Depressive States." *International Journal of Psychoanalysis* 16, no. 1: 145–174.

Klein, M. 1952. The Mutual Influences in the Development of Ego and Id: Discussants." *The Psychoanalytic Study of the Child* 7, no. 1: 51–68.

Kohut, H. 1976. "Creativeness, Charisma, Group Psychology." *The Search for the Self* 2: 287–301.

———. 2012. *The Restoration of the Self*. Chicago, IL: University of Chicago Press.

Krell, R. 1985. "Therapeutic Value of Documenting Child Survivors." *Journal of the American Academy of Child Psychiatry* 24, no. 4: 397–400.

———. 1993. "Child Survivors of the Holocaust: Strategies of Adaptation." *The Canadian Journal of Psychiatry* 38, no. 6: 384–389.

———. 2013. "The Resiliency of the Survivor: Views of a Child Holocaust Survivor/Psychiatrist." *Kavod* 3: 1–9.

———. 2019. "Resilience." In *The Handbook of Psychoanalytic Holocaust Studies: International Perspectives*, edited by Ira Brenner, 129–142. London and New York: Routledge.

Krystal, H. 1968. *Massive Psychic Trauma*. New York, NY: International Universities Press.

———. 1978. "Trauma and Affects." *Psychoanalytic Study of the Child* 33: 81–116.

———. 1981. "The Aging Survivor of the Holocaust: Integration and Self-Healing in Post-Traumatic States." *Journal of Geriatric Psychiatry* 14: 165–187.

——. 1984. *Generations of the Holocaust.* New York, NY: Basic Books.

——. 1988. *Integration and Self-Healing: Affect, Trauma, and Alexithymia.* Hillsdale, NJ: Analytic Press.

Kulka, R. A., W. E. Schlenger, J. A. Fairbank, R. L. Hough, B. K. Jordan, and C. R. Marmar. 1990. *Trauma and the Vietnam War generation: Report of Findings from the National Vietnam Veterans Readjustment Study.* New York, NY: Brunner/Mazel.

Landy, M. S., A. C. Wagner, A. Brown-Bowers, and C. M. Monson. 2015. "Examining the Evidence for Complex Posttraumatic Stress Disorder as a Clinical Diagnosis." *Journal of Aggression, Maltreatment & Trauma* 24, no. 3: 215–236.

Langer, L. L. 1980. "The Dilemma of Choice in the Deathcamps." *Centerpoint: A Journal of Interdisciplinary Studies* 4, no. 1: 249–254.

Langbein, H. 2003. *People in Auschwitz.* Translated by Henry Friedlander. Durham, NC: University of North Carolina Press.

Laplanche, J. 1999. "Notes on Afterwardness." In *Essays on Otherness*, edited by J. Fletcher, 260–265. London: Routledge.

Lassley, J. 2015. "A Defective Covenant: Abandonment of Faith among Jewish Survivors of the Holocaust." *International Social Science Review* 90, no. 2: 1.

Last, U., and H. Klein. 1980. *Holocaust Traumatization: The Transgenerational Impact.* Jerusalem: Yad Vashem.

Laub, D. 1992. "An Event without a Witness: Truth, Testimony and Survival." In *Testimony Crises of Witnessing in Literature, Psychoanalysis and History*, edited by S. Felman and D. Laub, 75–91. New York, NY: Routledge.

——. 1998. "The Empty Circle: Children of Survivors and the Limits of Reconstruction." *Journal of the American Psychoanalytic Association* 46, no. 2: 507–529.

——. 2002. "Testimonies in the Treatment of Genocidal Trauma." *Journal of Applied Psychoanalytic Studies* 4, no. 1: 63–87.

——. 2005. "From Speechlessness to Narrative: The Cases of Holocaust Historians and of Psychiatrically Hospitalized Survivors." *Literature and Medicine* 24, no. 2: 253–265.

Laub, D., and N. C. Auerhahn. 1989. "Failed Empathy—A Central Theme in the Survivor's Holocaust Experience." *Psychoanalytic Psychology* 6, no. 4: 377–400.

———. 1993. "Knowing and Not Knowing Massive Psychic Trauma: Forms of Traumatic Memory." *International Journal of Psycho-Analysis*, 74, no. 2: 287–302.

Laub, D., and S. Lee. 2003. "Thanatos and Massive Psychic Trauma: The Impact of the Death Instinct on Knowing, Remembering and Forgetting." *Journal of the American Psychoanalytic Association* 51, no. 2: 433–463.

Laufer, R. S. 1988. "The Serial Self." In *Human Adaptation to Extreme Stress: From the Holocaust to Vietnam*, edited by J. P Wilson, Z. Harel, and B. Kahana, 33–53. Boston, MA: Springer.

Leary, M. R., and J. P. Tangney. 2012. "The Self as an Organizing Construct in the Behavioural and Social Sciences." In *Handbook of Self and Identity*, edited by M. R. Leary and J. P. Tangney, 1–18. New York, NY: The Guilford Press.

Lee, B. S. 1988. "Holocaust Survivors and Internal Strengths." *Journal of Humanistic Psychology* 28, no. 1: 67–96.

Lenna, M. T., G. Domino, A. J. Figueredo, and R. Hendrickson. 1996. "The Prediction of Ego Integrity in Older Persons." *Educational and Psychological Measurement* 56, no. 6: 930–950.

Leon, G. R., J. N. Butcher, M. Kleinman, A. Goldberg, and M. Almagor. 1981. "Survivors of the Holocaust and Their Children: Current Status and Adjustment." *Journal of Personality and Social Psychology* 41, no. 3: 503–516.

Levi, P. 1959. *If This Is a Man*. New York, NY: Orion Press.

———. 1961. *Survival in Auschwitz: The Nazi Assault on Humanity*. New York, NY: Collier.

———. 1989. *The Drowned and the Saved*. New York, NY: Vintage International.

Levi, P. 1989. *The Drowned and the Saved*. New York, NY: Summit Books.

Levi, P. 1993. *Survival in Auschwitz: the Nazi Assault on Humanity*. New York, Toronto: Collier Books and Maxwell Macmillan Canada.

———. 1996. *Survival in Auschwitz: The Nazi Assault on Humanity*. Translated by S. Woolf. New York, NY: Touchstone.

Levi, P., and F. Camon. 1989. *Conversations with Primo Levi*. Evanston, IL: Northwestern University Press.

Levi, P., and P. Levi. 1979. *If This Is a Man, and, The Truce*. Harmondsworth, UK: Penguin.

Lifton, R. J. 1980. "The Concept of the Survivor." In *Survivors, Victims and Perpetrators: Essays on the Nazi Holocaust*, edited by J. E. Dimsdale, 113–126. New York, NY: Hemisphere.

——. 1967. *Death in Life: Survivors of Hiroshima.* New York, NY: Random House.

——. 1973. "Concept of the Survivor." In his *Home from the War: Vietnam Veterans: Neither Victims nor Executioners.* New York, NY: Simon & Schuster.

——. 1979. *Survivor Experience and Traumatic Syndrome: The Broken Connection.* New York, NY: Simon and Shuster.

Loevinger, J. 1987. *Paradigms of Personality.* New York, NY: W. H. Freeman.

Lomranz, J. 1990. "Long-Term Adaptation to Traumatic Stress in Light of Adult Development and Aging Perspectives." In *Stress and Coping in Later-Life Families,* edited by J. H. Crowther, S. E. Hobfoll, D. L. Tennenbaum, and M. A. Parris Stephens, 99–121. New York, NY: Hemisphere.

——. 2005. "Amplified Comment: The Triangular Relationships between the Holocaust, Aging and Narrative Gerontology." *International Journal of Aging and Human Development* 60: 255–267.

Lomranz, J., D. Shmotkin, A. Zechovoy, and E. Rosenberg. 1985. "Time Orientation in Nazi Concentration Camp Survivors: Forty Years After." *American Journal of Orthopsychiatry* 55, no. 2: 230–236.

Long, C., and G. Eagle. 2009. "Ethics in Tension: Dilemmas for Clinicians Conducting Sensitive Research." *Psycho-Analytic Psychotherapy in South Africa* 17, no. 2: 27–52.

Luthar, S. S. 1999. "Measurement Issues in the Empirical Study of Resilience: An Overview. In *Resilience and Development: Positive Life Adaptations,* edited by M. Glanz, and J. L. Johnson, 129–160. New York, NY: Plenum.

Luthar, S. S., D. Cicchetti, and B. Becker. 2000. "The Construct of Resilience: A Critical Evaluation and Guidelines for Future Work." *Child Development* 71, no. 3: 543–562.

Mahler, M. S., F. Pine, and A. Bergman. 2000. *The Psychological Birth of the Human Infant: Symbiosis and Individuation.* New York, NY: Basic Books.

Malkinson, R., and L. Bar-Tur. 2005. "Long Term Bereavement Processes of Older Parents: The Three Phases of Grief." *OMEGA: Journal of Death and Dying* 50, no. 2: 103–129.

——. 2000. "The Aging of Grief: Parents' Grieving of Israeli Soldiers." *Journal of Personal & Interpersonal Loss* 5, no. 2–3: 247–262.

Masten, A. S., K. M. Best, and N. Garmezy. 1990. "Resilience and Development: Contributions from the Study of Children who Overcome Adversity." *Development and Psychopathology* 2, no. 4: 425–444.

Mazor, A., Y. Gampel, R. D. Enright, and R. Orenstein. 1990. "Holocaust Survivors: Coping with Post-Traumatic Memories in Childhood and 40 Years Later." *Journal of Traumatic Stress* 3, no. 1: 1–14.

McDonnell, M., K. Robjant, and C. Katona. 2013. "Complex Posttraumatic Stress Disorder and Survivors of Human Rights Violations." *Current Opinion in Psychiatry* 26, no. 1: 1–6.

McCann, I. L., and L. A. Pearlman. 1990. "Vicarious Traumatization: A Framework for Understanding the Psychological Effects of Working with Victims." *Journal of Traumatic Stress* 3, no. 1: 131–149.

McFarlane, A. C. 1988. "The Aetiology of Post-Traumatic Stress Disorders following a Natural Disaster." *The British Journal of Psychiatry* 152, no. 1: 116–121.

———. 2007. "Resilience, Vulnerability: The Course of Posttraumatic Reactions." In *Traumatic Stress: The Effects of Overwhelming Experience on Mind, Body, and Society,* edited by B. A. van der Kolk, A. C. McFarlane, and L. Weisaeth, 155–181. New York: The Guilford Press.

McHugh, T., D. Forbes, G. Bates, M. Hopwood, and M. Creamer. 2012. "Anger in PTSD: Is There a Need for a Concept of PTSD-Related Posttraumatic Anger?" *Clinical Psychology Review* 32: 93–104.

Meierhenrich, Jens. 2020. "How Many Victims Were There in the Rwandan Genocide? A Statistical Debate." *Journal of Genocide Research* 22, no. 1: 72–82.

Nedelmann, C. 2012. "Introduction." In *Survival and Trials of Revival: Psychodynamic Studies of Holocaust Survivors and Their Families in Israel and the Diaspora,* by H. Klein, 10–15. Boston, MA: Academic Studies Press.

Nelson, D. R., W. N. Adger, and K. Brown. 2007. "Adaptation to Environmental Change: Contributions of a Resilience Framework." *Annual Review of Environment and Resources* 32: 395–419.

Niederland, W. G. 1964. "Psychiatric Disorders among Persecution Victims: A Contribution to the Understanding of Concentration Camp Pathology and Its After-Effects." *The Journal of Nervous and Mental Disease* 139, no. 5: 458–474.

———. 1981. "The Survivor Syndrome: Further Observations and Dimensions." *Journal of the American Psychoanalytic Association* 29, no. 2: 413–425.

Ochse, R., and C. Plug. 1986. "Cross-Cultural Investigation of the Validity of Erikson's Theory of Personality Development." *Journal of Personality and Social Psychology* 50, no. 6: 1240.

O'Rourke, N., S. Carmel, and Y. G. Bachner. 2018. "Does Early Life Trauma Affect how Depression is Experienced by Holocaust Survivors in Late Life?" *Aging & Mental Health* 22, no. 5: 662–668.

Orth, U., and A. Maercker. 2009. "Posttraumatic Anger in Crime Victims: Directed at the Perpetrator and at the Self." *Journal of Traumatic Stress* 22: 158–161.

Panter-Brick, C., and M. Eggerman. 2012. "Understanding Culture, Resilience, and Mental Health: The Production of Hope." In *The Social Ecology of Resilience: A Handbook of Theory and Practice,* edited by M. Ungar, 369–386. New York: Springer.

Paris, J. 2000. "Predispositions, Personality Traits, and Posttraumatic Stress Disorder." *Harvard Review of Psychiatry* 8, no. 4: 175–183.

Parker, I. 2005. *Qualitative Psychology Introducing Radical Research.* Mainhead: Open University Press.

Pedersen C. 2019. "Encountering Trauma 'Too Soon' and 'Too Late': Caruth, Laplanche and the Freudian *Nachträglichkeit."* In *Topography of Trauma: Fissures, Disruptions and Transfigurations,* edited by D. Schaub, J. Linder, K. D. Novak, S. Tam, and C. V. Zanini, 25–44. Leiden, Boston: Brill.

Perry, J. C., J. L. Herman, B. A. Van Der Kolk, and L. A. Hoke. 1990. "Psychotherapy and Psychological Trauma in Borderline Personality Disorder." *Psychiatric Annals* 20, no. 1: 33–43.

Prince, R. 2016. "Past Imperfect: Historical Trauma and Its Transmission." In *Ethics of Evil: Psychoanalytic Investigations,* edited by R. C. Naso and J. Mills, 203–232. London: Karnac.

Prot, K. 2010. "Research on Consequences of the Holocaust." *Archives of Psychiatry and Psychotherapy* 2: 61–69.

Pynoos, R. S. 1992. "Grief and Trauma in Children and Adolescents." *Bereavement Care* 11, no. 1: 2–10.

Pynoos, R. S., and K. Nader. 1993. "Issues in the Treatment of Post-Traumatic Stress in Children and Adolescents." In *International Handbook of Traumatic Stress Syndromes,* edited by J. P. Wilson and B. Raphael, 535–549. New York, NY: Plenum Press.

Pynoos, R. S., S. B. Sorenson, and A. M. Steinberg. 1993. "Interpersonal Violence and Traumatic Stress Reactions." In *Handbook of Stress: Theoretical and Clinical Aspects,* edited by L. Goldberger and S. Breznitz, 573–590. New York, NY: Free Press.

Pynoos, R. S., A. M. Steinberg, and A. Goenjian. 2007. "Traumatic Stress in Childhood and Adolescence: Recent Developments and Current Controversies." In *Traumatic stress: The Effects of Overwhelming Experience on Mind, Body, and Society*, edited by B. A. Van der Kolk, A. C. McFarlane, and L. Weisaeth, 331–358. New York, NY: The Guilford Press.

Resick, P. A., M. J. Bovin, A. L. Calloway, A. M. Dick, M. W. King, K. S. Mitchell, and E. J. Wolf. 2012. "A Critical Evaluation of the Complex PTSD Literature: Implications for DSM-5." *Journal of Traumatic Stress* 25, no. 3: 241–251.

Ricks, M. H. 1985. "The Social Transmission of Parental Behaviour: Attachment across Generations." *Monographs of the Society for Research in Child Development* 50, no. 1–2: 211–227.

Rising, D. 2020. "Germany to Give $662 Million in Aid to Holocaust Survivors." *AP News*. October 14. https://apnews.com/article/virus-outbreak-international-news-western-europe-germany-europe-fe70a989c90101e79ff8ee4d9abcf7b0.

Robinson, S., J. Hemmendinger, R. Netanel, M. Rapaport, L. Zilberman, and A. Gal. 1994. "Re-Traumatization of Holocaust Survivors during the Gulf War and Scud Missile Attacks on Israel." *British Journal of Medical Psychology* 67, no. 4: 353–362.

Robinson, S., J. Rapaport, R. Durst, M. Rapaport, P. Rosca, S. Metzer, and L. Zilberman. 1990. "The Late Effects of Nazi Persecution among Elderly Holocaust Survivors." *Acta Psychiatrica Scandinavica* 82, no. 4: 311–315.

Rutter, M. 1985. "Resilience in the Face of Adversity: Protective Factors and Resistance to Psychiatric Disorder." *The British Journal of Psychiatry* 147, no. 6: 598–611.

———. 1999. "Resilience Concepts and Findings: Implications for Family Therapy." *Journal of Family Therapy* 21: 119–144.

Rutter, M. 2012. "Resilience as a Dynamic Concept." *Development and Psychopathology* 24, no. 2: 335–344.

Rutter, M., E. Taylor, and L. Hersov. 1995. "Child and Adolescent Psychiatry: Modern Approaches." *Journal of the American Academy of Child & Adolescent Psychiatry* 34, no. 7: 964.

Sar, V. 2011. "Developmental Trauma, Complex PTSD, and the Current Proposal of DSM-5." *European Journal of Psychotraumatology* 2, no. 1: article 5622.

Schell, T. L., G. N. Marshall, and L. H. Jaycox. 2004. "All Symptoms are Not Created Equal. The Prominent Role of Hyperarousal in the Natural Course of Posttraumatic Psychological Distress." *Journal of Abnormal Psychology* 113: 189–197.

Shanan, J., and O. Shahar. 1983. "Cognitive and Personality Functioning of Jewish Holocaust Survivors during the Midlife Transition in Israel." *Archiv fur Psychologie* 135, no. 4: 275–294.

Shklarov, S. 2013. "Soviet Jewish Child Survivors. Identity and Resilience after Long Silence." *Kavod* 3: 1–6.

——. 2013. "Theory through the Eyes of the Child Survivors of the Holocaust." *Kavod* 3: 1–10.

Sicher, E. 1998. *Breaking Crystal: Writing and Memory after Auschwitz*. Chicago, IL: University of Illinois Press.

——. 2000. "The Future of the Past: Counter Memory and Post Memory in Contemporary American Post-Holocaust Narratives." *History & Memory* 12, no. 2: 56–91.

Sigal, J. J., and M. Weinfeld. 2001. "Do Children Cope Better than Adults with Potentially Traumatic Stress? A 40-Year Follow-Up of Holocaust Survivors." *Psychiatry: Interpersonal & Biological Processes* 64, no. 1: 69–80.

Silverman, P. R., D. Klass, and S. L. Nickman, eds. 1996. *Continuing Bonds: New Understandings of Grief*. Washington, DC: Taylor & Francis.

Solomon, Z., M. Bensimon, T. Greene, D. Horesh, and T. Ein Dror. 2015. "Loneliness Trajectories: The Role of Posttraumatic Symptoms and Social Support." *Journal of Loss and Trauma* 20, no. 1: 1–21.

Southwick, S. M., G. A. Bonanno, A. S. Masten, C. Panter-Brick, and R. Yehuda. 2014. "Resilience Definitions, Theory, and Challenges: Interdisciplinary Perspectives." *European Journal of Psychotraumatology* 5: 10.

Sossin, K. M. 2007. "Non-Mentalizing States in Early-Childhood Survivors of the Holocaust: Developmental Considerations regarding Treatment of Child Survivors of Genocidal Atrocities." *The American Journal of Psychoanalysis* 67, 1: 68–81.

Surkes, S. 2021. "Number of Holocaust Survivors in Israel Down to 180 000." *Times of Israel*, April 6, 2021.

Stammel, N., C. Heeke, E. Bockers, S. Chim, S. Taing, B. Wagner, and C. Knaevelsrud. 2013. "Prolonged Grief Disorder Three Decades post Loss in Survivors of the Khmer Rouge Regime in Cambodia." *Journal of Affective Disorders* 144, no. 1–2: 87–93.

Suedfeld, P., E. Soriano, D. L. McMurtry, H. Paterson, T. L. Weiszbeck, and R. Krell. 2005. "Erikson's 'Components of a Healthy Personality' among Holocaust Survivors Immediately and 40 Years after the War." *The International Journal of Aging and Human Development* 60, no. 3: 229–248.

Sutker, P. B., D. K. Winstead, Z. H. Galina, and A. N. Allain. 1991. "Cognitive Deficits and Psychopathology among Former Prisoners of War and Combat Veterans of the Korean Conflict." *American Journal of Psychiatry* 14: 7–72.

Tauber, Y. 1996. "The Traumatized Child and the Adult: Compound Personality in Child Survivors of the Holocaust." *The Israel Journal of Psychiatry and Related Sciences* 33, no. 4: 228–237.

Tedeschi, R. G., and L. G. Calhoun. 2004. "Posttraumatic Growth: Conceptual Foundations and Empirical Evidence." *Psychological Inquiry* 15, no. 1: 1–18.

Terr, L. C. 1995. "Childhood Traumas." In *Psychotraumatology: Key Papers and Core Concepts in Post-Traumatic Stress*, edited by G. S. Everly and J. M. Lating, 301–320. New York: Plenum Press.

Trappler, B., C. I. Cohen, and R. Tulloo. 2007. "Impact of Early Lifetime Trauma in Later Life: Depression among Holocaust Survivors 60 Years after the Liberation of Auschwitz." *The American Journal of Geriatric Psychiatry* 15, no. 1: 79–83.

Turner, S. 2004. "Emotional Reactions to Torture and Organized State Violence." *PTSD Research Quarterly* 15, no. 2: 1–7.

Valent, P. 1998. "Resilience in Child Survivors of the Holocaust: Towards the Concept of Resilience." *The Psychoanalytic Review* 85, no. 4: 516–535.

———. 2002. *Child Survivors of the Holocaust.* New York, NY: Brunner Mazel.

———. 2014. "Memories of the Holocaust: An Essay." *Kavod* 4: 1–8.

Van der Kolk, B. A. 1988. "The Trauma Spectrum: The Interaction of Biological and Social Events in the Genesis of the Trauma Response." *Journal of Traumatic Stress* 1, no. 3: 273–290.

———. 2007. "The Complexity of Adaptation to Trauma: Self-Regulation, Stimuli, Discrimination and Characterological Development." In *Traumatic Stress: The Effects of Overwhelming Experience on Mind, Body, and Society*, edited by B. A. Van der Kolk, A. C. McFarlane, and L. Weisaeth, 182–213. New York, NY: The Guilford Press.

———. 2007. "Trauma and Memory." In *Traumatic Stress: The Effects of Overwhelming Experience on Mind, Body, and Society*, edited by B. A. Van der Kolk, A. C. McFarlane, and L. Weisaeth, 279–302. New York, NY: The Guilford Press.

Van der Kolk, B. A., and R. E. Fisler. 1994. "Childhood Abuse and Neglect and Loss of Self-Regulation." *Bulletin of the Menninger Clinic* 58, no. 2: 145.

Van der Kolk, B. A., and A. C. McFarlane. 2007. "The Black Hole of Trauma." In *Traumatic Stress: The Effects of Overwhelming Experience on Mind, Body, and*

Society, edited by B. A. Van der Kolk, A. C. McFarlane, and L. Weisaeth, 3–23. New York, NY: The Guilford Press.

Van der Kolk, B. A., A. Hostetler, N. Herron, and R. E. Fisler. 1994. "Trauma and the Development of Borderline Personality Disorder." *Psychiatric Clinics* 17, no. 4: 715–730.

Van der Kolk, B. A., A. C. McFarlane, and L. Weisaeth, eds. 2007. *Traumatic Stress: The Effects of Overwhelming Experience on Mind, Body and Society*. New York, NY: The Guilford Press.

Van der Kolk, B. A., D. Pelcovitz, S. Roth, and F. S. Mandel. 1996. "Dissociation, Somatization, and Affect Dysregulation." *The American Journal of Psychiatry* 153, no. 7: 83.

Wardi, D. 1992. *Memorial Candles: Children of the Holocaust*. London: Routledge.

Wiesel, E. 1960. *Night*. New York, NY: Hill and Wang.

———. 1978. *A Jew Today*. New York, NY: Random House.

Wilson, J. P., Z. Harel, and B. Kahane, eds. 2015. *Human Adaptation to Extreme Stress: From the Holocaust to Vietnam*. New York, NY: Plenum Press.

Winnicott, D. W. 1960. "The Theory of the Parent-Infant Relationship." *International Journal of Psycho-Analysis* 41: 585–595.

———. 1965. "The Maturational Processes and the Facilitating Environment: Studies in the Theory of Emotional Development." In his *The Maturational Processes and the Facilitating Environment: Studies in the Theory of Emotional Development*, 1–276. London: The Hogarth Press and the Institute of Psycho-analysis.

———. 1969. "The Use of an Object." *International Journal of Psychoanalysis* 50: 711–715.

———. 1974. "Fear of Breakdown." *International Review of Psychoanalysis* 1: 103–107.

Winship, G. 2007. "The Ethics of Reflective Research in Single Case Study Inquiry." *Perspectives in Psychiatric Care* 43, no. 4: 174–182.

Witztum, E., and R. Malkinson. 2009. "Examining Traumatic Grief and Loss among Holocaust Survivors." *Journal of Loss and Trauma* 14, no. 2: 129–143.

World Health Organization. 2018. International Statistical Classification of Diseases and Related Health Problems *(11th revision)*.

Yehuda, R., B. Kahana, S. M. Southwick, and E. L. Giller. 1994. "Depressive Features in Holocaust Survivors with Post-Traumatic Stress Disorder." *Journal of Traumatic Stress* 7, no. 4: 699–704.

Appendix 1.
Ethical Clearance Certificate

UNIVERSITY OF THE WITWATERSRAND JOHANNESBURG

Division of the Deputy Registrar (Research)

HUMAN RESEARCH ETHICS COMMITTEE (MEDICAL)

R14/49 Farber

CLEARANCE CERTIFICATE	PROTOCOL NUMBER M050729
PROJECT	Integrity Versus Despair: The Experience of Aging Child Holocaust Survivors in South Africa
INVESTIGATORS	Ms. T. Farber
DEPARTMENT	SHCD/Psych010U
DATE CONSIDERED	05.07.29
DECISION OF THE COMMITTEE*	Approved unconditionally

Unless otherwise specified this ethical clearance is valid for 5 years and may be renewed upon applicatiön.

DATE   05.08.29   CHAIRPERSON . ⎯⎯⎯⎯⎯⎯⎯⎯⎯⎯⎯⎯⎯⎯⎯⎯⎯

(Professor P. E. Cleaton-Jones)

*Guidelines for "informed consent" attached where applicable cc: Supervisor: Prof G. Eagle

DECLARATION OF INVESTIGATOR(S)

To be completed in duplicate and ONE COPY returned to the Secretary at Room 10005, 10th Floor, Senate House, University.

We fully understand the conditions under which I am/we are authorized to carry out the abovementioned research and I/we guarantee to ensure compliance with these conditions. Should any departure to be contemplated from the research procedure as approved I/we undertake to resubmit the protocol to the Committee. I agree to a completion of a yearly progress report.

Appendix 2.
Turnitin Plagiarism Report

PLEASE QUOTE THE PROTOCOL NUMBER IN ALL ENQUIRIES

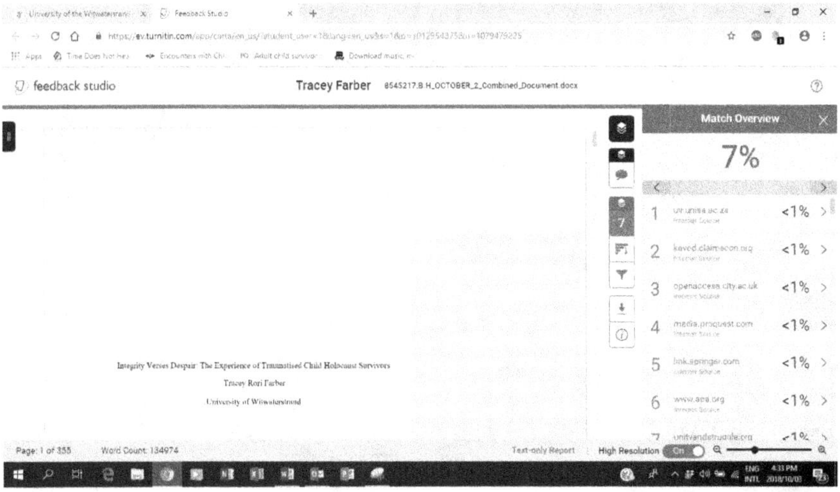

Fig. 6.

Index

www.ingramcontent.com/pod-product-compliance
Lightning Source LLC
Chambersburg PA
CBHW071730270326
41928CB00013B/2626